Marvel Comics' *Civil War*
and the Age of Terror

Marvel Comics' Civil War and the Age of Terror

Critical Essays on the Comic Saga

Edited by
Kevin Michael Scott

Foreword by Robert G. Weiner
Afterword by Marc DiPaolo

McFarland & Company, Inc., Publishers
Jefferson, North Carolina

LIBRARY OF CONGRESS CATALOGUING-IN-PUBLICATION DATA

Marvel Comics' Civil War and the age of terror : critical essays on the comic saga / edited by Kevin Michael Scott ; foreword by Robert G. Weiner ; afterword by Marc DiPaolo.
    p.   cm.
Includes bibliographical references and index.

ISBN 978-0-7864-9689-1 (softcover : acid free paper) ∞
ISBN 978-1-4766-2218-7 (ebook)

1. Comic books, strips, etc.—United States—History and criticism. 2. Superheroes in literature. 3. Politics in literature. 4. Ethics in literature. 5. National characteristics, American—History and criticism. 6. Graphic novels—History and criticism. 7. Marvel Comics Group. I. Scott, Kevin M., 1966– editor.

PN6728.C585M37 2015   741.5'973—dc23   2015023922

BRITISH LIBRARY CATALOGUING DATA ARE AVAILABLE

© 2015 Kevin Michael Scott. All rights reserved

No part of this book may be reproduced or transmitted in any form or by any means, electronic or mechanical, including photocopying or recording, or by any information storage and retrieval system, without permission in writing from the publisher.

Front cover image of an American flag on a building in New York City © 2015 Jupiterimages/Photos.com/Thinkstock

Printed in the United States of America

McFarland & Company, Inc., Publishers
Box 611, Jefferson, North Carolina 28640
www.mcfarlandpub.com

To Bob, Marc and, of course, Mike.
You would look great in capes.

Acknowledgments

Gratitude, first, to Margaret Ellen Scott, whose discovered love for comics brought me back. Without you, this book would not exist. No exaggeration.

Special thanks:

To Robert Paul Lamb and Mary Ann Scott, whose readings made this a stronger, wiser book.

To John Lent, the editor-in-chief of the *International Journal of Comic Art*, for generously allowing me to include in this volume the excellent essay by Travis Langley.

To the contributors to this volume, who showed unflagging willingness to craft, edit, and refine their work. The book improved with every email I received. To Tony and Marc I owe extra thanks for the thoughtfulness and intensity of their ideas and support.

To the library staff at Albany State University for all of their support. No resource escapes their gaze.

And to Rob Weiner, whose conversations and mentorship both intimidated me and made the project feel like something I could actually accomplish.

Table of Contents

Acknowledgments — vi
Key to Abbreviations — xi
Foreword
    Robert G. Weiner — 1
Introduction
    Kevin Michael Scott — 3

— PART I —
The SHRA: What the Marvel Universe Tells Us About American Legal Culture

The Superhuman Registration Act, the Constitution, and the Patient Protection and Affordable Care Act
    Ryan M. Davidson — 11

Whose Side Is the Law On? Living with Legalistic Absurdity in Marvel's *Civil War*
    Daniel Davis Wood — 26

— PART II —
Superheroics and the American Response to 9/11

Marvel's Illuminati: Who Watches the Watchmen?
    Mark Bousquet — 37

"You wish to know of war, old man?" Generational Conflict, Moral Compromise and Youth Rebellion in *Civil War: Young Avengers & Runaways*
    David Sweeney — 48

Whither Alpha Flight? The Nationalistic Response to Canada During the War on Terror
    Brenna Clarke Gray — 58

Freedom versus Security: The Basic Human Dilemma from 9/11 to Marvel's *Civil War*
    Travis Langley — 69

— PART III —
Political Philosophy and *Civil War*

Political (In)Visibility in the Marvel Universe and the Real World
   ANTHONY PETROS SPANAKOS   77

The Language of Common Sense: Thomas Paine and *Civil War*
   SCOTT CLEARY   90

Competing Authorities in the Nation State of Marvel
   KARL E. MARTIN   98

Iron Curtain Man versus Captain American Exceptionalism: World War II and Cold War Nostalgia in the Age of Terror
   KATHLEEN MCCLANCY   108

— PART IV —
Super-Powered, American and Marginalized: Triple Consciousness in the Marvel Universe

Battles of Family, Freedom and Femininity: Portrayals of Gender in Marvel's *Civil War*
   BRANDI HODO   121

Superdad: Luke Cage and the Heroic Fatherhood Ideal in the Contemporary Marvel Universe
   JEFFREY A. BROWN   130

— PART V —
Character(s) Revealed Through Trauma

Between Two Towers: The Struggle for the Soul of Spider-Man
   DANIEL J. O'ROURKE   143

Captain America in the 21st Century: The Battle for the Ideology of the American Dream
   JOHN MCGUIRE   150

— PART VI —
Graphic Narrative and Cultural Resonance

Visual Form and Meaning Making in Marvel's *Civil War*
   JOSEPH J. DAROWSKI   165

When Flaw Meets Form Meets Function: Narratology, Crossover Comic Events and a New Art Experience
   KEVIN MICHAEL SCOTT   174

— PART VII —
Teaching the Trouble: Pedagogy and *Civil War*

Teaching Ethics When Hero Battles Hero
   MARK D. WHITE   189

Illustrating *Pedagogy of the Oppressed*: A Freirian Approach to
  Teaching Marvel's *Civil War*
    SENECA VAUGHT   200

Afterword: Why Civil War *Matters, Why This Book Matters*
    MARC DIPAOLO   213
About the Contributors   221
Index   223

Key to Abbreviations

AF	*Alpha Flight*
ASM	*Amazing Spider-Man*
ATA	*Avengers: The Initiative*
CA	*Captain America*
CW	*Civil War*
CWCS	*Civil War: Choosing Sides*
CWFL	*Civil War: Front Line*
CWSB	*Civil War: Script Book*
CWTC	*Civil War: The Confession*
CWTI	*Civil War: The Initiative*
CWYAR	*Civil War: Young Avengers & Runaways*
DA	*Dark Avengers*
IIM	*The Invincible Iron Man*
MM	*Ms. Marvel*
NA	*The New Avengers*
NAI	*New Avengers: Illuminati*
SHRA	*Superhuman Registration Act*
SI	*Secret Invasion*
TB	*Thunderbolts*
UX	*Uncanny X-Men*

Foreword

ROBERT G. WEINER

> "Secrecy, being an instrument of conspiracy, ought never to be the system of a regular government."—Jeremy Bentham
>
> "Real liberty is neither found in despotism or the extremes of democracy, but in moderate governments."—Alexander Hamilton

There are those events in the history of comics that are significant and then there are those comics events that are *really important* (that deserve the emphasis). These are events that are worth talking about years (even decades) after they are published. I am talking about stories that continue to have relevance both for the writers and artists who create the comics, as well as for the fans who read and enjoy them and the scholars who study them. Ask the fanboys (and, increasingly, fangirls) what some of the major crossover events are in the history of mainstream superhero comics and you'd most likely get the standard responses: *Avengers: Kree Skrull War, Spider-Man: Death of Gwen Stacey, Clone-Saga, Batman: Knightfall, Death in the Family, Death of Superman, Fantastic Four: The Galactus Trilogy, Crisis on Infinite Earths, Fourth World Saga, X-Men: Dark Phoenix Saga,* and *Legion of Superheroes: The Great Darkness Saga* are just a few of the stories that might be mentioned in passing. *Civil War*, published in 2006 and 2007 by Marvel Comics, would also be among those. It encompasses nearly 200 individual comics and culminates in the "death" of Captain America.

While I have always argued that comics are a form of social history and can be viewed as primary historical documents, *Civil War* has a special kind of resonance. It is one of those comic book sagas that is certainly a reflection of its time, but it also has a timeless quality to it that will speak to generations twenty, fifty, a hundred years after it began publication (2006). Sure, one can see the series as a response to the concerns raised by the events of September 11, 2001, the USA PATRIOT Act, and the rise of modern-day terrorism. Certainly one can also see the parallels between the Negative Zone prison and Guantanamo Bay detention camp. However, the social and cultural resonance of the comic event goes much deeper than that because, at its core, *Civil War* is about the struggle between the "Common Good" and the "Right" to individual liberty and privacy.

With so much concern today over "Big Brother" in the form of the NSA and government spying on individual citizens and one's right to privacy, *Civil War* is more timely than ever. As long as we live in a world where identity theft and ease of access to one's personal information continues to be an ever-present issue, *Civil War* will continue to be a story that readers will go back to time and time again and scholars will find new points of analysis and relevance.

Readers and commentators have often seen Captain America and his team as the heroes of the story standing up for personal liberty and the rights of the individual. It is all too easy to vilify Iron Man and his team as the "evil" establishment group who are trying to force everyone else to conform to some unreasonable standard. We have to remember, though, that Iron Man truly believed that he was working in the interest of protecting the lives of American citizens and that his motives were pure. (Comic book readers are conditioned to root for the "super heroes," but *Civil War* makes this more difficult from the get-go by showing us that, in the Marvel Universe, the American people are overwhelmingly in support of the Superhuman Registration Act.) Is it honestly too hard to imagine in a world with super powered individuals that there would not be an attempt at some kind of checks and balances in the interest of public safety? The average citizen would certainly be afraid of these "Marvels." As some of the essays in this well-curated volume discuss, the morality of both sides is up for debate and both Cap's and Iron Man's teams make some dubious decisions. We know that just because someone's motives are pure does not necessarily make them morally correct. One can easily argue the questionable ethics of cloning Thor (for Iron Man's team) or adding the Punisher to Captain America's team. The subsequent events of both those actions had tragic consequences.

Kevin Michael Scott put together this fine collection with the purpose of giving the world an honest assessment of the *Civil War* series that digs deep into all aspects of society from the Cold War, to secret societies, ethics, comics theory, law, history, psychology, art, instruction, and the "kitchen sink" because that's in there in too. As the first academic collection based on this important "cataclysmic comics event," editor Scott has filled a much needed void in comics scholarship. This collection will continue to be relevant in the years to come.

Robert G. Weiner is a pop culture librarian at Texas Tech University where he serves the College of Visual and Performing Arts and Film Studies. He is the editor of *Captain America and the Struggle of the Superhero* (2009) and co-editor (with Robert Moses Peaslee) of *Web-Spinning Heroics* (2012) and *Graphic Novels Comics and in the Classroom* (2013) and the author of *Marvel Graphic Novels and Related Publications* (2008, all from McFarland) as well as numerous articles on film, music and comics.

Introduction

Kevin Michael Scott

It wasn't a particularly new, or original, observation that struck me as I wandered through the deeply impressive and deeply affecting 9/11 Memorial Museum only a few weeks after it opened, in the spring of 2014.

Things fall apart. The center cannot hold. Anarchy is loosed upon the world.

Walking through the memorial, I saw vast chunks of the original Twin Towers, now installed as exhibits. Two of the famous tridents. The granite staircase. The slurry wall. Even the very bedrock into which the Towers dug their toes for purchase.

It was simply astonishing that such things *could* fall apart, William Butler Yeats' apocalyptic vision notwithstanding. It had all seemed so solid, so permanent. Even now, removed from their purpose, these artifacts still do. Two of the most startling moments in the museum, though, are the videos of the Towers falling. The first video appears to you as you come around a corner, a surprise you know is coming. The short video, on a loop and perpetual, is edited into a vertical image and placed above your head, so that you must look up to see a tower fall.

Mere anarchy. The blood-dimmed tide is loosed. The ceremony of innocence is drowned.

Of course, Yeats wasn't talking about buildings, or anything necessarily physical, in his poem "The Second Coming."[1] He was interested in the ever-ongoing battle between Order and Chaos. Chaos, it seems, is always at the ready, hiding and preparing (like some kind of psychopathic super-villain) to break down the world.

Yeats composed the poem in the bloody wake of World War I. Whatever the apparent outcome, Chaos won that war. As much as a battle between the Allies and the Central Powers, it could be seen as a fight between modernity and *everything-that-came-before*. Certainly, everything that came after was different.

As it would be after 9/11.

The thing about 9/11, and things falling apart, is that, in order for it to have happened, things had to have been falling apart for quite a while. Systems fall apart. Values fall apart. So do principles. And after the Towers crumbled, the falling apart of systems and values and principles seemed to accelerate.

It would be too easy to take the liberal stance and see this falling apart as coming only from an American government opportunistically using the tragedy to serve its own domestic and global ambitions (which did happen). The American people more than participated in tearing chunks out of the body politic. We had been, for a time, suspicious of overseas adventures, but we found ourselves singing along with Toby Keith's jingoistic anthem, "Courtesy of the Red, White and Blue (The Angry American)" and supporting two new wars. We drove the Dixie Chicks out of the country and out of country music for exercising their right to free speech. (And the gendered nature of much of the hatefulness suggested an ugly truth: we seem to retreat into old, safe bigotries in moments of stress.) We mislabeled Park51 as the "ground zero mosque" and tried to block the proposed Muslim community center near ground zero because it had a prayer space (just as the Towers themselves had), curtailing even this expression of freedom of religion because *we happened not to like that one*.

Most significantly, we largely supported the formation of the Department of Homeland Security and the passage of the USA PATRIOT Act, both of which we knew would challenge some of our most cherished civil liberties. A most common refrain: if you're innocent, you have nothing to worry about. Over the next few years, plenty of Americans cried out against each of these developments, especially the attacks on our right to privacy, and this nascent protest extended across traditional political lines. (Indeed, if the election of Barack Obama to the presidency was the trigger, the PATRIOT Act was ammunition in the formation of the Tea Party Movement.)

By the middle of the decade, as faith in the Bush administration continued to fall for all but the most conservative, the United States was engaged in an extended period of national soul searching. Marvel's *Civil War* event, beginning in the fall of 2006, was perfectly suited to explore the multiple, complex, and even contradictory social and political conflicts confronting the nation at the time.

And, *boy, oh, boy*, did it.

In addition to addressing the civil liberties already discussed, *Civil War* took on a daunting variety of social and cultural phenomena: the state and impact of 21st-century journalism, Guantanamo Bay, the fearfulness of the American citizenry, the use of bad criminals to catch worse criminals, the creation of a new national police force with undefined powers, the redefinition of citizenship, trials without juries, incarceration without charges, and so on. *Civil War* earned the national attention it would receive.

Comics are now commonly acknowledged as art and as historically important. They are our American mythology, it is commonly said. Still, beyond whatever joy or handwringing results from the proliferation of superhero movies, it is rare that actual comics break through the barriers of condescension and into the public consciousness. Every now and then, publishers stage events that seem designed to create a little public attention. The death of this character. The resurrection of that one. Sometimes, a powerful story earns the attention fairly, such as the death of Superman storyline in 1992. Marvel garnered considerable attention in the early 21st century for acknowledging a changing American demography (and, implicitly, the comics industry's exclusionary history in its representation of race, gender, and religion) with its recasting of Thor as a woman, Ms. Marvel as a Pakistani teenager, and, most notably, Captain America as Sam Wilson, Steve Rogers' African American friend and partner.

Few comics events, though, have come anywhere close to garnering the attention enjoyed by Marvel with its *Civil War* storyline. A collaboration between writer Mark Millar and artist Steve McNiven, the central story is only seven issues long. From its conception, though, Marvel knew that the story would carry through the entire Marvel Universe, and the "Marvel *Civil War* event" involves more than a hundred comics. The sheer breadth of the story, achieved over eight months, allows for a depth of narrative and political allegory seldom available in the comic book form—or any other. (Furthermore, the consequences of the events in *Civil War* would create subsequent storylines, such as *Secret Invasion, Dark Reign*, and *Siege*, that would extend the cultural commentary and dominate the Marvel Universe for almost four years. Though focused on *Civil War*, this volume necessarily addresses these storylines as well, sometimes peripherally, occasionally in depth.)

All of the major news organizations covered *Civil War*, many during the run of the story, and even more after, when Captain America was killed at the culmination of a conspiracy involving an updated, neo-capitalist version of his World War II–era enemy, the Red Skull. While some sources responded to the series as another piece of popular culture now worth reviewing, most used the comic event to stage their own meditations upon American culture. The tagline for *Civil War* is "Whose Side Are You On?" It functioned both as an effective bit of marketing and a clever prediction of the effect the series would have on the culture—that of revealing readers' pre-existing ideologies. NPR's *Talk of the Nation* explored the connections between the story and contemporaneous stories about government wiretapping (see Conan). In its story "What the Death of Captain America Really Means," ABC News depicted Captain America as a martyr to an administration that governs through misdirection and "arguably lies" (Robinson). Fox News' coverage casts Cap as a victim of terrorism and his death as an attack on American values (see articles by Bonisteel). These are just a few examples of many.[2] Moreover, the series dominated conversation within the comic book community online, with dozens of websites and blogs dedicating themselves to conversation about the series and debate regarding its merit and meanings.

Most of the important figures behind *Civil War* have been clear that their intention with the series was not to promote any particular political position or ideology.[3] Rather, the intention was to dig into the core values behind American beliefs, to render the assumed more visible, and to get the reader to do some serious thinking about the culture that the story allegorizes. The very openness of the series invited the varied journalistic and public responses.

All of which brings us to this volume.

Comics scholarship has been steadily increasing in volume and sophistication; however, most of the scholarship is made up of either articles focused on individual works or longer projects covering larger issues in comics, such as form or the role of comics in cultural history. In recent years, comics scholars have begun to focus more squarely on individual characters, and a number of recent and excellent books have considered figures like Spider-Man, Batman, Superman, and, especially, Captain America from critical perspectives such as history, psychology, political science and literary criticism.[4] However, comics scholarship has yet to produce much in the way of book-length works covering single storylines or comic events, such as *Civil War*. Given the subject matter's clear reference to some of the most hostilely debated issues of the new century and the wide public appeal of the series, intensive scrutiny is clearly deserved.[5] It seems to me that, for comics scholarship to see itself as mature, it needs to move toward considering particular storylines in the way that scholars from all fields treat individual novels or movies. In short: extended, close analyses.

My goal with this book is to tackle the difficult process of contextualizing a series designed to be open and indeterminate. To that end, this volume brings together scholars from across many academic fields and interests. Writing about comics brings with it special challenges. The tendency of individual titles to be represented differently from issue to issue, the changing rosters of comics creators within even the same title, and the incomplete instruction in the *MLA Handbook* regarding citation and documentation are just a few. To increase readability, abbreviations for terms and titles that are used repeatedly have been employed.

This volume is divided into eight sections covering a variety of approaches to *Civil War*. Because the series and its tie-ins are so explicitly political, what these stories may have to say about the U.S. government and its actions takes a large portion of the attention of the scholars here. However, readers will find disagreement and stylistic diversity throughout.

Robert G. Weiner opens the book with a foreword that provides context and lays out the necessity of tackling explicitly political works in comics.

The entire premise of *Civil War* depends on a 9/11–like tragedy that leads to the passage, within the Marvel Universe, of the Superhuman Registration Act (SHRA), designed to bring all super-powered individuals under government control, a process that would include each hero revealing to the government his or her secret identity. In this volume's first part, "The SHRA: What the Marvel Universe Tells Us About American Legal Culture," practicing lawyer and legal scholar Ryan M. Davidson tackles the constitutionality of the SHRA by comparing its design and implementation to the more recent Patient Protection and Affordable Care Act ("Obamacare"). Daniel Davis Wood then takes a literary approach to the absurdity he identifies in the SHRA, surveying how various heroes interact with a law that expects and depends on what he sees as contradictory values and legal principles.

As its creators have acknowledged, *Civil War* grew out of U.S. political and cultural responses to terrorism, and the second and third sections contend with just these issues. In the second part, "Superheroics and the American Response to 9/11," scholars investigate some of the ways that the comic event explored how the nation processed its new vulnerability. Mark Bousquet investigates the parallels between the desire of the American people for their government to do something after 9/11 to the debates among the most powerful heroes in the Marvel Universe—who jokingly call themselves the Illuminati—to act preemptively in the face of globally disruptive events. David Sweeney examines how exactly these kinds of disruptive events create cultural gulfs between groups that, on the surface, should be allies, in this case, Marvel's established heroes and the next generation. In the wake of 9/11, the American government and its people reassessed their relationships with other nations, even their allies. Brenna Clarke Gray considers how even Canada came under fire both in the comics and out in her essay. Travis Langley uses the theories of eminent psychologist Erich Fromm to analyze how the *Civil War* event represents the often contradictory human desires for both freedom and security, especially in a troubled culture.

In the third part, "Political Philosophy and *Civil War*," scholars use the tools of political science to interrogate both *Civil War* and the country it represents. Anthony Petros Spanakos shows how the Marvel Universe is attempting to process an ongoing conflict common around the non-fictional globe: how common citizens, often "invisible," struggle to make their political will known. Scott Cleary shows how the core debates of *Civil War* have driven American political thinkers since the days of Thomas Paine. In his essay, Karl E. Martin sees Captain America and Iron Man as representing opposed conceptions of the nation state that serve different parts of society. Kathleen McClancy identifies covert nostalgia in the writing of both Captain America and Iron Man, a desire to recreate the easy morality of World War II–style conflicts.

The through-line of *Civil War* is the variety of debates about the nature of American freedom. In the fourth part, "Super-Powered, American and Marginalized: Triple Consciousness in the Marvel Universe," scholars wrestle with whether or not this freedom is equally available to all Americans, even if they are "super." Comics have long contained contradictions about gender, depicting female characters as strong and decisive, but also as sexual objects. Brandi Hodo explores this phenomenon in *Civil War* through the most significant female character in the Marvel Universe during the event, Ms. Marvel. Jeffrey A. Brown tackles the incorrect cultural belief in the "absent black father" and shows how an African American superhero central to the comic event, Luke Cage, provides a necessary counter narrative.

In the fifth part, "Character(s) Revealed Through Trauma," two scholars approach *Civil War* through close analysis of individual characters whose responses to the super-conflict are even more revealed in their own titular series than in *Civil War* itself. Daniel J. O'Rourke positions Spider-Man as Marvel's superheroic answer to the everyman, torn between the two mentors of Captain America and Iron Man and struggling to fulfill his responsibilities in an environment that muddies even the purest motives. In the character of Captain America, John McGuire finds a longstanding contest about the nature of the American Dream. In James "Bucky" Barnes' replacement of Steve Rogers as Captain America, McGuire sees a more contemporary and liberal vision of the American Dream.

While *Civil War* was popularly debated both for its philosophy and coherence, most readers, reviewers, and scholars have acknowledged that it is a compelling and provocative tale. The sixth part, "Graphic Narrative and Cultural Resonance," examines how the series' creators used the unique form of comics not only to tell their story but to explore key American conflicts. Joseph J. Darowski demonstrates that the narrative and thematic power of *Civil War* depends as much on the penciller, colorist, and inkers as it does on the writer. In my own essay, I argue that the *Civil War* event, with its dozens of involved titles and roughly one hundred tie-in issues, expands the traditional limits of narrative and provides an artistic expression of post–9/11 America unavailable to and unmatched by the other arts.

Because one common goal of both comics and comics scholarship is to demonstrate the value of graphic narrative, the final part, "Teaching the Trouble: Pedagogy and *Civil War*," presents both strategies and an argument for using Marvel's comic event as a teaching tool. Mark D. White identifies *Civil War* as a powerful investigation of ethics in practice and presents strategies for using the narrative in philosophy courses. Seneca Vaught builds upon the ideas of educational theorist Paulo Freire and argues that the classroom is an appropriate environment to promote social justice, with *Civil War* providing a compelling mechanism for that goal.

Finally, in the afterword, Marc DiPaolo offers a passionate, personal, and yet scholarly defense of the idea that comic book stories can wield enormous influence in their readers' lives.

While working on this book, I have been struck numerous times with how the editing process shares a few themes with both *Civil War* and the public response to it. The idea that smart, thoughtful people can disagree about some of America's foundational principles is likely the most profound example. On a more quotidian level, undertaking the editing of a book like this is a large endeavor, and, to harken back to the opening of this introduction, there are forces of Chaos that want to get in the way (proposals, bad junk mail settings, authors who are already incredibly busy). There are also, however, forces of Order at play (submission guidelines, shared research, and the same authors demonstrating creativity and commitment).

The Marvel Universe took almost four years to reassert order. In that time, many characters continued to suffer, and aspects of *Civil War* continued to exert significant influence for years after that. But, then, despite having ended the wars in both Afghanistan and Iraq and having replaced the president who presided over them as well as the passage of the PATRIOT Act, the real world legacy of 9/11 has rendered a full return to the status quo impossible (even if such a thing were desirable).

This brings me, once again, to my experience at the 9/11 Memorial Museum. One story the museum tells is of symmetry (which is Order). The first artifacts the visitor sees are two of the internal steelworks for the entryway tridents (truly, one of the few architectural flourishes in the original Towers). Still on the steelworks are messages written in sturdy paint, directing the construction workers on where and how to place them. Near the end of the museum experience is "the last column." It is the final structural column removed from the site, and it was covered in painted, written, and attached messages by the many recovery workers who spent many months cleaning up the site. So, bookending the experience are columns with messages, each containing hope, connection, and belief in the future. Humanity is visible in both.

Humanity in all its complexity and contradictions is also on display in *Civil War*, and, while I hesitate to speak for all of the scholars included in this book, I feel I can propose that at least one of the reasons we all chose to be scholars and to write about topics like this is because we want to take part in and promote artistic expressions like *Civil War*. The series takes American culture seriously, its politics and its fundamental values. It acknowledges the need of the country to change when it realizes its flaws and vulnerabilities, but it also recognizes the pain that inevitably accompanies that change. While the idea that comics are our modern mythology is not inaccurate, it is ironic, as the best stories, even when they are about characters who can destroy cities, are deeply human.

Notes

1. I have (obviously) been creative in my use of William Butler Yeats' poem "The Second Coming." That said, for my reading, I have used the version of the poem published in *Michael Robartes and the Dancer* (1920). The poem is widely available online in its various forms. I used PotW.org (Poem of the Week).

2. Articles about *Civil War* also appeared in *USA Today, The New York Times, The Pittsburgh Post-Gazette, Newsweek, The Washington Post, The San Francisco Chronicle, The Boston Globe*, and from the AP, among numerous others. Overseas, news services like the BBC, Der Spiegel, and Reuters understood the series and Captain America's death as sad commentary on contemporary American culture.

3. Interviews with the creators have made this clear on many occasions, but for a few examples, see Conan as well as Millar 33, 41, 65, and 93–95 for comments from Joe Quesada, Marvel editor-in-chief, Tom Brevoort, series editor, and Mark Millar, the writer of the flagship series.

4. For a few good examples (and *not* an exhaustive list), see Travis Langley's *Batman and Psychology: A Dark and Stormy Knight*, Jason Dittmer's *Captain America and the Nationalist Superhero: Metaphors, Narratives, and Geopolitics*, editor Mark D. White's *Superman and Philosophy: What Would the Man of Steel Do*, and *Web-Spinning Heroics: Critical Essays on the History and Meaning of Spider-Man*, from editors Robert Moses Peaslee and Robert G. Weiner.

5. As evidence for its public appeal, in an era when the most popular books often sell only a fraction of what average books sold in the 1980s and early 1990s, *Civil War* was held up as a hit for Marvel and for their bottom line. See Ellis.

Works Cited

Bonisteel, Sara. "Captain America Killed Off in Latest Comic." FOXNEWS.com. Fox News Network, LLC, 7 Mar. 2007. Web. 24 Dec. 2014.

_____. "Captain America Lives! Hero to Return in 2008." FOXNEWS.com. Fox News Network, LLC, 12 Oct. 2007. Web. 24 Dec. 2014.
Dittmer, Jason. *Captain America and the Nationalist Superhero: Metaphors, Narratives, and Geopolitics.* Philadelphia: Temple University Press, 2012.
Ellis, David. "Marvel Stock: Still a Hero?" CNNMoney.com. Cable News Network, 23 Feb. 2007. Web. 24 Dec. 2014.
Keith, Toby. "Courtesy of the Red. White and Blue (The Angry American)." Vevo.com. Vevo, LLC. Web. 24 Dec. 2014. Music video.
Langley, Travis. *Batman and Psychology: A Dark and Stormy Knight.* Hoboken: John Wiley & Sons, 2012. Print.
Millar, Mark, and Steve McNiven. *Civil War: Script Book.* New York: Marvel, 2007. Print. The *Script Book* is not paginated, so page numbers have been provided, beginning with the traditional summary and credits page as 1.
Peaslee, Robert Moses, and Robert G Weiner, eds. *Web-Spinning Heroics: Critical Essays on the History and Meaning of Spider-Man.* Jefferson: McFarland, 2012. Print.
Quesada, Joe, and Paul Lenkins. "Marvel Characters Split in 'Civil War' Series." *Talk of the Nation.* NPR.com. National Public Radio, 6 May 2006. Web. 24 Dec. 2014.
Robinson, Bryan. "What the Death of Captain America Really Means." abcnews.go.com. ABC News Internet Ventures, 8 Mar. 2007. Web. 24 Dec. 2014.
White, Mark D. *Superman and Philosophy: What Would the Man of Steel Do?* Hoboken: Wiley-Blackwell, 2013. Print.
Yeats, William Butler. "The Second Coming." *Michael Robartes and the Dancer.* Churchtown, Dundrum, Ireland: The Chuala Press, 1920. PotW.org. Poem of the Week. Web. 24 Dec. 2014.

Part I—The SHRA: What the Marvel Universe Tells Us About American Legal Culture

The Superhuman Registration Act, the Constitution, and the Patient Protection and Affordable Care Act

RYAN M. DAVIDSON

Marvel's *Civil War* event is perhaps one of the most *legally* interesting comics storylines of the new century, if not in comics history. Premised upon the passage of the Superhuman Registration Act (referred to both in the comics and this essay as the "SHRA"), the story can be viewed as the Marvel writers' attempt to deal with the legal and political aftermath of 9/11. The most deadly terrorist attack in American history led to a national discussion on the balance between liberty and security. The passage of the USA PATRIOT Act in 2001 and its renewal in 2006 has been a source of lasting controversy (see Berkay).

The *Civil War* arc has proven to be no less controversial. Fan reception was mixed at best from the start and did not improve in the years since the series was published. Indeed, Marvel itself seemed to regret some of the editorial and plot decisions made during the series, as some events which promised permanent change in the Marvel canon were undone very quickly. For instance, Spider-Man's revelation of his identity to the world was undone in the 2007-2008 *One More Day* storyline. The SHRA itself was repealed at the end of Marvel's *Siege* storyline in May 2010, leaving almost no trace of the seemingly monumental events of *Civil War*.[1]

It is the purpose of this essay to suggest that many of the problems with *Civil War* can be explained by two issues having to do with the way the writers handled the legal details of the story. First, there did not seem to be any consensus among the writers as to what the SHRA actually said. Indeed, one can even argue that individual authors—whether deliberately or inadvertently—fail to maintain a consistent notion of the SHRA. It should not be terribly surprising that a story arc predicated on a change in the law might run into problems when the law in question is not well or consistently defined.

Second, what legal details are present are often inconsistent with the legal environment in the real world. Granted, comic books depart from reality all the time; that's one of the main reasons we read them, after all. But many of the problems and inconsistencies that appear in the story could have been avoided entirely if the authors had been more careful about accuracy in the content, implementation, and enforcement of the SHRA. Simply put, even if we distill the SHRA down to its most basic, essential components (ignoring any inconsistencies with the story that this might produce), the resulting law would be problematic at best—if not outright unconstitutional. Given the current state of constitutional jurisprudence, it is quite difficult to see how Congress could pass a law which is both consistent with applicable United States Supreme Court holdings *and* have the effects that the SHRA seems to have in the story.

Part of the legal analysis has to do with very significant developments in statutory and constitutional law: the Patient Protection and Affordable Care Act ("ACA") and its treatment by the Supreme Court in *Nat'l Fed. of Ind. Bus. v. Sebelius* ("NFIB"). The implementation and enforcement (or the lack thereof) of the ACA illustrates very effectively why the SHRA is problematic and how some of the most significant points of plot conflict would have been entirely avoided if the SHRA had better reflected principles of federal constitutional and administrative law.

The Nature of the SHRA

Before going any further, we must have some understanding of what the SHRA actually *does*. The text of the law is never set forth in the comics in any meaningful way. This is not necessarily a bad thing, as statutes tend to make for rather tedious reading. A statute of this magnitude would likely take up dozens if not hundreds of pages.[2] But it does make efforts to analyze the SHRA somewhat challenging.

The most significant early discussion of the SHRA appears in *New Avengers: The Illuminati* #0 (*NAI*) published about two months before *Civil War #1* (Millar). Toward the end of *NAI #0*, Tony Stark (as Iron Man) addresses leading representatives of the most significant groups of super-human individuals then extant: Dr. Strange (Earth's Sorcerer Supreme), Charles Xavier (leader of the X-Men), Reed Richards (Mr. Fantastic of the Fantastic Four), Black Bolt (leader of the Inhumans), and Namor (King of Atlantis). Once they are gathered, Iron Man begins a discussion of the forthcoming law.

> STARK: Something larger than any issues we have is on the horizon ... and if I didn't come to you with it I would not be able to live with myself. This is an early draft of a bill that will hit the floor of the United States Congress in a month or two. It was slipped to me under the table. It's the Super Hero Registration Act. Anyone with powers—anyone in costume—any mutant—any of *our* kind is going to be required by law to reveal themselves to the United States government. In return, the registered hero will be given a job as a guard in the new S.H.I.E.L.D. World Security Force.... Refusing to do so will be considered a federal crime....
>
> DR. STRANGE: If a person wears a mask, how will they know who to—?
>
> STARK: S.H.I.E.L.D. is developing a special unit to hunt down anyone flagrantly disobeying the law.
>
> DR. STRANGE: Well, that's just disgusting.
>
> STARK: And I think we should all voluntarily support and obey this act before it even goes to a vote.... We should cooperate now, *before* it gets ugly. Before someone or *everyone* is made an example of [Bendis, *NAI* #0, 26].

Stark then proceeds to lay out the basic justification for the SHRA, which the other contributors to this collection have discussed in more detail than is necessary here. Suffice it to say that it is clear that the Marvel writers had finally decided to deal with the fact that neither the United States federal government nor the voting public is likely to put up with massively powerful individuals running around without any kind of government oversight.

Even now, the first time this version of the SHRA is introduced, consistency problems are evident. Perhaps a minor quibble, but if the various authors cannot even be consistent about the *name* of the key legislation behind the entire story, that does not bode well.

And, sure enough, it would not be long before other ambiguities and inconsistencies manifested themselves. In *New Avengers #22*, Stark goes with Ms. Marvel to confront Luke Cage (a sometime member of the Avengers) and his wife Jessica Jones on the eve of the SHRA going into effect. Despite being written by the very same author as *NAI #0*, Stark's discussion of the SHRA is somewhat different in this issue:

> STARK: At midnight, the Superhuman Registration Act becomes law. All heroes, including we Avengers, will be required to sign in. We'll all work for the United States Government. And the Avengers will be a fully sanctioned legal team with pay and benefits. Will you sign on?
>
> CAGE: [silence]....
>
> STARK: I need to know, Luke. Because at midnight, if you don't ... you and Jessica are effectively criminals. Again.
>
> CAGE: [silence]
>
> STARK: Now I talked to—wait—I talked to the powers that be. Your sordid past is all being swept under the rug. All that trouble in your youth ... none of it will affect your standing as a sanctioned Avenger.
>
> JONES: What about me, Mr. Stark? Yeah, I have powers too ... and you know what? I don't *want* to use them, and I have no plans to use them. *And* I don't want to work for the United States of Corporate Sellouts. What about someone like me?
>
> CAGE: Well, Mrs. Cage ...
>
> JONES: Jones.
>
> STARK: Well, Jessica, you'll sign in, and we'll deal with that when the time comes. You have a newborn baby. No one's going to ask you to go fight Doctor Doom.
>
> JONES: Bet your ass.
>
> M. MARVEL: Jessica, you're—
>
> JONES: Carol, don't! Just—you're military. You *like* being told what to do. We *don't*. In fact, we *hate* it [Bendis, *NA #22*, 2–3].

As the conversation proceeds, Cage compares Stark's threats to slavery and Jim Crow. Stark rejects the comparison without offering any concrete means of distinction. He and Ms. Marvel depart after Cage strongly implies that neither he nor his wife will comply with the law, Stark having threatened to send S.H.I.E.L.D.[3] agents to arrest Cage if he does not sign up. This is a threat he will make good on: S.H.I.E.L.D. agents arrive mere seconds after midnight.

There are definitely points of consistency between the discussions of the SHRA in *NAI #0* and *NA #22*. In both discussions, it is clear that super-humans are required to register with the federal government. Likewise, registration isn't the end of it: registered super-humans are seemingly going to be salaried federal employees working in legally-sanctioned hero teams. And the authorities will not take kindly to super-humans who decline to sign up.

But even in just these two issues, we start to see inconsistencies, or at least unresolved details, despite having been written by the very same author only perhaps four months apart. The name of the Act has changed, for one thing. And whereas in *NAI #0* Stark suggests that registered super-humans will be working for the S.H.I.E.L.D. World Security Force, in *NA #22* they will apparently be working directly for the federal government. In the comics, S.H.I.E.L.D. is usually depicted as some kind of United Nations–affiliated security force. Working for the UN and working for a U.S. federal entity are very different, legally speaking.[4] Joe Quesada, Marvel's editor-in-chief from 2000 to 2010, never seems to have sat the writers down and worked out how the SHRA was supposed to work.

Stark also indicates that every super-human is required to register, whether or not they intend to actually use their powers. Yet compare that to the following exchange from *Ms. Marvel* #7, published two months later. Ms. Marvel is meeting with Anya Corazon (the future Spider-Girl) and Anya's father in an attempt to convince Anya to register. At the time of the conversation, the SHRA has been in effect for some months. Anya has not registered and has been cruising around Brooklyn like she always has. Yet rather than arresting her on sight, Ms. Marvel seems almost conciliatory:

> Ms. Marvel: The important thing is that you haven't done *anything* wrong. Since the Super-human Registration Act went into effect, the only times you've been seen in public are when you're traveling around Brooklyn. Although you *could* be ticketed for appearing in public in *costume*—
>
> Anya: But it's *not* a costume. It's a part of me—
>
> Ms. Marvel: What I mean is, you've not been breaking any laws big enough for anyone to care about. If you come clean right now, register and—
>
> Mr. Corazon: No! This is *craziness*! My daughter is too young to—
>
> Ms. Marvel: There is *no* lower age-limit on the S.H.R.A. Mister Corazon. If someone with powers and abilities is going to *legally* use those powers and abilities, then they must be *registered* and *trained*, no matter *how* old they are [Reed, MM #7, 11].

This is a very, *very* different depiction of the SHRA than seen previously. In *NA* #22, Tony Stark demands that Cage and Jones register *immediately*, and S.H.I.E.L.D. agents knock on Cage's door as *soon* as the SHRA goes into force. In *MM* #7, Ms. Marvel describes Anya's failure to register as not constituting a violation of any law "big enough for anyone to care about." The perspectives could not be more different. Further, this discussion strongly implies that a super-human who decides to simply not use his powers might not be required to register at all. This is specifically what Jessica Jones asked Stark in *NA* #22 and Stark clearly did not consider failure to register to be an option for anyone. His dialog there suggests some potential flexibility in the employment requirement, but none whatsoever for the registration requirement.[5]

As to the employment requirement, in *NAI* #0 it was suggested that registered super-humans would become agents of S.H.I.E.L.D. In *Civil War* #5, this too was "amended." When escorting Daredevil to "Project 42," the story's Negative Zone version of Guantanamo Bay, Stark first mentions what would become the Fifty-State Initiative (later simply "the Initiative"): "Our big idea is fifty super-teams spread over all fifty states, each one licensed and accountable to the taxpayer" (Millar, *CW* #5, 20). The gist of the idea is that super-humans registered under the SHRA would be assigned to these federal teams, one per state, to create blanket coverage of the entire country. This would form the premise of the new series *Avengers: The Initiative*, which saw a thirty-five issue run ending in 2010. So which is it? S.H.I.E.L.D. or the Initiative? And what is the relationship, if any, between the two agencies? It's all rather muddled.

All in all, it does not seem possible to construct an entirely consistent picture of the SHRA from the various comics. There simply does not appear to have been sufficient editorial control to impose a coherent vision of the details of the law on the Marvel writers' stable. The most stripped-down version of the law that is most consistent with most of the discussions in the comics would seem to contain the following elements: (1) mandatory registration of *all* super-humans whether or not they used their powers (the "registration requirement"), and (2) the creation of the Initiative to employ those super-humans as federal security operatives (the "employment requirement"). Space being limited, it is these two elements upon which we will focus in exploring the legal implications of the SHRA.

The SHRA and the Constitution

Having identified these two elements as the core of the SHRA, we can move on to an analysis of their constitutionality. Under current Supreme Court jurisprudence, it seems likely that the law would run into significant judicial problems almost right away.

Can the Federal Government Require Super-Human Registration?

The most fundamental question presented by the SHRA is whether Congress has the authority to pass a law that requires super-humans to register with the federal government. This is essentially a question of federalism, i.e., whether the Constitution has authorized Congress to enact such a law (and implicitly for the other branches to enforce it).

This essay cannot and is not intended to be a primer on constitutional law, so this decision from Chief Justice William Rehnquist will have to suffice:

> We start with first principles. The Constitution creates a Federal Government of enumerated powers. See Art. I, § 8. As James Madison wrote, "The powers delegated by the proposed Constitution to the federal government are few and defined. Those which are to remain in the State governments are numerous and indefinite" [*United States v. Lopez* 552].

In other words, Congress does not have what is called "police power," i.e., unlimited jurisdiction to legislate about "health, safety, and morals" simply on the basis of its perceptions of what constitutes good public policy. Rather, the federal government's power to act is limited to those powers specifically granted to it by the Constitution.[6] Conversely, state governments *do* have police power and may thus issue and enforce legislation on any matter which the Constitution does not specifically reserve for the federal government.

An example would be zoning laws/ordinances. States and municipalities may pass and enforce extraordinarily restrictive and exacting ordinances regarding the use of land as long as those ordinances do not violate various constitutional protections, e.g., restricting the freedom of speech (*Schad v. Borough of Mt. Ephraim*), discriminating on the basis of race (*Buchanan v. Warley*), or amounting to the seizure of private property (*First Eng. Evangelical Lutheran Church v. Los Angeles*). By contrast, the federal government can only impose those same kinds of land-use regulations with respect to federal property.[7]

The most likely enumerated power for the SHRA would be the Commerce Clause, which gives Congress the power to "regulate Commerce with foreign Nations, and among the several states, and with the Indian tribes" (U.S. Const. art. I, sec. 8, cl. 3). Under the Supreme Court jurisprudence prior to 1995, a super-human registration act would have seemed plausible enough.

Here, some of the aforementioned consistency problems come home to roost. Specifically, the question of whether the SHRA applies to *every* super-human (the "broad" version of the requirement) or merely to those who wish to use their powers in public (the "narrow" version) turns out to be hugely important. If all super-humans are required to register, the SHRA may well be unconstitutional, as recent Commerce Clause jurisprudence suggests that the Supreme Court, under its current configuration, would take a dim view of such a requirement.

Simply stated, the broad version of the SHRA registration requirement would be that every super-human within the U.S. is required to register with the federal government, whether or not they use or intend to use their powers in public. Yet in two relatively recent Supreme Court decisions, the Court has ruled against requirements being imposed directly upon individuals as such. Again, Congress does not have general police power and cannot pass legislation simply because a particular bill appears to be good policy. The states may do that, but federal law must be tied to a power enumerated in the Constitution.

Something like super-human registration would certainly seem to be permissible under *Wickard v. Filburn* (1942) and its progeny. *Wickard* is the case in which the Supreme Court began upholding components of the New Deal as proper exercises of the Commerce Power. Prior to *Wickard*, attempts to create economic recovery programs of the sort that are mostly uncontroversial today were uniformly struck down as unconstitutional. (See, for example, *U.S. v. Butler* [1936] and *A.L.A. Schechter Poultry Corp. v. U.S.* [1935].) *Wickard* essentially ushered in the modern era of the expansive federal administrative state.

But in 1995, the Supreme Court handed down *Lopez*, striking down a federal law premised upon the Commerce Clause—the Gun Free School Zones Act of 1990. In *Lopez*, the Court held that the mere fact that an activity might arguably have an *effect* on interstate commerce, however tangential, was insufficient to justify federal regulation of that act without something further. "The possession of a gun in a local school zone is in no sense an economic activity that might, through repetition elsewhere, have ... a substantial effect on interstate commerce" (*Lopez* 549). Further, even bracketing the requirement of a "substantial effect" upon interstate commerce, the law "contain[ed] no jurisdictional element that would ensure, through case-by-case inquiry, that the firearms possession in question has the requisite nexus with interstate commerce" (549). In short, the activity of "possessing a gun in a school zone" was not sufficiently connected with interstate commerce to permit regulation in and of itself, and Congress did not draft the law in such a way that would permit the courts to distinguish between individual instances of such activity which did affect interstate commerce and those which did not. As such, the Court held that the law exceeded Congress's Commerce Clause authority and was therefore unconstitutional. Congress acted quickly, passing a version of the law that made it illegal to possess a gun which "has moved in or otherwise affects interstate commerce" (18 U.S. Code, Sec. 922 [q][2][A]).

Similar reasoning was used in *U.S. v. Morrison*, when the Court struck down a portion of the Violence Against Women Act of 1994 for lack of any "jurisdictional element" connecting federal criminalization of certain kinds of gender-related violence to Congress's authority to regulate interstate commerce (598).

But where things get really interesting is *Nat'l Fed. of Ind. Bus. v. Sebelius*, the Supreme Court's first ruling on the ACA. The case deals with a number of issues, not all of which are relevant here, but one of the main issues has to do with whether Congress can order private individuals to buy health insurance on the private market, as the ACA purports to do in 26 U.S. Code, section 5000A. The final ruling involved no less than *six* opinions, and the implications of the case are still working themselves out.

Very briefly, four Justices voted in a dissent to strike section 5000A entirely as an unconstitutional exercise of Congress's Commerce Clause Power. The dissenters' argument is essentially that notwithstanding the fact that the health insurance market is arguably inextricably connected to interstate commerce, and notwithstanding the fact that Congress can regulate entirely intra-state participation in that market, Congress could not regulate the *failure to participate in that market entirely* (NFIB, Scalia, J., dissenting). In short, the dissenters would preclude Congress from imposing any sanction whatsoever on an individual who refuses to buy health insurance.

Chief Justice Roberts did not join that opinion, leaving it with only four votes. This is why it is a dissent rather than the majority opinion or a concurrence. But Roberts implied in what is officially the majority opinion that he agrees with the dissenters on that point. The net result is that it looks very much like there *are* five votes for the proposition that Congress may not regulate economic *inactivity*, only economic *activity*, and only where that activity is linked in some way—however nominal—to interstate commerce.

What does this mean for the SHRA? Well, parsing the various opinions in NFIB, together with *Lopez* and *Morrison*, the "broad" version of the registration requirement would probably not pass Supreme Court muster at this point in time. The Court would not seem to be concerned about super-humans like Luke Cage and Jessica Jones who simply decide to stay home and not use their powers in public. But there would seem to be broad support among the Justices for a registration requirement for super-humans who do use their powers in public, particularly if said super-humans were engaged in some sort of crime-fighting or security activity. A requirement for those super-humans simply using their powers in private *might* be upheld, but a requirement for using said powers for other people's benefit *certainly* would.

This has important implications for the plot of the story. One of the main reasons the "Pro-Reg" side wound up looking so unreasonable is that they made no exceptions for super-humans who just wanted to be left alone, either because they had retired from their public activities or had never had any to begin with. The notion that people who are minding their own business and not bothering anybody should be free from government supervision and regulation resonates pretty strongly with many comic book readers, and indeed the American public in general. So if the authors had spent a little more time getting this particular detail right, Tony Stark wouldn't need to send the S.H.I.E.L.D. SWAT team in to Luke Cage's apartment at a minute after midnight, and the writers could spend time debating the actual merits of the SHRA rather than showing just how big of a jerk Tony can be. Unfortunately for the plot, this means that some of the more poignant conflicts do not need to happen at all.

Is the Initiative Constitutional?

From there we turn to the question of whether a federally-organized series of superhero teams stationed around the country and manned by super-humans forced to register under the SHRA would be legal. The answer is that it might be *constitutional*, but still not *legal* under the current state of affairs. In one sense, the Initiative has a lot more constitutional support for it than either the broad or narrow versions of the registration requirement. But that very constitutional support turns out to be what likely rules out anything like the Initiative from actually becoming law.

As discussed above, under a Commerce Clause analysis, the broad registration requirement that every super-human must register with the federal government whether or not they use their powers is probably unconstitutional. As the narrow version would probably involve skipping some of the bigger character conflicts, that's not an entirely satisfactory solution either. Besides, if only public super-humans need to register, will there be enough registrants to adequately man the Initiative?

But Congress absolutely *does* have the power to "raise and support armies" (U.S. Const. art. I, sec. 8, cl. 12) and to "make rules for the government and regulation of the land and naval forces" (cl. 14). As depicted, the Initiative is part of S.H.I.E.L.D., and several characters make reference to Initiative members being federal employees, apparently with generous benefits packages. This is a promising beginning.

The key point is that, under the War Powers Clause, Congress has the authority to institute a compulsory national draft. The Supreme Court has interpreted the draft power to be an inherent component of what it means to "raise and support armies." The Supreme Court has upheld the draft against challenges from a fairly wide variety of legal theories, including the Thirteenth Amendment prohibition of involuntary servitude and First Amendment protections for freedom of religion and speech (the *Selective Draft Law Cases* decision of 1918) and has upheld the legitimacy of the draft during peacetime (the *Holmes v. U.S.* decision of 1968). The Court has, to date, never found an opportunity to hold that Congress had exceeded its authority under the draft power.

That being the case, why could Congress not sidestep the Commerce Clause issues entirely by relying upon the unambiguous and more extensive grants of authority under the War Powers Clause? Why not just use the draft power both to ground the registration requirement of the SHRA *and* secure the services of a sufficient number of super-humans to fully man the Initiative? Indeed, under current jurisprudence there is no reason to think that a draft specifically targeting super-humans would be improper. The Selective Service System only requires men eighteen years old and older to register for the draft, and the Supreme Court has upheld that limited requirement (*Rostker v. Goldberg*).

It turns out there is a reason, and that reason is at least as much political as strictly constitutional. The constitutional aspect is that while Congress does have extensive draft powers, there is one limitation that has been so axiomatic that it has never been directly addressed: draftees must be drafted *into the military*. There is no question that Congress can draft people into the Army, the Navy, the Marines, and the Air Force. That's happened before and it can happen again. But Congress has *never* attempted to draft anyone into non-military federal service. There is, therefore, no case law on point. But it seems reasonable to think the Supreme Court would take a very dim view of any attempt by Congress to employ the War Powers Clause for anything but "raising and supporting armies." So while Congress could use the War Powers Clause to justify the SHRA and the Initiative, it could only do so if the Initiative were part of the United States military.

That, as it turns out, creates a huge *political* problem, one sufficiently thorny that even something as significant as the emergence of super-humans might well not be adequate to overcome. Simply put, both state governments *and* Congress are very, *very* uncomfortable with the use of federal military forces on U.S. soil, for a variety of reasons, and Congress has passed laws that severely restrict such deployments.

In the aftermath of the Civil War (the real, historical one), there was a period of military rule over the "rebel states" authorized by the Reconstruction Acts. This was not entirely unjustified, as in the early 1870s, many Southern state governments actively and explicitly refused to enforce law and order during federal elections, allowing local officials to overtly suppress the African American vote. Federal troops were deployed in an effort to curb such abuses. The problems that arose as a result are far too complex and multi-faceted to treat here, but suffice it to say that by the late 1870s, the country was well and truly ready for the end of domestic federal military rule.

In response, Congress passed the Posse Comitatus Act, the gist of which is that the federal troops may not be used in law enforcement or domestic governance matters on U.S. soil except in very limited circumstances. The text in relevant part reads as follows:

> Whoever, except in cases and under circumstances expressly authorized by the Constitution or Act of Congress, willfully uses any part of the Army or the Air Force as a posse comitatus or otherwise to execute the laws shall be fined under this title or imprisoned not more than two years, or both [Posse Comitatus Act].

Essentially, the use of federal military troops on U.S. soil is prohibited except where specifically authorized.

There are a few standing authorizations for such deployments. The President may obviously deploy the armed forces to defend against foreign invasion. He is, after all, the commander-in-chief, and it seems unlikely that Congress could restrict such deployments even if it wanted to. There is also the Insurrection Act of 1807 and the three Enforcement Acts of 1870 and 1871,[8] together with a few others. These laws give the president the authority to use federal troops domestically in certain circumstances.

For instance, federal troops may be used to enforce federal law if state governments refuse to do so. This is basically what happened in Little Rock in the late 1950s, motivating President Eisenhower to have the 101st Airborne escort a group of nine African American children to school over the opposition of the Arkansas state governor. Similarly, the president may honor the request from the governor or legislature of a state for the use of federal troops to restore civil order. This provision was invoked to quell the 1992 Los Angeles riots in the wake of the Rodney King verdict. But in the absence of a specific, explicit congressional authorization, the president may not use federal armed forces to enforce the laws on U.S. soil.[9]

Unfortunately, the Initiative does not seem like it would fall into any of the available exceptions. For one thing, they would not seem to authorize the creation of dedicated federal military units garrisoned in every state for the purpose of preventing largely *domestic* super-human misbehavior. If the Initiative was exclusively and solely tasked with keeping America safe from Latverian Doombots and Skrull invaders, that would be one thing. There have been strategic bomber units in the Midwest on more-or-less constant standby for fifty years now, but their commanders are not focused on domestic threats. By contrast, the Initiative is most certainly supposed to be dealing with problems that have historically been handled by local law enforcement.

Further, the Initiative is not deployed only when civil order breaks down. It seems that in the Marvel Comics universe, state and local governments are pretty much open for business most of the time. Granted, there are certainly specific instances when things seem to get out of hand, e.g., *World War Hulk*, but one could reasonably expect state governments—which would still be functional even under those circumstances—to issue a request to the president to use federal forces for the duration of the emergency. That is a very different thing from having a super-human crew on standby, ready to go in every time a super-villain makes an appearance and whether or not the governor has asked for their help.

Indeed, the notion that a state governor would make a request that a standing federal force of super-humans be stationed in his state to be used there on a regular basis seems contradictory to the entire justification for the SHRA. Remember, the SHRA was passed because super-humans operating in Connecticut blew up an elementary school. The sense of the voting public is said to be that there are just too many super-humans running around civilian areas these days. Indeed, a common critique of superheroes throughout comics history is that if it were not for do-gooder super-humans parading around, ordinary criminals would have no motivation to aspire to super-villain status. *Expanding* the number of super-humans operating in civilian areas does not seem to be the most obvious political consequence of such sentiments.

Combine that with the country's rather entrenched resistance to the domestic use of federal troops and the possibility of a new exception to the Posse Comitatus Act really seems like a political non-starter. The American public, state governments, and members of Congress have proven to be far too suspicious of the domestic use of federal troops to be willing to create a specific exception for the Initiative.

This creates something of a catch-22 for the SHRA. On one hand, the Commerce Clause problems could be avoided by basing the law on the War Powers Clause, with the result that the Initiative would become merely another branch of the U.S. armed forces. As this is not that far off from how the Initiative is portrayed in the comics, it is a truly attractive option. But on the other hand, making the Initiative part of the military would tend to preclude its domestic use under current political arrangements, because it does not seem as if the Initiative can fit into any of the available exceptions to the Posse Comitatus Act.[10] On the gripping hand, if the Initiative is *not* part of the armed forces, opening it up for use domestically, then the SHRA cannot be based on the War Powers Clause, because Congress may only draft people into the military. Again: the very fix that makes the SHRA work would prevent it from working as described in the comics.

The SHRA and the ACA

The constitutional and political problems with the SHRA are interesting enough, but it turns out that there is a *very* timely example from the real world which, I would argue, shows that the comics' bungling of their legal foundation is actually what causes a lot of the stories' plotting problems. Specifically, the disastrous rollout of Healthcare.gov shows just how much administrative law goes into acts as complicated as the SHRA.

The two laws may seem to have nothing whatsoever to do with each other, and in terms of content, that's largely true. The SHRA has to do with super-human registration and the creation of a federal, multi-state domestic super-human fighting force. The ACA reformed the private health care insurance market, particularly individual plans, and created a series of health care exchanges and subsidies. But in their *structure*, there is a certain degree of similarity. Both laws involve an unknown but potentially very large number of citizens registering with the government in ways that no one has ever had to do before. Both laws involve the government evaluating registrants and sorting them into newly-created categories. And both laws theoretically contain previously unheard of penalties for those that decline or refuse to comply.

Recall in *NAI* #0 that Tony Stark was supposedly at Luke Cage's house the night before the SHRA was to go into effect. At a minute after midnight, Stark says, Cage will be in violation of the law unless he registers. And sure enough, five minutes after midnight, in go the S.H.I.E.L.D. capekillers.

Now wait just a minute. *It's the middle of the night.* Is it absolutely imperative that

Cage register *now*? Can it not wait until morning? Or maybe next week? What if Cage has a day job and cannot get to the registration office until he has a day off? What if his son has a cold, Jessica has to work, and he needs that day off to stay home with the kid? Is Stark *seriously* going to send in the capekillers because a family man doesn't want to deal with bureaucratic red tape *while he is supposed to be in bed*?

Apparently so. With the result that a lot of readers and critics thought the problem with *Civil War* was *not* the SHRA as such, but the fact that the only way to generate any kind of controversy about the SHRA was to make "Pro-Reg" characters into massive jerks regardless of what their prior characterization would suggest. Tony Stark is, admittedly, more than a little arrogant. But Mr. Fantastic has historically been a kind and reasonable man. Suggesting, creating, and enforcing the use of a secret negative zone prison for rebellious super-humans, some of whom are his *friends*, is not really in character for him. But Captain America needed to be able to take a principled stand, so Mr. Fantastic gets to hold the "villain ball" for this one.

More substantively, if the SHRA is going into effect at midnight ... how was Cage supposed to register in the first place? He could not have gone to the registration office (more on that in a minute) earlier that afternoon, because *there was no registration requirement yet*. That only came along when the SHRA became law.

Further, as we see in a very entertaining vignette involving Howard the Duck, registration itself is not a simple matter (see Templeton). Of *course* it isn't. Registering your *car* involves a maddening amount of paperwork; how could registering as a *super-human* be otherwise? Leaving aside the question of just which government is going to be responsible for registration,[11] it cannot simply be a matter of walking in to the office, giving your name to the clerk, and going home. There are going to be forms to fill out, questionnaires to take, identification to secure, and so forth. This is going to take at least a couple of hours. *How is Cage supposed to register until those processes and documents have been created?* Stark is functionally threatening Cage with arrest for refusing to do something that he could not do even if he wanted to.

What we are dancing around here is the fact that laws as complex as this one take time to implement—just like the ACA has. That act was passed in 2010, but it was not until the end of 2013 that individuals were supposed to be able to sign up to purchase health insurance on the exchanges. Even given two and a half years of lead time, the rollout of the federal and most state exchange websites was, by all accounts, a disaster mitigated only by the Obama administration's questionably legal extensions instituted by what amounts to executive fiat.

Whatever one thinks about the merits of the ACA as such, it is easy to see *why* the Administration has done what it has in delaying implementation of various provisions of the Act. The intuition here is that it is just not *fair* to cancel someone's health insurance plan, order them to buy health insurance on an exchange, threaten to penalize them if they fail to do so, and then not have the exchanges working when the requirement goes into effect. This intuition lines up very nicely with legal doctrines surrounding due process, which is a right guaranteed by the Fifth and Fourteenth amendments. No penalties may be imposed without due process of law, and a penalty for violating a requirement that cannot be reasonably complied with would violate that protection.

But implementation issues aside, the way the ACA is written reflects the real-world process of giving the various regulatory agencies responsible time for turning words on paper into a functional, reliable system that people can use to buy actual health insurance products, for the IRS to develop the rules and forms for reporting and accounting for compliance, and for state departments of insurance and insurance companies to develop and implement the insurance regulations and policies that people can actually buy.

Granted, creating health insurance exchanges for millions of users in all fifty states is almost certainly a harder technical and administrative task than managing super-human registration. One year into implementation, healthcare.gov does not seem to be truly finished. It does not seem like super-human registration would take two years to get going,[12] and the public probably wouldn't have stood for it anyway. But those registration forms *do* still need to be drafted. Employees need to be hired/assigned and then trained on the registration process. Entirely new government offices might need to be opened. Implementing the registration requirement of the SHRA does not seem like it could take *less* than two or three months, at the very minimum. Six to nine is far from unreasonable. More if the registration requirement extends even to those who do not use their powers.

So, if the SHRA had a built-in period between the act becoming law and the registration requirement going into effect, the conversation between Stark and Cage in *NAI* #0 would have gone something more like the following:

STARK: The SHRA goes into effect tonight.
CAGE: Yes, I know.
STARK: And you're going to have to register.
CAGE: When?
STARK: In ninety days.
CAGE: What if I decide I don't want to register?
STARK: Well, no need to make up your mind now. You've got three months after all.
CAGE: Right, but what if I have made up my mind and don't want to register?
STARK: There will be a modest fine, and you'll still have to register. And if you don't register within *180* days, then I may have to come back here with some friends.
CAGE: Fine, look, we're eating dinner here. It's my turn to put the kid to bed. Can we do this some other time?
STARK: Sure. You should be getting the paperwork in the mail when it's available. Make sure you send it in.

Basically, if the SHRA had been depicted as being written the way real laws with similar administrative elements are actually written, the capekillers do not get sent in until the "anti-reg" characters have had several months to register at their leisure. There is still the potential for a plot-advancing dramatic standoff, with Stark confronting Cage as the clock ticks down. But it would be set several months after the SHRA became law. The focus in that situation would be about *the merits of registration*, i.e., the whole point of *Civil War*, rather than the fact that Stark is being completely unreasonable in demanding instant and immediate compliance from a family man in the middle of the night.

Conclusion

Marvel Comics is, on one hand, to be commended for attempting to deal with pressing social and political issues head on. In 2006, the country was still significantly engaged in a public conversation over the balance between liberty and security, a conversation that is still going on. They are further to be commended for taking seriously the fact that governments are not likely to let super-humans wander around unsupervised for very long. Entities as powerful as the Hulk, Iron Man, and the Green Goblin would provoke a legal and political response almost immediately.

But the execution of the *Civil War* event leaves much to be desired. There does not seem to have been any consensus among the writers as to what the SHRA actually *does*, and even individual writers occasionally seem to shift their thinking without explanation. Further, the depiction of the law involves constitutional, political, and administrative problems, and these problems wind up being what causes a lot of the main plot conflicts instead of what the authors were probably trying to get at, i.e., the social, political, and philosophical motivations for the SHRA as such. Iron Man (and Tony Stark) do not need to be unreasonable and fascistic for the SHRA to be problematic, and indeed, making them out to be such clouds the genuine issues that *Civil War* was probably intended to get at. One can only hope that future explorations of these issues will be based on a more considered stance on real-world legal structures.

Notes

1. Marvel has always taken a more mythological approach to its continuity than DC's more historiographic one, with events fading in and out of canon over time rather than being rewritten by periodic, continuity-spanning "crises" which wipe the slate clean for the entire comics line. Marvel took only three years to almost completely reverse, undo, or otherwise eliminate most of the events of *Civil War*, which is much faster than usual for the publisher.

2. The USA PATRIOT Act, for instance, takes up some 131 pages in the official version published by the Government Printing Office.

3. The acronym for Marvel's international peace keeping organization, *Supreme Headquarters, International Espionage, Law-Enforcement Division*.

4. This is all that will be said about S.H.I.E.L.D. in this essay. Though it does represent a major locus of legal complication in the *Civil War* story, this has more to do with the fact that the precise nature, jurisdiction, and organizational structure of S.H.I.E.L.D. have never been completely nor consistently described. Indeed, the legal issues involved with the organization merit an essay in their own right. In light of that, it seems reasonable to bracket the legal problems in *Civil War* that have to do with S.H.I.E.L.D. and its role in enforcing the SHRA, as such issues do not arise out of the *Civil War* series itself. Thus, for the purposes of this essay, it is assumed—rightly or wrongly—that S.H.I.E.L.D. is, for all intents and purposes, a part of the executive branch of the United States federal government.

5. As an aside, Ms. Marvel has seemingly introduced a new requirement of the SHRA: a ban on appearing in a costume in public. This had not been previously mentioned, and it does not seem to come up again. There is no discussion of the legality or regulation of costumes in *Civil War* other than Ms. Marvel's comment here. Contrast with the Keene Act from Alan Moore's *Watchmen*, which targets "costumed vigilantism" rather than "super-humans." The setting of *Watchmen* contains many of the former but only one of the latter, and unlike, say, Captain America, or even arguably Superman, there is not any practical way of making Dr. Manhattan do anything he does not want to do.

6. Or, in practice, implied to have been so granted as the Constitution is interpreted by the courts.

7. This is, of course, something of a simplification, as there are a host of federal regulations that do wind up impacting land use, especially environmental regulations. But these are not zoning regulations per se, i.e., they are not land use regulations as such. The federal government is simply not in the business of deciding how high buildings can be, or whether a new construction project will overload the local traffic grid. Indeed, zoning is so intensely local a proposition that it is hard to imagine how the federal government could operate effectively in that capacity. To be sure, federal lawsuits regarding local zoning ordinances are far from uncommon. One ongoing example (as of the writing of this essay) would be *Undercliff Cottage, LLC v. FHRE, LLC*. But even there the parties are not asking the federal government to assume direct and ongoing responsibility for land use planning, merely that the local land use authority be required to comply with some tangentially-related federal law.

8. The third of these acts is significant for introducing 42 U.S. Code, section 1983, the first statute that specifically authorizes civil actions alleging the deprivation of civil rights. It has proven to be one of the most important civil rights laws in American history.

9. For a general discussion on constitutional powers which, like the war powers, are shared by both

Congress and the President, see *Youngstown Sheet & Tube Co. v. Sawyer* (particularly the concurring opinions of Robert Jackson and Felix Frankfurter).

    10. It is worth pointing out that in 2006, the Insurrection Act was amended (the John Warner National Defense Authorization Act for Fiscal Year 2007, section 1076), dramatically expanding the potential scope of the Act in such a way that might have made the Initiative a little more workable. Whereas the former and current state of the law require a *state* government to make the determination that it is incapable of maintaining public order, the 2006 amendments would have permitted the *President* to make that determination on his own. These amendments were repealed in 2008 (National Defense Authorization Act for Fiscal Year 2008, section 1068). The result is, interestingly enough, that for the very brief period during which *Civil War* was published, the Initiative *might* have been viable under the War Powers Clause. But the very fact that even a mundane expansion of domestic federal military power was so unpopular that Congress repealed it at the first available opportunity illustrates just how much resistance there is to the domestic use of federal troops.

    11. In *Civil War: Battle Damage*, we see that states have passed various enabling acts in support of the SHRA, and some of them may have created their own registration requirements—assuming the SHRA was not pre-emptive. The text does not give us nearly enough to work with to get that far into the weeds, but that issue is another facet of the regulatory complexity involved here.

    12. Though given the verities of federal bureaucracies, there is no reason to think it *could not*. Here's a hypothetical *Marvel* "What If…?" storyline: the SHRA passes, but it takes so long for S.H.I.E.L.D. and the other agencies to work all the kinks out of the registration process that the Skrull invasion of 2007–08 is well underway before the Initiative is up and running and the SHRA gets repealed before registration even becomes possible. Less "civil war," more "death by bureaucracy."

Works Cited

A.L.A. Schecter Poultry Corporation v. United States. 295 U.S. 495. 495–551. No. 854. U.S. Supreme Court. 1935. Web.

Bendis, Brian Michael (writer), Alex Maleev (penciller), and Dave Stewart (colorist). *New Avengers: Illuminati* #0 (March 2006), Marvel Comics. Print.

Bendis, Brian Michael (writer), Leinil Yu (artist), and Dave McCaig (colorist). *New Avengers* #22 (Sept. 2006), Marvel Comics. Print.

Berkay, Max. "Marvel Comic's Civil War: An Allegory of September 11 in an American Civil War Framework." *Traces: The UNC-Chapel Hill Journal of History* (2013). Web.

Buchanan v. Warley. 245 U.S. 60. 60–82. No. 33. U.S. Supreme Court. 1917. Web.

Byrd, Ronald (writer), and Scott Kolins (inker and penciller). *Civil War: Battle Damage* (March 2007), Marvel Comics. Print.

18 U.S. Code. Sec 922. 1996. Web.

Enforcement Act of 1870. 16 Stat. 140, ch. 114. 31 May 1870.

Enforcement Act of 1871. 16 Stat. 443, ch. 94. Feb., 1871.

Enforcement Act of 1871 (Third Enforcement Act). 17 Stat. 13, ch. 31. 20 Apr. 1871.

First English Evangelical Lutheran Church v. Los Angeles. 482 U.S. 304. 304–339. No. 85-1199. U.S. Supreme Court. 1987. Web.

Gun Free School Zones Act of 1990. Pub. L. 101647. 104 Stat. 4789. 29 Nov. 1990. Print.

Holmes v. United States. 391 U.S. 936. 936–945. No. 1072. U.S. Supreme Court. 1968. Print.

Insurrection Act. 2 Stat. 443. 10 U.S. Code 331–335. 1807. Print.

John Warner National Defense Authorization Act for Fiscal Year 2007. Pub. L. 109-364. 120 Stat. 2083. 17 Oct. 2006. Web.

Madison, James. "Federalist No. 45." *The Federalist Papers*. Ed. Clinton Rossiter. New York: Signet Classics, 1961.

Millar, Mark (writer), and Steve McNiven (penciller). *Civil War* #1–7. (May 2006–Feb. 2007), Marvel Comics. Print.

National Defense Authorization Act for Fiscal Year 2008. Pub. L. 110-181. 122 Stat. 3. 28 Jan. 2008. Web.

National Federation of Independent Business v. Sebelius. 567 U.S. ____. 1–59. No. 11-393. U.S. Supreme Court. 2012. Web.

Patient Protection and Affordable Care Act. Pub. L. 111–148. 124 Stat. 119. 23 Mar. 2010. Web.

Posse Comitatus Act. 18 U.S. Code. Sec. 1385 (original at 20 U.S. Code. Sec. 152). 1878. Print.

Reed, Brian (writer), Robert Delatorre (penciller), and Chris Sotomayor (colorist). *Ms. Marvel* #7 (Sept. 2006), Marvel Comics. Print.

Rostker v. Goldberg. 448 U.S. 1306. 1306–1311. No. A-70. U.S. Supreme Court. 1980.

Schad v. Borough of Mount Ephraim. 452 U.S. 61. 61–67. No. 79-1640. U.S. Supreme Court. 1981. Print.

Selective Draft Law Cases. 245 U.S. 366. 366–390. Nos. 662, 664, 665, 666, 681, and 769. U.S. Supreme Court. 1918.
Templeton, Ty (writer), Roger Langridge (artist), and J. Brown (colorist). *Civil War: Choosing Sides* (Oct. 2006), Marvel Comics. Web.
Undercliff Cottage, LLC v. FHRE, LLC. 2:14-cv-00110. District of Maine. Filed Mar. 27, 2014.
United States v. Butler. 297 U.S. 1. 1–78. No. 401. U.S. Supreme Court. 1936.
United States v. Lopez. 514 U.S. 549. 549–644. No. 93-1260. U.S. Supreme Court. 1995. Web.
United States v. Morrison. 529 U.S. 598. 598–666. No. 99-5. U.S. Supreme Court. 2000.
U.S. Constitution. Art. I, Sec. 8, cl. 3 (Commerce Clause). Web.
_____. Art I, sec. 8, cl. 11 (War Powers Clause). Web.
USA PATRIOT Act. Pub. L. 107–56. 115 Stat. 272. 26 Oct. 2001. Web.
Wickard v. Filburn. 317 U.S. 111. 111–133. No. 59. U.S. Supreme Court. 1942. Web.
Youngstown Sheet & Tube Company v. Sawyer. 343 U.S. 579. 579–589. No. 744. U.S. Supreme Court. 1952. Web.

Whose Side Is the Law On?
Living with Legalistic Absurdity
in Marvel's *Civil War*

Daniel Davis Wood

In the months building up to the publication of the first issue of Marvel's *Civil War*, and once again on the front cover of that issue, readers were asked a question that served as the tagline for the series as a whole: "Whose side are you on?" Following the passage of the Superhuman Registration Act (SHRA) and its requirement that all Marvel superheroes subject themselves to government oversight and accountability, the two sides available for readers to establish a sense of allegiance were, of course, the supporters of registration, led by Iron Man, and the opponents of registration, led by Captain America. But the stylistic simplicity of that question—those five words offering only a binary choice—whitewashed the moral and political complexity of the issue at hand, suggesting that the matter of choosing a side in this conflict would be, for readers, inevitable and therefore obligatory, and in any event straightforward. The only hint of the possibility that one might remain impartial or ambivalent toward the issue of registration appeared halfway through the series when Dr. Strange refuses to take a side and remarks, "There is no right or wrong in this debate" (Millar 150). Aside from those words, the absence of all traces of acceptable neutrality elsewhere in the series effectively coerced readers, by the omission of political options, into taking a stance on registration and choosing one set of heroes to side with.

But on what basis, exactly, were readers supposed to choose which set of heroes to side with? Some readers were no doubt guided by emotions and affections to simply take the side of their favorite characters almost reflexively and without careful thought. It is easy, and almost instinctual, to know oneself as a reader with a soft spot for Spider-Man, for example, and then to follow his lead as he chooses a side in the conflict. Other readers, conversely, were perhaps guided more by reason and ended up taking the side of the characters who put forth the most persuasive justification for their own political stances, regardless of whether those characters are in any way likeable. To speak personally on this issue, while I have always found Iron Man a more compelling character than Captain America, I felt that Steve Rogers made a more persuasive case for resisting superhero registration than Tony Stark did for supporting it. But then, of course, there must have been some readers who found themselves little moved by either personalities or persuasion—readers as uninterested in playing favorites as in following superheroic discourses—insofar as they held fast to certain political principles prior to opening the first issue of *Civil War*, and they simply sided with whichever heroes espoused, adopted, and defended them.

Across the existing critical analyses of the series, regardless of whether many critics would number themselves among the latter category of readers, there exists now a broad consensus that, at the very least, the characters involved in the conflict over superhero registration were guided by political principles and that, for readers, the two sides were intended to allegorize arguments over political principles in cultural discourses contemporaneous to the publication of the comics. For instance, as Rebecca Wanzo puts it, the conflict that split apart the Marvel Universe arose "from post–9/11 debates about the PATRIOT Act and citizen surveillance" (93). More specifically, as Francisco Veloso and John Bateman write, "*Civil War* is not rooted in the conflict of good versus evil personified by heroes and villains, but is instead motivated by a conflict of values and challenges to the system mirroring well both the landscape of dissent surrounding the PATRIOT Act and the need not to alienate potential dissenters" (431).

For the readers of "numerous media sources" that followed the serialized ups and downs of the conflict throughout late 2006 and early 2007, its aftermath seemed to be, as Bond Benton observes, far too obvious:

> [It was] a thinly veiled (and some might suggest hackneyed) attempt to create a metaphor for the concerns of a population increasingly uncomfortable with both the power and judgment of its government.... Politically motivated opportunists preying on the fears of a nation? A conflict based in part on questionable intelligence, arguably lies? [It] appears to be a fairly transparent effort to parallel the debates over the Iraq War, the PATRIOT Act, the Bush domestic surveillance program and other controversial programs in the post–September 11 period in the United States [75–76].

Benton goes on to characterize the conflict as one that stems from a principled disagreement between those heroes who see registration as "a responsible obligation" and those who oppose it "on the grounds that it violates civil liberties and threatens the privacy constitutionally guaranteed to all citizens" (79), and similar views have been expressed in almost identical terms by Veloso and Bateman (430) as well as Travis Langley (426) and Jason Dittmer (150). Langley builds his principled analysis of the conflict on the political theorizations of Erich Fromm, while Dittmer alone concedes that there may be something too convenient, too contrived, about the discourse from which the conflict erupted. He argues that by forcing superheroes to either support or oppose registration, *Civil War* presents readers with what Veloso and Bateman call "a dichotomy of values" which finally advances a "reductionist" view of some extraordinarily complex political issues (431).

But while that may be the case for readers, skewing our ability to choose a side in the conflict on the basis of informed deliberation, the same cannot be said of the characters involved in the conflict. After all, every law, real or hypothetical, is essentially reductionist, since everyone to whom it applies must at bottom either be for it as it is passed or against it as it is passed, without occupying any middle ground except in purely rhetorical terms. Yet even if some readers of *Civil War* were guided toward choosing a side on the basis of political principle, why should the above critics assume that the superheroes would do likewise? Although Captain America and Iron Man and their respective followers may have occasionally professed to be adhering to principles whose violation they cannot abide, why should critics not take a critical approach to what these characters say? Why, in other words, have we so far overlooked the extent to which the various superheroes chose sides in the conflict on the basis of rational self-interest rather than principle? And, to follow on from that, why not consider which aspects of registration and the registration legislation might have affected the self-interests of different superheroes in different ways so as to move some heroes to support it while others rebelled against it?

In these pages, I look at several problems with the SHRA to argue that political principle played very little role in the choosing of sides in *Civil War*, and that, as a result, to read the series as an allegory of its contemporaneous political discourses is to downplay, if not wholly dismiss, the particularities of and variations between the characters involved in it. Another way of saying this is that the focus on the series' political allegorization is sustainable only by a continued abandonment of interest in the subtleties, the artistry, and the requirements of its narrative. Given the series' political context and its overtly political content, of course, it may seem counterintuitive to advance an argument of this sort, but I hope to advance it by first considering both sides of the registration divide and then focusing on why the dissenters are moved to dissent and, more specifically, why their particular natures, their particular powers and origins, offer them much stronger motivations to dissent than their politics do. I eventually arrive at case studies of five major heroes affected by registration in different ways—Iron Man, Captain America, Thor, the Hulk, and Spider-Man—in order to look at the particular problems each of them faces as a result of the registration legislation. Overall, then, I do not contend that criticism of and opposition to the SHRA are somehow misguided, but I do intend to suggest and to show that they rest on shaky foundations when grounded in the rhetoric of political principles at the expense of an analysis of the circumstantial particularities of those involved in the registration dispute.

As readers unaffected by the drama of *Civil War*, watching events unfold from the extradiegetic space of the text, it is easy for us to side against the SHRA for any one of a number of reasons: because it practices a form of legislative persecution, because its legal validity is questionable if not altogether disputable, and, of course, because its implementation cannot be categorized as anything less than catastrophic. Opponents of the act might feel that it possesses anti-humanistic associations, as Travis Langley notes (429–430), given the history of comparable registration acts already passed in the Marvel Universe. As these acts have typically targeted the mutant population, they have been driven less by political principle than by bigotry toward minority groups, and the SHRA may be simply a larger scale expression of the same brute fears that led to their passage. Or opponents might simply contend that the act is plainly unconstitutional. Like Bond Benton (79), some might view the requirement that superheroes reveal their secret identities as a violation of fundamental guarantees of personal privacy—even though such guarantees are only implied, not explicitly enumerated, in the United States Constitution—while others might share my view that it is unconstitutional because it undercuts the Constitution by legitimizing unconstitutional behavior, offering official legal sanction to administrators of justice who operate far outside the justice system established in the Fourth, Fifth, and Sixth Amendments to the Constitution. Or, finally, opponents might point out that the implementation of the act unleashed extraordinary chaos and carnage, and that its supporters made ethically dubious responses to the resistance it attracted. These responses include, after all, genetically manipulating Thor without his consent (Millar 94) as well as effectively offering amnesty to mass-murdering super-villains (Millar 101–102) and creating a prison in the Negative Zone specifically to house political opponents. They also include, most egregiously, the hypocritical determination of the act's supporters to remain above the law: "I just read [the President] the Riot Act," Reed Richards tells Tony Stark, "and told him I wouldn't play a part in our big finale unless I had an absolute guarantee that Sue and Johnny wouldn't face arrest.... He said he'd give us twelve immunities" (Millar 140). Even without being privy to the text of the act, then, readers of *Civil War* have no shortage of good reasons to oppose it.

If this is the case, however, then on what grounds does the act receive support? The event used to justify the passage of the act is the massacre of school children at the hands of villains who are provoked to attack innocents by the media-hungry New Warriors. The implications are that irresponsible superheroism resulted in the deaths of the very people who were supposed to be *protected* by heroes, and that superheroic behavior must therefore be subject to government approval and oversight. But a close reading of *Civil War* reveals that there are more reasons than this one behind the support for registration. In fact, by my count, there are at least three other reasons given for supporting it.

The first reason is voiced by Goliath, despite his opposition to registration, when he acknowledges that registration may be justified by "Philly getting bombed" and "the Hulk trashing Vegas" (Millar 15), references to the Winter Soldier's metropolitan firebombing of Philadelphia in *Captain America* #6 and #8 (Brubaker) and the Hulk's rampage through Nevada in *Fantastic Four* #533–535 (Straczynski). Registration, from this perspective, institutes a means of controlling carnage caused by superheroes rather than by super-villains. The second reason is voiced by the mother of one of the children killed in the New Warriors incident, a woman who spits on Tony Stark and disparages his private funding of superheroes. "Who's been telling kids for years that they can live outside the law as long as they're wearing tights?" she asks him. "Joe Billionaire here says all you need are some powers and a badass attitude, and you can have a place in his private super-gang" (Millar 17–18). Registration therefore also institutes a means of diminishing the privatization and implicit corruption of the United States justice system. The third reason is voiced by Tony Stark himself, when he concedes that the New Warriors have done discredit to superheroes *en masse* and he says that registration is a way of "making [superheroes] more legitimate. Why shouldn't we be better-trained and publicly accountable?" (Millar 22). "[R]egulating our behavior," he admits elsewhere, is in fact "[t]he compromise we offered [S.H.I.E.L.D. and the federal government]" (Millar 117) in order to secure what is elsewhere referred to as a way of "giving us all a future" (Millar 130).

Registration thus garners supporters by virtue of its potential to legitimize otherwise illegitimate superheroic activity. But since none of these reasons for supporting registration are precisely the same as the reasons used to justify the passage of the SHRA (in the wake of the New Warriors debacle), their expression suggests that registration has a more nuanced and multifaceted set of justifications and thus a broader base of support than it may at first appear to possess. And since these qualities do not allow opponents of registration to write it off simply by excusing or rationalizing the New Warriors debacle, supporters of registration are able to characterize themselves as pragmatists while tarring their opponents as fools who are "not meeting new contingencies" and remain "living in the past" (Veloso and Bateman 438).

In fact, however, opponents of registration have a *very* pragmatic reason for taking their position. They, too, have three grounds for objection, three lines of argument that have little to do with principled defenses of civil liberties and the right to privacy. First, as several heroes point out, registration is non-consensual and so, to a large extent, coercive with an element of indentured servitude to it: Sue Storm describes it to Namor as "a superhuman draft" (Millar 142) while, elsewhere, Luke Cage describes it as tantamount to slavery and segregation (Bendis 2–3). Secondly, building on this aspect of registration are the concerns that its establishment of a formal alliance between superheroes and the government—the breaking of which is a punishable offense for the heroes—empowers the government to define the purposes toward which superheroic activities should be directed. Captain America describes it as *de facto* contract employment in a fledgling government militia, a slippery slope toward superheroes receiving proactive assignments from government agencies rather than independently engaging in responsive action when faced with a destabilization of the existing social order: "Super heroes need to stay above that stuff," he says, "or Washington starts telling us who the super-villains are" (Millar 26). Thirdly, though, it is the likely response of super-villains toward the registration of superheroes that most strongly leads some heroes to oppose registration—and in this reason for opposition lies the heart of the problem.

Prior to revealing his secret identity, Spider-Man voices concerns about using coercion to force all other heroes to reveal theirs. He worries that by exposing himself, by making his private self public, he will incur reprisals from super-villains targeting his private life. Sue Storm, before she becomes an opponent of registration, tries to reassure him: "The secret identity thing isn't such a big deal," she says. "The Fantastic Four have been public since the very beginning, and it's never really been a serious concern" (Millar 23). But Spider-Man remains rightly unconvinced. "Yeah, well," he replies, "[it's] not [a concern] until that day I come home and find my wife impaled on an octopus arm and the woman who raised me begging for her life" (Millar 23). His anxieties are echoed in that conversation by Daredevil, and, in a later scene, Captain America warns Maria Hill that despite his own more principled opposition to registration, most of the resistance is coming from "the heroes who work close to the streets like Daredevil and Luke Cage" (Millar 25). Far from matters of political principle, then, the foremost problem with the SHRA seems to be that the act itself is too principled, too committed to total and absolute registration, and too weak in terms of pragmatic application to distinguish between the different types of *villains* that different heroes customarily face and to consider how those villains might react differently toward those heroes if the heroes' identities were to be exposed.

It is easy for Sue Storm to say that having one's secret identity made public "isn't such a big deal" because she and the remaining members of the Fantastic Four customarily face large-scale and generally depersonalized threats. Galactus, Thanos, Doctor Doom, and the Mole Man all occupy a level of super-villainy far removed from the day-to-day and face-to-face contact with the people they seek to harm and the heroes who seek to stop them: they operate, respectively, on intergalactic, cosmic, international, and subterranean scales, not on the metropolitan or urban scales of more petty super-villains. For Spider-Man and Daredevil, however, it is far less easy to say that the revelation of one's secret identity is of little consequence. Dr. Octopus, the Vulture, Bullseye, the Kingpin, and others of their ilk are one-on-one antagonists with no-holds-barred personal vendettas against the heroes they cross, villains who would not hesitate to launch personal reprisals against Peter Parker, Matt Murdock, and heroes of their stature. Indeed, Kingpin sends an assassin after Parker *and* his family immediately after the conclusion of the conflict.[1] On this side of the superhero divide, as Veloso and Bateman write, "the opinion is constructed that the means are not justified by the ends" (438), rendering universal and mandatory superhero registration a disproportionate means of regulating superheroic activity.

This is where readers first catch a glimpse of the major fault in the SHRA: its foundation on the principle of universal registration leaves it ill-equipped to make room for the circumstantial particularities of each member of the vast pantheon of heroes in the Marvel

Universe, and as a result it incites a rebellion against registration among those heroes whose particularities would make them the most adversely affected by a revelation of secret identities. If we, as readers, acknowledge the pre-existing self-interests of the various superheroes prior to giving any credibility to the principled positions they espouse, adopt, and defend, then we must also acknowledge that the heroes' civil war is driven by forces that exist prior to, and are entirely independent of, whatever allegorical meaning we may read into the resultant political conflict. Ironically, among the supporters of registration there was one who identified a problem similar to the problem of the diversity of superheroic self-interests before the conflict erupted. As Travis Langley notes,

> After Congress proposes superhero registration in *Fantastic Four* #335 and wants Reed Richards, leader of the Fantastic Four, to develop superhuman detection technology, Richards speaks before a congressional panel in the following issue to argue the philosophical problem with such a proposal and to demonstrate the sheer impracticality of establishing operational criteria for defining and detecting any super-powers [430].

This is, of course, typical of Reed Richards, missing the forest for the trees by worrying over the scientific problems with detecting a diversity of super-powers rather than worrying over the responses to registration on the part of diverse superheroes facing diverse super-villains. But when we recognize this problem at the heart of *Civil War*, this failure to respect particularities and differences in a law that applies equally to radically different people, related problems become apparent elsewhere. How can it be the case, for instance, that the Winter Soldier's firebombing of Philadelphia and the Hulk's rampage through Las Vegas are sufficiently equitable to the New Warriors' provocation of super-villains so as to equally justify superhero registration? It is true that the New Warriors acted irresponsibly, and perhaps even to an extent that warrants some regulation.

The Winter Soldier, however, firebombed Philadelphia under the control of the villainous General Lukin, not acting as an independent superhero and therefore not subject to the SHRA at all, and the Hulk rampaged through Las Vegas because Nick Fury and S.H.I.E.L.D. tricked him into going to Nevada, which effectively leaves those government representatives as culpable for the destruction as the Hulk himself—and as responsible as the New Warriors for the provocation of a disaster. More intriguingly, though, when the problem of simplistically equating disparate superheroes causes troubles for the supporters of registration, those troubles are explicitly aired but then brushed aside rather than resolved. "I just can't understand why our Thor-clone killed a man," Ant-Man complains after Tony Stark's genetic monstrosity electrocutes Goliath. "Is he missing a human conscience? Do we need to fuse him with Donald Blake or Jake Olson to have him function properly?" (Millar 101).[2] These are the sorts of questions that Stark and his supporters should have been asking before adopting their preferred stance on registration—as are corollary questions such as how the Thor clone could be physically and psychologically bound to the terms of registration, and who exactly would be so bound if he was indeed fused with another person.

Civil War is rife with these and other difficulties, double-binds, and absurdities, all arising from the disjuncture between an absolutist law and the particularities of superheroic self-interests. One need only look at some of the more prominent Marvel superheroes in order to further illustrate the point, and to see how further variations on this disjuncture cause an already problematic law to collapse under the incompatibility of its principled strictures with its practical application.

Consider, first, Iron Man. Supporting registration ostensibly as a means of legitimizing superheroic behavior, he cannot adopt this position purely as a matter of principle or out of disinterested pragmatism, since he, above all other superheroes in the Marvel Universe, is the one most likely to adopt exactly this position, the one most guided toward this position by his own vested interests. Because Iron Man's super-powers are self-developed and externalized, created by Tony Stark and separable from his body in a way that offers him the possibility of not acting as a superhero at all, Iron Man by definition operates outside the justice system established in the Constitution and therefore operates above the law.[3] This brand of superheroic behavior gives Stark the greatest possible incentive to support registration as a means of legitimizing superheroism—superheroism in general, as well as his own brand—so that, far from leading a moral crusade in support of registration, Stark's self-interest drives him to ameliorate his "tense relationships with the government" (Veloso and Bateman 430) by obtaining governmental legitimization of his heretofore unregulated use of advanced weaponry. His history and his superheroic particularities effectively foreclosed the possibility of Stark ever speaking out against the *SHRA*. For series writer Mark Millar, it would have been implausible to have Stark behave any other way.

Captain America, on the other hand, adopts an opposing position on the issue of registration largely because his distinct self-interests lead him into doing so. As a "sickly boy transformed by American medical ingenuity to become a peerless soldier" (Benton 76), Steve Rogers' superheroic particularities were sanctioned by the American government from the very beginning. Francisco Veloso and John Bateman contend that, because Captain America "gained his powers as part of an experiment carried out by the U.S. Government to create super-soldiers who could win the war against Germany," "having him as a leader *against* the Registration Act brings interesting overtones" to *Civil War* (430)—with "interesting" here connoting something surprising about his opposition to registration.

But Captain America was always destined to oppose registration in much the same way that Iron Man was destined to support it because, in the 1940s, his creation by the very government that now requires registration prospectively invested him with the legitimacy that registration would now otherwise afford him. In other words, he does not need the one thing that the SHRA offers to those who abide by it because he has possessed as much from the moment of his creation, which leaves him absolved of the incentive to register that motivates the self-created Iron Man. Indeed, the requirements of the SHRA may well be unconstitutional when applied to Captain America because they are tantamount to *ex post facto* demands, entailing a governmental about-face on the issue of registration which effectively invalidates the informed consent that Steve Rogers must have granted the government before he submitted himself to the super soldier serum all those decades ago. For Captain America, then, registration is redundant at best and, at worst, illegal—and so, in any event, it is not something he would ever support, regardless of whatever political principles he might hold.

Other difficulties with the SHRA become apparent in the cases of heroes like Thor and the Hulk, both of whom do not have *secret* identities to be revealed so much as they have *double* identities that raise questions of legal culpability. It is true, of course, that neither of these heroes appears in *Civil War*, since the Hulk has been exiled to the planet Sakaar (see Pak) and Thor is technically dead before the conflict erupts, but the SHRA is nevertheless complicated by their very existence in several important ways. Early in J. Michael Straczynski's relaunch of the *Thor* comic series, which takes place in the immediate aftermath of *Civil War*, Thor relocates the Kingdom of Asgard to rural Oklahoma and so attracts the ire of an increasingly authoritarian Iron Man. "Things have changed around here while you were—gone," Iron Man tells him. "It's real simple, Thor. You either work with the government, for the government, or you're against the government. There's no middle ground" (Straczynski, *Thor #3*, 6). But how can a deistic entity like Thor possibly count as a citizen to be bound by the laws of a single human nation? Indeed, how could he be bound any more than God himself or, at the other end of the legal spectrum, an animal lacking all understanding of human legal responsibility? Thor dwells in an entirely different realm to that of mankind and its laws—and, more importantly, the fact that the law requires force in order to be upheld means that those who possess superior force can simply evade or disregard the law.

This is the lesson that Iron Man quickly learns when Thor refuses to comply with registration and backs up his refusal with a display of force that leaves Iron Man decimated. In response, Iron Man accepts that there may be a "compromise position" after all: "If we treat Asgard as a separate entity, like a diplomatic mission or embassy, then it's not officially United States territory.... That would put Asgard and anyone who lives there outside of the jurisdiction of the Registration Act" (15). As Iron Man admits, this is a rationalization intended above all to make sure that his superiors "don't lose face" (15), particularly since it merely plays semantics with the definition of United States territory, but it highlights the point that entities like Thor—entities who are not really human, let alone super-human—cannot be bound by the SHRA because their use of super-powers is part of their essential nature, as much as sleeping, eating, and breathing are a part of ours.[4] The only way that Thor could possibly be subject to the act is if registration was forced upon Donald Blake so as to regulate his transformation into Thor, but this situation would not involve the registration of the superhero himself—and this point applies also to entities such as the Hulk, with added complications. To the extent that Bruce Banner's transformation into the Hulk is involuntary, can Banner be justifiably held responsible for the actions of the Hulk, including the rampage through Las Vegas, and can he therefore also be subject to registration? Entities so dramatically empowered as to no longer count as human beings cannot fall under the jurisdiction of the Superhero Registration Act, and still less can they do so when they are contained within human hosts who disappear when they emerge, and yet the act itself is not qualified to accommodate, exempt, or otherwise make provisions for them.

By this logic, the only major superhero who could conceivably be made subject to the SHRA without facing any significant difficulties is Spider-Man. Unlike Tony Stark, of course, Peter Parker should not be required to register simply as a matter of principle because, whereas Stark becomes a superhero after transforming himself into one, Parker never asked to be bitten by the radioactive spider that imbued him with his super-human abilities. In practice, however, Parker makes a conscious decision to use his abilities and could just as easily decide not to use them, and it seems to me that this sort of entirely independent administration of justice—a form of justice intended to provide supplementary services to an established justice system riven by perceived weaknesses and shortcomings—is precisely what the SHRA is intended to countervail.[5] As painful as it may be for Peter Parker not to act on his belief that his possession of great power invests him with a responsibility to use it for the common good, his altruistic intentions do not offset the damage he does to the long-term stability of the justice system via repeatedly engaging in what is effectively illegal super-powered vigilantism.

It is impossible to say what problems the Marvel Universe would face if this sort of vigilantism was simply outlawed, since the preponderance of super-powered antagonists is itself a problem that super-powered vigilantism already addresses. Yet it is also impossible to suggest that lawmakers acted irrationally or irresponsibly in fighting for the passage of the SHRA, since, in the pre–*Civil War* Marvel Universe, superheroism had flourished for so long with so little regulation that it had effectively invalidated the justice system belonging to the government that those same lawmakers represent. The flaw in the actions of the lawmakers was the expediency with which they drafted and approved the registration legislation, an expediency driven by the sense of a need for urgent action in the wake of the New Warriors debacle. What lawmakers should in fact have acted on was not the aftermath of that debacle, not the urgency they felt, but rather the sustained and incremental accession to the actions of independent administrators of justice who, solely by virtue of possessing super-human abilities, establish themselves as adjudicators of societal disturbances acting on senses of presumed omniscience and omnipotence instead of respecting the slow, complex, and cumbersome dictates of due process. Had lawmakers paid more attention to the daily undermining of the established justice system as distinct from the outrage unleashed by the New Warriors, they might have attempted to address a longstanding political problem without succumbing to the rush and overreach of the SHRA.

What this all means, finally, is that the legal dilemmas that led to the passage of the SHRA far predated the debacle that precipitated it, in much the same way that the circumstantial particularities that led the Marvel superheroes to take sides on the issue of registration far predated the legislation that precipitated their division. *Civil War* was, in other words, woven into the fabric of the Marvel Universe well before it actually broke out. Where is the space, in this view of the conflict, for advancing a politically principled understanding or allegorization of events, aside from simply adopting the principles underpinning contemporary judicial processes, which are at any rate enshrined in the Constitution? The hostilities of *Civil War* thus do not mark the commencement of some extraordinary event in the Marvel Universe—an event that forces those involved in it to search deep within themselves for the principles they hold dear—so much as it marks the culmination of theoretical conflicts embedded in the Marvel Universe long before the SHRA divided the Marvel superheroes and asked its readers which side they would stand on.

Notes

1. While the SHRA does not mandate making all super-powered individuals reveal their identities to the public, as did Peter Parker, considering how often the secret halls of S.H.I.E.L.D. and the American government are penetrated in the Marvel Universe, it is certainly understandable that any superhero might consider registering tantamount to publicly revealing a secret identity.

2. Henry Pym's question is particularly creepy and arrogant as it simply assumes the moral authority to make such decisions for Blake or Olson, fusing their bodies to a part-organic, part-mechanical cyborg "clone" of the Norse Thunder God. Such arrogance is often depicted as part of the pro-registration side's philosophy—a clear certainty of their essential rightness, and the consequent permission that carries to act however necessary to "win."

3. After the events of the *Extremis* storyline in 2005–2006 in *Iron Man*, Tony's armor is infused within him. Arguably, he no longer has the ability to simply take off his armor and not be a super-human. However, this is dealt with very inconsistently, given we see people like Thor rip pieces off of him in fights. He regularly removes his own mask and sets it aside, which would not be logically possible (without further explanation) if the armor were a part of him. So, during *Civil War*, the character of Iron Man is treated as a mere human in a sophisticated machine.

4. Arguably, this would be just as true for mutants, whose powers are literally in their DNA. However, Millar and the editors of *Civil War* both acknowledge this potential narrative problem and set it aside by having (nearly all) mutants opt out of the social conflict from the beginning, their long-term experience with efforts to create a Mutant Registration Act having left them with little optimism about the outcome.

5. Of course, the issue of whether super-powered people would need to register if they committed to never using their powers is also dealt with inconsistently in the *Civil War* tie-in storylines. For example, see Ryan Davidson's discussion earlier in this volume of the two approaches taken by Ms. Marvel to this issue.

Works Cited

Bendis, Brian Michael (writer), Leinil Yu (penciller), and Dave McCaig (color art). "New Avengers: Disassembled, Part 2." *New Avengers* #22 (September 2006), Marvel Comics. Web. Accessed 1 July 2014.

Benton, Bond. "Redemptive Anti-Americanism and the Death of Captain America." *Studies in Communication Sciences* 13 (2013): 75–83. Print.

Brubaker, Ed (writer), Steve Epting (penciller), and Frank D'Armata (colorist). "Out of Time, Part 6." *Captain America* #6 (June 2005), Marvel Comics. Web. Accessed 1 July 2014.

_____. "The Winter Soldier, Part 1." *Captain America* #8 (September 2005), Marvel Comics. Web. Accessed 1 July 2014.

Dittmer, Jason. "Captain America in the News: Changing Mediascapes and the Appropriation of a Superhero." *Journal of Graphic Novels and Comics* 3.2 (2012): 143–157. Print.

Langley, Travis. "Freedom versus Security: The Basic Human Dilemma from 9/11 to Marvel's *Civil War*." *International Journal of Comic Art* 11.1 (Spring 2009): 426–435. Print.

Millar, Mark (writer), Steve McNiven (penciller), and Dexter Vines (inker). *Civil War*, Collected ed. (April 2007), Marvel Comics. Print.

Pak, Greg (writer), Carlo Pagulayan (penciller), and Jeffrey Huet (inker). "Planet Hulk: Exile, Part 1." *The Incredibile Hulk* #92 (February 2006), Marvel Comics. Web. Accessed 1 July 2014.

Simonson, Walt (writer), Rich Buckler (penciller), and Romeo Tanghal (inker). "Death by Debate." *Fantastic Four* #335 (December 1989), Marvel Comics. Web. Accessed 1 July 2014.

Straczynski, J. Michael (writer), Olivier Coipel (penciller), and Mark Morales (inker). "Everything Old Is New Again." *Thor* #3 (September 2007), Marvel Comics. Web. Accessed 1 July 2014.

_____, Mike McKone (penciller), and Andy Lanning and Cam Smith (inkers). *Fantastic Four* #533–535 (January–April 2006), Marvel Comics. Web. Accessed 1 July 2014.

Veloso, Francisco, and John Bateman. "The Multimodal Construction of Acceptability: Marvel's *Civil War* Comic Books and the PATRIOT Act." *Critical Discourse Studies* 10.4 (2013): 427–443. Print.

Wanzo, Rebecca. "The Superhero: Meditations on Surveillance, Salvation, and Desire." *Communication and Critical/Cultural Studies* 6.1 (Mar. 2009): 93–97. Print.

Part II—Superheroes and the American Response to 9/11

Marvel's Illuminati: Who Watches the Watchmen?

Mark Bousquet

We do not believe it is possible to defeat all terrorist attacks against Americans, every time and everywhere.
—The 9/11 Commission Report, p. 365

For every crisis, there is a response. In the wake of the 9/11 terrorist attacks on the United States, Congressman Jim Sensenbrenner (R-WI) introduced H.R. 3162, more commonly known as the PATRIOT Act.[1] Sensenbrenner's legislation passed the United States House of Representatives by a vote of 357–66, moved to the Senate, where it passed by a 98–1 margin, and then was delivered to the desk of President George W. Bush, who signed the bill into law on October 26, 2001. From the morning of the attacks on September 11, 2001, it took one month and twelve days for H.R. 3162 to be introduced, but then only three days for the bill to become law. While much of those 42 days between the attacks and the bill's introduction were spent negotiating the details of the bill to ensure smooth passage, it is nonetheless surprising how quickly Congress can move when so motivated to *do something*. Forty-two days is a veritable blink of an eye in terms of gathering, assessing, and analyzing a terrorist attack, to say nothing of crafting detailed legislation, yet only 66 representatives and one senator opposed the PATRIOT Act. The Senator was Russ Feingold (D–WI), who took to the Senate floor to urge his fellow politicians that "we must examine every item that is proposed in response to these events to be sure we are not rewarding these terrorists and weakening ourselves by giving up the cherished freedoms that they seek to destroy" (*Congressional Record*, S11019). With cleanup efforts at the World Trade Center in New York City and the Pentagon in Washington, D.C., still underway, and a nation still dealing with the tragedy and demanding answers and responses from the government, examining "every item" was not going to happen, and despite legal challenges and public pressure, large sections of the PATRIOT Act remain in place 13 years later.

The ability to compress and decompress time allows for an event like Marvel's *Civil War* to rage white hot over a seven-month period (July 2006–January 2007), and then become quickly folded into the larger history of the company and its fictional universe. In this macro-historical context, the *Civil War* is no more or less significant than other events that promised to change the Marvel Universe forever, before returning comfortably to a reasonable facsimile of the status-quo: *Avengers Disassembled* begat *House of M* begat *Civil War* begat *Secret Invasion*. Everything is the Most Important Event in Marvel Comics History until the next event starts a few months later. Yet in the micro-historical context, each event is incredibly significant for the way they rearrange established pieces for short-term gains (both narratively and economically). While there is an illusion of change in superhero comics that is rarely matched by the actual narrative events with any sense of permanence (a character's death all but guarantees a character's rebirth; a hero's turn to the dark side is just the prologue to their story of redemption), that doesn't render the temporal changes insignificant. Instead, the high energy and company-stated importance of the crossover event allows Marvel to constantly keep their characters fresh in the guise of a constant upheaval that will ultimately put almost everything back where it came from. As Joe Quesada, the editor-in-chief of Marvel Comics, told *The New York Times* prior to the release of *Civil War*, "Stagnation means death" (Gustines).

In this vein, Marvel's *Civil War* crossover event can be seen as the company's compacted response to the 9/11 terror attacks. It is wrong to think of *Civil War* as simply 9/11 retold with capes, however. Writer Mark Millar insisted to *The New York Times* that "the political allegory is only for those that are politically aware. Kids are going to read it and just see a big superhero fight" (Gustines). There are fundamental differences in the type of attack that launches each story (a planned and coordinated terrorist attack meant to cause public fear and damage to a nation's infrastructure versus a super villain's snap decision to escape capture by a superhero team filming a reality show) and who the United States identifies as the people who need to be held responsible (foreign nationals versus American citizens). Where 9/11 is critically important in our understanding of Marvel's *Civil War* is the public's demand for the government to *do something*. In his remarks speaking out against the PATRIOT Act, Senator Feingold concluded that "this bill still does not strike the right balance between empowering law enforcement and protecting civil liberties" (*Congressional Record*, S11019); this is the heart of the battle between heroes in *Civil War*, the passion play of a scared, angry, and vengeful nation looking to prevent the very thing the *9/11 Commission Report* clearly states is an impossibility.

Another manner in which time and space bend to the whims of the publishing industry that is important to understanding *Civil War* is the concept of the "retcon," or "retroactive continuity." Shepherded into comics lingo by the legendary Roy Thomas during his work on DC's *All-Star Squadron* in 1983, the retcon has become a popular (and profitable) narrative strategy for comic companies looking to mine the popular stories of the past by offering fans a new understanding of what they already know, or in some cases, a new history that alters a character's past.[2] Thanks, in large part, to the company's shorter history and the efforts of continuity-conscious editors like Mark Gruenwald and in-house archivist/historian Peter Sanderson, continuity was held in high regard at Marvel Comics through the '80s and '90s. Even in the years of *Civil War*'s production and release, creators knew they had a solid foundation on which to build their stories; in discussing the differences between the two big superhero publishers, artist Alex Ross said, "Continuity really, really matters with Marvel. The various events that have happened to their characters haven't been retconned continually and, generally, you can treat most of what Kirby, Lee and Ditko did as canon" (Weiland).[3] At Marvel, then, retcons generally work in the manner of "filling in the gaps" rather than erasing the company's established history; stagnation may mean death, but making something unrecognizable is temporal, as characters typically revert back to the foundations of previous creative generations.[4]

Marvel's use of the retcon in *Civil War* comes in the form of *New Avengers: Illuminati*, a separate series operating outside of *Civil War* but existing largely to support the choices made by characters in *Civil War*.[5] This makes *Illuminati* a unique type of retcon in that it is less about altering specific stories as it is creating a secret history; it does this not to change our understanding of the *past* nearly as much as it is to enhance our understanding of the *present*. *NAI #0* is filling in gaps we didn't even know were there—gaps, as it turns out, we need to have filled in to rationalize the contemporary actions of characters. It is a prime example of the original use of the term "retroactive continuity." The inventor of the term, Elgin Frank Tupper, argues that "[Wolfhart] Pannenberg's conception of retroactive continuity ultimately means that history flows fundamentally from the future into the past, that the future is not basically a product of the past" (100). *NAI #0* is an example of future needs building the historical past. Instead of crafting a story based on specific historical moments, Marvel enlisted writer Brian Michael Bendis and artists Alex Maleev and Jimmy Cheung to create a new super-group that had not previously been seen, linking the 1971–1972 *Kree-Skrull War* event to 2006's *Civil War*.[6] The *Illuminati* mini-series is a purpose-built justification for the *Civil War* actions of Tony Stark, Reed Richards, Stephen Strange, Black Bolt, and, by the proxy figure of Prince Namor, Captain America; by setting themselves above not only humanity but every other hero, the Illuminati justifies Stark placing himself in charge of all heroes, Reed's capitulation to sidekick status, Strange's role as conscientious objector, Black Bolt's dis-involvement, and Captain America's/Namor's fury.

The Illuminati: "We're the law enforcement of this planet"

Released six weeks prior to the publication of *Civil War* #1, the *New Avengers: Illuminati* one-shot establishes a secret coalition of leaders from around the Marvel Universe for the Tony Stark-expressed purpose of creating a "unified structure" of heroes to prevent events like the Kree-Skrull War (KSW) from happening (Bendis, *NAI #0*, 3).[7] Tony has invited six participants to the meeting: Charles Xavier (founder of the X-Men), Prince Namor (of the undersea kingdom of Atlantis), Black Bolt (King of the Inhumans), Dr. Stephen Strange (Sorcerer Supreme), Reed Richards (leader of the Fantastic Four), and T'Challa (the Black Panther and King of Wakanda).[8] Stark's suggestion that the KSW was "our fault" is not readily accepted, and he explains, "We knew all the players. We knew what they were capable of. We knew that these alien races have been at war with each other for—forever. And we knew that key members of both races had set up shop right here on planet Earth. Of course it would come to a head" (Bendis, *NAI #0*, 2). Stark wonders if having a "more unified structure" would have prevented the Kree and Skrull from even thinking about bringing their war to Earth. Framing his idea in the shadow of the apocalyptic statement, "when the Earth is attacked again," Stark lays clear that "we're the ones who will defend it," and that "to the rest of the universe, we're the law enforcement of this planet. I'm saying, maybe we should gather together and do just that" (Bendis, *NAI #0*, 3). When Namor repeatedly asks who Stark is referring to when he uses the term "we," Stark posits nothing short of a private political state comprised of capes. "The heroes," he answers. "Us. All of us. The X-Men, the Avengers, the Inhumans, the Fantastic Four, everyone else ... we should gather. We should make our own delegation" (Bendis, *NAI #0*, 3). Note that at this point, Stark is suggesting the creation of an open delegation comprised of all heroes, and not a secret organization of just the assembled participants. The creation of the Illuminati comes during the meeting, and how these seven men move from an open delegation to a secret society begins to reveal how their roles will be defined during the civil war.

Tony's idea of a superhero delegation has him in full dreamer mode, seeing only the positives of the outcome and not the details it will take to get there, which is where the others enter the discussion. Namor is the most openly hostile to the idea, flatly stating, "No" to the idea of sharing information between all the factions of superheroes. It is clear from his response that Namor embraces his role as an outsider, constantly framing his rebukes with a "you" for every "we" Iron Man deploys. "You can't even control the groups you're already in," Namor chides. "How on Earth could you hope to control them as a larger body?" (Bendis, NAI #0, 4). Now on the defensive, Stark says this is why he has called this meeting, to discuss how to make it work. Namor again says, "No," but the others now find a voice and we see instantly how the retroactive continuity starts to work; Bendis' depiction of the individual members of the Illuminati is not a wholesale revision of these characters as much as it puts an emphasis on their representation in *Civil War*. Namor's role is to be openly hostile, creating the position that Captain America will inherit once the hostilities begin. Reed is instantly focused on the governance of the potential coalition, and Strange brings up the frustrations coming from the inevitable bureaucracy, doubting the "best super heroes" would want to deal with that kind of system. Through this back-to-back questioning, however, the road is being paved from Stark's all-inclusive delegation to the elitist Illuminati. It is Reed who changes the language from "delegation" to "coalition," suggesting an internal group rather than external representation. Dr. Strange's addition is subtle, but significant, already trimming the numbers down to the "best" of their community. Namor's bluster forces the group into compromise mode, and Reed starts to fall in line while Strange displays hesitation; bluster, capitulation, and disinterest will follow these three men throughout *Civil War*.

It is Charles Xavier who delivers the keenest insight into what will drive Tony Stark during the conflict: his incessant need to please the public.[9] If there is any aspect of any of these characters that undergoes the greatest alteration in Bendis' *Illuminati* and Mark Millar's *Civil War*, it is Tony Stark being led around by the chain of public opinion. Xavier notes how during KSW, "the Skrulls tried to turn the public against you. And they came close. It's a new feeling for you, that animosity. Am I right?" After Stark agrees, Xavier compares what he's experiencing for the first time with the daily reality of being a mutant: "As a mutant ... we feel what you're feeling right now ... every day. All day. I know exactly how you feel. And you want to turn that feeling into something—something positive. And that's noble. But this idea...." (Bendis, NAI #0, 4).[10] Stark tries to rally him to his cause by suggesting that the inclusion of mutants could help "smash down barriers" and "install trust in mutants all around the world" (Bendis, NAI #0, 5).[11] Stark's response to Xavier's analysis shows that he still feels the public is on his side and that he (and the other heroes) can lead the public to a better place, yet he will spend the entirety of Civil War on the other end of that dynamic.

It is Namor's antagonism that eventually drives the formation of the secret society by pointing out that creating a greater public face for their community will inevitably invite greater scrutiny. "How many convicted criminals and supposed ex-mutant terrorists do you have on the Avengers right now?" he asks Iron Man, turning the Avengers' long history of offering people a second chance against him (Bendis, NAI #0, 5). It is not just Stark that comes under Namor's gaze; he has questions for others, too. He wants to know how Xavier "screens" the mutants he lets into his school, and what Black Bolt has done with his brother, Maximus, who was an "architect of the Kree invasion" (Bendis, NAI #0, 6). "And you want to shine a spotlight on all of this?" Namor asks the group. "You think you can put these people up as role models and delegates for the entire planet Earth. That is completely deluded" (Bendis, *NAI #0*, 6). The response is complete silence, but in tearing down Stark's concept of the "unified structure," Namor has unwittingly opened the door to the closed circle of elites.[12] Reed takes his first steps into the role of Stark's sidekick, as the guy who helps Tony implement all of his visionary ideas, by bringing the matter back to the less-controversial idea of sharing information.[13] "A meeting just like this could have saved a lot of peoples' lives," he suggests, and the tide finally turns in favor of doing something instead of continuing the status-quo (Bendis, *NAI #0*, 6). Strange focuses on the need for private meetings, Reed iterates it would only be for major events, and now Namor finds himself drawn in, stating he could "trust the people in this room," but insisting it would only be them: no teammates, "no family. No wives" (Bendis, *NAI #0*, 7). He looks at Reed as he makes this last demand, as Namor's desire for Reed's wife, Susan, has long been out in the open; to get Namor to buy in, Reed has to accept his conditions, but to accept his conditions drives a wedge between him and Susan that Namor would not have a problem exploiting, if the opportunity arose.

After the group agrees to private meetings and allowing Xavier to scan their minds to ensure this privacy, everyone assembled votes yes, with the exception of the Black Panther; given the Pannenbergian idea of future needs constructing the historical past, it falls to the previously silent T'Challa to deliver the warning of the "possible" future that will inevitably play out. "I am telling you now," he declares. "End this. Walk away from this table and go home" (Bendis, *NAI #0*, 9). His argument walks two paths: public opinion and dissension in the ranks. On the first point, he argues the reason the Skrulls were able to turn the public against heroes was "because deep down everyone knows that this could happen, and now it has" (Bendis, *NAI #0*, 9). By setting themselves up as the secretive elite that makes planet-altering decisions, the assembled group is creating an unsustainable situation. "What happens when you disagree?" T'Challa asks. "When one of these Earth-changing moments finds you all at odds with each another, here in a secret meeting?" (Bendis, *NAI #0*, 9). T'Challa leaves without answering the question, but Reed and Strange again step in to set-up their eventual role in *Civil War*: Reed thinks it is a "one of the best ideas I've ever heard," thus committing himself to the cause even before there is a cause, and Strange declares if T'Challa's scenario comes to pass, "we do walk away," which is exactly what he will do (Bendis, *NAI #0*, 10). Though Bendis does not write *Civil War*, he certainly knows what is going to happen from the story meetings at Marvel's annual creative retreat, and what he sets up here helps Mark Millar deliver the characterizations of Tony, Reed, Strange, and Namor/Cap in his series. Writing as contemporaries but in different parts of the Marvel chronology, the needs of Millar's future are given seed in Bendis' past.[14]

Tony Stark: "We aren't living in 1945, anymore"

Tony Stark's arc in *Civil War* is one of an unchecked visionary (or futurist, as Stark has taken to calling himself) being pushed forward by public opinion. Stark sits at the heart of Pannenberg's retroactive continuity; readers of Marvel Comics since the KSW have not seen a Tony Stark that has been championing the kinds of reforms issued forth in the wake of the super villain Nitro blowing himself up and killing over 600 residents, including 60 schoolchildren, to avoid capture by the New Warriors. To create the appropriate narrative justification for this alteration in Tony's approach, Brian Michael Bendis emphasizes the visionary, public-conscious aspect of the character in *Illuminati*.[15] At the end of the *Illuminati* one-shot (after the Hulk has been exiled to space but prior to Nitro's explosion), Tony calls the group together to inform them of the *Superhero Registration Act*: "Anyone with powers—anyone in costume—any mutant—any of our kind is going to be required by law to reveal themselves to the United States government.... You will still get to be a super hero, but you'll have to answer to someone. Refusing to do so will be considered a federal crime" (Bendis, *NAI #0*, 27).[16] The group's response ranges from hostile (Namor) to offended (Strange) to skeptical (Reed), but Stark pushes forward, declaring, "I am a futurist" (Bendis, *NAI #0*, 27). He lays out a nightmare scenario where "a hero, probably a young one ... some carefree, happy-go-lucky, well-meaning young person, with the best of intentions, will do something wrong ... and people will be hurt or killed because of it. And it'll either happen on live TV, or be recorded," and "it'll play over and over ... all over the world" (Bendis, *NAI #0*, 27). This, of course, is almost exactly what happens in *Civil War #1*, when cameras recording a New Warriors reality show record Nitro's explosion. The group now splinters: Namor, Dr. Strange, and Black Bolt all refuse to go along with Tony's plan, while Reed falls into his role of sidekick.[17]

Tony's futurist-driven support for the SHRA is given fuel by his newfound desire to please the public, which is given a representative voice in the figure of Miriam Sharpe, the mother of one of the children killed by Nitro. Sharpe places the blame on Stark for actions that he had no direct connection to or control of, and this falls under the same 9/11-esque auspices of the desire to blame someone and do something to get revenge, even if those connections are tenuous, at best. After memorial services for the victims of Stamford Connecticut, Sharpe accosts Stark by spitting in his face and accusing him of being responsible. After Stark insists the New Warriors had nothing to do with him, Sharpe asks, "Who finances the Avengers? Who's been telling kids for years that they can live outside the law as long as they're wearing tights? Cops have to train and carry badges, but that's too boring for Tony Stark.... The blood of my little Damien is on your hands right now" (Millar, *CW #1*, 14–15). Legal analyst Kent Roach explains how "before 9/11, it seemed relatively clear that a state had to give directions to or have control of a terrorist group before being held responsible for the acts of terrorism," but in the post–9/11 world, the United Nations has "arguably expanded the right of self-defense against states that harbor terrorists" (30). Sharpe's invective against Stark follows this same logic, in that his actions are indirectly responsible for Nitro because his actions are indirectly responsible for the existence of the New Warriors. He can be held accountable, in Sharpe's eyes, because his name, reputation, and money have essentially encouraged younger heroes to act without guidance or reproach.

With his adversaries in the Illuminati removed from the *Civil War* playing field, Tony Stark's main antagonist arrives in the form of Captain America, and with his long-time friend and colleague, Tony fuses his futurist/public-dictated arguments in their first one-on-one interaction during the conflict. Steve Rogers is the perfect foil for Stark in this conflict; it is Cap's position as the man from the past thrust forward from the past into the present that best highlights their positions on opposite sides of the Registration Act.[18] Captain America and the anti–Registration forces have been fully embracing an old school approach to being a superhero, having Nick Fury build them new secret identities to allow them to continue to operate as they have been for decades.[19] Stark immediately attacks this idea; after Captain America rebukes Spider-Man for questioning his principles (and thus, his old school ethics), Stark admits he knows this is an "enormous change from the way we've always worked," before insisting, "we aren't living in 1945 anymore. The public doesn't want masks and secret identities. They want to feel safe when we're around, and there's no other way to win back their respect" (Millar, *CW* #3, 13). Stark's framing of the argument as a world fundamentally different than the pre–Nitro explosion, and thus one that needs new solutions to old problems, is reminiscent of the approach to the post–9/11 world by President George W. Bush's White House. In a speech given at the White House near the fifth anniversary of the September 11 attacks (and just weeks prior to the publication of *Civil War* #4), the president declared, "We watched the twin towers collapse before our eyes, and it became instantly clear that we'd entered a new world and a dangerous new war" (Bush). Like Stark, Bush trumpets a new way of thinking as the only way to victory, stating, "[O]ur government has changed its policies and given our military, intelligence and law enforcement personnel the tools they need to fight this enemy and protect our people and preserve our freedoms" (Bush). And like the president, Stark relies on his own either/or logic—for him, you either have to be for the SHRA, or you are against it. There is no other option in Stark's mind, which is a curious position for a visionary to take, except when they are having their actions created by public opinion.

Reed Richards: "Please fix this"

In 1982, Thomas Dolby released a synthpop single entitled, "She Blinded Me With Science," and in 2006, Reed Richards was not a man blinded by science, but a scientist blinded by the futurist visions of Tony Stark. Since the early days of the Fantastic Four, Reed has born the weight of his failures; specifically, being responsible for leading Susan Storm, Johnny Storm, and Ben Grimm into a cosmic radiation storm that gave them their superpowers, and being unable to reverse that process and give his best friend, Ben, his normal life back. On some level, then, it must have been comforting for Reed to be involved with the Illuminati. Not only was he surrounded by other brilliant minds and world leaders, but he had a man, in Tony Stark, completely willing to tell Reed what to do, and support his marathon sessions in a laboratory.[20] As an inventor, as a man with an incurable desire to fix and improve and invent things, it is natural for Reed to join the pro–Registration side of the conflict: the actions of Nitro caused a problem, after all, and problems need to be fixed. Reed's role in *Civil War* is to be Tony's most-trusted lieutenant, and Reed is happy to play this role until it costs him his wife; it is only after Sue leaves him to join Cap's forces that Reed begins to be more than Tony's adoring sidekick.

New Avengers: Illuminati uses Namor to create a wedge between Reed and Sue, and *Civil War* picks up on this thread by having Reed ignoring Sue in favor of concentrating on his work for Tony Stark. Reed's occasional preference for the company of his lab over his friends and family is one of the character's historical traits, and so Millar and Bendis' use of Pannenberg's retroactive continuity is less to create a new back story as it is to clear out other interpretations of the character and focus the audience specifically on this attribute. It is the Thing who watches Reed and Sue's children as Sue enters the lab to confront Reed over what he's doing, as Johnny Storm is in the hospital, a victim of a public assault in *Civil War* #1. Reed is in total adoration mode this early in the conflict, insisting, "Tony's big plans for the superhuman community is the most exciting thing we've ever worked on, Sue.... I haven't been this excited since I saw my first black hole" (Millar, *CW* #2, 6). Sue's response is an attempt to appeal to Reed's humanity through humor; she cracks, "Yeah, well, maybe I'd be excited, too, if his genius plan didn't mean jail for half of our Christmas card list" (Millar, *CW* #2, 6). Reed relies on his own scientific projections of what will happen if heroes don't register, deflecting humanity with science, and when Sue finds a computer disk labeled, "42," her interest is rebuked, as her husband tells her, "that's classified information" (Millar, *CW* #2, 7). When T'Challa briefly enters the storyline to confront Reed over Spider-Man publicly unmasking himself at a Stark-orchestrated press conference, Reed again insists Stark's plan is their "only chance," which leads to the Wakandan King offering a "word of advice. Call Susan" (Millar, *CW* #3, 3–4). We see here how Millar and Bendis are using Pannenberg's retroactive continuity with Reed: the specific wedge that Namor creates in *Illuminati* by insisting on absolute secrecy is given physical form in the classified "42" disk, and even though Reed does not tell T'Challa of the disk, the Panther sees the widening of the wedge.

Reed's return to his more traditional self comes only after Sue leaves him a "Dear John" letter informing him she is joining the anti–Registration forces, which forces his scientific and emotional halves to find a compromise with one another. Under the direction of Stark, Reed has built a cyborg clone of the Thunder God, Thor, and that invention proceeds to kill Bill Foster (the current Goliath) during the battle in which Iron Man and Captain America first confront one another. Stark's forces are on the verge of victory before Sue steps in and allows for Cap's side to escape by constructing an invisible force shield. Sue's letter to Reed details her reasons for leaving, starting with her feelings of shame at both Reed and herself: "Our hands are soaked in Bill Foster's blood and you're so blinded by your graphs and social projections that you can't even see it" (Millar, *CW* #4, 20). Though she is taking Johnny with her, Sue is leaving their children with Reed; ostensibly, this is done because living underground is "obviously no place for Franklin and Valeria," but Sue is still betting on Reed's humanity (and guilt) to save him, "begging" Reed to "give them the time you have so often denied them in the past" (Millar, *CW* #4, 21). She ends her letter by making one final appeal, this time hitting Reed the Scientist, not the Husband, imploring him to "please fix this" (Millar, *CW* #4, 21). Almost instantly, Reed begins to lament the conflict, admitting, "sometimes, I wish we'd never gotten involved" and tying this to Sue's absence (Millar, *CW* #5, 19). Reed is now caught between his desire to please both Tony and Sue as the scientist in him believes in the former while the emotional side needs the latter. He spends 36 hours in the lab attempting to fix the cyborg/clone Thor, but he also leverages his importance to Tony's side by getting the president of the United States to agree to give them 12 "immunities," making it clear one of them will be for Sue (Millar, *CW* #6, 5). Reed's arc in *Civil War* ends with Sue's return, a perfect illustration of the push and pull inside the Marvel Comics offices to balance Joe Quesada's edict that "stagnation means death" with the need to honor the company's legacy.

Stephen Strange and Conclusion: "There is no right or wrong"

There are, of course, always two reasons why stories unfold the way they do: the internal rationale of the characters and the external needs of the creators. Externally, it is important for Dr. Stephen Strange, Sorcerer Supreme of Earth, to be removed from the conflict. Just like Professor Xavier, the Hulk, and Black Bolt, Strange has the power to end the conflict on his own. Internally, Strange decides to become a conscientious objector to the Civil War. After declaring that the SHRA is "giving in to other people's ignorance and fear,"

Strange retreats to the Arctic, where, according to his manservant Wong's statement to pro–Registration supporter Hank Pym, he hopes that "he might resolve your differences by fasting for forty nights" (Bendis, *NAI #0*, 31; Millar, *CW #3*, 4). As the war rages, Uatu the Watcher visits Strange in the Arctic and asks, "Are you not tempted to simply end it? With your great power, you could stop this quarrel with a gesture or a whisper" (Millar, *CW #6*, 15).[21] Strange insists this is why he must "stay above the fray" and that "there is no right or wrong," yet when the conflict is over and the pro–Registration forces have won after Captain America surrenders, Dr. Strange joins the rebellious New Avengers, in violation of federal law.[22]

Stephen Strange is a metaphor for the dangers of inaction during a time of national conflict. He is the stand-in for the politicians who allowed the PATRIOT Act to be rushed through Congress without doing their due diligence. In the years since the enactment of the PATRIOT Act, even its most ardent supporters have sometimes found themselves opposing the implementation of the bill's policies. One of the bill's primary authors, Congressman Jim Sensenbrenner, released a statement in 2013 questioning the actions of the FBI: "While I believe the PATRIOT Act appropriately balanced national security concerns and civil rights, I have always worried about potential abuses.... Seizing phone records of millions of innocent people is excessive and un–American" (Sensenbrenner). Senator Feingold's assertion that the PATRIOT Act never properly balanced security and civil liberties highlights the difficulty in attempting to stop something that, according to the 9/11 Commission, cannot ever fully be stopped. Tony Stark's actions in Civil War attempt to do the same, going to great lengths to mollify the public's response to a super-villain doing what super-villains do—blow things up, hurt people, kill people. It is a pity that during Stephen Strange's response to the public's desire for the heroes to *do something* was to *do nothing*, an act that neither honored the memory of those killed in Nitro's self-explosion nor helped to save the lives of heroes caught up in the *Civil War*.

Notes

1. The USA PATRIOT Act is an acronym that stands for "Uniting and Strengthening America by Providing Appropriate Tools Required to Intercept and Obstruct Terrorism Act of 2001."
2. The first use of the term "retroactive continuity" was in Elgin Frank Tupper's book, *The Theology of Wolfhart Pannenberg* (London: Westminster Press, 1973).
3. Ross is referring to Stan Lee, Jack Kirby, and Steve Ditko, three primary architects of the first decade of Marvel Comics.
4. This was typically the case, but not always. During his run on *West Coast Avengers*, John Byrne radically and controversially altered the history of the Vision, literally and figuratively ripping the character to pieces.
5. Two items. First, *New Avengers: Illuminati* consists of a one-shot (since labeled issue #0), followed by a five-issue limited series. Second, while the series is entitled *New Avengers: Illuminati*, the group has little to nothing to do with the New Avengers. It is simply a convention of contemporary branding to attach a new series to a popular series. In terms of the internal world of the Marvel Universe, the Illuminati was formed years before the New Avengers had even come into existence. Only the final issue occurs after the New Avengers were formed.
6. The Kree-Skrull War took place in *Avengers* (Volume 1) 89–97 in 1971–72. It involved an intergalactic war fought by two alien races: the militaristic Kree and the shape changing Skrulls. To return to the discussion of time, the Illuminati mini-series thus weaves its way through 35 years of published history. What this means to the internal time of the Marvel Universe is, frankly, anyone's guess, and that guess will soon be wrong. In the continuity-obsessed 1980s, Marvel fronted the idea of a "seven-year universe," that is, everything that had happened since Fantastic Four #1 had happened within the last seven years. This has long since been abandoned. Now, it is best just not to think too hard about it.

7. The first actual appearance of the Illuminati was in *New Avengers* (Volume 1) 7, also written by Brian Michael Bendis. See Brian Michael Bendis (writer), Steve McNiven (artist), Mark Morales (inker), "The Sentry! Part 1 of 3," *New Avengers* (Volume 1) #7 (July 2005), Marvel Comics, Web, 13 July 2014.

8. Technically, it is Iron Man who invites them, as Stark's identity is not publicly-known at this point, nor does he share this information with them during the meeting.

9. Charles Xavier will spend the entirety of the Civil War off the planet Earth, so his participation in this issue represents his only significant contribution to the event.

10. In point of fact, and taking into account the hyper-malleable treatment of time in superhero comics, during the era of the KSW, the X-Men's comic had ceased printing new stories due to low sales. From issue #67 through #93 (1970–1975), *X-Men* reprinted earlier stories that did not feature the same level of anti-mutant bigotry from the Marvel Universe public as later stories.

11. Note that Stark is trying to widen out the group, moving away from Strange's "the best heroes" to helping mutants on a planetary scale.

12. Not that Namor would have a problem with this; if anyone in the room is comfortable with the idea that he is better than others, it is the Atlantean Prince.

13. I will discuss this shift in Reed's character more fully in short order, but while it is hard to think of Reed as a sidekick, I do think it is a reasonable evolution—or extension—of his ability to lose himself in his work. Tony is simply able to exploit that desire to solve problems for his own purposes better than anyone else.

14. In the back-half of this one-shot, the Illuminati conspire to remove a major, unpredictable piece from the *Civil War* landscape by exiling the Hulk into deep space. Marvel made certain to remove heroes whose involvement could dramatically shift the balance of power, and thus Hulk, Xavier, and Thor play no direct role in the conflict.

15. It is important to recognize that Tony's actions in Civil War are not wholly out of character and could be seen as a natural progression of the character's worldview. What has been altered, however, is the emphasis on these attributes and the creation of a backstory that specifically supports them. Instead of going back and highlighting specific moments from *Iron Man* and *Avengers* comics of the past, Bendis and Millar simply invented the backstory they needed. Why send new readers scurrying to the comics shops to hunt through back issues when you can simply place all the history they need right next to *Civil War* on the New Release shelf?

16. Charles Xavier is not present at the meeting, as he has disappeared following the events of a previous crossover event, *House of M*. Round and round it goes.

17. Unable to let things go, Tony calls on the Illuminati to come together again at the end of *Civil War*, to warn them that the Skrulls have come back and are already living among them, thereby setting up the next crossover event, *Secret Invasion*.

18. While Captain America is widely regarded as the leader of the Avengers, the group has traditionally been funded by Tony Stark.

19. This is, of course, a completely naive response to the SHRA, one that seems designed to bring the conflict to a head, rather than being a logical response of how to approach their current situation. Also, Stark is aware of what they're doing and has laid a trap to draw the anti–Registration forces out, which creates this confrontation.

20. It is easy to read the Tony/Reed relationship in terms of the public perceptions of Steve Jobs and Steve Wozniak, the visionary leader and highly-skilled programmer.

21. Uatu the Watcher is a cosmic character who watches the major events of universe unfold with a vow of non-interference.

22. Strange's purpose in working with the rebel Avengers after the end of the Civil War is a bit different. If he had participated in the conflict, he would have fought for one side, for a particular goal, which he did not wish to do, but afterward, he is more in a protective mode, keeping his friends from being captured. It is more than a semantic difference.

Works Cited

Bendis, Brian Michael (writer), Jim Cheung (penciller), and Mark Morales (inker). *New Avengers: Illuminati* #1–4 (Dec. 2006–Aug. 2007), Marvel Comics. Web. 13 May 2014.

Bendis, Brian Michael (writer), and Alex Maleev (penciller). *New Avengers: Illuminati* #0 (Mar. 2006), Marvel Comics. Web. 13 May 2014.

Bendis, Brian Michael (writer), Steve McNiven (penciller), and Mark Morales (inker). "The Sentry! Part 1 of 3." *New Avengers* (Volume 1) #7 (July 2005), Marvel Comics. Web. 13 July 2014.

Bendis, Brian Michael, Brian Reed (writers), Jim Cheung (penciller), and Mark Morales (inker). *New Avengers: Illuminati* #5 (November 2007), Marvel Comics. Web. 13 May 2014.

Bush, President George W. "Speech on Terrorism." Transcript Printed in *The New York Times*. Sept. 6, 2011. Web. 15 July 2014.
Gustines, George Gene. "The Battle Outside Raging, Superheroes Dive In." *The New York Times* (Feb. 20, 2006). Web. 9 July 2014.
Millar, Mark (writer), Steve McNiven (artist), and Dexter Vines (inker). *Civil War #1–7* (May 2007–Feb. 2007). Marvel Comics. Web. 10 May 2014.
National Commission on Terrorist Attack. *The 9/11 Commission Report: Final Report of the National Commission on Terrorist Attacks Upon the United States*. Washingtonm D.C.: GPO, 2004. Web. 1 June 2014.
Roach, Kent. *The 9/11 Effect: Comparative Counter-Terrorism*. Cambridge: Cambridge University Press, 2011. Print.
Sensenbrenner, Jim. "Author of PATRIOT Act: FBI's FISA Order Is Abuse of PATRIOT Act." Congressman Jim Sensenbrenner Congressional Website. June 6, 2013. Web. 21 July 2014.
Tuper, Elgin Frank. *The Theology of Wolfhart Pannenberg*. London: Westminster Press, 1973.
United States Government. Congressional Record, Volume 147. Washington, D.C.: GPO, 2001. Web. 15 July 2014.
Weiland, Jonah. "WWC: Alex Ross Talks 'The Return' to Marvel." *Comic Book Resources*, Aug. 11, 2007. Web. 20 May 2014.

"You wish to know of war, old man?" Generational Conflict, Moral Compromise and Youth Rebellion in *Civil War: Young Avengers & Runaways*

DAVID SWEENEY

Created by writer Brian K. Vaughn and artist Adrian Alphona, *Runaways* (2003–2009), although firmly located in the Marvel Universe, always felt as if it could exist comfortably in its own self-contained world. As such, the series recalled the titles *Hitman* by Garth Ennis and John McCrea (1996–2001) and Warren Ellis and Jon Cassady's *Planetary* (1998–2009) that occupied distinct niches of, respectively, the DC and Wildstorm universes. Like *Hitman* and *Planetary*, *Runaways* features super-powered characters who do not wear traditional superhero costumes; instead the Runaways resemble the cast of a television teen melodrama such as *Dawson's Creek* or more accurately, given that they do have powers, *Buffy the Vampire Slayer*. (Indeed, in a kind of creative exchange program, Vaughn wrote the second story-arc of the "canonical" Season 8 *Buffy* comic book while *Buffy's* creator, Joss Whedon, wrote the second volume of *Runaways* in which he further distanced the series from the Marvel Universe by setting part of his run in late–19th-century New York.) As Richard Reynolds has observed, costume is "the crucial sign of superheroism" (26), and dispensing with it can be taken as the expression of a desire to deviate from the conventions of the superhero genre, or indeed to present an *opposition* to them. Opposition is also an important theme in the series: the Runaways reject their parents on discovering that they are super-villains who expect their children to follow in their footsteps, which leads to a general suspicion about adulthood and the loss of integrity it seems to involve. This is particularly evident in the title's *Civil War* crossover with *Young Avengers* (2006), written by Zeb Wells, in which various Runaways make derogatory references to the "adults" and "grown-ups" (the characters also sarcastically put these terms in quotation marks) who have created the tension between superheroes.

Although of an age with them, the Runaways are also sceptical about the Young Avengers who are modeled on, as their name indicates, their adult counterparts in the Avengers, with Nico comparing them to "kids who listen to their parents' music—you just don't trust them" (Wells, *CWYAR #2*, 21). The Young Avengers' use of traditional superhero costumes is also singled out by the Runaways as a particular reason to not to trust them. The Young Avengers, then, are presented as *obedient* children—to their parent figures and to the conventions of the superhero genre, whereas the Runaways, the team—and *Runaways*, the series—stand in opposition to both. However, the fact that Runaways are involved in a crossover with *Young Avengers*, as part of a company-wide "event," and that their narrative is set within the Marvel Universe, reminds us that this is not an independent series but, like *Hitman* and *Planetary*, a company owned property: *Runaways* is *compromised* by its corporate status, which is thematically consistent with the series' depiction of adulthood as the participation, even for superheroes, in the apparently beneficent, but ultimately restrictive, status quo that is neoliberal capitalism which even the Runaways as "dropouts" cannot fully escape, in either the Marvel Universe or in the actual world.

The Runaways' rejection of their parents, and adults generally, transforms them from peer group into surrogate family. Of course, the depiction of youthful superheroes as a family unit is hardly unprecedented in the history of the genre, with such series as *X-Men*, *Legion of Superheroes*, or *Teen Titans* having previously represented super-teams in this way and also having engaged with the theme of inter-generational conflict. But what is significant in the *Civil War: Young Avengers & Runaways* crossover is the presentation of *intra* as well as inter-generational antagonism: the Young Avengers are ridiculed for their imitation of adult role models and this can be interpreted as a comment on the inherently conservative nature of both the superhero genre and the American comic book industry in general.

Using Harold Bloom's concept of the agon in which he argues that a "strong" writer will always strive to create work in opposition to the influence of that which has gone before, Geoff Klock describes the fight between characters modelled on "classic pulp heroes" and analogues of the Justice League of America in the first issue of *Planetary* as a poetic representation of "the battle in which the contemporary superhero replaced these classic pulp heroes" in the entertainment marketplace (157). Ellis and Cassady present this conflict to suggest a future for the superhero genre to be achieved by breaking away from established generic conventions to revisit the "essential idea" behind the superhero (Klock 156 n330) and rediscover the novelty of the genre. We might think of this in Deleuzian terms as an attempt to repeat the difference that made superheroes so powerful in the first place before generic and industrial conventions limited their development. Similarly, CWYAR can be read as statement of opposition to the superhero publishing industry, with its emphasis on decades of continuity in service to the ageing fan base that sustains it. The Young Avengers exist in the shadow of their adult counterparts, whereas the Runaways attempt to flee the legacy of their forebears, both in the series and in the genre, taking the "essential idea" of the youthful super-powered peer group as surrogate family into the 21st century in the process.

The Return of Marvel Boy

It is significant that *CWYAR* should feature the character Noh-Varr, created by Grant Morrison and J.G Jones for their six-issue series *Marvel Boy* (2000–2001). The series was published by the imprint, Marvel Knights, which allowed creators to experiment with established characters outside of the demands of ongoing Marvel Universe continuity, Noh-Varr being the sixth iteration of Marvel Boy, a character dating back to the Golden Age. Writing in 2002, Klock identified *Marvel Boy* as an exemplar of the emerging "pop comic," an attempt to break the comic book medium and the superhero genre out of the ghetto of fandom and into the mainstream, a situation which has indeed come to pass (even if *Marvel Boy* is not one of Morrison's or Jones's best known works). As the title of the series indicates, youth is a central theme of *Marvel Boy*, with Noh-Varr—whose name, of course, is a play on *nova* meaning *new*—represented as something of a rebellious teenager, a trait exemplified by his *monumental* vandalism of New York to spell out a rude message visible to an orbiting S.H.I.E.L.D. satellite (Morrison, *Marvel Boy #2*, 20). Noh-Varr is placed in conflict with Midas, an "obsessive and domineering father figure" whose costume is modelled on that of the original, Silver Age Iron Man (Klock 174). Noh-Varr's own costume design, while not dissimilar to traditional superhero styles, is closer to a uniform, Noh-Varr having been the youngest crew member on a Kree spaceship. Morrison also uses uniforms as replacements for traditional costumes in his run on *New X-Men* (2001–2004) which Klock also identifies as a "pop comic" in large part because of this departure from generic convention: removing the costumes actually changes the *nature* of the X-men, or rather reveals that they were never truly superheroes, at least not in the traditional sense (173).

This change was short-lived, however, with Whedon immediately returning the characters to their costumes when he took over from Morrison and *New X-Men* became *Astonishing X-Men*. Ironically, although the title of Morrison's run emphasised its novelty, the series continued the numbering from the main *X-Men* comic it was designed to modernize. (Morrison was recruited by Marvel editor-in-chief Joe Quesada who, in partnership with Jimmy Palmiotti, had created Marvel Knights, and his appointing of Morrison, known for his often subversive approach to superheroes, can be seen as a continuation of the imprint's experimental ethos). Whedon's run, although a direct continuation of *New X-Men* began with an issue #1. This is, of course, a fairly common tactic in the comic industry to solicit new readers and attract collectors, but one cannot help but feel that the impact of *New X-Men*, its very novelty, was diminished somewhat by its numbering. Furthermore, while Whedon's series provided more traditional superhero fare, and although it was bedevilled by lengthy delays due to his television and film commitments, it benefitted from a consistency in the artwork (by *Planetary*'s John Cassady) that had been absent in *New X-Men* after the first 3-issue story arc (#114–#116), further diminishing the impact of the series.

In *CWYAR*, we learn that Noh-Varr's own father-figure, or nearest equivalent, the benign "Living Database" Plex, has been destroyed by the Warden, a sadistic figure whose old age is evident in his liver-spotted face, thinning hair and ample gut, following Noh-Varr's capture and delivery to the Cube as depicted in the final issue of *Marvel Boy*. We discover that he has been brainwashed to believe the Warden *is* Plex and is effectively the warden's slave. Noh-Varr is set against both the Runaways and the Young Avengers, almost defeating them until he is incapacitated by cross-team co-operation. The teams then remove the Warden's mind control, allowing Noh-Varr to take his revenge by enslaving the false father figure. *CWYAR* closes with an epilogue showing Noh-Varr triumphant, reprising his proclamation, made prematurely at the end of *Marvel Boy*, that the Cube is "the capital city of the New Kree Empire" (Wells, *CWYAR #4*, 25).

In the context of the generational conflict represented in the crossover, this reprise can be read as a reassertion of the importance of the on-going development and modernisation of the superhero genre and of the "pop comic" generally (and *Marvel Boy* in particular which, as I say above, is not one of Morrison's best known works despite his "superstar" status in the industry and high mainstream media profile). While *Runaways* may not have been as formally innovative as *Marvel Boy*, its defiance of established superhero conventions, its absorption of other genres much as TV melodramas like Whedon's *Buffy, the Vampire Slayer* did, and Marvel's decision to market the series to young adults as part of their Tsunami imprint rather than to their existing readership, make it a significant entry in the history of recent pop culture. (Notably, the category description on my digest-sized collected editions identifies them as Action/Comedy/Teen Romance.)

> "We may be dumb, we may be young, but we're not scum"
> —Ange, Little Brother (Doctorow 157)

During his torture of the Young Avenger Wiccan, the Warden takes great pleasure in goading him into making a death threat, remarking, "And so our youth become killers.... Perhaps we do have a war on our hands" (Wells, *CWYAR* #4, 10). Considering Young Avengers as a post–9/11 text, it is difficult not to read this statement as an indictment of the Bush administration for the number of young lives lost in the "War on Terror," particularly given the Warden's description of the young super-humans as "new toys to play with" (Wells, *CWYAR* #4, 4). The line of dialogue that gives this paper its title—"You wish to know of war, old man?"—is delivered to the Warden by the Runaway Xavin, a Skrull trained to be a warrior from birth. Xavin then exclaims, "I have no innocence! I have no ideals!" (Wells, *CWYAR* #4, 11), a further indictment, in the context of the wider narrative of *Civil War*, of the brutalising of warfare on the young.

Similarly, throughout the crossover, the Runaways hold the view that the "Civil War" is a situation created by "adults" and another reason to avoid growing up, which is contrasted with the Young Avengers' involvement in Captain America's resistance movement. The inevitable genre expectations do rear their inevitable head; *CWYAR* doesn't completely dispense with superhero conventions and an alliance is formed between the two previously combative teams. Yet the Runaways' position remains unchanged at the end of the crossover, with Nico explaining the team's position to the tellingly named Patriot, the Young Avengers' version of Captain America:

> I saw a bunch of people who work for the United States government ... people who probably think *they're* the good guys. You play grown-up long enough and you lose your perspective on right and wrong. Why not put it off for as long as possible? [Wells, *CWYAR* #4, 23].

It is useful here to compare *CWYAR* with another post–9/11 text, Cory Doctorow's dystopian young adult novel, *Little Brother*, published in 2008, a year after the end of *Civil War*. The novel depicts the response by a group of teenagers to a major terrorist attack in San Francisco in the near future and a subsequent youth uprising against the government after civil liberties are suspended by the Department of Homeland Security (DHS).

Its title is, of course, a reference to the Party leader, Big Brother, in George Orwell's classic depiction of totalitarianism, *1984* (as is the net handle, "W1n5t0n" used by *Little Brother*'s narrator, Marcus, in homage to Winston Smith, the protagonist of *1984*). A hacker from an affluent Californian background, like the Runaways themselves, Marcus is held and interrogated by the DHS following the terrorist attack. After he is finally released, he retaliates by setting up an underground communication network, the "Xnet," which is named for the repurposed Xbox game consoles involved but is also a pleasing, if accidental, reminder of the generational conflict of the *X-Men* (particularly Grant Morrison's "Riot at Xavier's" storyline in *New X-Men* #135–#138, which focuses on the super-intelligent teenage mutant Quentin Quire's challenge to Professor Xavier's authority). At a rally to recruit members of the network, Marcus' ally, Ange, addresses the crowd, proclaiming, "[T]hey're turning into adults younger and younger out there. Back in the day, they used to say, 'Never trust anyone over 30.' I say, 'Don't trust any bastard over 25!'" (158).

Like the Runaways, the members of the Xnet feel aggrieved at been involved in a situation created by adults. Adulthood is to be avoided as it involves not only a compromise of integrity but also the collaboration in a culture of suspicion and obedience. However, the members of Xnet refuse to merely flee from their situation, although the theme of travel as an escape from a restrictive normality is present in the novel in Marcus's reading of, and quotation from, Jack Kerouac's classic Beat novel *On the Road* which I will return to below.

The use of re-purposed Xboxes for the Xnet is significant: Marcus explains that his model, the (fictitious) Universal, "was the first Xbox that Microsoft decided to give away entirely for free" (78). Despite this, the model proves to be as unpopular as its games, produced exclusively by companies who have paid an exorbitant licensing fee to Microsoft, "were really expensive and not a lot of fun" (86). He describes Microsoft as a "razor-blade business" involved in "[g]iving away one thing to sell another" (86). Marcus lives in an economy of abundance but the neoliberal favouring of corporate controlled intellectual property over open sourcing reveals this abundance to be illusory. Doctorow made *Little Brother* available for free through his website using a Creative Commons license, encouraging readers to "remix" the text and hosting the results, which is in sharp contrast with the work-for-hire context and company-owned status of comics like *Runaways*, a situation with which Brian K. Vaughn, who now only produces creator-owned work—such as his series *Saga* (beginning in 2012) through the independent publisher Image—is undoubtedly familiar.

Warren Ellis does continue to produce company owned work, such as his current Marvel series *Moon Knight* (vol. 3). But he also makes reference to *Civil War* in an afterword to his creator-owned, independently published superhero mini-series, *Black Summer* (#0). *Black Summer* is, itself, very much a post–9/11 text, as it makes direct reference to that event and opens with the execution, by a patriotic superhero, of George W. Bush for crimes against the American people (Ellis, *Black Summer #0*, 4). Ellis writes that *Black Summer* poses "a much bigger question than, say, asking if super-human combatants in America should be registered with a Federal agency," something that can only be achieved with "the freedom of doing a piece of superhero fiction outside the auspices of company ownership and the weight of continuity" (10–11). Like Marcus, Vaughn and Ellis realise the compromises involved in dealing with corporate entertainment. Indeed, Doctorow perhaps knows this best of all: *Little Brother*'s sequel, *Homeland*, was also made available for free online via creative commons, but Doctorow was forced to take it down by Fox, who claimed it was infringing on their, completely unrelated, TV series of the same name, an event which resulted in Doctorow calling for the head of Fox CEO, Rupert Murdoch (Biggs).

The slogan on the paperback edition of *Little Brother*—"Big Brother is watching you. Who is watching back?"—is recalled in the tagline from the 2013 film, *The East*: "Spy on us, we'll spy on you." Like *Little Brother*, *The East* features a group of "culture jammers" who use surveillance technology against the powerful. *The East* also evokes a Kerouac-esque sense of the freedom of travel in an early scene that depicts a group of young dropouts who have hopped a freight train and are entertaining each other with banjos and acoustic guitars. With their worn clothes, dirty faces, tattoos, and piercings, the drop-outs resemble a cross between Depression-era hobos and 21st-century hipsters similar to the subjects of the photographs in Mike Brodie's book, *A Period of Juvenile Prosperity*, taken during his own five-year period riding the railways, which he began in 2003 at the age of 18. In an interview with Sean O'Hagan for *The Guardian*, Brodie named Mark Twain's teenage adventurer Huckleberry Finn as the inspiration for his travels, but also compared some of the other young people he encountered on the rails to Kerouac. The title of Brodie's book, and many of the images themselves, represent dropping out as an *enriching* experience, a view which Marcus seems to share even if he does not participate in a peripatetic lifestyle. Nevertheless, *Little Brother*'s celebration of youth as a time to be relished before the inevitable compromises of adulthood under neoliberalism places it in a tradition of American teenage existential fiction to which *Runaways*—and *Young Avengers*, *X-Men* and *Teen Titans*—also belongs.

Not of course that the Runaways are ever truly vagabonds: with their high-tech, and possibly sentient, vehicle, the Leapfrog, which had belonged to their super-villain parents, the team do not have to resort to freight hopping. Nor do we see them forage for discarded food by "dumpster diving" as is also depicted in *The East*. Instead, at the start of *CWYAR*, we see them stop off at a farmer's market to shop for provisions. Here they encounter both a pair of heavily armoured security guards, who debate the validity of their stationing at such a genteel location, and Flag-Smasher, a rather silly, vulgar–Marxist super-villain originally conceived in 1985, during the height of the Cold War, as a sort of Communist equivalent of Captain America's Nazi nemesis, the Red Skull. Having already bested Flag-Smasher previously, the Runaways easily defeat him when he engages the guards as a prelude to, it would appear, attacking the market. During the fracas, Flag-Smasher proclaims his rejection of American Sovereignty and demands of the Runaways, "Haven't you fools read Marx?"(Wells, *CWYAR #1*, 8). Victor admits he has not, nor even attended history class generally. The whole, brilliantly executed and hilarious, scene is in keeping with the light tone of the *Runaways* series but also that of the core *Civil War* books written by Mark Millar, with their emphasis on presenting political debate between the conflicting superhero factions even as they engage in combat. However, the use of the farmers' market as a setting should not be overlooked. As Greg Sharzer (2012) has observed, such examples of small-scale "localism" may appear to challenge neoliberalism and its agenda of globalisation, but in fact operate using the same basic economic strategies of cost-cutting and profit maximisation as large corporations.

While not wishing to appear as joylessly doctrinaire as Flag-Smasher, and though I admit to being touched by the excitement of the Runaways' youngest member, eleven-year-old Molly, at the prospect of tasting lemons that "are actually sweet" (Wells, *CWYAR #1*, 2), I nevertheless share Sharzer's view that farmers' markets, and similar small scale organisations, are often as illusory as the "razor blade" businesses Markus describes in *Little Brother* in their concealment of the true exploitative nature of capitalism. For Roland Barthes, wine, the quintessential French drink, could not be an "unalloyed blissful substance" in the 1950s unless one was "innocent" of the knowledge that much of its production took place in colonial Algeria (61). Similarly the "quality" produce and family friendly environments provided by farmers' markets—the entrance to the Santa Monica market, as accurately represented in the first panel of *CWYAR*, resembles the gateway to a theme-park—ultimately serve to make capitalism acceptable, particularly when presented as examples of a "good life" which opponents to capitalism—as caricatured in Flag-Smasher—would seek to destroy. But as already noted, the Runaways, like Marcus in *Little Brother*, come (mostly) from affluent Californian backgrounds, so their visiting a farmers' market is a perfectly understandable attempt to continue an aspect of the lives they have been forced to leave behind through no fault of their own, and they can hardly be blamed at their young age for not having engaged with the complexities of neoliberalism (nor could Marcus in *Little Brother*).

> *"I believe in the Propaganda of the Deed"*
> —Abigail Beryl Burns, *Iron Man* #18 (Gillen 22)

Laurie Penny, a young British feminist and leftist writer, and associate of Doctorow, in 2011 addressed the existential conflict of neoliberalism in her article, "Dropping out won't fix the world: It is possible to drink your Starbucks latte with your politics intact?" Penny takes issue with the "notion peddled by right-wing commentators ... that you cannot have any serious, sustained objections to fiscal feudalism and its discontents if you happen to have grown up in a detached house, or attended an elite university, or if you once, in a moment of weakness late at night, found yourself walking out of a well-known conglomerate with a box of suspicious chicken pieces coated in unmentionable sauce and wondering what your life had become" (Penny).

Penny argues that "[i]f capitalism is a disease, everything and everyone is infected" and so attempting to remove oneself from society will only allow the status quo to continue. A comics reader, Penny has received perhaps the fan's highest accolade, serving as the inspiration, along with fellow writer and feminist Abigail Brady, for the *Iron Man* character Abigail Beryl Burns, created by the writer Kieron Gillen. The character's online identity and later superhero name, Red Peril, recalls Penny's Twitter handle, Pennyred, while, visually, Burns combines Penny's "emo" dress sense with Brady's hairstyle. In her first appearance, in *Iron Man* #18, Burns lists the threats to the world as "neoliberal policy. Impotency of democracy. Impossibility of envisioning a world outside of capitalism. Corporate hegemony. The usual" (Gillen 22). She also states her belief that things "can be better" and her belief in the "propaganda of the deed," a phrase which recalls Quentin Quire's sloganeering in *New X-Men* (22). This leads to Burns being selected to become Mandarin-Seven and "save the world from Tony Stark," Stark being, of course, a corporate CEO (23).

Although Burns eventually backs off from Stark and becomes a superhero, Gillen's use of the character to channel Penny's views brought a political complexity to *Iron Man* seldom found in mainstream superhero comics. Even as Red Peril, the character remains an activist; in this she differs from the Runaways, who tend to *react* to the situations in which they find themselves. But then, so do most superheroes, which is one of the reasons Warren Ellis has been so critical of the genre—he has spoken of having "hated the fact they [superhero comics] present a society where nothing can change because it takes superhuman effort to keep things the way they are" (Salisbury, 63)—and why his series *The Authority*, illustrated by Bryan Hitch (#1–12) was so radical: its superheroes *changed the world*.

However, the Runways' decision to flee can also be seen as a challenge to superhero conventions: as young people traumatised by the revelations that the comfortable lives they have enjoyed were the result of their parents having, as Nico puts it, "squeezed Los Angeles for so long" (Wells, *CWYAR #1*, 3) and that they too possess powers which might also tempt them into evil, the Runways taking to the road is perhaps a more convincing act than their immediately deciding to fight crime. That said, their confusion over their abilities also recalls that quintessential teenager, Peter Parker, and his own moral quandary over how to use his abilities before deciding to become Spider-Man (he briefly considered a career as a wrestler to make money).

"I am the face of civil disobedience!"
—Flag-Smasher, *Civil War: Runaways & Young Avengers*, #1 (Wells 7)

Like Peter Parker, the Runaways come to realise that with great power comes great responsibility and by the time of *Civil War* they have decided to protect Los Angeles from the villains who have attempted to take over the city after the death of their parents (*Runaways* #17). To an extent, this decision made the series a more traditional superhero comic, its departures from generic convention notwithstanding.

It is in their role as Los Angeles' protectors that the Runaways engage with Flag-Smasher at the Santa Monica farmers' market. Just before the fracas, as he is challenged by the security guards, Flag-Smasher proclaims his belief in super-beings as "the last *truly* independent power structure!" (Wells, *CWYAR* #1, 4). As ridiculous a character as Flag-Smasher undoubtedly—and intentionally—is, his anti-nationalist, anarchist beliefs are not dissimilar to those of Ellis's version of *The Authority*. As Klock has observed, under Ellis, The Authority's responsibility *was* to change the world, into a "finer place" (137). "*The Authority* is the zenith of the superhero qua power fantasy, and the degree to which readers enjoy the title is the degree to which they participate in the genre for precisely this reason" (137). *The Authority*'s novelty, what makes it for Klock a "revisionary" narrative that escapes the influence of superhero tradition, is in its refusal to provide a *comforting* narrative. Rather, the emphasis is upon *excitement* and the, as Klock puts it, "obscene glory of the superhero/superego" (139).

When Ellis left *The Authority*, he was replaced by *Civil War*'s architect, Mark Millar, who transformed the team into celebrities who indulge in a hedonistic, even decadent lifestyle—one is a heroin addict—and lend their names and likenesses to a variety of commodities, while continuing to influence—or interfere in, depending on your point of view—geo-politics. This inevitably leads to retaliation from the powers-that-be and the replacement of the Authority by a team of duplicates representative of, and obedient to, the G-7 nations. As is now well known, Millar suffered from censorship from DC Comics, which had acquired the title's publisher, Wildstorm, in 1999, and even had his run interrupted for four issues for a storyline written by Tom Peyer, which led to Millar's resignation from the company. Wildstorm was originally an imprint of Image Comics, an independent publisher which, as Klock has observed, presented a "genuine break from the big publishing houses" when it was launched in 1992 (144).

As with Ellis's *Black Summer*, published by the independent Avatar Press, Image provided freedom, from both the standards of the major publishers (early Image comics were often criticised for excessive violence and the near-pornographic depiction of women) and the weight of continuity. Ellis was recruited to the company in the mid–1990s along with Alan Moore, writer of *Watchmen*, often considered the "greatest comic of all time." This brought a degree of respectability to the company, although it continued to produce considerably more extreme content than either DC or Marvel would have accepted. After Wildstorm's acquisition by DC, and following Millar's departure, *The Authority* lost the intensity of its first two years and the title was cancelled in 2010. Some of the characters have since been integrated into DC's "New 52[qm] continuity but they have become pale imitations of their former selves in order to fit into DC's moral universe. This is perhaps an example of what Abigail Beryl Burns means by "corporate hegemony" (Gillen 22).

Runaways is a much more humane text than *The Authority*, as we might expect from a series aimed at young adults and released by a mainstream publisher. The Runaways want to protect their city from those who would seek to "squeeze" or destroy it, but in in doing so they perpetuate the neoliberal status quo that conceals the exploitative truth of capitalism beneath the pleasures of an (apparent) economy of abundance. Like Barthes' wine, the "actually sweet" lemons Molly desires can only be an "unalloyed" pleasure if one is innocent of the conditions of their production. But Molly *is* innocent: her dramatic function in *Runaways* is to remind the others of their own youth even as circumstances draw them ever closer to the dreaded state of adulthood. Innocence and ignorance are not the same thing, of course, and while we may read *Civil War* as a post–9/11 text, we can also look back on it now as a pre-financial crisis narrative. I personally would have greatly enjoyed seeing the Runaways encounter the Occupy movement or the Anonymous hackers, or, indeed, Red Peril, in their role as Los Angeles' protectors, but alas the series was cancelled in 2009 just as the true extent of the catastrophe, and the reasons for it, were becoming apparent.

In Patrick Meaney's documentary about Warren Ellis, *Captured Ghosts*, the author describes the desire by some superhero fans for a real life Superman to have intervened in 9/11 as "anti-evolutionary," seeing this response as a retreat into comforting fantasy rather than attempting to engage with the complexities and contradictions of global capitalism. Superhero comics are, of course, products of capitalism and, as the subtitle to Gerard Jones' *Men of Tomorrow: Geeks, Gangsters and the Birth of the Comic Book* reminds us, this includes the involvement of organised crime. In *The Threepenny Opera* Brecht presents the gangster, Macheath, and the respectable businessman, Peachum, as mirror images of each other. For Brecht, there was no real difference between the characters, except that Peachum—like all capitalists—was adept at concealing the criminality behind his wealth. Peachum has in fact made his fortune through his exploitation of London's beggars. "Who is the bigger criminal," Brecht asks us, "he who robs a bank or he who founds one?" (act 3, scene 3). This is a difficult question for anyone to answer when things seem to be going well, particularly a superhero, but if *Runaways* was still in publication today it strikes me that it would be the perfect vehicle to engage with the relationship between neoliberal capitalism and popular culture. Perhaps the nearest recent equivalent was Gail Simone and Freddie Williams II's Occupy Movement-influenced series *The Movement* (2013), set in the DC Universe, in which a super-powered teenager collective oppose police and government corruption in their city and attempt to create their own micro-culture free from adult interference. Timely though it was, *The Movement* lacked *Runaways*' warmth and humour. It was also cancelled by DC after a year.

In the final, pre-epilogue page of *CWYAR*, Nico re-states to Patriot her position that "when the world goes crazy, you run. You runaway" [*sic*] (Wells, *CWYAR* #4, 23). By now, of course, the Runaways are settled in Los Angeles, so Nico's statement is a reassertion of her, and the others,' belief that, to borrow a phrase from Richard Linklater's American "Indie" film classic, *Slacker* (1991) "withdrawing in disgust is not the same as apathy." The Runaways *do* care: about each other, about their city. They are dropouts who still participate in society, which does not make them hypocrites. Rather, in their own way, the Runaways are activists, a collective attempting to find a new way of living, different from the normative model of the nuclear family that has betrayed them. They listen to their own music; they wear their own clothes. That the series was cancelled is itself an expression of market logic—the title was presumably not selling enough copies to be profitable—and a fate that can befall any company owned property. It is my dream that the characters could flee again, from Marvel, back to Vaughn and Alphona who would continue their journey.

As I said at the beginning of this essay, they never really needed to be a part of the

Marvel Universe, although as *Civil War: Young Avengers & Runaways* proves, in order for it to develop the Marvel Universe needs them to be a part of it.

Works Cited

Barthes, Roland. *Mythologies*. London: Vintage, 2000. Print.
Biggs, John. "Fox shuts down Cory Doctorow's book Homeland in overzealous DMCA move." *Tech Crunch*. AOL Inc. 21 April 2013. Web. 19 July 2014.
Brecht, Bertolt. *The Threepenny Opera*. New York: Grove Press, 2005. Print.
Brodie, Mike. *A Period of Juvenile Prosperity*, 2d ed. Santa Fe: Twin Palms, 2013. Print.
Deleuze, Gilles. *Difference and Repetition*. London: Continuum Impacts, 2004.
Doctorow, Cory. *Little Brother*. London: HarperVoyager, 2008. Print.
The East. Dir. Zal Batmanglij. Perf. Brit Marling, Alexander Skarsgard, and Ellen Page. Scott Free Productions, 2013. Film.
Ellis, Warren (writer), and John Cassady (artist). *Planetary* #1–27. La Jolla, CA: Wildstorm, 1998–2009. Print.
Ellis, Warren (writer), Bryan Hitch (penciller), and Paul Neary (inker). *The Authority* #1–12. La Jolla, CA: Wildstorm. 1999–2000. Print.
Ellis, Warren (writer), and John McCrea (artist). *Hitman* #1–60. New York: DC Comics, 2009–2012. Print.
Ellis, Warren (writer), and Juan Jose Ryp (artist). *Black Summer* #0. Rantoul, IL: Avatar, 2007. Print.
Gillen, Kieron (writer) and Joe Bennett (artist). *Iron Man* #18. New York: Marvel, 2013. Web. 6 Sept. 2014.
Klock, Geoff. *How to Read Superhero Comics and Why*. New York: Continuum, 2002. Print.
Morrison, Grant (writer), and J. G. Jones (artist). *Marvel Boy* #1–6. New York: Marvel Knights, 2000–2001. Print.
Morrison, Grant (writer), and Frank Quitely (artist), *New X-Men* #114–154. New York: Marvel, 2001–2004. Print.
O'Hagan, Sean. "Mike Brodie's freight train photographs: 'It's a romantic life, at least in the spring and summer.'" *The Guardian*. Guardian News and Media. 30 Mar. 2013. Web. 18 July 2014.
Penny, Laurie. "Dropping Out Won't Fix the World: It Is Possible to Drink a Starbucks Latte with Your Politics Intact?" *New Statesman*. New Statesman. 14 Nov. 2011. Web. 18th July 2014.
Reynolds, Richard. *Superheroes: A Modern Mythology*. London: B.T. Batsford, 1992. Print.
Salisbury, Mark. *Writers on Comic Scriptwriting*. London: Titan Books, 1999. Print.
Sharzer, Greg. *No Local: Why Small Scale Alternatives Won't Change the World*. London: Zero Books, 2012. Print.
Simone, Gail (writer), Freddie Williams II, (penciller), and Chris Sotomayor (colorist). *The Movement* #1–6. New York: DC Comics, 2013–2014. Print.
Slacker. Dir. Richard Linklater. Perf. Linklater, Kim Krizan, and Mark James. Orion Classics, 1990. Film.
Vaughn, Brian K. (writer), Adrian Alphona (penciller), and Craig Yeung (inker). *Runaways* #17 in *Runaways Digest Vol. 3: The Good Die Young*. New York: Marvel, 2005. Print.
Warren Ellis: Captured Ghosts. Dir. Patrick Meaney. Sequart and Respect! Films, 2011. Film.
Wells, Zeb (writer), and Stefano Casellis (artist). *Civil War: Young Avengers and Runaways* #1–4. New York: Marvel, 2006. Print.
Whedon, Joss. *Runaways Digest Vol. 8: Dead End Kids*. New York: Marvel, 2009. Print.

Whither Alpha Flight?
The Nationalistic Response to
Canada During the War on Terror

BRENNA CLARKE GRAY

Within the lead up to Marvel's *Civil War* event, one of the most shocking moments for the Canadian comics reader was the destruction of Alpha Flight team at the hands of The Collective in *New Avengers #16*. Jason Dittmer asserts in his essay "Captain America's Empire: Reflections on Identity, Popular Culture, and Post–9/11 Geopolitics" that Captain America literally embodies the nation for the Marvel Comics reader (627). So too does Alpha Flight embody Canada, especially insofar as it reflects a marginal Canadian space in the larger American Marvel Universe. Alpha Flight is notable as one of the very few Canadian superhero teams in mainstream comics, with a legacy dating back to the 1970s. As part of Wolverine's backstory, Alpha Flight has a significant role in the Marvel canon—but of course, part of the power and excitement about a series like *Civil War* is that anything is possible and nothing is sacred.

On a socio-cultural level, though, what does it mean for Marvel to kill off these Canadian superheroes—effectively Canada's answer to The Avengers—in their clearly post–9/11-inspired world event? In what ways might the destruction of Alpha Flight parallel the American cultural distrust of Canada in the immediate post–9/11 era? After all, this was a period when rampant untruths about Canadian sovereignty and security ran unchecked in American media and government statements, as Chantal Allan has documented in her book *Bomb Canada and Other Unkind Remarks in the American Media* (2009). Just as American pundits and politicians were asking if Canada was really such a true ally after all—from the false belief that the 9/11 terrorists entered the U.S. from Canada to the anger over Canada's refusal to pursue war in Iraq—Marvel was stripping Canada of her superheroes and denying their role as an ally in the post–*Civil War*, S.H.I.E.L.D.-dominated new world order.

When Alpha Flight is reformed as Omega Flight, this continued distrust of Canadian allies is apparent as the restructuring heavily de–Canadianizes the team, going so far as to have USAgent—whose role in the reformed team is to represent the American government—essentially lead the once all–Canadian team. In sending USAgent to Omega Flight, S.H.I.E.L.D. asserts Canada's supposed vulnerability in the post–*Civil War* era and her need for protection. This vulnerability reflects the (incorrect) perception popular on Fox News and in other media outlets that Canada's insecurity and vulnerability to terrorists was a pressing threat to America. It also reflects a notion of American-led security as the only meaningful protection, thus reducing the concept of the ally at all in a period when America found itself increasingly willing to go it alone in the context of international diplomacy.

In this essay, I argue that Alpha Flight's destruction, reshaping, and resurrection within and after the Marvel *Civil War* event both reflects and critiques American cultural responses to Canada as a perceived failed ally, both in terms of national security and in the Iraq conflict, in the immediate post–9/11 era.

Alpha Flight and Why They Matter

According to 2006's *The Marvel Encyclopedia*, Alpha Flight is "Canada's foremost Super Hero team," first emerging in the pages of *Uncanny X-Men #120* in 1979[1] as part of a response to "superhuman activity within the United States" (DeFalco 11). Those early appearances placed Alpha Flight in opposition to the X-Men, as their first task within the pages of the comics is an assignment from Prime Minister Trudeau to repatriate the missing Weapon X, better known to comics readers as Wolverine (Claremont, *UX #120*, 1). They are aligned very tightly, in these early appearances, with the Canadian government and its prevailing ideology, though their relationship to government policy would ebb and flow over the years; indeed, as the series progressed, members of Alpha Flight would find themselves at odds with the government over Quebec separatism, neo-fascist ideology, and more, leading Dale Eaglesham, penciller for the 2011 revival of *Alpha Flight*, to note that the title "has always been one of the most progressive comic books out there" (qtd. in Iannacci 102). But whether or not *Alpha Flight* aligned with Canada's real-world government policy on a given issue, the team always strongly aligned with Canada, particularly in relation to the land and the people.

Alpha Flight has had various incarnations over the years, but the makeup at the time of the *Civil War* event included Guardian, Sasquatch, Vindicator, Shaman, Puck, Puck II, and Major Maple Leaf[2] (Bendis, *NA #16*, 13–14; *NA #17*, 8). Throughout the various runs of *Alpha Flight* (1983–94, 1997–9, 2004–5, 2011–2) totaling 170 issues, the creative team has sought to represent Canadian demographics, including French-speaking, First Nations, black, and gay characters, characters from all the regions of Canada, and characters struggling with mental health issues and issues of political ideology. These representations are not perfect, and often slip into essentialism, but compared to the larger history of Canadian superheroes, what Bart Beaty has termed the "fighting civil servant" (428) marked primarily by his whiteness and maleness, this is progress. This attempt to be representative, especially within a landscape like superhero comics where Canadian faces are typically not seen at all, is part of the larger significance of the title.

Alpha Flight has been variously successful; certainly its original 130 issue run was the most financially successful for Marvel. In his *Marvel Comics: The Untold Story*, Sean Howe notes that the first issue of Alpha Flight "sold terrifically and put a record-breaking thirty thousand dollars in his [penciller John Byrne's] pocket" (265). Other runs have shuttered due to insufficient sales; the 2011 mini-series was extended to an ongoing comic only briefly before "market forces shattered what had perhaps been a decision based on wishful thinking" (Pak, *AF #8*, 23). And yet for Canadians, Alpha Flight has larger cultural resonances, perhaps best explained by the paucity of superheroes in Canadian media; as Ryan Edwardson notes, superhero comics remain "a cultural arena where New York overwhelms New

Brunswick, and one rarely sees a maple leaf" (199). While this statement is certainly true of other global markets, the significance in Canada is heightened by language and geography: the vast majority of media consumed by English-speaking Canadians is American in origin. As Edwardson argues, "in mass culture one can find mass national identity" (186).

While it might seem odd that Canadians would relate strongly to an American-produced and often-stereotypical representation of themselves, in the vacuum that is the dearth of Canadian superheroes, this is perhaps less surprising. As Vivian Zenari notes in considering the significance of Wolverine's Canadian citizenship, for example, the American-created Wolverine is referred to in Canadian media as "our greatest symbol of national pride" (53); this reference, albeit slightly tongue-in-cheek, speaks to the power of representation for a minor nation like Canada, even when, as Zenari and Beaty have both noted, these representations are steeped in stereotypes (Zenari 60; Beaty 435). The Canada in these comics is "the imagining of another country" that "it is easy to be cynical about" (Zenari 58). And yet Canadians do buy and respond favourably to these representations when they can access them. Representation of one's own experiences, however flawed, is exceptionally powerful.[3] Further, Canadian identity has often been typified by antagonism with the United States rooted in "chronic insecurities regarding the state's cultural and political uniqueness in the continental setting" (Dittmer and Larsen, "Captain Canuck" 739), and this antagonism is certainly embodied by Alpha Flight's early battles with the X-Men.

The history of superhero comics in Canada is short, starting only in the 1940s with "the wartime importation ban on non-essential goods that removed American comic books from Canadian newsstands" (Beaty 429). Prior to that, Canadians had been content to consume American comic books, but the ban saw an opportunity for Canadian publishers to launch characters like Nelvana of the North and Johnny Canuck. These comics were popular while they were the only game in town, but the more famous names of American superheroes combined with the high cost of producing comics in Canada led to these titles folding within a few years of the end of the war. In the 1970s, another attempt to create a nationalist superhero emerged with Captain Canuck, but it was more symbolically than commercially successful; while most Canadians can name Captain Canuck, in four runs over 40 years the comic only totaled 23 issues, and repeatedly shuttered due to financial concerns. Part of what makes Marvel's Alpha Flight and Wolverine so beloved in Canada, then, is the lack of competition: there just are not that many Canadian superheroes to choose from, and the American origin of these characters is less significant to Canadian readers than one might anticipate.[4] Those who seek to construct a domestic canon of superhero comics, like John Bell, tend to downplay the significance of these comics; Bell writes in *Guardians of the North* that, although creator John Byrne was a Canadian artist who relocated to the U.S., "*Alpha Flight* belonged too much to the American superhero tradition to really answer the need for Canadian superheroes" (31). Bell's scant two paragraphs on the Marvel team barely acknowledge that Alpha Flight's economic success in Canada compared to the homegrown titles he foregrounds might indeed suggest that Alpha Flight answered a significant need for comics fans in Canada. Indeed, in spite of its status as an American publication, Jason Dittmer and Soren Larsen have termed *Alpha Flight* "arguably the most successful Canadian nationalist superhero comic" ("Aboriginality and the Arctic" 58).

If, as Jason Dittmer argues in his study of post–9/11 Captain America, "the seemingly innocent nature of the comic book medium contributes to its battle over American identity because it usually operates beneath the gaze of most cultural critics" (628), it seems to me that the articulation of Canadian identity through Alpha Flight is doubly important: consumed by more Canadians than any other Canadian nationalist superhero,[5] it operates beneath the gaze not only of Canadian cultural critics, but outside the purview of Canadian cultural producers. As such, it provides a meaningful lens through which to interrogate American perceptions of Canadian identity and U.S.-Canada relations.

U.S.-Canada Relations in the Post–9/11 Era

Scholars do not write about anti–Canadianism in media often, because it is typically dwarfed by scholarly discussions on both sides of the border about anti–Americanism (in fact, my word processor acknowledges anti–Americanism as a word, but not anti–Canadianism). But U.S.-Canada relations have grown out of a long history of misunderstanding the fundamental underpinning of both nations. Canada has never fully understood America's desire for rebellion, and American has never fully understood that Canada does not feel oppressed by its continued relationship with Britain. From the pre–Canadian colonies disinterest in the Revolutionary War to Canada's defense of itself in the War of 1812, this misunderstanding framed the early relationship between Canada and the U.S. But as Chantal Allen suggests, this has not disappeared over time: "The roots of negativity towards Canada unavoidably trace back to the United States' turbulent relationship with Britain" and Canada's continuing ideological connection to Mother Britain on issues like health care, education, and social welfare (xii). This explains why a large percentage of anti–Canadianism in mainstream American news emerges from right-wing pundits: "For many in Conservative circles, Canada is the prime example of what *not* to become.... While some blue-blooded journalists muse of Canada as utopia, others in the conservative media see it as a mediocre hell" (104). While there have been extended periods of positive Canada-U.S. relations, these ideological differences often make themselves known in moments of contrast or disagreement.

By 2006, when the *Civil War* event occurred, U.S.-Canada relations had been battered by a series of missteps in the period following the September 11 attacks. This was informed by politics and personality: Canadian Prime Minister at the time of the attacks, Jean Chrétien, a once-impoverished left-of-center Catholic French-Canadian lawyer, seemed to find little common ground with a right-wing fundamentalist Texan child of privilege like President George W. Bush. Canada was also in the midst of legalizing same-sex unions and relaxing restrictions on marijuana use. But beyond issues of personality and ideology, there was major unrest rooted in untruths about Canada's role as a global haven for terrorists[6] and Canada's eventual decision not to join the "Coalition of the Willing" in entering Iraq. Questions started to burble in Washington and in the American media: could Canada no longer be a reliable ally? Could Canada, in fact, be an enemy? It is these questions that echo in the representation of Canada in Marvel's *Civil War* event; with the destruction of Alpha Flight, we are left with a nation that cannot police its own borders and, as a result, emerges as inherently suspect and in need of the control of the United States.

In Canada, there were also questions about the nature of the relationship between the two nations. Canadians felt slighted when George W. Bush "neglected to mention Canada when thanking nations for supporting the United States after the attacks" in spite of the fact that "33,000 passengers" from diverted aircraft had been hosted by businesses and individuals across Canada after air travel was halted on September 11 (Allen 80; 79).[7] Similarly, Canadians felt that their national sacrifice in Afghanistan was under-appreciated by America, especially when four Canadian soldiers were killed by American pilots in a friendly-fire incident and "President Bush was slow to offer public condolences" (84). These incidents, in 2001 and 2002, respectively, helped to keep public support in Canada for American aggression in Iraq low, which, coupled with Jean Chrétien's public doubts about the presence of weapons of mass destruction in Iraq, led to Canada's decision not to support the Iraq War. This led to a marked increase in the distrust of Canada represented in the American media.

Examples of the kind of rhetoric echoed in the pages of Marvel's *Civil War* event represent the kind of distrust and suspicion that marked this period in U.S.-Canada relations. At the extreme end, Fox News host Neil Cavuto actually framed a discussion around the headline: "Canada: An Enemy of the United States?" (qtd. in Allen 94). Also on Fox, the always controversial Anne Coulter noted that the U.S. "could have taken them [Canada] over so easily" (qtd. in Allen 92), while on the supposedly less ideologically-driven CNN, Tucker Carlson announced that "the United States does not need Canada" (qtd. in Allen 91). Outside of the shock tactics of cable news, even print publications like *The Washington Times* ran stories with headlines like "Can Canada really be considered our 'friend' anymore?" (qtd. in Allen 95). And beyond the media, politicians like Hilary Clinton and others have repeatedly and erroneously "mentioned that the 9/11 terrorists crossed into the United States from Canada" (101). Aside from these claims related to policy and governance, insults got personal, with pundits on various cable outlets referring to Canada as "your retarded cousin," "a joke," full of "Muslim crazies," and home to "the worst Americans" (qtd. in Allen 94; 95; 95; 92). It is perhaps not surprising, given this deluge of commentary, that according to Pew, warm feelings toward Canadians dropped almost 20 percent in this period (98). We certainly see this suspicion and anxiety, and indeed much of this rhetoric, borne out in *Omega Flight*.

From Alpha to Omega: De-Canadianizing Canada's Premier Superhero Team

The death of Alpha Flight is really a footnote to the larger *Civil War* event, but because it represents one of the event's few interactions with real-world nation states outside of America, it is particularly instructive. In light of the significance of Alpha Flight to Canadian audiences and the tone and rhetoric surrounding U.S.-Canada relations, a close reading of the building of Omega Flight in the wake of Alpha Flight's death demonstrates the ways in which *Civil War* reflects post–9/11 geopolitics vis-à-vis the world's longest undefended border.

The death of Alpha Flight is nothing if not unceremonious. In fact, the whole thing takes only two pages to occur. There is no epic, glorious final fight to the death for these characters[8]; instead, what we see repeated in *New Avengers #16* and *#17* are large-panel images of the dead Alpha Flight team (Bendis, *NA #16*, 14; *NA #17*, 8; *CWTI* 6, 7). Their death is entirely wrapped up in issues of border security: they are asked to stop an energy trail that has destroyed the city of North Pole, Alaska and is en route to the lower 48 states; that they are unable to do so places America at risk, thus representing a geopolitical situation where Canada's inability to protect itself directly threatens the United States. When faced with the crisis, the president immediately orders that The Avengers be called in; when he is told, "If the Canadian super team had no effect, then what could—," he responds, "It's Captain America. He'll take this down. He always wins" (Bendis, *NA #16*, 15). The expectation here is that the American option is by definition bigger, faster, stronger, and more capable of defense. That Iron Man and Ms. Marvel are able to stop Michael Pointer, once a mailman and now the earthly vessel for The Collective (a body that has absorbed all the power of the Mutants de-powered in *House of M*), all on their own where the entire team of Alpha Flight has failed suggests the level of weakness of the Canadians (we discover later that Sasquatch has survived, but the mechanism by which this has occurred is not clear) (Bendis, *NA #17*, 17–18). Narratively, of course, Alpha Flight is used here as simple cannon fodder: Marvel needs to kill off a team powerful enough to demonstrate the depth of the threat and recognizable enough to sell some issues, but not anyone currently integral to the unfolding plot lines. As the most recent run of *Alpha Flight* had folded due to poor sales about a year prior to the lead-up to the *Civil War* world event, they were well positioned for Marvel's needs.

It is significant, as far as Canadian sovereignty as represented in the world of *Civil War* is concerned, to note that the formation of Omega Flight comes about as part of the post-*Civil War* Initiative, which Mr. Fantastic explains is a project with the goal of placing registered superhero teams in each of the fifty states (Millar 24). And also Canada; in fact, *Civil War: The Initiative*, a one-shot follow-up to the main series, opens with Michael Pointer and his assignment to Omega Flight (Bendis, *CWTI* 2). As a result, rhetorically or strategically, no distinction is made between seeking out a team to mind Rhode Island and the formation of Alpha Flight. The suggestion here is potent in its lack of overt discussion: for the purposes of national security from the perspective of S.H.I.E.L.D., Canada effectively is the 51st state. This echoes generations of anxiety about a lack of significant or meaningful difference between Canada and the U.S. and Canada's historical fear of annexation. Anne Coulter's remarks on Fox News that Canada does not "even need to have an army, because they are protected, because they are on the same continent as the United States" finds itself reenacted in the pages of *Civil War: Choosing Sides* (Allen 92). Tony Stark is clear about the strategic reasons for protecting Canada:

> The Canadian government no longer has the assets to deal with the hordes of super-villains currently flooding their borders. Canada supplies the U.S. with 20 percent of its oil. A good deal of our energy and infrastructure is tied directly to Canada. Their security is a top priority for S.H.I.E.L.D. We need [...] to protect those interests [Oeming, *CWCS* 28].

To this end, Stark sends USAgent to lead the Initiative team in Canada. USAgent's disgust here is clear, asserting that he "serves Uncle Sam" and not "Major Maple Leaf" (Oeming, *CWCS* 29), which seems a particularly callous remark given that Major Maple Leaf, a character from the 2004 incarnation of *Alpha Flight*, was one of the members killed in *New Avengers #16*.

There is a fair amount of this callousness to swallow for the Canadian characters involved in the reframing of Alpha Flight as Omega Flight. For example, as part of his penance, Michael Pointer is asked to wear Guardian's suit and join Omega Flight; Pointer, remember, is the vessel The Collective use to destroy Alpha Flight. The members of Omega Flight who knew Alpha Flight, like Shaman's daughter Talisman, are asked not only to forgive Pointer but to accept his adoption of the Alpha Flight leader's costume; they are told that "the Americans don't know what to do with him" and therefore they must accommodate

(Oeming, *OF #1*, 9). And even the name Omega Flight, which S.H.I.E.L.D. imposes upon Sasquatch, is fraught: Omega Flight was the team of villains that fought, and occasionally killed, Alpha Flight in the 1983 iteration of the comic. As Sasquatch reminds the Canadian Security Intelligence Service operative who finds him, "Omega Flight? They were our enemies" (Oeming, *OF #1*, 7). There is a notion that things have gotten so grave that no indignity is too much in the name of national security. And to be sure, the security in question is not only Canada's, but America's.

The problem for Canada is that, in the wake of the Superhero Registration Act that frames the conflict of the *Civil War* event, all those super-humans who do not want to register, either because they want to live like old-school superheroes or because they are super-villains who want to escape the watchful eye of S.H.I.E.L.D., have found their way to Canada. This suggests just the kind of porous border seen in post–9/11 rhetoric, and suggests that Canada cannot manage her own border security. Of course, to S.H.I.E.L.D., both groups are in contravention of the law, and so Canada is viewed as a safe haven for lawlessness and a land filled with powered individuals that America simply did not know what to do with anymore. The sense that Canada is a nation ready to be taken over by these lawless figures is exemplified by the Wrecking Crew, who wait at the border for their chance for "beer, banks, and broads" and to "crank the profile up to ten and there's nothing to stop us" (Oeming, *OF #1*, 6). There are multiple panels throughout the series showing Canadians being attacked, stores being looted, and crime running rampant; one of the prime minister's aides remarks, "With the heavy hammer coming down on them in the States, they see Canada as a safe harbor, easy pickings.... And maybe we are" (Oeming, *OF #1*, 2). Canadians are not able to manage this deluge of corruption and crime, and the comic even shows Canadian politicians looking to America to rescue them from the crisis; as the prime minister phrases it, "The U.S. started this mess. They'll help clean it up" (3). This loss of sovereignty is swift and unchallenged, reminiscent of rhetoric suggesting Canada waits for and expects America to rescue her from peril.

There are moments when the remaining Canadian superheroes attempt to assert their strength, but these moments are often undercut by the accompanying visual representations. For example, in *Omega Flight #1*, Sasquatch attempts to deal with the Wrecking Crew, who have been killing innocent civilians and causing property damage. As he battles them, he asks: "You thought you could come up here and raid my country? You thought we can't defend ourselves? That we are weak? You thought wrong!" (Oeming, *OF #1*, 16). But though these statements express strength and power, in the very next panel Sasquatch is chained up and finds himself powerless against yet another massive explosion; he screams that he "won't let it happen again" but is powerless to actually protect his own nation (17). Indeed, in the next issue, Sasquatch goes on to be tortured by the Wrecking Crew, and it is only with the help of the new American members of Omega Flight that he is able to be rescued.

It is not as if the few Canadians on Omega Flight do not object to the Americanization of their team, but there is a sense of inevitability to the whole process. Talisman, in particular, fights the decision, and especially the indignity of having Pointer join the team. But the flip side, which Iron Man tries to convince the team of, plays on Canadian perceptions of moral authority and superiority[9]: only Guardian's suit is powerful enough to contain and control the collected evil of The Collective (Bendis, *CWTI* 8). In fact, Iron Man even labels Michael Pointer as Weapon Alpha, which fans of the series will know was Guardian's original code name (Bendis, *CWTI* 2) But does Iron Man really believe this, or is it just, as quoted earlier, that they do not know what else to do with him? And as Talisman notes, the symbolism regardless is just no good: "An American wearing the Guardian suit? ... Sounds like Manifest Destiny to me" (Oeming, *OF #3*, 7). Again we hear echoings of the long history of misunderstanding and insecurity that construct the relationship between Canada and the U.S.

Throughout the series, Canadian government structures are derided and questioned. Even CSIS, the Canadian equivalent of the CIA, is considered relatively powerless; when the Wrecking Crew is arrested, Omega Flight is asked to "get them into CSIS custody until S.H.I.E.L.D. can pick them up" (Oeming, *OF #5*, 18). Even Canadian prisons, then, are ineffective holding cells for the caliber of criminal that has flooded across the Canada-U.S. border. And the Canadian imagery that abounds in *Omega Flight* suggests a nation in peril. Consider the cover of *Omega Flight #2*, which offers a white background with a red maple leaf, emblematic of the Canadian flag. But the leaf, filled with silhouettes of the characters, is off-center and unbalanced, and appears to be bleeding (Kolins). The splatter that runs down the page is reminiscent of a maple-leaf-shaped bullet hole in a strikingly white chest. The flag itself is dying. This imagery is repeated on Michael Pointer's cell in *Omega Flight #4*, covered in these upside-down and bloodied maple leaves (Oeming, *OF #4*, 4).

In each of these examples, we can see the echoes of the kind of rhetoric that dominated the discourse of U.S.-Canada relations in popular consciousness in the immediate post–9/11 period. The death of Alpha Flight in the line of duty suggests that Canada is incapable of defending herself. The porous nature of the border represents threats to both Canadian and American security. The terrorizing of Canadians by super-villains demonstrates the fear that Canada is a save haven for terrorists. The Americanization of Alpha Flight as Omega Flight suggests a lack of ability to respond to a threat within Canadian law and order. And Tony Stark's control over Omega Flight through S.H.I.E.L.D., especially with his imposition of such a symbolically nationalist American hero as USAgent,[10] suggests the distrust of Canada as an ally of America and the need for America's watchful eye. Taken together, the themes, images, and events of *Civil War* deftly represent American anxieties about Canada's role as an ally through this time period, while simultaneously allowing, through the outbursts of the dissenting Canadian superheroes and the Canadian politicians, a space to interrogate Canadian anxieties about American geopolitical power.

Epilogue: Chaos War and the Resurrection of Alpha Flight

I would be remiss in discussing Alpha/Omega Flight's arc if I did not address their resurrection in a recent major world event for Marvel, the Chaos War series. Alpha Flight returns in *Chaos War #5* with a number of other superheroes who are brought back from the dead as part of the larger chaos of the fighting gods, and they go on to star in a 9-issue mini-series called *Alpha Flight*. Does the relaunch of *Alpha Flight* suggest that we have entered a positive cycle in the relationship between the U.S. and Canada, at least in the public consciousness?

In the most recent *Alpha Flight* reboot, Alpha Flight is reunited as the all–Canadian cast of Guardian (not Michael Pointer's version), Vindicator, Sasquatch, Marrina, Northstar, Aurora, and Snowbird (eventually, Puck also returns, and Vindicator defects). Very little reference is made to *Omega Flight* or the events of *Civil War*; upon resurrection, Guardian says, "I remember facing a naked man?" and this is the only reference to their obliteration at the hands of Michael Pointer (Pak and Van Lente, *CW #5*, 7). This time, instead of being tools of the American government at the behest of the Canadian, they find themselves standing against a fascist regime known as Unity; in the process, they have been branded "domestic terrorists" (Pak and Van Lente, *AF #5*, 3). This is a clear return to the original ethos of the Alpha Flight team, and the decision to avoid discussion of *Omega Flight* suggests a series reboot. The true enemy in this series is fascism and a government that lies and manipulates a global terror crisis in order to control the population; the real goal, then, for Alpha Flight, is to fight for Canadian liberty against the wishes of the government (Pak and Van Lente, *AF #4*, 18–19). Where *Omega Flight* dealt with the anxieties of national borders and the role of the ally, *Alpha Flight* pushes the narrative even further to set up a narrative that demands critical thinking and resistance to government oppression for all people. *Alpha Flight* succeeds in the "restoration of Free Canada" only with the support of the population (Pak and Van Lente, *AF #8*, 19).

Perhaps, then, where *Omega Flight* was the post–9/11 story of anxiety and suspicion, *Alpha Flight* offers a story of cooperation and public engagement for the era of Occupy and Idle No More[11]; the population does not fear mistreatment by the government but instead triumphs over it.

Notes

1. The character who would come to be Guardian, leader of Alpha Flight, first appeared on the pages of *Uncanny X-Men #109* the year before.
2. This makeup of Alpha Flight is a combination of characters from the 1983 and 2004 runs of the comic and would not be replicated in the post–*Chaos War* 2011 series.
3. Jason Dittmer and Soren Larsen do a good job of reflecting on this idea in their study of audience responses to *Captain Canuck*, a Canadian-produced superhero comic of the 1970s. *Captain Canuck* positioned itself as offering an alternative to American-produced comics, and in its pages readers "recognized this identity, found it seductive, and claimed it" (741). When the comic moved to less nationalist themes to attract U.S. readership, it lost support at home (743).
4. Interestingly, Canadians have also been willing to domesticate and repatriate Superman as a Canadian nationalist superhero, giving him his own Canadian stamp in 1995; that creator Joe Shuster was born in Canada "alone was sufficient for Superman to be deemed Canadian" even though he left when he was eight (Edwardson 197). There is an old joke in Canadian cultural circles that if an author penned the Great American Novel while flying over Canada en route to Europe, Canadians would fete it as our own. This is not so far off the mark.
5. Certainly, Wolverine is the Canadian superhero who has had the greatest popular success, having been a major anchor at Marvel since the 1980s, but he does not fit the definition of a nationalist superhero. Wolverine's Canadian nationality makes for an interesting backstory but is tangential to who he is. A nationalist superhero, conversely, operates on behalf of the nation and often under the national flag. This is why Alpha Flight can function as a nationalist superhero for Canada even while it is created by a major American corporation like Marvel.
6. It is worth noting, of course, that the rumor that recurred often in the immediate aftermath of the September 11 attacks, that the hijackers had entered the U.S. from Canada, was entirely untrue and had never been verified before becoming part of the common knowledge, repeated ad nauseum, in the news cycle of the day.
7. I rely on Chantal Allen's meticulously researched quotations throughout this section, but I have verified their accuracy myself. Dozens more examples than those I have highlighted here can be found in her *Bomb Canada* monograph.
8. There is also no mourning for Alpha Flight. Even Wolverine's entire emotional response is to say, "Damn" (Bendis, *#17*, 7). This seems odd considered Wolverine's long and varied history with this team that makes up a significant portion of his backstory.
9. Bart Beaty draws on the idea of Canadian presumptions of moral superiority—Canadian chauvinism—in his "The Fighting Civil Servant" (434).
10. This is particularly salient when you consider that Captain America was, by this point in the *Civil*

War event, dead. This suggests that America's only remaining nationalist superhero, USAgent, is sent to Canada, demonstrating the level of importance Tony Stark places on controlling the replacement force for Alpha Flight.

    11. The Occupy and Idle No More movements were interrelated grassroots initiatives protesting, respectively, income inequality and the treatment of indigenous people in settler nations like Canada, the United States, and Australia. Occupy started 2011 in the United States as Occupy Wall Street, while Idle No More began in Canada in 2013 as something of a follow-up movement to it. Both movements were marked by grassroots, collectivist organizations against existing power structures, and were notable for their momentum and successful engagement with social media; the movements differ because Occupy was largely critiqued for a lack of coherent message, where Idle No More has been very specific in laying out its demands, particularly in Canada. Alexander Hudson explores this comparison more thoroughly in "Next Steps for the Idle No More Movement: A Public Law Perspective," published in *Aboriginal Policy Studies*.

Works Cited

Allen, Chantal. *Bomb Canada and Other Unkind Remarks in the American Media*. Edmonton: Athabasca University Press, 2009. Print.
Beaty, Bart. "The Fighting Civil Servant: Making Sense of the Canadian Superhero." *American Review of Canadian Studies* 36.3 (2006): 427–439. Print.
Bell, John. *Guardians of the North: The National Superhero in Canadian Comic-Book Art*. Ottawa: National Archives of Canada, 1992. Print.
Bendis, Brian Michael (writer), Mike Deodato (penciller), and Jose Pimentel (inker). "The Collective." *New Avengers #17–18* (May-June 2006), Marvel Comics. Web. 2 July 2014.
_____, Steve McNiven (penciller), and Dexter Vines (inker). "The Collective: Prologue." *New Avengers #16* (April 2006), Marvel Comics. Web. 2 July 2014.
Bendis, Brian Michael, Warren Ellis (writers), and Marc Silvestri (penciller). "Civil War: The Initiative." *Civil War: The Initiative* (April 2007), Marvel Comics. Web. 2 July 2014.
Claremont, Chris (writer), and John Byrne (artist). "Home Are the Heroes." *Uncanny X-Men #109* (February 1978), Marvel Comics. Web. 2 July 2014.
_____. "Shoot-Out at the Stampede." *Uncanny X-Men #121* (May 1979), Marvel Comics. Web. 2 July 2014.
_____. "Wanted: Wolverine, Dead or Alive." *Uncanny X-Men #120* (April 1979), Marvel Comics. Web. 2 July 2014.
DeFalco, Tom, ed. *The Marvel Comics Encyclopedia*. New York: DK, 2006. Print.
Dittmer, Jason. "Captain America's Empire: Reflections on Identity, Popular Culture, and Post–9/11 Geopolitics." *Annals of the Association of American Geographers* 95.3 (2005): 626–643. Print.
_____, and Soren Larsen. "Aboriginality and the Arctic North in Canadian Nationalist Superhero Comics, 1940–2004." *Historical Geography* 38 (2010): 52–69. Print.
_____. "Captain Canuck, Audience Response, and the Project of Canadian Nationalism." *Social and Cultural Geography* 8.5 (October 2007): 735–753. Print.
Edwardson, Ryan. "The Many Lives of Captain Canuck: Nationalism, Culture, and the Creation of a Canadian Comic Book Superhero." *The Journal of Popular Culture* 37.2 (2003): 184–201. Print.
Howe, Sean. *Marvel Comics: The Untold Story*. New York: Harper Perennial, 2012. Print.
Hudson, Alexander. "Next Steps for the Idle No More Movement: A Public Law Perspective." *Aboriginal Policy Studies* 3.1/2 (2014): 149–163. *Google Scholar*. Web. 3 September 2014.
Iannacci, Elio. "Superheroes Vs. Right-Wing Canada." *Maclean's* 124.20/21 (2011): 102. *Academic Search Complete*. Web. 3 July 2014.
Kolins, Scott. Cover art. *Omega Flight #2*. (July 2007), Marvel Comics. Web.
McCann, Jim (writer), Reilly Brown, and Salvador Espin (pencillers). "Chaos War: Alpha Flight." *Chaos War: Alpha Flight* (November 2010), Marvel Comics. Web. 2 July 2014.
Millar, Mark (writer), and Steve McNiven. *Civil War #7* (January 2007), Marvel Comics. Web. 4 July 2014.
Oeming, Mike Avon (writer), and Scott Kolins (artist). "Alpha to Omega." *Omega Flight #1–5* (June-October 2007), Marvel Comics. Web. 2 July 2014.
_____. "USAgent in: Choosing Sides." *Civil War: Choosing Sides* (October 2006), Marvel Comics. Web. 2 July 2014.
Pak, Greg, Fred Van Lente (writers), Dale Eaglesham (penciller), and Andrew Hennessy (inker). "Born on the First of July." *Alpha Flight #2* (September 2011), Marvel Comics. Web. 2 July 2014.
_____. "Powered and Dangerous." *Alpha Flight #3* (October 2011), Marvel Comics. Web. 2 July 2014.
_____. "Pride of a Nation." *Alpha Flight #1* (August 2011), Marvel Comics. Web. 2 July 2014.
_____. "With Many, Strength." *Alpha Flight #4* (November 2011), Marvel Comics. Web. 2 July 2014.

Pak, Greg, Fred Van Lente (writers), and Dale Eaglesham (penciller). "The Last Refuge." *Alpha Flight #5* (December 2011), Marvel Comics. Web. 2 July 2014.
_____. "A Murder of Crows." *Alpha Flight #6* (January 2012), Marvel Comics. Web. 2 July 2014.
_____. "Pride of a Nation (Redux)." *Alpha Flight #8* (March 2012), Marvel Comics. Web. 2 July 2014.
_____. "Re-Union." *Alpha Flight #7* (February 2012), Marvel Comics. Web. 2 July 2014.
Pak, Greg, Fred Van Lente (writers), Ben Oliver and Dan Green (artists). "Alpha Flight." *Alpha Flight #0.1* (July 2011), Marvel Comics. Web. 2 July 2014.
Pak, Greg, Fred Van Lente (writers), Koi Pham (penciller), Thomas Palmer and Bob McLeod (inkers). "The End Is Here." *Chaos War #5* (March 2011), Marvel Comics. Web. 2 July 2014.
Zenari, Vivian. "Mutant Mutandis: The X-Men's Wolverine and the Construction of Canada." *Culture and the State: Nationalisms. Vol 3*. James Gifford and Gabrielle Zezulka-Maillouxm eds. Edmonton: CRC Humanities Studio, 2004. 53–67. Print.

Freedom versus Security: The Basic Human Dilemma from 9/11 to Marvel's *Civil War*

Travis Langley

Marvel Comics' seven-issue series *Civil War* depicted superheroes battling superheroes over whether or not to comply when newly passed legislation requires all super-powered persons in the United States to register with the federal government, thereby revealing their true identities to authorities. After a tragic incident in which errors by young superheroes result in hundreds of civilian deaths, the community of superheroes disagree over whether to support the law as a way of taking responsibility or to oppose regulation as a civil liberties issue and because maintaining secret identities can protect their families and themselves from their many enemies (Millar, *Civil War* #1).[1]

While he intended for the series to read first and foremost as a superhero story, author Mark Millar acknowledged undercurrents of allegory intended to add depth and resonance along with some degree of political commentary regarding political and social realities of the post–9/11 world such as privacy issues, controversial wiretapping, and the wide variety of compromised civil liberties rising out of the Patriot Act (Newsarama). Regardless of criticisms about rushed storytelling (S. Miller; St. Louis; Trabold), weak plot (Gonzalez; Hayes; Sacks), continuity errors (Belk; George & Schedeen), and characters that were acting out of character (AICN; Amacker; Little; Sacks), the series sold well (J. Miller), stimulated discussions (AICN), and generated mainstream publicity which, according to Marvel Comics executive editor Tom Brevoort, galvanized existing readers, drew new readers, and brought back lapsed fans (Weiland).

In the course of the story, superheroes who register with the government must enforce laws including the Superhuman (also called Super Hero) Registration Act, and they must therefore pursue and arrest unregistered super-powered opponents of the law. After government agents pull weapons on Captain America merely for expressing reservations about hunting his fellow heroes, he becomes a fugitive and soon leads the anti-registration opposition. Over the course of the seven-issue series and throughout other comic book series set in this same fictional world, heroes die, villains die, civilians die, government agents die, authorities release unrehabilitated criminals in order to sic them on rebel superheroes, the government funds construction of a massive extradimensional prison to hold the rebels even though they had never built such a structure to contain super-villains, anti-registration heroes defy laws the public expects them to uphold, and leading pro-registration heroes amass wealth from associated government contracts (Millar, *Civil War* #4; Jenkins, *Civil War: Frontline* #11; Straczinski, *The Amazing Spider-Man* #535). Does a world where the deconstruction of the superhero reaches such heights (or depths) leave room for the heroes to become heroic again? Can fallen icons dust themselves off and shine once more?

Answering these questions may require examination of a more basic issue: Was there ever anything heroic about these characters' conflict in the first place?

The Basic Human Conflict

Psychologist Erich Fromm held that the basic human dilemma involves contradictory desires for both freedom and security. Having left his native Germany after the Nazi Party came to power, Fromm contemplated how and why the German populace, beaten down by the economic and social turmoil of the Great Depression, had traded away their freedoms in exchange for security under a malignant, dictatorial regime. Fromm's quest to understand his homeland's mass irrationality had begun previously as a teen who had found himself astonished by the hysterical fanaticism that blazed through the German nation during World War I. Observing changes among his family, friends, neighbors, and educators, he wondered why "decent and reasonable people suddenly go crazy" (qtd. in Evans 57). After the war, he became "obsessed with the question of how war was possible, by the wish to understand the irrationality of human mass behavior, by a passionate desire for peace" (Fromm, *Beyond the Chain of Illusion* 9).

After immigrating to the United States in order to escape the Nazi menace, Fromm worked with psychoanalyst Karen Horney, whose ideas heavily influenced his theory development. Horney taught that the need for safety (meaning security and freedom from fear) dominated childhood, and that properly nurtured individuals who felt safe while receiving love, acceptance, trust, and encouragement to grow could develop independent, integrated, unified adult personalities (*The Neurotic Personality of Our Time*). Fromm, who rarely acknowledged the great extent of Horney's influence upon his own work, saw that this inherent need to feel safe would inherently conflict with the desire to feel free. He contended that western individuals in the 20th century, possessing greater freedom than in any previous era, would experience greater loneliness, alienation, and feelings of insignificance than people of ages past. Those who failed to become close to others without giving up freedom and personal integrity, Fromm held, could only regain feelings of security by renouncing freedom, surrendering individuality, and giving up liberties of many kinds. Although relinquishing their rights would not foster forms of self-expression or promote personal development, doing so would remove the anxiety of feeling alienated from other people and would help individuals to the comfort of feeling more safe and secure even if the safety and security were merely illusions. "Powerful tendencies arise to escape from this kind of freedom into submission or some kind of relationship to man and the world which promises relief from uncertainty, even if it deprives the individual of his freedom," said Fromm (*Escape from Freedom* 37).

Civil Freedom versus Homeland Security

When motivated by losses in either freedom or security, people often relinquish the other. Feeling vulnerable in the wake of the attacks of September 11, 2001, many American citizens accepted a lessening of liberties in the forms of wire tapping, e-mail monitoring, lengthier airplane boarding procedures, broadened government ability to engage in search and seizure, expanded regulation of financial transactions, and easing of restrictions on foreign intelligence gathering on United States soil. Passed with minimal debate only 45 days after 9/11, the USA PATRIOT Act (or simply Patriot Act) dramatically expanded law enforcement agencies' authority in every one of these areas (Department of Justice, n.d.). Civil liberties groups and the Justice Department, among others, have debated the law's potential for abuse of individuals' rights against the perceived imminent need to empower authorities in their efforts to protect citizens from terrorism (Abramson). Even the administration implementing the controversial wiretapping measures experienced sharp division among its people over issues like warrantless eavesdropping (Kellman).

Those who defend the regulations which others consider to be erosions of freedom have argued that law-abiding citizens have nothing to fear, that extra security protects the innocent while helping to curtail the guilty. Related to this and to Fromm's assertion that modern society leads people to feel disconnected from each other is the extent to which the greatest infringements on liberties intrude upon "other people's" freedoms. To the nation's three hundred million citizens, the hundreds of individuals held at Guantanamo Bay Naval Base's military prison (nicknamed "Gitmo") for five years or more without benefit of trial or even formal charges are aliens, 375 of whom are *suspected* al Qaeda or Taliban loyalists (Marlantes) and some of whom—worried Americans fear—might each readily kill thousands. To keep the monsters contained, many accept the chargeless imprisonment of faceless, foreign strangers. Former President Clinton and others have called for the facility to be "closed down or cleaned up" (Barber & Taylor), and while the current administration has finally agreed that the facility should be shut down, officials remain undecided about what to do with the detainees. Gitmo, therefore, goes on.

In the fictitious *Civil War* storyline, the analogous containment of rebel superheroes in an extradimensional prison off U.S. soil where no lawyers, no courts, no legal recourse can ever net their liberation leads Spider-Man to decide that he has backed the wrong side in the registration conflict. Even though revealing his identity to the public and registering with the government had seemed the responsible thing to do, he decides that taking sides against individuals who want the protection of anonymity while fighting super-powered criminals and siding with those who would imprison other heroes for being unlicensed heroes is simply wrong (Millar, *Civil War* #5; Straczinski, *The Amazing Spider-Man* #535). Erich Fromm (*Escape from Freedom*) extolled the virtues of individuals taking such independent action, of their using reason to establish moral values and evaluate moral dilemmas rather than adhering to values imposed by others. While automaton conformity can displace the burden of choice from oneself and onto society and obedience can relieve one of the burden of decisions and responsibilities by turning them over to authority figures, taking responsibility for one's own decisions and actions fosters freedom, independence, and maturity, and Spider-Man has long since decided that he cannot stand by without striving to shape the course of events around him, that having great power meant that he must take great responsibility (Lee, *Amazing Fantasy* #15, 11).

On both sides of the *Civil War* conflict are characters taking responsibility for their respective positions, others simply following those who have taken the lead, and then those who change their positions. While the majority of the American public depicted in this fictional world prefer that the superheroes register, receive training, and accept government regulation, the heroes themselves cannot easily settle the issue among themselves. The series has ended, but the story cannot. As Fromm said, the basic human dilemma of freedom versus security is never-ending.

Superhuman Registration

The topic of registering superhumans is not new to *Civil War*.

Marvel Comics publications first mentioned the concept in *Uncanny X-Men* #141 without referring to a registration act until *Uncanny X-Men* #181. When a Mutant Registration Act becomes law in Marvel's fictional world, requiring all mutants to register their powers like registering deadly weapons regardless of the nature of any specific power, the act affects mutant characters throughout a variety of ongoing series as a meaningful issue in their lives, and yet after Claremont departed from writing *Uncanny X-Men*, mention of the act becomes rare, with no clear confirmation as to whether the act has been repealed or is simply no longer enforced until *Civil War*.

Whereas *Uncanny X-Men* and related series had equated the Mutant Registration Act with racism and bigotry, each discussion of non-mutant superhero registration within the comics has focused on issues of practical application and personal freedom. Marvel Comics stories did not address the possibility of broader registration for super-powered individuals other than mutants until 1989, raising, addressing, and settling the issue (for the time being) all within two months. After Congress proposes superhero registration in *Fantastic Four* #335 and wants Reed Richards, leader of the Fantastic Four, to develop superhuman detection technology, Richards speaks before a congressional panel in the following issue to argue the philosophical problem with such a proposal and to demonstrate the sheer impracticality of establishing operational criteria for defining and detecting any super-powers (Simonson). In Marvel's fictional United States, the issue of superhero registration then simply dies for sixteen years in real world time, although Canada comes to require it during the interim (Furman, *Alpha Flight* #120).

Government regulation of costumed, super-powered crimefighters is not an issue unique to Marvel Comics. Retroactive continuity (a "retcon") for the original super-team, the Justice Society of America, holds that they disbanded and retired for a time rather than submit to a McCarthy-era House of Representatives committee's demand that they unmask to prove their loyalty to their country ("Justice Society of America")—a plot device also seen in the 1983 motion picture *The Return of Captain Invincible*. The limited series *Watchmen*, the ongoing comic book series *Astro City*, and the 2004 film *The Incredibles* all depict outright bans on superhero activities.

"*Sed quis custodiet ipsos custodies?*" asked the poet Juvenal in *Satire VI*, meaning, "But who will guard the guardsmen themselves?" and often translated as "Who watches the watchmen?" Alan Moore asked the question in his groundbreaking limited series *Watchmen*, as did the Tower Commission in their report assessing the Reagan administration's Iran-Contra scandal. People want protection. People also want protection from their protectors because of the inherent potential for power's—much less super-power's—abuse. In fictional worlds where their protectors hide behind masks, accountability can be difficult to impose. In fictional worlds where heroes sometimes go rogue, get possessed, turn insane, or turn out to be villains, people are right to be wary.

In separate series that fans find strikingly similar in many regards, Marvel Comics and DC Comics each explored what can go wrong when superheroes reign and proliferate without restriction, both in alternate universe stories featuring versions of the Justice League: respectively *Squadron Supreme* and *Kingdom Come*. Both stories depict deadly conflicts that eventually arise when superhumans dominate, regardless of whether those superhumans generate chaos by running unrestrained or actively impose order upon their world, and each tale ends with heroes realizing they must not operate unchecked by the non-super humankind whom they serve. Like *Civil War*, both of these series deconstructed their masked heroes, tearing them down and apart in order to examine with new eyes.

Deconstruction versus Reconstruction

Fromm pointed out that social upheaval of the Renaissance and Protestant Reformation had to shatter medieval stability before people of Western civilization could enjoy greater freedom with its opportunities for self-expression, personal development, and power over their own lives. Before World War II, he had seen people relinquish liberties, individuality, and integrity for the security Nazi Germany offered. That security had to be stripped down to nothing before they could psychologically rebuild afterward.

In the fictional *Civil War*, the side fighting for security wins—officially, at least. The seven-issue series concludes with the anti–Registration camp's surrender. Captain America, their leader, orders his allies to stand down during a fight that they were winning physically but losing philosophically (Millar 21). For either side to beat the other outright would require them to break the other heroes. It would require a villainous act. For either side to surrender while losing would have given neither the chance to do something heroic at the end. Quite possibly the only way for either side to end the story heroically was to give up while winning a mêlée, which is exactly what Captain America does.

Although time has passed since *Civil War* finished its seven-issue run, the story goes on. It may, in fact, never end. Just as the American Civil War left scars that still linger to this day, the superheroes' conflict must impact the fictional characters of Marvel's Earth in ways they cannot forget and may never emotionally overcome. Just as the Marvel mutants' struggles reflect the endless nature of real world civil rights issues, the registration issue reflects the basic human dilemma that will not go away. People will not cease to weigh issues of freedom versus security. Too much of either prompts some people to seek the other, so the human race works its everlasting balancing act, and narrative need requires no easy balance. Stories, whether fictional or not, require conflict.

So the rebels back down. Some accept amnesty upon their surrender. Some leave the country. Some go underground and become leaderless vigilantes lacking long-term plans. Some simply do not recover. Captain America—the symbol of America, the company's longest-lasting high profile hero, and often the moral compass for their super-human community—soon dies, assassinated on his way to court (Brubaker 17), a brutal coda to the superheroes' Civil War.

Whether a former sidekick from the 1940s, an insane substitute from the 1950s, a shapeshifting Skrull from another world, or a mock talk show host from New York becomes the custodian of Captain America's shield, readers expect Steve Rogers to wield it again one day. However, regardless of widespread skepticism about the permanence of any comic book death, especially that of a character as important as this (Cronin; Gross; Kratina), his return must not be an easy thing. He may need to stay gone for quite some time—which will also let him regain his status as a man out of his time. Repercussions will last a long time. Heroes who have gone underground have many stories to offer in their post–Civil War fugitive state. For Cap's return to have meaning, readers and other characters need time for his death to become a long settled fact.

Shifting our gears from one psychological theorist to another, we point out what Joseph Campbell (1949) said well: Heroes must descend into the darkness, through the depths and in a deeply meaningful way, before they can emerge fully mature. For the growth of Captain America's fellow heroes and all inhabitants of the world where they dwell, this means that they all need time to feel painful repercussions of their whole Civil War before they can come back as something better. Beyond denial and anger, past bargaining, depression, and acceptance awaits a hero's emergence and rebirth. Captain America's return may require a resurrection more messianic than usual for a comic book hero, or his death will be cheapened and his return's impact diminished.

Staying gone for some time might also help Captain America refresh his status as a man out of his time. Marvel's other heroes need time to hurt before they really heal. Those now struggling to create a better world because they naturally need to rebuild will need time to learn that renewal cannot come quickly. Their speediest efforts to rebuild their collective body while still missing the heart must fall painfully short in order to force the "winners" themselves to reexamine their stand. For Cap's return to inspire true reconstruction, both sides must reach a point when they need him most. Conversely, for true reconstruction to occur, Captain America must rise again, one way or another.

Fall precedes triumph precedes fall precedes triumph. Both lows and highs provide contrast so that the stories can carry on.

Conclusions

In relating Marvel Comics' *Civil War* to Eric Fromm's basic human dilemma, we see how character motivations on both sides of the fictional conflict can arise from positive human qualities because Fromm's image of human nature is ultimately optimistic, holding that people on either side are struggling to find what is best for all. Fromm (*The Sane Society*) held that the moral victories which produce true, mature, and rational societal change do not come about by force. To think that one might beat someone else into seeing one's rationale is itself an irrational expectation. At *Civil War*'s end, Captain America sees this too.

The American Civil War's aftermath saw a leader's assassination and turbulent Reconstruction. After severe deconstruction of these superheroes, they cannot quickly reconstruct. Until time passes, they will remain too close to these events to look back in retrospection. Right now, they may be hurting and, with their war declared over, think it's time to move on, but like people suffering post-traumatic stress, they might have to suffer for some time before they can realize that they never let themselves feel the pain deeply enough to let themselves heal. As comic book scribe Kurt Busiek and superhero scholar Peter Coogan (198) have remarked, deconstructing heroes should mean tearing them down and learning from the pieces, coming to understand them better in order to move beyond darkness and cynicism, to reconstruct them and build them into something better.

However, the heroes will have to learn not only from their Civil War but from considerable aftermath as well if they are to grow stronger for it.

Note

1. This essay began as a presentation for the Comics Arts Conference held as part of San Diego Comic-Con International and then evolved into an article for the *International Journal of Comic Art*, from which this is reprinted with permission (Vol. 11, no. 1 [Spring 2009]: 426–435). At that time, Steve Rogers was considered "dead" in the comic book stories, having been assassinated in the aftermath of *Civil War*. We have chosen to print it in its original form because it remains relevant as fans speculate on what might become of Cap in the Marvel Cinematic Universe. As America changes, so does Captain America's place in it.

Works Cited

Abramson, Larry. "The Patriot Act: Alleged Abuses of the Law." NPR.com. NPR. 20 July 2005. Web. 9 Apr. 2007.
AICN. "AICN Comics Roundtable Review: The @$$holes on *Civil War, Annihilation*, and Marvel!!!" *Ain't It Cool News*. Ain't It Cool, Inc. 12 Oct. 2006. Web. 20 June 2007.
Amacker, Kurt. "Character Consensus and the Evolution of Heroes." Mania.com. Mania. 4 Oct. 2006. Web. 11 June 2007.
Barber, Lionel, and Paul Taylor. "Clinton Adds Voice to Criticism of Guantanamo." *Financial Times*. Financial Times, Ltd. 19 June 2005. Web. 23 June 2007.
Belk, Travis. "Comic Book Delays." BellaOnline. Minerva WebWorks, LLC. 2007. Web. 19 June 2008.
Brubaker, Ed (writer) and Steve Epting (art). "The Death of the Dream." *Captain America* #25. (Apr. 2007), Marvel. Web. 20 Jan. 2015.
Campbell, Joseph. *Hero with a Thousand Faces*. New York: Pantheon, 1949. Print.
Coogan, Peter. *Superhero: The Secret Origin of a Genre*. Austin: MonkeyBrain, 2006. Print.
Cronin, Brian. "*Captain America* #25 Review." CBR.com. Comic Book Resources. 7 Mar. 2007. Web. 12 May 2007.
Department of Justice. "The USA PATRIOT Act: Preserving Life and Liberty." Department of Justice Website. U.S. Department of Justice. 2007. Web. 23 June 2007.
Evans, Richard Isadore. *Dialogue with Erich Fromm*. New York: Harper & Row, 1966. Print.
Fromm, Erich. *Beyond the Chain of Illusion: My Encounter with Marx and Freud*. New York: Simon & Schuster, 1962. Print.
_____. *Escape from Freedom*. New York: Rinehart, 1941. Print.
_____. *The Sane Society*. New York: Rinehart, 1955. Print.
Furman, Simon (writer), Pat Broderick (penciller), and Bruce Patterson (inker). "The Clampdown: Part Three." *Alpha Flight* #120 (May 1993), Marvel. Print.
George, Richard, and Jesse Schedeen. "Comic Book Reviews for November 15, 2006." IGN.com. IGN Entertainment. 15 Nov. 2006. Web. 19 June 2007.
Gonzalez, Guy LeCharles. "What If *Civil War* Was Good?" loudpoet.com. Guy LeCharles Gonzalez. 22 Nov. 2006. Web. 11 June 2007.
Gross, Joe. "Comics: On the 'Death' of Captain America." Austin260.com. The Austin American-Statesman. 7 Mar. 2007. Web. 30 June 2007.
Hayes, Phillip. "*Civil War* #1–#6." Paperback Reader.com. Paperback Reader. 2007. Web. 14 June 2006.
Horney, Karen. *The Neurotic Personality of Our Time*. New York: Norton, 1937. Print.
Jenkins, Paul (writer), Ramon Bachs (penciller), and Johns Lucas (inker). *Civil War: Front Line* #1–11 (7 June 2006–28 Feb. 2007), Marvel. Web. 29 Dec. 2014.
Juvenal. *Juvenal: The Satires*. Ed. John Ferguson. London: Duckworth, 2003. Print.
Kellman, Laurie. "Ashcroft: Official Fought Over Snooping." ABC News.com. ABC News. 21 June 2007. Web. 23 June 2007.
Kratina, Al. "*Captain America* #25." ComicBookBin.com. Coolstreak Cartoons, Inc. 12 Mar. 2007. Web. 30 June 2007.
Lee, Stan (writer), and Steve Ditko (artist). "Spider-Man!" *Amazing Fantasy* #15 (10 Aug. 1962), Marvel. Web. 28 Dec. 2014.
Little, Paul John. "What's So Civil 'Bout War Anyway?" PLAYBACK:stl.com. Big Fat Cat, LLC. 9 Mar. 2007. Web. 14 June 2007.
Marlantes, Liz. "Gitmo May Close, but Fate of Detainees Uncertain." ABC News.com. ABC News. 23 June 2007. Web. 23 June 2007.
Martinez, Luis. "Terror Detainees Revolt at Guantanamo." ABC News.com. ABC News. 19 May 2006. Web. 23 June 2007.
Millar, Mark (writer), Steve McNiven (penciller), and Dexter Vines (inker). *Civil War* #1–7 (May 2006–Feb. 2007), Marvel Comics. Web. 25 Dec. 2014.

Miller, John Jackson. "Comic Book Sales Charts and Analysis." CBGXtra.com. Comic Buyers Guide. 2006–2007. Web. 4 May 2007.

Miller, Seth David. "No Civil War." *Mostly Muppet*. Mostly Muppet. 22 Sept. 2006. Web. 14 June 2007.

Newsarama. "Civil War and Peace of Mind with Mark Millar (Part 2)." Newsarama.com, LLC. 2006. Web. 19 June 2007.

Sacks, Jason. "Civil War: A Negative Review in Seven Parts." *Silver Soapboxes*. Comics Bulletin. 2006. Web 11 June 2007.

St. Louis, Hervé. "Review: Civil War #3." ComicBookBin.com. Coolstreak Cartoons, Inc. 23 July 2006. Web. 14 June 2007.

Simonson, Walter (writer), Ron Lim (penciller), and Mike DeCarlo (inker). "Dark Congress!" *Fantastic Four* #336 (Jan. 1990), Marvel. Web. 21 Dec. 2014.

Straczinski, J. Michael (writer), Ron Garney (penciller), and Bill Reinhold (inker). *Amazing Spider-Man* #535 (Sept. 2006), Marvel. Web. 21 Dec. 2014.

Tower Commission. *Tower Commission Report: The Full Text of the President's Special Review Board*. New York: Bantam, 1987. Print.

Trabold, Jim. "Ultimate Marvel Handbook #184." *Comics Nexus*. Inside Pulse. 7 Oct. 2006. Web. 14 June 2007.

"Justice Society of America." *The Unofficial Guide to the DC Universe*. The Unofficial Guide to the DC Universe. 2007. Web. 21 June 2007.

Wallace, David. "Line of Fire Reviews: Amazing Spider-Man #535." *Silver Bullet Comics*. Silver Bullet Comics. 29 Sept. 2006. Web. 20 June 2007.

Weiland, Jonah. "2006, the Year That Was: Part 1." *CBR News*. Comic Book Resources. 11 January 2007. Web. 20 June 2007.

Part III—Political Philosophy and *Civil War*

Political (In)Visibility in the Marvel Universe and the Real World

ANTHONY PETROS SPANAKOS

Marvel's *Civil War* opens and closes a battle. It is a battle between Iron Man and Captain America, a battle between Iron Man and his allies and Captain America and his allies, a battle between the right of a state to legitimately monopolize coercion within its territory and the right of a people to not be wholly exhausted by the decisions of a representative political body which seeks to intervene into both the private lives of that people and to monopolize the notions of justice that it believes should motivate that people.[1] What if the battle did not open and close with *Civil War*? What if the eruption into the ordinary—which is the essence of plot[2]—that *Civil War* produces is an intervention *into* a battle, a battle already in progress, a battle that was on-going before the *Civil War* and one that went on after *Civil War* ended?[3]

Marvel has consistently asked readers, "What if?" It even uses this counterfactual for the *Civil War* itself. In one such story it asks what if Captain America led *all* heroes against registration and, in another, what if Iron Man lost. It is not surprising that *Civil War*, written by Mark Millar, garnered two "What ifs" since it is a Marvel Universe-changing event. As the other essays in this volume suggest, the terrorist attacks of September 11, 2001 and the responses in the U.S. and the rest of the world can be seen as the sort of world-changing event in which questions of "what happened" must also consider "what if," where the evident comes to terms with the latent (but potential).[4] Somewhere in between is the invisible, the subject of this essay. This essay examines what the seeing of the invisible non-superhero reveals about the *Civil War* with the hope that unearthing its presence in *Civil War* offers insight into the politics in the U.S. and the world since September 11, 2001. Have recent political events made those at the margins of politics more visible, agents capable of determining their destinies? Or do they remain invisible, rounded up only when a name is necessary for a victim, one which justifies the action of politicians and other elites?

Three Stages, Which Protagonists?

The plot of *Civil War* might be periodized as follows: one, an explosion occurs prompting the Superhuman Registration Act (hereafter SHRA) which divides superheroes (and, indeed, villains) in two (*CW #1–2*); two, the pro–SHRA heroes almost defeat the anti–SHRA heroes (*CW #3–4*); and three, the anti–SHRA heroes almost defeat the pro–SHRA heroes before standing down (*CW #4–7*). While this is a stylized outline, it is not an unfair one. The reader is tempted to see Iron Man and Captain America as the protagonists in each of these three stages. Captain America resists Maria Hill (and arrest, stage 1, *CW #1*, 23), is almost killed by Iron Man (stage 2, *CW #3*, 20), and almost kills Iron Man before standing down (stage 3, *CW #7*, 19–20). Similarly, Iron Man goes to Washington to promote the SHRA (stage 1, *CW #1*, 31), almost kills Captain America (stage 2), and almost is killed by Captain America (stage 3). Missing here are very important determinant actors who are mostly invisible but central to *Civil War*.

The SHRA is the result of innocent men, women, and children being victims of inter-superhero violence. That is, the spillover effects of an on-going battle within a certain group in society (superheroes and villains) reach a tipping point and force an intervention into the politics of the ordinary. The shock and awe of the super (hero or villain) vis-à-vis the unpowered/normal people have always been present, but they have been largely glossed over historically in comic books.[5] In *Civil War*, the violence committed against the innocent is gruesome. Although Marvel shows only the damage to physical buildings, there are no images of the slain innocents—only silhouettes of children playing as the explosion goes off and a group of survivors who are revealed once Marvel Girl telekinetically lifts rubble that had been obscuring a staircase (*CW #1*, 10–11). Unlike all the other acts of violence—including the hard-to-believe battle between former friends and the apparent willingness of superheroes to kill[6]—this is the only violence that is *not* depicted. It might not be visible because it is un-representable, the assumption being neither artists nor fans could handle it, but the violence against the men, women, and children in Stamford may also be invisible because it happens to a "them" who are only important in so much as they motivate the actions of an "us," the groups which truly merit attention, praise, and/or condemnation. And, yet, while these victims of Stamford are invisible, it is their death and the change in public opinion among an equally invisible American citizenry that prompts the SHRA, the purported *raison d'être* of *Civil War*.

The victory of the pro–SHRA forces is prevented by the action[7] of the Invisible Woman (*CW #3*, 10).[8] Her intervention is decisive, though it is not pure battleground maneuver. Her decision represents a shift from personal disagreement with her husband to public political objection. In acting publicly to defend to anti–SHRA group, she demonstrates a refusal to allow her husband's political decisions to drive her own, her concern with family and friends (her brother, losing her husband to his rationalism, the life of her friend Goliath) over the political orders (the law) decided by others. The Invisible Woman makes herself visible—literally by encapsulating one band of combatants in an invisible force field—stealing victory from what had been, by default and/or inaction, her presumed side. It also leads to her switching sides, and it is decisive in turning the tide of war against pro–SHRA forces.

Finally, the victory of the anti–SHRA forces is prevented by the intervention of masses of men (and one woman) who restrain Captain America (from crossing an ethical line he would never cross otherwise) and prove to him that his actions are not for the *polis* as a whole (*CW #7*, 18–20). His victory would have required not only killing his friend but destroying New York City, where the battle takes place.[9] The danger to the city is shown, again, in terms of damage to physical infrastructure, though one can make the reasonable assumption that such damage to buildings, highways, and automobiles can hardly happen without taking human lives in the process. The people, who have heretofore been largely represented rather than visible,[10] suddenly appear and bring Captain America to his "senses" and, in so doing, deliver victory to the pro–SHRA forces.

In each of these three moments invisible actors are decisive and intervene in a political *status quo*. But what does it mean to be invisible?

Invisible Men, Women and Children

In a world of superheroes, invisibility refers to the ability to make one's self (and perhaps others one touches) unseen. Susan Storm, the Invisible Woman, can do this (as well as produce invisible force fields). Invisibility is a *power*, a capability, something that can be deployed. Outside of such a world, it is usually a constraint. This is borne out by other literary figures known for their invisibility. Dostoevsky's underground man is paradigmatic. He approaches a bar where a brawl is in process and, while trying to involve himself, an officer "took me by the shoulders and silently—with no warning or explanation—moved me from where I stood to another place, and then passed by as if without noticing. I could even have forgiven a beating, but I simply could not forgive his moving me and in the end just not noticing me" (Dostoevsky 49). He notes that he "had been treated like a fly" (Dostoevsky 49), one of the various similes he uses so as to show that he was not seen as a man. The underground man contrives various plots to force the officer to notice him, to recognize him *qua* man, but even after two years he is unsuccessful. He later tries to draw some of his former classmates into a duel. But he is eminently unsuccessful; no one, not even his manservant, will condescend to treat him as an equal. When a prostitute shows him sympathy, he is incapable of responding without bile (and regret).

The underground man is not only not visible (i.e., recognizable) as a man, but his identity is largely determined by others. Even in his autobiographical account in which he sets out to establish who he is and that he should be taken seriously and recognized as a man, he constantly prevaricates, shows himself absurdly concerned with the (potential) reader's impression of him, trying to please and scandalize the reader in a way that only heightens how ultimately important the reader's recognition of him is. In this way, he is not only invisible, but, when he is visible, it is according to the way others perceive him. He has no agency, and his attempts to assert himself end in folly, shame, and anger, driving away the few people who show him goodwill.

The underground man's efforts to provoke confrontation in a public space through bumping into another and forcing the latter's recognition of him are echoed in the opening of Ralph Ellison's *Invisible Man*. In the introduction, Ellison's narrator confesses "[to] whom can I be responsible and why should I be when you refuse to see me?.... Responsibility rests upon recognition, and recognition a form of agreement" (Ellison 14). Danielle Allen's brilliant reading of Ellison as political theorist begins with the story of Elizabeth Eckford, a girl who, like millions of other children in the United States, entered a new school in September of 1957 (Allen 3). Eckford, however, was prevented from entering Central High School of Little Rock by the Arkansas National Guard. While the *Brown v. Board of Education* Supreme Court decision gave her the right to attend the high school, her act of trying to go to school despite the protestors and National Guardsmen who obstructed her path constituted an effort for someone whose political membership was largely framed by others. The simple act of going to school, and in Allen's rendering, the choice of outfits, was political; it involved an act of affecting the way in which one was recognized. In his unfinished

Three Days Before the Shooting,[11] Ellison has one of his white characters explain how even banal actions constitute political insurrection for some.

> Don't you Yankees recognize that everything the nigra *does* is political.... If you catch a nigra in the wrong section of town after dark, he's being political, and that's because he knows he's out of his place. If he brushes against a white person on the street or on a stairway, *that's* political.... If a nigra owns more than one shotgun, rifle, or pistol, it's political. If he forgets to say "sir" to a white man or tries to talk Yankee talk, if he drives to doggone fast or too doggone slow ... all these things are political, and don't ya'll forget it! [Ellison 53–54].

Later, the voice of the white narrator recalling the collapse of an inter-racial relationship he had, declares, "History, both past and future, haunted my mind. It was no longer merely an Hegelian abstraction, for I had been plunged into its bewildering interior" (Ellison 102). That is, Hegel's master-slave dialectic and the aggressive contest for recognition became concrete (see Hegel and Kojève).

Frantz Fanon's reading of this dialectic leads him to conclude that the colonized "native" has been created by the colonizer. The former is wholly determined—physically, emotionally, materially, morally—by the latter.[12] "The native is declared insensible to ethics; he represents not only the absence of values, but also the negation of values" (Fanon 41). As such, "decolonization is the creation of new men.... [T]he 'thing' which has been colonized becomes man during the same process by which it frees itself" (Fanon 37). This liberation comes only through violence because drawing the colonizer's blood forces the former's hand in recognizing that the latter is also a man while it also allows the colonized to overcome the pyscho-neurotic self-imperiling conditions of colonialism (Fanon 45, 293).

But Luke Cage has "unbreakable skin." And while all comic book characters have some sort of weakness, few of them can be physically harmed by the normal men, women, and children of the polity. The efforts at recognition of the non-super must take a different form. They may not be able to force the superhero to see them as being equals, but they may still affect the latter's perception.

Jacques Rancière distinguishes "police'"—regulatory and administrative efforts which are not only *status quo*-oriented but which deliberately depoliticize populations—from "politics"—eruptions into a *status quo* during which actors who "did not count" previously must suddenly be included in the counting (by which he means the literal and/or metaphorical register of citizens. See *Dissensus* and *Hatred of Democracy*). "The essential work of politics is the configuration of its own space. It is to make the world of its subjects and its operations seen" (*Dissensus* 37). In this way, politics produces a new "partition of the sensible" in that it disturbs previous cognitive mappings of politics and makes new possibilities visible. Understanding politics as such, one wonders whether the "uncounted" in *Civil War* and their intervention into superhero politics as usual or the attacks of September 11, 2011 produced new "partitions of the sensible." This may be the way that the unpowered and/or downtrodden make themselves visible.

Counting the Uncountable in Civil War

Consider the counting. Readers are never told how many died in Stamford. Captain America estimates it as "eight or nine hundred" (Millar, *CW #1*, 10).[13] This rough approximation (with a range of some 12.5 percent) is contrasted by the precision of numbers in the pages that follow. Immediately after *assuming* such a high number of deaths, there is a *certain* sense of relief, if not triumph, when 6 surviving children are found (Millar, *CW #1*, 11).[14] Later S.H.I.E.L.D. commander Maria Hill tells Captain America that "twenty-three of your friends are meeting ... to discuss how the super-people should respond to the president's solution" (Millar, *CW #1*, 23) and, poignantly, she wants to know how many will be in support (Millar, *CW #1*, 21). The vagueness of the numbers of dead and the demand for precision on the part of the state's security apparatus is not surprising. But it does demonstrate that the invisible people—those who are not counted—need not be counted, even after so terrible an occurrence, while the "ones who matter' must be accounted for precisely. On first blush, the six surviving children seem to undermine such a position. But they do quite the opposite because they restore the non-super-powered to the position of being objects "rescued" by superheroes, not agents capable of action on their own. They remain beings who are determined by action on another stage, a stage which is lit and attended, unlike the one where they perform.

Even after the tragedy, the people never speak for themselves. They simply are represented by one mother who, typically, falls for the charms of Tony Stark. Instead, intra-superhero debate is highlighted, a talking head is shown, and certain political institutions are briefly given voice. That is, the "people" remain in the space of representation: it must be assumed that their beliefs, fears, and reasoning are being presented to the reader through the mouths and actions of others. Such an assumption is not necessary about the superheroes. The reader sees the plurality of views within the "superhero community," but no such concern is shown for the non-superhero.[15]

While the people intervene to "end" the civil war, they do not change their own status in the process. After Captain America is captured, the people only appear as arms waving in support of the new state-sponsored superhero teams (Millar, *CW #7*, 23). They only give acclamation to decisions made elsewhere. More disturbing, perhaps, is that this acclamation comes during a press conference, a space that is easily manipulated, suggesting that the "people" may have been staged again (Laclau 76–124). They remain representable only by being separated from their political identity to a form established and defined by another.[16] While Rancière hopes that politics leads to a partition of the sensible and a new "counting" within society, *Civil War* does not seem to do that. The non-powered remain in the background cheering or jeering, still uncounted, relying on others to speak and act for them.

The resolution of *Civil War* is a restoration of the lack of agency of the people, of the invisible. The ending—with people as spectators—bookends nicely with *New Avengers: Illuminati*, the prequel to the *Civil War* series. In that story, the Black Panther hosts Iron Man, Mr. Fantastic, Prince Namor, Black Bolt, Professor X, and Doctor Strange because Iron Man wants to form a super-super-group (one that represents the entire superhero community) to address issues bigger than those faced by individual superheroes or super-groups (like the Avengers or Fantastic Four). The Black Panther immediately rejects the idea and walks out.[17] During the second meeting, Namor rejects the idea and briefly squares off against Iron Man. When Iron Man warns of an impending superhero registration act in the third meeting, all of the participants except Mr. Fantastic reject Iron Man's call to have a super-super-group. There are two main claims made by the Black Panther, Namor, and the others. First, that this select group, the "Illuminati," may misjudge friend and foe. Second, that this group is not necessarily representative. The second point suggests an unexpected irony.

Democracy, Rationality and Representation

In the modern world, democratic governments chosen through rational discourse in commercially open polities are considered to be most legitimate and representative of the people. This is a rationalization of forms of legitimacy (see Weber). And yet, of those present, the voices of those from traditional, *ie* non-rational, forms are the ones who most legitimately represent their people and who seem most ethical. Consider that three are monarchs (Black Panther, Namor, and Black Bolt) and it is among this group where there is the most resistance and where there is the greatest questioning of whether such a group is just and representative. These men are indeed the legitimate representatives of their people. Resistance later comes from Professor X and Doctor Strange who represent charismatic and mystical authority (Professor X's claim to leadership is more credible given his status among the X-Men specifically, and mutants more generally, whereas Dr. Strange can make no claim among magicians or other creatures). The only proponents of "the only rational" solution are Iron Man and Reed Richards, representatives of the military-industrial complex and a notion of science that is divorced from tradition, charisma, and any relation to polity or ethics.

When Iron Man reminds Namor that he, like Namor, is a warrior, Namor elides the comment saying "You're a warrior. I'm a king." In his hubris, Iron Man responds, "Not up here you're not" (Bendis 19). Iron Man is a genius. He knows that what Namor has said is true: one is a king, one is not. His response aims to rob Namor of the legitimacy of the office of king by limiting it to the place where he is king. The statement is logically false. Namor remains a king as long as he holds his throne. He may not be a king of a specific territory but he is no less a king when he is outside of his kingdom. Were that so, monarchs could only conduct relations with other monarchs through intermediaries and could never leave their territory.[18] Why make so fallacious a statement? The problem is Iron Man not Namor. Iron Man has no claim to rule nor to make decisions. Whereas Namor can represent Atlantis, Black Bolt the Inhumans, and the Black Panther the people of Wakanda,[19] Iron Man's leadership is the result of neither election nor selection (by someone other than himself). He has been the on again/off again leader of the Avengers, but so have many other heroes. The only thing he has consistently done is bankrolled the Avengers, for which he is attacked by Mrs. Sharpe (Millar, *CW #1*, 14–5). Indeed, he makes his case on the grounds of its rationality, not his authority as representative of anything other than reason, and his most extensive argument—the one that previews the opening of *Civil War*—asserts that his power is that he can see the future and knows how to prepare for the future (Bendis 30–32). That is, he is an entrepreneur who knows what people will want and need in the future and can profit by offering it at the right time. He is not representing anyone, only responding to what people may want (putting aside the morality of those wants). The government purchases Stark Industries weapons, but he cannot claim that the U.S. should attack—say, Afghanistan—because there will be a need for regime change in Afghanistan. Such a claim of a pre-emptive strike by a government faces considerable scrutiny (even if elected), but certainly few would countenance a similar statement made by an arms dealer.

And what is Reed Richards doing there? He is the leader of the Fantastic Four, whose name suggests how limited his constituency is. But he does not even speak on behalf of those people. Quite the contrary. When he and Iron Man are left alone in the room as the only two who are committed to the policy conclusions that pure rationality leaves them, he tells Iron Man, "I have to go home and fight with my wife about this for the rest of my life" (Bendis 33). This is the first time that he mentions his wife (and he does not mention the other Fantastic Four). Instead, wives and family are only mentioned by the monarchs (Namor on page 9 and Black Panther on page 11). The Black Panther says pointedly, "You just decided all by yourselves that you are the earth's protectors. And that you, and *only* you, not your teammates or family are trustworthy enough to include in the process" (Bendis 11). The problem is that Richards—as presented in the *Civil War* arc—cannot involve his wife in the process. He is a tragic figure as he cannot explain to his wife his work, as it is inexplicably complex, despite it having such an immediate impact on their world and their marriage.

For Rancière, one of the chief puzzles of recent decades is how democracy has become the only legitimate form of government while politics has become increasingly less democratic (a theme addressed in both *Hatred of Democracy* and *Dissensus*). Even within democracies, more and more decisions are made by non-elected bodies (central banks, technical commissions), corporate and private actors have increasing influence over public decision-making, and traditional representative institutions (parties, unions) are seen as ineffective and/or untrustworthy. Mr. Fantastic embodies this dilemma: to know what is correct but to be unable to communicate and convince others, whether Prince Namor or his wife, the Invisible Woman. In one evening, he and Iron Man came up with 100 ideas to make the world better (Millar, *CW #7*, 27), but he could not figure out how to keep his family together, nor how to persuade others of the virtue of those ideas (which are largely pursued in secret).

But he is not the only figure involved in keeping the family together. Indeed, presuming that he strips the Invisible Woman of her agency as an actor, the family then would live and die with *his* efforts, making her invisible once again. But *Civil War* is a story in which she becomes visible and asserts her agency, and, in doing so, she leaves her husband despite her desire to keep the family together and her love for her husband. The Invisible Woman is not only central to the plot but she most intensely experiences on a personal level the effects of the SHRA. Without her knowledge, her husband makes the decision to put into motion a superhero response to the *SHRA* before it is even proposed (Bendis 1). Her brother is attacked by uppity, non-powered people outside a club as retribution for the Stamford violence (Millar, *CW #1*, 16–17). This violence foreshadows the death of Goliath at the hands of the robot Thor, although, notably, whereas superhero violence ultimately leads to death, the violence of the non-superhero only sends the Human Torch to the hospital. The power of the people is either limited or it is better capable of pulling back from ethical precipices.

After Bill Foster (Goliath)[20] is killed and the Invisible Woman protects the anti–*SHRA* heroes, she writes a note to her husband and leaves home. In that note, she is capable of communicating directly with her husband who is more comfortable with data than people. Because she is "*ashamed* of you ... and myself for supporting your fascistic plans," she decides to join the resistance (Millar, *CW #4*, 18). The rest of the note seems personal, as opposed to political (she says her leaving is "not another cry for attention"). She knows that the underground is not a good environment for their kids, and she does not want him to think she is "a bad wife or, worse still, a bad mother," and she reminds him that she loves him "more than anything in the world" (Millar, *CW #4*, 18–19). Before signing off, she writes, "please fix this." This refers to something in the singular (as opposed to "these") that is close at hand (as opposed to "that"). For Reed, the political and personal are separable—how else can he side with Iron Man and expect to fight with his wife for the rest of his life? Indeed, comic books all too often separate the visible actions of superheroes—

their spectacular battles across cityscapes—from the less visible personal relations between them, to say nothing of the even less visible non-superhero characters. For "Sue" (the nickname—personalized—that the Invisible Woman uses to sign off), "this" is all part of one big problem, equally political and personal, impacting the visible and invisible.

"This" is a reference to what has been set in motion by his "fascistic plans." For the student of history, fascism has very precise meaning. Rhetorically, it recalls what many people consider the least democratic and most belligerent regimes in the 20th century, known for their rigid and violent enforcement of conformity within their society as well as their expansionary efforts outside. Reed could—and perhaps would—quibble with the word. A comparison of his plans to those of Mussolini, Salazar, or Hitler, or, more fairly, to scientists who might have supported the regimes of those, would not pass any real standards of social science rigor. She, of course, knows that she cannot communicate with him at an intellectual level; she can only hope that she can at an emotional level. And yet, in the panel after she leaves the Baxter Building (where the Fantastic Four is based), the reader looks at the face of a sad Ben Grimm (a member of the Fantastic Four) looking out the window. Reed is still asleep. On the next page, Reed is walking around in a lab coat with Tony Stark talking about defections—the number is "more than we can afford" (Millar, *CW #4*, 20). Her letter, apparently, has not impacted his work.

She is smart enough to know that she cannot rely purely on an emotional connection. She also appeals to his ego/intelligence. She writes, "I'm doing this for the best of reasons and pray that your genius can *resolve* this thing before one side ends up slaughtering the other" (Millar, *CW #4*, 20). And she turns out to be correct (at least, during the *Civil War* arc). His algorithm which sought to predict the likely turn of events may have been correct, but it did not "resolve" the civil war. Something else was necessary. Captain America needed to be shown the error of his ways not by superheroes but by the *people*, and then it is just as, if not more, necessary that those people have to slip back into the background. His model could have predicted the latter because that is what non-superheroes do in comic books and indeed, that is what the people do in most of the world, including in its most democratic polities.

Before addressing the disappearance of the people, it is worth noting that Reed writes his own letter to Sue (whom he calls "my dear, sweet Susan") in which he expresses that nothing he has accomplished means anything without her and he asks her to return (Millar, *CW #7*, 25). She does. The people always seem to return, the invisible intervenes and then goes back to being invisible, taken for granted. Or, at least, that is the lesson of *Civil War*.

Partition of the Sensible

This may not be the lesson of post–September 11 politics. It is not surprising that, in recent years, there have been many translations of Jacques Rancière's work into English. Also, not surprising, is the rock star-like popularity of Marxists Michael Hardt and Antonio Negri (for their works, *Empire*, *Multitude*, and *Commonwealth*). Negri's notion of "constituent power" (1, 12), the creative power of a people that undergirds and is beyond any form of government (any "constituted power"), has been central to the various protesting "people" who have erupted throughout the world. Unlike *Civil War*'s invisible people who intervened into politics but went home without producing a new "partition of the sensible," ceding its authority to others to represent them, a politics of rebellion of peoples who suddenly refuse representative forms and bodies that previously governed them has emerged (Douzinas 9).

Due to space constraints, it will be impossible to cover all or even some of such movements in depth. Rather, I will try to sketch out a few notable examples of where the invisible has intervened into politics as normal and asserted its authority, demanding to be counted in a new audit of society, contributing to a new "partition of the sensible." There is no effort to present a causal argument about how the events of or reactions to 9/11 generated this new partition of the sensible. Rather, the goal in the rest of this essay is to map out how the uncounted and invisible have become visible and demanded a re-count.

While Barack Obama was not elected president because of the demands of an invisible part of the population, a significant subset of what had been increasingly apathetic and disengaged publics felt that, for the first time, a politician represented them. This representation was less the result of candidate Obama's proposed policies as it was the result of who he was, or, at least, who he was perceived to be. Indeed, biography was not only part of his appeal, it was explicitly part of his marketing strategy (Smith). While his background obviously spoke to professional African American men, the traditional "invisible men" à la Ellison, it also touched other outsiders, young people of different races, other racial and ethnic minorities—professional and non-professional. At the same time, what the Obama presidency makes very clear, while he has seen the invisible, he did so on his own terms (and those made possible by the political, economic, and cultural structures available. See Coates). The invisible did not force the "establishment" to see them; it simply had a more empathetic head of state.

A more persuasive case might be made for both Tea Party and Occupy Wall Street activists, people who had been largely invisible and/or taken for granted by elites (heroes) and institutions (comic book story arcs) on their respective ends of the political spectrum. Although activists within the group may resent the common grouping (and their ability to impact policy may vary significantly), they share a very intense sense that they have been ignored by elites and institutions and that both of these need to be challenged regularly through the contestation of public space in order to make change according to the "authentic" will of the people. Of course, there are private funders and intellectuals who have worked within these groups (again to differing degrees), which may challenge the reading that these groups represent the "pure" voice of the people. Nevertheless, the groups have forced political leaders of the left and right to re-consider strategies, undermining some party-favored candidacies, forcing certain issues onto the political agenda, and modifying the way other issues are addressed. They have also affected the way that elites and non-elites see the political world. One now finds demands on behalf of "the 99 percent" or against the "1 percent," terms that suddenly have clear political meaning. Similarly, conservative radio has shifted to incorporate considerable criticism of members of the Republican Party who are seen as betraying the conservative goals of Tea Party supporters. The effort to promote division within political conservatives while the White House is held by the Democratic Party is noteworthy.

Perhaps a still better case may be made for broad categories such as Islam, political Islam, the Middle East and North Africa, and Central Asia. While none of these terms was absent from political discussions prior to September 11, 2001, there is no question that a new partition of the sensible emerged which directly affected these terms and, importantly, in which previously invisible actors played a key role in the formation of that new partition. This was not simply a question of "demonizing"—as there were plenty of mainstream critiques of and warnings against such behavior. Indeed, what is evident is that Islam, one of the world's largest religions in terms of declared adherents, became not only visible to the entire world but became present, an unexpected (and often unwelcome) neighbor of sorts. The forced awareness of the existence of Islam happened alongside competing efforts to characterize it and to make sense of its relationship to the political (see Esposito and De Long-Bas). Similarly, the Middle East, which previously was generally seen in the West as a space of Arab and Jew conflict was suddenly a region that intruded into one's own household (at least among many in the U.S., if not also in Europe). Although Afghanistan and Pakistan (and India) are frequently assumed to be part of the Middle East, Central and South Asia have also become more part of the U.S. (and Western?) political imagination. But this is not just a matter of new dangerous places that "hate us," but places where U.S. political machinations and involvement are made increasingly visible to U.S. (and other) citizens (see Spanakos 26–28).

The terrorists and the various governments in the Middle East, North Africa, Central and South Asia, and the peoples there who have implicitly and explicitly supported and rejected them, intruded into politics as usual, demanded to be counted, forced consideration, and changed the way the world thinks of politics. The terrorist attacks, from the perspective of the terrorists and the political spaces where they originated, were not *ex nihilo* incursions but were part of a long tradition of resistance to Western imperialism. Contextualizing the attacks within history does not justify them, but it does give insight into a long-term scrum within the Middle East that was largely invisible to the U.S. public. Previously, that public considered Middle East conflicts as between different peoples from whom it was distinct and, therefore, capable of acting as intermediary and periodic peacemaker. Such a view assumes a certain neutrality on the part of the U.S. and a distance from political struggles among local actors, positions that actors on various sides of the conflict would probably reject. But the assumption of neutrality and innocence has been rendered incredible and this is evident even in mainstream, popular level representations.

When Marvel's *Civil War* asks readers to "take sides," it tries to make both sides equally rational, right, and just (as numerous essays in this volume demonstrate). In the various *Iron Man* films, the role of a U.S. government that has been coopted by the military-industrial complex and made complicit in the crimes of Muslim Afghanistan is laid bare (Spanakos 21). Thus, in the first *Iron Man* film, Afghan terror groups and warlords fight each other and U.S. soldiers with Stark industry weapons. Not only are U.S. weapons turned against the U.S., but Stark's intellectual property is turned against his own person when he is a prisoner of an army armed with his weapons. Escaping the U.S.-armed Afghan soldiers forces him to work in a cave with a fellow prisoner to develop the first Iron Man prototype. An encounter with the terrorist leads Stark to return to the U.S. and want to give up arms production. Walt Kelly's famous statement, "We have met the enemy and he is us," first used for an Earth Day poster in 1970, takes on a novel meaning in that the U.S. is not only the cause of its own problems due to what it has done to the physical environment, but because of its relations with other humans as well.

The attacks of September 11 not only made "political Islam" part of the quotidian discourse of media political pundits and more popular barroom philosophers, it also raised questions of "What are we doing there?"; "Should we send more or fewer soldiers?"; "Are we a democratizing force and/or an occupying army?"; "Why are not more foreign states more assertively defending our policies?"; "Can they have democracies and do we have the right to push such decisions on them?"; "Is an invasion of Iraq, Afghanistan, Iran, Libya, and/or Syria necessary to fight terrorism?"; "Do we need support from other Arab and Muslim countries for our foreign policy plans?"; and "How can we win the (political) hearts and minds of Muslims?" On a more mundane level, there was considerable debate surrounding the location of a Mosque and Islamic cultural center near the site of the future World Trade Center. The debate gave opportunity for various voices in favor and against the location. In the process, even opponents of the site recognized some important new realities: that there are significant numbers of Muslims within the United States; that there is diversity within this group on important political issues; and that not extending American baseline political obligations to Muslims needed to be carefully crafted.

A more direct claim could be made of the various outpourings of popular contestation in non-democratic governments in the Middle East. Perhaps most paradigmatic of the invisible forcing the powerful to recognize them is when Mohamed Bouazizi immolated himself in December 2010 as a protest of the personal humiliation experienced at the hands of a woman working for the Tunisian state. The digital capture of the event allowed the image of an otherwise nameless man, suffering a universally comprehensible indignity to become viral—seen and experienced by multitudes, over and over. The response to his protest was the most immediate inspiring cause of the various popular protests that spread across the Middle East and North Africa, leading to an important period of regime change and political realignments (see Haddad and Schwedler).

As much as the Arab Spring protests were against autocratic rulers who made themselves unaccountable to the people and, as such, did not take the "people" into account, similar demands were made in other countries (Ukraine, Thailand), including in more democratic spaces (Turkey, Brazil, Venezuela, Spain, Greece). In each case, massive numbers of people went into the streets to protest governments that were believed to have ignored or betrayed the people's interests. Occupying public space was part of a broader strategy to remind rulers that the people were there, watching them, and are the ultimate holders of power and legitimacy. Although each of these protests responds to local conditions and aims at different policy responses, they share this notion of trying to impose a new political count. This might very well have been what the "invisible" tried to do in *Civil War*.[21]

Notes

1. A Weberian state contending with anti-statist tendencies, whether libertarian, anarchist, or otherwise.
2. See Aristotle.
3. For examples, see Marvel's *Siege, Dark Reign*, and *The Heroic Age* storylines.
4. Agamben builds on Aristotle's notion that potentiality involves both the potential to be and not to be, to do and not to do, Agamben looks to bring the "potentiality" of texts into "actuality." De la Durantaye writes "The philosophical element—rich in potentiality—is that which, while present, goes unstated in a work and is thereby left for others to read between the lines and formulate in their own" (9). The current essay seeks to do this with *Civil War*.
5. Alan Moore and Dave Gibbons' *Watchmen* (1986–87) and Frank Miller's *Dark Knight Returns* (1986) are clear outliers here. A less cynical but no less dramatic depiction of this can be seen in Kurt Busiek and Alex Ross's *Marvels* (1994).
6. Although superhero comics rely on constant physical confrontations, killing an opponent is an ethical taboo which has historically been eschewed.
7. "Action" is used in the singular to highlight the sudden and unexpected agency of the Invisible Woman. Of course, her action is established through multiple actions on her part.
8. Hercules does play a role but it is the Invisible Woman who protects the entire anti-*SHRA* group and gives them time to teleport away.

9. This may be the physical version of Socrates's claim in *Crito* that he would destroy Athens by escaping its judgment.

10. An important exception is Mrs. Sharpe, the mother of one of the murdered children, who is in the enviable position of spitting on Tony Stark (*CW #1*, 14).

11. See Ricouer.

12. For Fanon, this is why the colonizer is so preoccupied with the veil, which becomes a sort of impermeable barrier to efforts to mark and define the colonial subject.

13. Elsewhere it is claimed to be "over 600."

14. Note that the non-powered emergency personnel only can access and save the children because of the intervention of Marvel Girl. She, literally, removes the stones/wreckage which blocked them from being able to "search and rescue," i.e., to do their jobs.

15. The *Front Line* series written by Paul Jenkins gives some insight into "normal" people but it is largely centered on the possibly heroic action of one investigative reporter's refusal to cooperate with the state.

16. This might comfort Edmund Burke, but it would madden Jean-Jacques Rousseau, given his commitment to the ideal of the social contract.

17. As an African, the Black Panther is likely to be especially sensitive to the idea of a privileged elite making decisions for others. This also resonates with the mutants and Inhumans, but Professor X and Black Bolt do not immediately speak up.

18. Xenophon's Hiero suggests that this is a problem faced by tyrants, a suggestion confirmed by Simonedes who argues that good rulers (monarchs) do not face a similar challenge (*Hiero*). Isocrates's advice *To Nicocles* offers a more radical alternative as the monarch's rule is legitimated in reciprocity with citizens.

19. One could argue that these are hardly the largest or most important polities to be represented, but that only strengthens the concerns of the Black Panther.

20. It should be noted that this Goliath was previously "Black Goliath," a nod, in 1975, to Marvel's effort to engage with civil rights and to respond to questions of the visibility of non-white superheroes. I am grateful to Kevin Scott for this note.

21. The author is grateful to Kevin Scott for his leadership on this project and his excellent comments on an earlier draft of this chapter.

Works Cited

Allen, Danielle S. *Talking to Strangers: Anxieties of Citizenship since* Brown v. Board of Education. Chicago: University of Chicago Press, 2004. Print.
Aristotle. *On Rhetoric: A Theory of Civic Discourse*. Trans., intro., notes, and appendices by George A. Kennedy. New York: Oxford University Press, 1991. Print.
Bendis, Brian Michael (writer), Alex Maleev (penciller), and Dave Stewart (colorist). *New Avengers: Illuminati* #0 (Mar. 2006), Marvel Comics. Print.
Coates, Ta-Nehisi. "Fear of a Black President." The Atlantic.com. Atlantic Monthly Group, 22 Aug. 2012. Web. 29 May 2014.
de la Durantaye, Leland. *Giorgio Agamben: A Critical Introduction*. Stanford: Stanford University Press, 2009. Print.
Dostoevsky, Fyodor. *Notes from the Underground*. Trans. Richard Pevear and Larissa Volokhonsky. New York: Vintage, 1994. Print.
Douzinas, Costas. *Philosophy and Resistance in the Crisis: Greece and the Future of Europe*. Malden, MA: Polity, 2013. Print.
Ellison, Ralph. *The Invisible Man*. New York: Vintage, 1995. Print.
_____. *Three Days Before the Shooting...*. New York: The Modern Library, 2011. Print.
Esposito, John L., with Natana J. De Long-Bas. "Modern Islam." *God's Rules: The Politics of World Religions*. Ed. Jacob Neusner. Washington, D.C.: Georgetown University Press. 2003. 159–184. Print.
Fanon, Frantz. *Wretched of the Earth*. Trans. Constance Farrington. New York: Grove Weidenfeld, 1963. Print.
Haddad, Bassam, and Jillian Schwedler. "Editors' Introduction to Teaching about the Middle East Uprisings." *PS: Political Science & Politics* 46.2 (2013): 211–216. Print.
Hardt, Michael and Antonio Negri. *Commonwealth*. Cambridge: Belknap Press, 2011. Print.
_____. *Empire*. Cambridge: Harvard University Press, 2000. Print.
_____. *Multitude: War and Democracy in the Age of Empire*. New York: Penguin, 2004. Print.
Hegel, G.W.F. *Elements of the Philosophy of Right*. Ed. Allen W. Wood. Trans. H.B. Nisbet. Cambridge: Cambridge University Press, 1991. Marvel Comics. Print.
Jenkins, Paul (writer), Roman Bachs (penciller), and John Lucas (inker). *Frontline* #1–11 (June 2006–Feb. 2007), Marvel Comics. Print.

Kojève, Alexandre. *Outline of a Phenomenology of Right*. Trans., Intro., and notes by Bryan-Paul Frost and Robert Howse. Ed. Bryan-Paul Frost. Lanham, MD: Rowman & Littlefield, 2007. Print.

Laclau, Ernesto. *On Populist Reason*. New York: Verso. 2005. Print.

Millar, Mark (writer), and Steve McNiven (penciller). *Civil War* #1–7 (May 2006–Feb. 2007), Marvel Comics. Print.

Negri, Antonio. *Insurgencies: Constituent Power and the Modern State* Trans. Maurizia Boscagli, with a new foreword by Michael Hardt. Minneapolis: University of Minnesota Press, 2009. Print.

Rancière, Jacques. *Dissensus: On Politics and Aesthetics*. Ed. and Trans. by Steven Corcoran. New York: Continuum. 2010. Print.

———. *Hatred of Democracy*. Trans. Steve Corcoran. New York: Verso. 2009. Print.

Ricoeur, Paul. *The Course of Recognition*. Trans. David Pellauer. Cambridge: Harvard University Press, 2005. Print.

Rockhill, Gabriel, and Philip Watts, eds. *Jacques Rancière: History, Politics, Aesthetics*. Durham: Duke University Press, 2009. Print.

Smith, Zadie. "Speaking in Tongues." New York Review of Books.com. NYREV, Inc., 26 Feb. 2009. Web. 26 February 2009.

Spanakos, Anthony P. "Exceptional Recognition: The U.S. Global Dilemma in *The Incredible Hulk, Iron Man*, and *Avatar*." *The 21st Century Superhero: Essays on Gender, Genre and Globalization in Film*, eds. Richard Gray II and Betty Kaklamanidou. Jefferson, NC: McFarland, 2011. 15–28. Print.

The Language of Common Sense: Thomas Paine and *Civil War*

SCOTT CLEARY

> *"As Millar said, Cap smells of 1776. He's about the ideals of the nation, rather than the reality."*
> —Tom Brevoort, *Civil War Companion*

Named moral godfather of the internet by *Wired* magazine, quoted by President Barack Obama in his historic first inaugural address of 2009, and claimed by all sides in an increasingly fractious American political climate, Thomas Paine is a man, it seems, whose time has come again. Or perhaps it has always been his time; Paine's impact on American radicalism and humanism, global revolutionary thought, eighteenth-century prose, and, as one scholar has very recently posited, the very concept of "right" and "left" in American politics, has filtered by a kind of osmosis into our collective and contemporary cultural understanding. It should come as no surprise that, if not the image, then the ideas and politics of Thomas Paine are evident across Marvel Comics *Civil War* event. While it is certainly true that Paine was a major player in the revolutions in America and France (and globally) at the end of the eighteenth century, and not the nineteenth century conflict that inspired the comics event, it is nonetheless the case that Paine's ideas about identity, the nature of government and its authority, the role of government in regulating rights, and the balance between security and liberty all form the basis for an exploration of these same ideals in *Civil War*. Indeed, if we are to cast the conflict between Captain America and Iron Man as driven by ideological differences more than inherently oppositional character traits, then the political philosophy of Thomas Paine offers a potential answer to *Civil War*'s most vexing question: whose side are you on?

While Millar's comment seems to make the calculation an easy one—John Adams' comment that "without Paine's pen, Washington's sword would have been raised in vain" is the ancestor of Millar's "smell of 1776"—and posits Captain America as the purest representative of Paine's ideas in *Civil War*, it is in fact Tony Stark who first invokes Paine in *The Amazing Spider-Man #532*. While convincing Peter Parker to join him in supporting the upcoming Superhuman Registration Act (SHRA) and appealing to their shared genius in cultural "evaluation," Stark claims, "More than anyone else here, you and I have a great deal in common, Peter. We're both scientists, levelheaded, practical…. We don't just react, we **evaluate**. We have similar temperaments, and we speak the same language…. The language of common sense" (Straczynski, *AMS* #532, 19). That language of common sense is, somewhat paradoxically, a language of the intellectual elite; a function of Stark's—and to a much lesser extent—Peter's genius and his manipulative way of framing the reality that he as a technocrat futurist determines as much as he "evaluates." Stark is neither ideologue nor idealist in the Civil War; instead, prophet-like, he is a man who assesses information and the cultural zeitgeist in order to predict, and by predicting, shape the future. It is no coincidence that as Iron Man, the first superhero Stark defeats as the opening salvo to the war is Prodigy. In what Sophia Rosenfeld has called the "fixing of a paradoxical conception of common sense to a democratic vision of politics as authoritative cause and effect," Stark invokes that very "conception" of common sense while facing a similarly paradoxical, middling hero whose name suggests his natural superiority (683–684). That is the calculus of common sense for Stark, namely that by merging an intellectual ideal that seems logically irrefutable with an essentially American democratic urge, he has found the perfect means of both demonstrating the righteousness of the Superhuman Registration Act, and "fixing" the terms by which the world and its superheroes would be governed.

By so using common sense as his world-building philosophy in the Civil War, Stark invokes not only a storied tradition of political philosophy, but the American Revolution and Thomas Paine's great contribution to it: *Common Sense*. Arguably the intellectual lynchpin of the revolution, *Common Sense* was published in January 1776 when the ebb of the war was firmly against the Americans. In it, Paine makes his seminal arguments concerning the abolition of the monarchy and the purpose and role of government, couched in the classical language of nature vs. society[1]:

> Some writers have so confounded society with government as to leave little to no distinction between them, whereas they are not only different, but have different origins. Society is produced by our wants, and government by our weakness; the former promotes our happiness positively by uniting our affections, the latter negatively by restraining our vices. The one encourages intercourse, the other creates distinctions. The first is a patron, the last, a punisher [4].

Sadly, Paine does not have Frank Castle in mind when calling government a punisher. Government is a "necessary evil," and one that creates laws to secure and enforce communal bonds that often splinter because of humanity's generally vicious nature. Government as both necessary and necessary enforcer is, in Stark's language of common sense, a politically valuable complement to his technocratic vision, which in the persona of Tony Stark understands and values government as a social and economic necessity, but as Iron Man enforces the laws (or leads government forces like S.H.I.E.L.D.) that are required because of (super)human nature in itself and as lived in community. He says as much in the Illuminati meeting held prior to *Civil War*: "If the earth is attacked again … **when** the earth is attacked again…. **We're** the ones who will defend it. There is no one else. No army is ready. So, to the rest of the universe we're the law enforcement of this planet. I'm saying—maybe we should gather together and do just that" (Bendis, *NAI #0*, 3). "Security," Paine says, is the "true design and end of government, and it unanswerably follows that that whatever form thereof appears most likely to ensure us, with the least expense and greatest benefits is preferable to all others" (5). Stark eloquently articulates within the self-described bounds of his own superheroism (futurist and technocrat) that security is the only truly meaningful function of government in a world of superheroes, and that the SHRA is the necessary condition of security in an increasingly volatile world. However, more than mere security, the SHRA both recognizes and reifies the distinguishing power of government, a mode of reflecting a highly stratified society but also of controlling it by making and enforcing distinctions within it that, in the case of *Civil War*, transcend the traditional categories of superhero and supervillain.

While it may then be fairly said that Tony Stark holds a fundamentally Paineite vision of government, his other actions made in the name of such a vision, namely the manipulation of Peter Parker into revealing his identity, bugging the enhanced Spider suit he gives Peter, and building and funding the Negative Zone prisons for anti-registration heroes mean that either Stark stopped reading *Common Sense* roughly halfway through, or he failed to see that for Paine the government as open, public security state is merely one function in a suite of governmental roles and responsibilities, and that to focus on it exclusively would be to foster tyranny. Indeed, if government is the condition of modern life lived among fellow humans and superhumans in the Marvel Universe, as well as demigods and mutants, then what Stark ignores is what Paine viewed as the concomitant state of humanity: society. It is a classical argument for political theorists, and in *Civil War* it can be seen in the words of the perhaps appropriately named Thinker. In *Fantastic Four #542*, Reed Richards describes to his long time nemesis, Thinker, the elaborate, ingenious equations that created the strategic need for the SHRA, a panoptical vision of society that continually ends in disaster or tragedy, to which the SHRA is the only, inevitable solution. Reed, like Stark, sees his own genius as much as the plan itself than as the solution, but Thinker is not convinced, largely because in his macro-social calculations, Richards has failed to account for one variable: the individual. "Your methodology," Thinker begins, "is, as you say, useless for predicting the actions of any single person. I have another technique for that. It's called common sense" (Straczynski, *FF #542*, 22). The Thinker sees that in trying to shape and manipulate societal trends, Richards has removed an essential component of common sense from its application to any political or social process. Not only does it evacuate common sense of its democratic meaning, but it refuses the essential individualism that is both activated and sacrificed within the democratic process. In short, it removes the revolutionary possibilities of grassroots democracy and confuses government and (specifically in Reed's case) data-driven policy for society and the bonds of common good around which it is typically formed.

Society is for Paine the prior and necessary condition of government. Humanity coheres in progressively larger groups before vice inevitably forces government upon those groups. So, if Paine is an advocate for the inevitability of government, then what the superheroes who oppose registration represent is society, in all its affective potential. It is perhaps no coincidence that various iterations of superhero teams have taken some variation of the term society for their own, because as superheroes they have often operated not beyond government or even outside of government oversight but as prior entities to the need for government itself. Society is mutually beneficial, joined by wants and shared values such as the justice, goodness, and right that superheroes generally defend and are the functions of what society desires heroes to believe in and to model just behavior.[2]

True, *Civil War* seems to complicate that with the tragedy at Stamford, but the story equally counters it with those characters who best symbolize the anti-registration forces. Captain America, who "smells of 1776" according to the architect of the event. The naive Peter Parker who is manipulated by Stark. Four of the original X-Men. Characters all who have stood outside the mainstream but sought the "affections" of those with whom they share a mission and a world-view. Note too that Paine says, contrary to the distinguishing function of government, society encourages "intercourse," or the very mixing and integration of views, opinions, and beliefs that, at their best, these societies represent and enact, and even a nascent democratic sensibility that seeks to unify and not divide or coerce.

Paine is so insistent on this point that he elaborates further in *Common Sense*: "Here then the origin and rise of government; namely, is a mode rendered necessary by the inability of moral virtue to govern the world. Here too is the design and end of government: freedom and security" (6). As Paine has structured his argument, government is necessary for security against human vice, but in specific terms of humanity's moral failure, government must also guarantee freedom simultaneously with security. The Marvel Universe is an interesting test case for this, and *Civil War* its fertile testing ground. Beyond contemporary, post–9/11 anxieties about the relationship between freedom and security, the Marvel Universe seems to make much the same claim. Governments need to guarantee security because we live together, but our freedoms because of occasionally egregious assaults against moral virtue. Of course, such virtue is the hallmark of many heroes so it is no surprise that Captain America most clearly articulates its modern vision:

> I believe in the fundamental freedoms accorded us by our constitution, Ben. I believe we have right to bear arms, a right to defend and a right to choose. I have sworn an oath to defend America from external forces and from **within**. If that means standing against my own government, rejecting a bogus law passed by my own superiors, then I suppose that's what it means [Jenkins 9].

The debate between Sally Floyd and Captain America in "Embedded: Part Eleven" is *Common Sense* distilled. The Captain represents society and virtue as acts and entities prior to government, which can be legitimately resisted if the laws they make do not necessarily square with what the function of government ought to be. Sally represents the world needing to be governed above all else, a world that demands punishment in the form of government because it values celebrity above heroism. The sheer energy and anger of her argument makes Captain America seemed old fashioned, out of touch, too idealistic, and more beaten than he already is.

But let it never be said that moral virtue is nothing if not idealistic. Indeed, the long speech Captain America gives to Peter in *Amazing Spider-Man #537*, concerning the value of a single man's conscience as both counterweight to anarchy and duty to government, framed as it is against their previous fight in *Amazing Spider-Man #534*, not only echoes Thinker's complaint about Richard's project, it also suggests that while the pro-registration forces rely too heavily on the governmental role of security, they in no way represent its necessary corollary of freedom because they mistake the role of government for the good of society. The structural differences among the *Civil War* comics echoes this. More than Tony's public proclamations at press conferences and congressional hearings, as in *The Amazing Spider-Man*, Captain America's philosophy of liberty and freedom comes in societal settings, less formalized and more dependent upon shared experiences where individual belief and expression are dominant modes of communication.

Utterly reeking of 1776 in those passages, Captain America invokes the intellectual crutch upon which security stands: freedom in general but rights in particular. The Negative Zone Prison and the ordeal of Robbie "Speedball" Baldwin are trenchant examples of violated rights as they relate to imprisonment, but from a purely ideological standpoint, Captain America's speeches argue for the broader palette of rights beyond the treatment of prisoners. Indeed, this discourse of rights, and specifically rights guaranteed by constitutions, references Paine's most famous work, *Rights of Man*. Published in 1791, while Paine was in France participating in the French Revolution, *Rights of Man* was a work that fit into the larger continuum of rights and rights language that emanated from enlightenment thinkers and brought to the English-speaking world the best formulation for the nature, extent, and necessity of rights in modern democracies. Paine, like many of those other thinkers, ties the concept of rights to the idea of a constitution, and it is interesting to note that in *Civil War*, it is the anti-registration forces alone who refer to rights and constitutions at any length. Although admittedly a loose coalition—Battlestar mentions privacy rights in terms of his secret identity, and Captain America refers to some contemporary "hot button" rights, such as the right to bear arms and "choice"—the anti-registration heroes counter Stark's language of common sense with constitutional language. Such anti-registration arguments for rights argue against pro-registration arguments for obedience to laws, which as Paine points out and history has proven, may or may not be constitutional. Paine himself is clear:

> A constitution is not a thing in name only, but in fact. It has not an ideal, but a real existence, and wherever it cannot be produced in a visible form there is none. A constitution is a thing *antecedent* to a government, and a government is only a creature of a constitution. The constitution of a country is not the act of its government, but of the people constituting a government [278].

The heroes' self-identified roles in the anti-registration camp, akin as they are to societal and not governmental structures of their comic world, understand the Civil War in exactly those terms. They advocate for and refer to the originary document of their rights, as prior to the formation of government, the very thing upon which government is based and by which it can fall. The implications of Paine's constitutional arguments for rights impacts the heroes directly and is the subtext of their plaintive arguments. Given its medial, post-society/pre-government place in the formation of democracies, a constitution does not create rights; it only guarantees rights that naturally occur within individuals in a society.

By invoking constitutions and rights, the anti-registration forces are in fact appealing to the most fundamental kind of rights for Paine: our natural rights. Paine's argument, as in *Common Sense*, rests on a dual nature of rights:

> Natural rights are those which appertain to man in right of his existence. Of this kind are all the intellectual rights, or rights of the mind, and also those rights of acting as individual for his own comfort and happiness, which are not injurious to the natural rights of others. Civil rights are those which appertain to man in right of his being a member of society. Every civil right has for its foundation some natural right pre-existing in the individual, but to the enjoyment of which his individual power is not, in all cases, sufficiently competent. Of this kind are all those that relate to security and protection.... The natural rights which he retains are all those in which the *power* to execute is as perfect in the individual as the right itself. Among this class, as is before mentioned, all are intellectual rights, or rights of the mind.... The natural rights which are not maintained, are all those in which, though the right is perfect in the individual, the power to execute them is defective [276].

The argument is elegant. We retain intellectual rights and all that within our scope of power we can actuate. Those we cannot, we grant to society to execute and protect. In so doing we "exchange" our natural rights for civil rights.

Indeed, as Paine goes on to say, this natural/civil rights continuum enumerates three distinct premises:

> First, that every civil right grows out of a natural right; or, in other words, is a natural right exchanged. Secondly, that civil power ... is made up of the aggregate of that class of the natural

rights of man, which becomes defective in the individual in point of power, and answers not his purpose, but when collected to a focus, becomes competent to the purpose of everyone. Thirdly, that the power produced from the aggregate of natural rights, imperfect in the power of the individual, cannot be applied to invade the natural rights which are retained in the individual, and in which the power to execute is as perfect as the right itself [276].

The views of the anti-registration forces seem easily to align with those expressed by Paine. Freedom of thought and belief are inviolate, and are so because they are natural rights within our power. Only those rights which *humans* (emphasis mine) are able to execute imperfectly are those that they can exchange, but Paine is careful to assure in the second premise that the value of the exchange is twofold. First, it allows our rights to be actuated in a context where they can do the most good. Second that most good is done for the most amount of people, since in Paine's view, all individuals at the behest of government give up the same natural rights, for the same amount of protection for those rights.

I emphasize *human* above because the powered superheroes of the Marvel Universe complicate these concepts of natural and civil rights. The idea that natural rights are limned by our power to execute them seems to understand power not so much as a biophysical capability but more so an organizational ability to achieve the optimum result of the right. A comic universe full of telepaths, clairvoyants, demigods, and Watchers seems to suggest a special category of rights for the super powered, and this is linked directly to Paine's view of moral virtue, its human failure, and *Civil War*'s focus on the identity of the heroes in the anti-registration camp. It is simplistic to say that what makes a hero is his or her power, but that is especially so in terms of their natural rights and the powers by which they are exercised. Heroes and superheroes have capacities that exceed those of the normal human, and thus seem to have a broader suite of natural rights which they do not need to exchange for civil rights because they have precisely the power to actuate them. Yet they willingly take their enhanced natural rights and exchange them for civil rights, thus making their contribution to society greater, in the Paine sense, and the burden on them heavier.

Two examples in *Civil War* bear this out. The first is the murder of Goliath by the Thor-clone. The murder sends shockwaves around the Marvel Universe, demonstrates the moral turpitude of the pro-registration forces (particularly Reed Richards), and exemplifies in contrast the very heart of the hero's moral virtue, namely that he rarely attempts to judge the worthiness of a life, merely their acts. Not coincidentally, Paine uses such judgment as the litmus test of the rights exchange: "A man, by natural right, has a right to judge his own cause; and so far as the right of the mind is concerned, he never surrenders it: but what availeth it him to judge, if he has not the power to redress?" (276). An exchange between S.H.I.E.L.D. Director Maria Hill and Iron Man offers a similar take:

> One of my agents was going over a report and he said to me—"You know all those people Norman Osborn killed as Green Goblin? When does it become Spider-Man's fault?" And I said, "Why would it be Spider-Man's fault?" He said, "Spider-Man's the one who has Osborn by the throat three times a year, but he never does what he has to do. He webs him up, they throw him in jail, then Osborn breaks out and he goes on another homicidal rampage" [Bendis 12].

Hill's typically cavalier response says it all. Spider-Man and all other superheroes have it in their power to redress; to refuse giving criminals over to the justice system, and by extension the government, and literally executing them as they see fit.[3]

And since for many heroes their public and secret identities are the price they pay for willingly exchanging rights they have it in their power to keep as superheroes, then it is not surprising that, as Battlestar asserts in *Civil War: Frontline*, it is identity that is the essential right contested in the Civil War.[4] Certainly Paine would see identity and selfhood, or perhaps self-understanding, as an inviolable intellectual right and thus one which, as he states in premise three above, the full weight of government cannot destroy by leveraging it against those rights which have been exchanged and civilized. By demanding that heroes and superheroes unmask, the pro-registration forces and the government that urges them on are violating the most fundamental rights any person or superhuman can hold: identity. This is liberty of conscience framed in a Marvel Universe way. The ability to maintain a secret identity is a function of conscience in that universe, and if there is any mark of the pro-registration camp's failure to live up even to its own claims of legitimate authority or governmental security, than it can be no greater than that one.

So, while no two superheroes seem to agree on why they oppose the SHRA, they don't ultimately need to in Paine's political philosophy. Collectively, they are contesting a law that violates both their civil and their natural rights, a kind of uber-law that decimates their societal role (as defined by Paine) and negates the freedom that such laws are meant to secure. Their resistance is as much justified as Paine's own was during the American Revolution, the war that rarely gets mentioned in the series.[5] And to a great degree, this clear violation of foundational rights, as portrayed in *Civil War*, inevitably returns to the foundational notions of common sense expressed in the series by Tony Stark and Thinker, especially when considered as the conflict between "a set of commonplace, collectively held assumptions, the quotidian assumptions of a pre-existing community of everyday people, or ... a basic human faculty that allowed individuals to make elemental judgments about ordinary matters in the first place, judgments that sometimes aligned themselves with conventional wisdom but more often than not did not" (Rosenfeld 633). Stark's original claim to a language of common sense shared with Peter Parker assumes the first definition yet consists of the latter, a destructive disconnect that disregards and decimates that which is a natural right (judgments about ordinary matters) and replaces it with the urge to go against "conventional wisdom," which for Stark is *his* vision for the Marvel Universe. It is a conversion of rights without the exchange, the protective guarantee, or the intercursive structure Paine insists upon for a healthy society and a functional government that resists tyranny. Thinker's claim for common sense encapsulates the individualism that feeds into the formation of society and which, for the anti-registration forces, is the last, best form of resistance to tyranny. It is the virtue of that resistance which makes for common sense: it empowers a natural right through a basic human faculty and resists the conventional wisdom espoused and normatively defined by Stark, S.H.I.E.L.D., and all government forces in *Civil War*. Nothing could be more elemental.

Notes

1. Nature here for Paine means the state of humanity before the formation of communities and community bonds that cohere into that which we call "society." Nature, then, is a "pure" opposite of society, where humanity has no obligation to sacrifice rights for a perceived greater good.
2. I take it as no coincidence that Christopher Nolan's trilogy of Batman movies also focuses on this idea of wants as they relate to superheroes and society.
3. The Punisher becomes an interesting counter argument to this, but it could be argued that he is a non-powered hero, certainly an anti-hero, and thus not subject to the argument.
4. While the shooting of Aunt May in *The Amazing Spider-Man* #538 suggests that the identities are often hidden for family safety, I hope to argue that there are deeper philosophical and political reasons such secrecy is necessary and unfairly targeted by the pro-registration forces.

5. The flashback panels in the "War Correspondence" issues of *Civil War: Frontline* run the gamut of American wartime experiences, from the Civil War to Vietnam, and even include an anecdote from the English Civil War (1642–1649). Yet, they show nothing from the revolutionary period, despite its centrality to American history and the rights discussed in *Civil War*. It is, to say the least, a curious omission.

Works Cited

Bendis, Brian Michael (writer), Alex Maleev (artist), and Dave Stewart (colorist). *New Avengers: Illuminati* (May 2008), Marvel Comics. Print.

Jenkins, Paul (writer), Ramon Bachs (penciller), and John Lucas (inker). "Embedded." *Civil War: Frontline* (Apr. 2007), Marvel Comics. Print.

Paine, Thomas. *The Complete Works of Thomas Paine*. Ed. Philip Foner. NewYork: The Citadel Press, 1945. 2 vols. Print.

Rosenfeld, Sophia. "Thomas Paine's Common Sense and Ours" *The William and Mary Quarterly*. Third Series. Volume 65, No.4 (Oct. 2008). 633–668. Print.

Straczynski, J. Michael (writer), Ron Garney (penciller), and Bill Reinhold (inker). *The Amazing Spider-Man #532–538* (May 2006–Feb. 2007), Marvel Comics. Print.

Straczynski, J. Michael and Dwayne McDuffie (writers), Mike McKone (penciler), and Andy Lanning, Kris Justice, and Cam Smith (Inkers). "We Used to Go to Hyperspace Just for Donuts." *Fantastic Four #542* (Jan. 2007), Marvel Comics. Print.

Thomas, John Rett. "Marvel Spotlight: Mark Millar/Steve McNiven." *Civil War Companion* (Jan. 2007), Marvel Comics. Print.

Competing Authorities in the Nation State of Marvel

Karl E. Martin

*"For so long, these masked marvels have saved lives and fought
off villainous threats. But now, questions are being asked.
Some demand to know who they are, what gives them the right—
the authority—they seem to possess"*
—Jim McCann, Opening Shot (12).

The conflict between Captain America and Iron Man over the Superhuman Registration Act (SHRA) and its enforcement, as it is played out in the Marvel comic event *Civil War*, is rooted in two competing visions of the nation-state. In a number of speeches and in his actions, Captain America makes the claim that the superheroes themselves, in fact all citizens, have the capacity and responsibility to make their own moral judgments. He further argues that no actions of the nation-state should be allowed to interfere with the individual's moral judgment. No moral authority can stand in judgment over the individual's conscience. In giving voice to this vision, Captain America becomes the embodiment of the American nation-state as it was envisioned by the Anglo-American, middle class nationalists who dreamed it into existence. Conversely, Iron Man argues that superheroes have too great a potential to disrupt society, creating chaos and destruction even when they do not intend to do so, to be allowed to determine right or wrong on their own; therefore, they should only be allowed to function under the authority and supervision of the nation-state and in service of an international economic structure that can best function when individual nation-states are politically stable. Significant irony accompanies the position each man takes. Captain America, in spite of his talk about the freedom of the individual, cannot imagine the actions of an American individual of good conscience that would conflict with the interests of his idealized nation-state; by so doing, he assumes a vision of the nation-state that may no longer exist in the minds of his fellow citizens. It certainly does not exist in the imagination of Tony Stark. Meanwhile Iron Man, who claims to be acting in the name of the nation-state, is actually serving the interests of a trans-national capitalist class whose interests transcend the nation-state. The creators of the comic event have created a world more complex than either of the primary heroes engaged in the struggle over the SHRA can truly negotiate. In doing so, they have provided readers of the *Civil War* comic event an opportunity to reflect on the complexity of two competing visions of the modern nation-state and the expression of moral authority possible within each vision.

Following the groundbreaking scholarship of Benedict Anderson's *Imagined Communities*, we can understand the modern nation-state as "an imagined political community— and imagined as both inherently limited and sovereign" (6). Anderson quotes Ernest Gellner as arguing, "Nationalism is not the awakening of nations to self-consciousness: it *invents* nations where they do not exist," and he adds emphasis to the term "invents" to argue that Gellner's term is misleading because it assumes that other communities exist that are not "invented" (6). Anderson prefers the terms "imagined" or "created." But the two theorists share a common central idea. The nation-state is not a "natural" entity. Anderson goes on to argue, "The nation is imagined as *limited* because even the largest of them ... has finite, if elastic, boundaries, beyond which lie other nations" (7). Middle class nationalists on both sides of the Atlantic in the eighteenth and nineteenth centuries "imagined" the nation-state as a "natural" political structure that corresponded to what was intended by nature and where rational males could live in a type of "state of nature" where they were in harmony with the world. In contrast, Anderson argues that the nation-state, like all political and cultural structures, is a construction of human beings and not a "natural" state.

Building on the scholarship of Anderson, historian David W. Noble has examined the development of these nation-states and argues, "Between 1770 and 1830, ... middle classes on both sides of the Atlantic were defining themselves as citizens rather than subjects." As citizens of various nations, "they could escape the artificial worlds of the aristocratic and peasant classes and achieve a classless and artless relationship with nature.... Paradoxically, the middle classes in each modern nation saw their individual and rational relationship with nature as exceptional" while viewing the cultures of other nation-states as artificially constructed. Americans, for example, would claim, "Their cultures had grown out of their national landscapes, those virgin lands whose naturalness and purity were protected by national political boundaries" (xxvi).

When Steve Rogers becomes Captain America as a result of an experiment to create super soldiers to defeat the Nazis in World War II, he becomes the embodiment of this ideal of the nation-state. As his name suggests and his origin story confirms, Captain America identifies with the American nation-state more fully than anyone else in the Marvel universe. "The government turned Rogers into their special costumed agent, Captain America, who represented traditional American ideals and the will to fight for them" (Saunders, Scott, March, and Dougall 18). Rogers becomes a citizen-soldier, a free and autonomous citizen who freely chooses to serve and sacrifice for his nation-state. Rogers volunteered to serve his country in any way he could, willingly submitting to the experiment that gave him his powers. Professor Reinstein, the scientist who created the serum used to transform Steve Rogers into Captain America, tells the observers of his experiment, "Observe this young man closely. Today he volunteered for army service, and was refused because of his unfit condition! His chance to serve his country seemed gone!" When the serum takes effect, the doctor tells Rogers, "We shall call you Captain America, son! Because, like you— America shall gain the strength and the will to safeguard our shores!" (Simon 6). Although many of Captain America's World War II adventures take place in Europe, like a good middle class nationalist, he is first commissioned to safeguard America's shores, the limited boundaries of the imagined nation-state. But of course America's involvement in World War II meant much more than simply protecting America's national boundaries and drew America into European affairs in ways that undercut the claim that American national identity was rooted solely in the landscape of the nation-state. Involvement in World War II urged Americans to embrace an internationalist agenda. Following World

War II, America's role in the world grew infinitely more complex and American politicians and cultural leaders had to negotiate their way through the Cold War and willingly assume an expanded role in the world. But Captain America spent much of this time frozen in the Arctic ice. When he emerged to join the Avengers, he brought with him an older and more straightforward understanding than his fellow superheroes of what it meant to exercise the role of a citizen in a modern nation-state.

When "artist Jack Kirby and writer Stan Lee ... revive Captain America for a new generation of readers" (Saunders, Scott, March, and Dougall 18) in 1964, Captain America is already a throwback not only to what now is commonly called the Greatest Generation but more importantly to a vision of the citizen rooted in the nineteenth century. His role in the *Civil War* comic event is informed by values even older than the values he developed while fighting in World War II.

Having missed much of the Cold War and the tumult of the early sixties, Cap is able to more innocently embody the values of heroism and patriotism than many of the other superheroes in the Marvel universe. Most notably, he does not suffer the angst of having acquired his powers through some freak accident of which he wanted no part like Spider-Man or the Hulk—the latter being the victim of an accident perpetrated by agents of the nation-state itself. As a consequence of his origins, Captain America does not deal with the moral ambiguity faced by many of his fellow superheroes in the Marvel universe. He is the dream of the Enlightenment philosophers—the free and independent citizen who voluntarily chooses to identify with the nation-state. The clarity of Cap's values plays a crucial part in his role in the *Civil War* series.

One aspect of Captain America's personality that clearly marks him as an anachronism, as a straight-forward hero in an ambiguous world, is his assumption that his fellow Americans share his values so completely that they do not even need to speak of them. The imagined community of Cap's world is one marked by a natural harmony of interests. Thus, if Americans are allowed to be free and exercise their will, they will all will the same thing, all embrace the same vision of the good. As rational citizens, they intuitively know the proper path to take, the moral actions to practice. Noble argues that by 1800, those who defined themselves as citizens of modern nation-states "imagined that modern nations would be rooted in timeless space" (1). The citizen of the modern nation-state, in this formulation, has stepped out of the flow of history so that he has been formed, not by the ebb and flow of that history, but by the timeless national landscape of his birth. Functioning from within this paradigm, Captain American assumes that the values he embraced would apply equally well in the twenty-first century as they did in 1941 or, for that matter, in the nineteenth century.

When the SHRA passes, Cap does not need to register his identity with the government, for his identity is known by all. As a rational citizen of a republic, Cap long ago made his choice and willingly endures its consequences. His transparency, of course, comes at a cost. He is constantly at risk of attack from his enemies and, consequently, cannot establish intimate connections with others without putting them at risk. Superheroes such as Spider-Man guarded their identities for so long in part to protect their intimate loved ones who were already in their lives when they became superheroes. Illustrating the risk registration poses for someone like Spider-Man, the creators of the comic event provide readers with one of the most heartbreaking losses of the *Civil War* storyline—Spider-Man's Aunt May. Cap avoids intimate relationships in part to keep those in his life safe, but in so doing he once again exhibits the characteristics of the idealized nation-state citizen, the male who is radically free to follow the dictates of his conscience without repercussions for others. Speaking of the dangers he faces, Cap tells Sharon, "I accept these things, not gladly, but I accept them, because Captain America is who I am and I understand what comes with that. But not everyone is like me. Not everyone is willing to risk what I have. Should they be denied the right to make that choice?" (Brubaker, *CA #22*, 14). Nick Fury, one of Cap's closest allies in the fight against the SHRA, echoes the primacy of the freedom of choice. He tells Bucky, "But havin' your government force you to work for them? Havin' 'em make your friends join up, and give up their secrets? Just 'cause they wanna make the world a better place? That ain't the America I bled for" (Brubaker, *CA #23*, 11). For both Cap and Fury, it seems, the freedom of choice supersedes even the final goal—a better world. Their imagined community is one in which, given the right to choose, the good man or woman will choose to serve and sacrifice. To force these heroes to serve violates the most basic of principles, for it treats citizens as subjects. By doing so, it violates the principle upon which the modern nation-state was founded—the rights of the citizen to define for himself his relationship with his nation.

The decision to make Captain America the primary spokesman for the opposition to the SHRA provides wonderful dramatic tension, for it places the very embodiment of the nation-state at odds with the current leadership of that nation-state. It places the heart and soul of the nation-state outside of its current embodiment. Therefore, the true identity of the nation is found outside of its legal definition of the appropriate citizen. By so doing, it harkens back to the foundational vision of the American nation-state (and the other modern nation-states who paradoxically believe themselves exceptional as well), that the cultural and political national landscape of a bounded territory produces the appropriate citizen for that nation-state and prepares him to live out his role as a citizen. Captain America does not need to learn anything from a source outside the national tradition.

The irony of Cap's position is mentioned throughout the comics that contribute to the *Civil War* saga. When Sharon argues that Cap is outside the law and that America was founded on the rule of law, Cap counters by arguing, "It was founded on breaking the law because the law was wrong" (Brubaker, *CA #22*, 15). Echoing the argument put forward by Henry David Thoreau in his "Civil Disobedience," Captain America argues for an intuitive sense that informs those who are free to make such judgments for themselves regarding what is right and wrong.[1]

He has found Thoreau's source of truth, the truth that informs all legal statutes rightly established, in the intuition of the reasoned citizen. Arguments regarding the merits of superhero registration do not resonate with Cap because they all involve coercion and thus violate the very first principle of the American republic and all other modern nation-states. When Captain America first breaks with the registration movement, he does so when Maria Hill, acting head of S.H.I.E.L.D., attempts to coerce him into service. Hill seems to assume that Cap will willingly hunt down those superheroes who resist registration. When he mentions the names of some who might resist, Hill asks, "So nobody you can't handle?" Cap clearly resists the suggestion that he can be coerced, and the confrontation escalates. When Hill suggests she is only asking Cap to "obey the will of the American people," Cap accuses her of playing politics: "Superheroes need to stay above that stuff or Washington starts telling us who the super-villains are." Hill responds by saying, "I thought super-villains were guys in masks who refused to obey the law" (Millar, *CW #1*, 22–23). The confrontation becomes violent as Cap is forced, he believes, to fight his way off the S.H.I.E.L.D. Helicarrier or submit to a moral authority he believes to be illegitimate.

Captain America's reaction to Hill's use of the term "the will of the American people" links this scene to the most significant justification Cap offers to explain his actions. The justification is also one that links Cap to an older formation of the American nation-state. In part six of "The War at Home," after Spider-Man has broken with Iron Man and joined the resistance, he asks Cap, "How does a man who is the country react when the country goes a different way?" (Straczynski, *ASM #537*, 12). What follows is an exceptionally long exposition for a graphic novel wherein Cap explains himself by quoting a passage from Mark Twain that was, he tells Spider-Man, so important to him that he memorized it as a young man. The quotation is from Twain's "Papers of the Adam Family" which Captain America quotes fairly accurately. Cap quotes Twain as asking, "In a republic, who is 'the country'? Is it the government which is for the moment in the saddle? Why, the government is merely a temporary servant; it cannot be its prerogative to determine what is right and what is wrong, and decide who is a patriot and who isn't. Its function is to obey orders, not originate them" (13). Cap goes on to quote Twain's critique of monarchies. "In a monarchy, the king and his family are the country; in a republic, it is the common voice of the people. Each of you, for himself, by himself and on his own responsibility, must speak" (14).[2] One would be hard-pressed to find another passage from American literature that more fully articulates the vision of the middle class nationalists who dreamed of an American nation-state formed out of the national landscape. The voice of the common people is enlivened by the national landscape in which they live.

Cap continues to quote Twain: "Each must for himself alone decide what is right and what is wrong, and which course is patriotic and which isn't. You cannot shirk this and be a man. To decide it against your convictions is to be an unqualified and inexcusable traitor, both to yourself and to your county, let men label you as they may" (Straczynski, *ASM #537*, 14). Twain's use of the phrase "and be a man" is instructive here, for it echoes the dream of the Anglo-American nationalists who founded the nation in the eighteenth century. The dream of the Enlightenment philosophers was that by stepping out of the time-bound, traditional, and profane cultures of Europe and coming to the "New World," white males could step out of the flow of history and its formation and into a sacred space of a pristine national culture where reason alone would be their guide.

In a striking panel, Captain America finishes quoting Twain while he is drawn as looming above Spider-Man who gazes up at him in an almost worshipful stance. Cap tells Spider-Man that this quotation from Twain is the final word:

> Doesn't matter what the press says. Doesn't matter what the politicians or the mobs say. Doesn't matter if the whole country decides that something wrong is right. This nation was founded on one principle above all else: The requirement that we stand up for what we believe, no matter the odds or the consequences. When the mob and the press and the whole world tell you to move, your job is to plant yourself like a tree beside the river of truth, and tell the whole world—"No, you move" [Straczynski, *ASM #537*, 15].

The quotation has great resonance, for it echoes both Psalm 1 where the blessed of God are described as being "like a tree firmly planted by streams of water" (*New American Standard Bible* Psalm 1:3) and Thoreau who wrote that those who seek the source of truth find where it feeds a lake or pool and, "gird up their loins once more, and continue their pilgrimage toward its fountainhead" (223).

Even when he surrenders and allows himself to be arrested—not as Captain America but unmasked as Steve Rogers—Cap does not surrender his core principles. He merely recognizes that the fight is costing his country too much, costing his fellow citizens too much.

He tells Falcon, "They're right. We're not fighting for the people anymore, Falcon. Look at us. We're just fighting" (Millar, *CW #7*, 21). In *Civil War: The Confession*, Captain America remains defiant to the end. In his last conversation with Iron Man, Captain America tells him, "We maintained the principles we swore to defend and protect. You sold your principles. You lost before you started" (Bendis, *CWTC* 20). He then goes on to again quote Twain, this time from "What Is Man?" He accuses Iron Man of bringing on the war and asks him, "I want to know what the hell made you think this was your job to do? Who made you the moral compass of us?" (21). Stark could easily answer Cap on his own terms, that he searched his conscience and determined that he was acting in the best interest of his nation, but that would not be fully consistent with Iron Man's vision of the nation-state. To explore Iron Man's motivation, we must revisit Noble's analysis of the development of the nation-state, for we will find that Tony Stark has a very different understanding of the world than does Steve Rogers. And in Stark's understanding, his actions make perfect sense.

While Captain America has clear and strongly expressed reservations regarding the SHRA, the creators of the comic event leave it to a minor character in the drama, Cable, to truly sound the alarm regarding the destructive potential of the passage and enforcement of the act. Cable speaks with the authority of "a soldier from the future" (Nicieza, *Cable and Deadpool #31*, 2) and tells Cap, "I know this goes beyond secret identities and registration. This will grow into the use of super-humans as an organized, totalitarian military patrol" (Nicieza, *Cable and Deadpool #30*, 14). Cable even confronts the United States President with his warning. As a follow-up to the SHRA, the president has proposed a Fifty States Initiative that will place superheroes throughout the nation in a policing capacity. Cable tells the president that "the Fifty States Initiative will pave the road toward a totalitarian state and a real Civil War—one whose effects on super-humans will engulf all American civilians—and ultimately the world" (Nicieza, *Cable and Deadpool #31*, 16). Cable's warning cannot be easily dismissed, yet to keep Iron Man from becoming nothing but a one dimensional villain, he must be presented as having a motivation for his support of the SHRA that considers the risk of the future Cable predicts yet considers the risk worth taking. Iron Man's motivation is made coherent when his contrasting vision of the nation-state is considered.

David W. Noble argues that World War II was a watershed event for the bourgeois elites who had claimed that the national landscapes of their individual nation-states allowed citizens to develop as distinctive, even exceptional, individuals. Prior to the war, they had maintained a belief in a certain level of cultural isolationism. The nation was treated as a bounded, sacred space. "The bourgeois elites in the United States and in the other major industrial nations converted during the 1940s from a self-conscious isolation to a self-conscious internationalism. They converted from seeing their nations as expressions of the state of nature to seeing the international marketplace as the state of nature" (xxvii). In light of Noble's analysis, we can examine the extent to which Tony Stark—often described as a "billionaire industrialist"—sees the transition to the protection of an international marketplace and all that transition entails as natural and inevitable while Captain America finds it to be a dangerous abandonment of national ideals.

As mentioned above, if he wanted to, Iron Man could certainly justify his actions employing the same rhetoric as Captain America. Like Cap, Iron Man is a loyal American who has searched his conscience and determined where he must stand. He sums up his position in a public service announcement he records in support of the SHRA. After the devastation at Stamford, the public has lost trust in their heroes. "But the very people we're pledged to serve no longer trust us," Iron Man proclaims. "Now, we desperately seek an opportunity to regain a measure of that trust—registration gives us that opportunity" (Knauf and Knauf 8). What is fascinating then is how seldom Iron Man resorts to the language so natural to Captain America. His use of an alternative rhetoric, I would argue, is rooted in his competing vision of the role of the nation-state. Unlike Captain America, he has converted to internationalism, so even when he employs nationalistic rhetoric, he is employing it to a very different end.

In a fascinating backstory related in the stand-alone issue *New Avengers: Illuminati*, Iron Man's conversion to internationalism is pushed back to the years following World War II. Iron Man has gathered Dr. Strange, Dr. Xavier, Reed Richards, Black Bolt, Prince Namor, and Black Panther to a secret meeting. In a plot development made plausible by the intergalactic nature of the Marvel universe, Iron Man makes reference to the Kree and the Skrull using the earth as a battleground. In the light of such a threat, neither individual heroes nor heroes closely associated with a single nation-state will be sufficient to defend the earth. Iron Man tells his colleagues: "If the earth is attacked again ... when the earth is attacked again we're the only ones who can defend it. There is no one else. No army is ready. So, to the rest of the universe we're law enforcement of this planet" (Bendis, *NAI* 4). In Iron Man's logic, we find the rhetoric employed by the academic historians Noble analyzes who convert from nationalism to internationalism following World War II. The international marketplace is a natural space whose development was inevitable—it is as natural as the earth itself. The economic elites of every nation-state rely on the stability of the international marketplace to ensure their well being, yet no single nation-state is powerful enough to secure the marketplace's freedom. In fact, individual nation-states seeking their own security above all else pose the greatest threat to the stability of the international marketplace.[3]

The inevitability—and therefore the naturalness—of the emerging international marketplace is further supported by two minor storylines in the comic event. In *CWTC*, Iron Man reveals his motivation while talking to Captain America's lifeless body. He relates that he once traveled back in time while doing battle with Dr. Doom to the time of King Arthur. In the midst of this wild adventure, he was given a glimpse of the future and saw a world where superheroes were battling one another (Bendis, *CWTC* 6–8). All of the behind-the-scenes maneuvering Iron Man has been doing to ensure the passage of the SHRA has been informed by this vision of a bleak future he witnessed. A similar vision informs the actions of Reed Richards (whose actions seem even more difficult to accept at times than do the actions of Iron Man). In *Fantastic Four #542*, Richards claims that his practice of "psychohistory" (adapted from Isaac Asimov's *Foundation*) allows him to use mathematical modeling to predict the future. His work convinces him of a coming cataclysm if the SHRA is not passed and an international order established (McDuffie 20–23). No convincing counter argument to these positions taken by Stark and Richards are offered to readers of *Civil War*, yet their position is resisted by many of the most compelling characters in the saga.

Iron Man's conviction that an international space must be created also helps explain his willingness to work so manipulatively behind the scenes. Captain America confesses to Sharon, "And while I love my country, I don't trust many politicians. Not when they're having their strings pulled by corporate donors. And not when they're willing to trade freedom for security" (Brubaker, *CA #22*, 15). In contrast to Cap's position, Iron Man is more than willing to cooperate with anyone he believes will help him achieve his final goal. He works not only with politicians but with such notorious Marvel villains as the Green Goblin and Kingpin, with the apparent clone of Thor, and with the entire Thunderbolt outfit (all of whom were once villains). All of these compromises are necessary, for, as Tony Stark tells Peter Parker, "we live in a time when everyone has had to make sacrifices of their privacy. Wiretaps. Increased surveillance. Random searches at airports. Did you think we would be immune to that for long? After what happened at Stamford?" (Straczynski, *ASM #532*, 12). It is not until the very end of the *Frontline* series that readers get a complete picture of just how much Stark has worked to manipulate the entire process.

Yet Stark's manipulations are ultimately judged appropriate, perhaps even heroic by journalists Sally Floyd and Ben Urich, arguably the most objective and toughest critics of all those involved in the conflict of the passage and enforcement of the SHRA. In their final interview with Tony Stark, Floyd and Urich confront Stark with a story they promise they will never print. They know Stark has manipulated all of the events, waiting for the inevitable chaotic incident to push forward the SHRA. He has used the round up of unregistered superheroes as a justification for building the prison in the Negative Zone that will eventually house super-villains and terrorists who would disrupt the stability of the international marketplace. He has even pushed the United States to the brink of war with Prince Namor's Atlantis in order to rally the nation-state together against a common foe to further convince his fellow citizens of the need for international alliances. Floyd tells Stark, "You sacrificed your status as a friend, colleague and hero for the greater good of the country" (Jenkins, *CWFL #11*, 21). Stark does not deny any of what Floyd tells him. His only reaction is to slump to the floor weeping at the extent of the required sacrifice. But one last problem remains—Floyd claims Stark did all that he did "for the greater good of the country." If this is true, "country" does not mean for Stark what it does to Captain America. Indeed, while Stark employs the rhetoric of nation-state interests, he actually acts on behalf of the sacred international marketplace.

A Federal Marshall tells Speedball, the minor figure most responsible for the disaster at Stamford, that the SHRA has been signed into law. Speedball is offered the following deal: "Our offer is as follows: That you register with local and federal officials as a costumed vigilante and that you subsequently work for S.H.I.E.L.D., following our specific directives. You will assist in the training of S.H.I.E.L.D. agents to track and subdue unregistered individuals. You will do so willingly, and in good faith, or you will be seen in contempt of this agreement" (Jenkins, *CWFL #2*, 18). The odd aspect of this deal is the complex relationship between the authority of the nation-state and the authority of S.H.I.E.L.D. as an international organization. Speedball is being disciplined by the nation-state but will be forced to serve the multi-national organization. This international project reflects Iron Man's vision.

The tension between the authority of the nation-state and the authority of international entities is also evident when Iron Man takes Spider-Man on a tour of the Negative Zone prison. Iron Man tells him, "This place is not on American soil. American laws don't touch here. American lawyers don't come here" (Straczynski, *ASM #535*, 12). Yet the prison incarcerates those deemed criminals by an act of the United States Congress signed into law by the president. The authority of the nation-state has been compromised, turned over, in fact, to an international body that Stark will eventually lead because the threats to the international community—where international capitalism is practiced—is too fragile to be protected by any single nation-state. In the standalone book *Civil War: The Initiative*, we are told, "Now, the Civil War is over, and Tony Stark has been named the Director of S.H.I.E.L.D., the international peacekeeping force. He has set into motion The Initiative, a plan for training and policing superheroes in this brave new world" (Bendis and Ellis 2).

For Captain America, his worst nightmare has come true—the freedom of the superhero as super citizen in a republic has been compromised. The individual is no longer left to determine for himself or herself the moral course of action. Captain America voices his fears well when he says, "They want superheroes to be controlled by the government. They want us to be puppets to a corporate shill structure, like everything else on the planet. They don't see that we're all that's left keeping them truly protected and free" (Bendis, *NA #21*, 4). Iron Man's perspective could not be more different. He tells his fellow members of the Illuminati, "Anyone with powers—anyone in costume—any mutant—any of our kind is going to be required by law to reveal themselves to the United States government. In return, the registered hero will be given a job as a guard in the new S.H.I.E.L.D. world security force. You will still be a superhero but you'll have to answer to someone. Refusing to do so will be a crime" (26). Iron Man may not be thrilled at this development, but he deems it necessary.

At the end of the saga, Captain America is apparently dead and Iron Man is an emotional wreck because of the price he has paid to bring about what he considers to be a necessary change in the world of superheroes. The reader is left to contemplate the fate of the Marvel universe and our own world. The values associated with a limited and clearly demarcated nation-state seem passé. The evolution from a world dominated by powerful nation-states to a world dominated by somewhat secretive international authority figures appears complete, and it seems necessary. Iron Man may be despondent because of the actions he has taken, but all alternative paths seem closed. Will the internationalist agenda Tony Stark helps put into place bring American citizens and others around the globe the blend of security and freedom they crave? Like all great works of art, the *Civil War* comic event poses a penetrating question it does not answer. We are left to contemplate the options for ourselves as we consider whether the modern nation-state has given way to an internationalist capitalist marketplace. But one thing seems disturbingly clear—unlike the Marvel universe, our world is not being watched over by superheroes.

Notes

1. The creators nicely contrast Cap's position with the position of Reed Richards who argues directly against civil disobedience. When Sue argues that the SHRA is wrong, Reed tells her, "Fine. Then change it. But until you can do that, we obey it. That's what we do, remember?" (Straczynski, *FF #540*, 6).

2. As if to highlight the arbitrary nature of authority under a monarch, the creators of *Civil War* open *Wolverine #45* with this quotation from Michel Foucault, "The king [shall] take revenge for an affront to his very person. The right to punish, therefore, is an aspect of the sovereign's right to make war on his enemies" (Guggenheim 2). In the nation-states as they are understood by Captain America and Wolverine, this right to punish has been transferred to the moral superhero who clearly has the right on his or her side.

3. In the *Civil War* comic event, the Black Panther story line best illustrates the tension between the interests of a truly independent nation-state and the development of an international marketplace. Resisting the expansion of an international marketplace, Black Panther announces during a visit to the United States, "The threat is there whether we want it or not. I would rather stop it here [within the borders of the United States] before the United States starts expanding their brand of 'public safety' across the globe" (Hudlin 10).

Works Cited

Anderson, Benedict. *Imagined Communities: Reflections on the Origin and Spread of Nationalism*. Rev. ed. New York: Verso, 1991. Print.

Bendis, Brian Michael (writer), Howard Chaykin (artist), and Dave Stewart (color artist). "New Avengers: Disassembled: Part One." *New Avengers #21* (June 2006), Marvel Comics. Web. 18 July 2014.

Bendis, Brian Michael (writer), Alex Maleev (artist), and Jose Villarrubia (color artist). "Civil War: The Confession." *Civil War* (Nov. 2007), Marvel Comics. Web. 18 July 2014.
Bendis, Brian Michael (writer), Steve McNiven (penciler), and Dexter Vines (inker). "Illuminati." *The New Avengers* (Mar. 2006), Marvel Comics. Web. 18 July 2014.
Bendis, Brian Michael, Warren Ellis (writers), and Marc Silvestri (penciler). "The Initiative." *Civil War* (Mar. 2007), Marvel Comics. Web. 18 July 2014.
Brubaker, Ed (writer), Mike Perkins (art), and Frank D'Armata (color art). "The Drums of War." *Captain America #22* (Sept. 2006), Marvel Comics. Web. 18 July 2014.
_____. "The Drums of War, Part Two." *Captain America #23* (Oct. 2006), Marvel Comics. Web. 18 July 2014.
Guggenheim, Marc (writer), Humberto Ramos (penciler), and Carlos Cuevas (inker). "Vengeance." *Wolverine #45* (Aug. 2006), Marvel Comics. Web. 21 July 2014.
Holy Bible (New American Standard Bible. Grand Rapids: Zondervan, 1995.
Hudlin, Reginold (writer), Koi Turnbull (penciler), and Don Ho (inker). "War Crimes: Part One." *Black Panther #23* (Dec. 2006), Marvel Comics. Web. 21 July 2014.
Jenkins, Paul (writer), Ramon Bachs (penciler), and John Lucas (inker). "Embedded: Part Two." *Front Line #2* (June 2006), Marvel Comics. Web. 18 July 2014.
_____. "Embedded: Part Eleven." *Front Line #11* (Feb. 2007), Marvel Comics. Web. 18 July 2014.
Knauf, Daniel, Charles Knauf (writers), Patrick Zircher (penciler), and Scott Hanna (inker). "Civil War." *Iron Man #13* (Nov. 2006), Marvel Comics. Web. 18 July 2014.
McCann, Jim (writer). *Opening Shot: Sketchbook* (May 2006), Marvel Comics. Web. 18 July 2014.
McDuffie, Dwayne (writer), Mike McKone (penciler), and Andy Lanning and Cam Smith (inkers). "We Used to Go to Hyperspace Just for Donuts." *Fantastic Four #542* (Jan. 2007), Marvel Comics. Web. 18 July 2014.
Millar, Mark (writer), Steve McNiven (penciler), and Dexter Vines (inker). "Civil War." *Civil War #1* (May 2006), Marvel Comics. Web. 18 July 2014.
_____. "Civil War." *Civil War #7* (Feb. 2007), Marvel Comics. Web. 18 July 2014.
Nicieza, Fabian (writer), Staz Johnson (penciler), and Klaus Janson (inker). "Casualties of War." *Cable & Deadpool #31* (Aug. 2006), Marvel Comics. Web. 18 July 2014.
_____. "The Hero Hunter." *Cable & Deadpool #30* (July 2006), Marvel Comics. Web. 18 July 2014.
Noble, David W. *Death of a Nation: American Culture and the End of Exceptionalism*. Minneapolis: University of Minnesota Press, 2002. Print.
Saunders, Catherine, Heather Scott, Julia March, and Alastair Dougall, eds. *Marvel Chronicle: A Year by Year History*. New York: DK, 2008. Print.
Simon, Joe (writer), and Jack Kirby (inker). "Meet Captain America." *Captain America #1* (March 1941), Marvel Comics. Web. 18 July 2014.
Straczynski, J. Michael (writer), Ron Garney (penciler), and Bill Reinhold (inker). "The War at Home: Part One." *The Amazing Spider-Man #532* (May 2006), Marvel Comics. Web. 18 July 2014.
_____. "The War at Home: Part Four." *The Amazing Spider-Man #535* (Sept. 2006), Marvel Comics. Web. 18 July 2014.
_____. "The War at Home: Part Six." *The Amazing Spider-Man #537* (Jan. 2007), Marvel Comics. Web. 18 July 2014.
Straczynski, J. Michael (writer), Mike McCone (penciler), and Andy Lanning and Cam Smith (inkers). "Some Words Can Never Be Taken Back." *Fantastic Four #540* (Oct. 2006), Marvel Comics. Web. 21 July 2014.
Thoreau, Henry David. *Collected Essays and Poems*. New York: Library of America, 2001. Print.
Twain, Mark. *Collected Tales, Sketches, Speeches, & Essays 1891–1910*. New York: Library of America, 1992. Print.
_____. *Letters from the Earth*. Ed. Bernard Devoto. New York: Harper and Row, 1962. Print.

Iron Curtain Man versus Captain American Exceptionalism: World War II and Cold War Nostalgia in the Age of Terror

Kathleen McClancy

The Marvel Universe's 2006–7 *Civil War* event begins when a super-human battle destroys the town of Stamford, Connecticut. This level of destruction is nothing new for comic books; splash pages predictably feature large-scale property damage in mainstream superhero titles. What makes this battle exceptional is that the damage is not limited to property. Hundreds of civilians also lose their lives, including 60 school children. The catastrophe leads to an outcry for better regulation and accountability of super-humans, and in short order, the United States passes the Superhuman Registration Act (SHRA), a law requiring any person with super-human abilities to register their names with the government. This new law sparks the eponymous war between superhero factions, as many superheroes refuse to comply with a law they consider to be a violation of their civil rights and invasion of their privacy. The story is an obvious allegory for the government policies of the "War on Terror" and to public debates over the USA PATRIOT Act; Captain America's unregistered forces are considered dangerous terrorists by the pro-registration group led by Iron Man, while even some within Iron Man's camp fear the Act's corresponding increase in government surveillance and control over their personal lives. But beyond the 21st century parallels, the narrative also echoes concerns from periods of 20th century American history. Captain America refuses to conform to the Act because of his own experiences during World War II; he sees this increase in government power as a step toward fascism. Iron Man, on the other hand, has a much more *realpolitik* view of the position of these super-humans of mass destruction that reflects the character's Cold War origins. In effect, the battle between these two characters becomes a conflict between ideologies, and *Civil War* becomes a debate between two different approaches to framing the War on Terror through America's recent past.

That a mass-market comic book crossover[1] would echo this tension between two competing nostalgic narrative frames for the War on Terror should come as no surprise; in the wake of September 11, American culture has struggled to find an adequate narrative to describe this new kind of war, and the two most common frameworks in use have come from the U.S.'s two most defining 20th century conflicts. When the Civil War ends with

Iron Man victorious, it replicates the eventual domination of a Cold War framing narrative over the earlier positioning of the September 11 attacks as a modernized version of Pearl Harbor. However, while the story rejects Captain America's naïve refusal to move beyond a simplistic, good-versus-evil, World War II understanding of the War on Terror, *Civil War* also challenges the appropriateness of the Cold War as a model. Iron Man explains his actions throughout the storyline by relying on the rhetoric of mutually assured destruction, but his insistence on viewing the situation through a Cold War lens nearly causes a cataclysm itself when he unleashes his own WMD, a clone of the Norse god Thor. *Civil War* thus illustrates how using any nostalgic frame, whether from World War II or the Cold War, as a model for the War on Terror is not only inappropriate but dangerous.

In the immediate aftermath of the attacks on the World Trade Center and the Pentagon, the most common comparison drawn by news media and political sources was to Pearl Harbor. Peter Jennings first made the analogy on ABC News shortly after the collapse of the first tower ("Special Report"); that afternoon, Senator Christopher Dodd also referenced Pearl Harbor, and the comparison became standard by that evening (Reynolds and Barnett 93). While this comparison is not particularly apt in literal terms—Pearl Harbor was an attack on military bases undertaken by a nation-state as a result of a crippling embargo, while September 11 was an attack on largely civilian populations undertaken by a terrorist group driven by ideological concerns—it is appropriate in emotional terms, given both the suddenness of the attack and its scale. Furthermore, the images from the attacks—the footage of the burning and then collapsing Towers, shown in a continual loop on what seemed to be every single television station—encouraged the idea that the attacks were both catastrophic and ubiquitous, not an isolated incident but the beginning of a war. Comparing the attacks to the nostalgic memory of Pearl Harbor as a symbol motivated a narrative of American innocence and of American greatness while also suggesting that they were only the opening salvo of a much longer fight. Locating the attacks as a repetition of Pearl Harbor rewrote them as a catalyst for American greatness instead of just a tragedy.

This analogy for the attacks soon broadened beyond Pearl Harbor, and the "Global War on Terror" (GWOT) came to be described in terms lifted from the mythology of World War II as a whole. Two days after the attacks, conservative columnist Ann Coulter wrote a *National Review* editorial explicitly describing both the attacks and her suggested response in world war terms, comparing terrorists to the Wehrmacht and concluding: "We weren't punctilious about locating and punishing only Hitler and his top officers. We carpet-bombed German cities; we killed civilians. That's war. And this is war." And in his 2002 State of the Union address, President Bush famously employed the term "Axis of Evil" to refer to three countries he described as supporting and promoting terrorism, in the process referencing World War II through the choice of the word "Axis" while transposing the characterization of World War II as a conflict of good versus evil to the contemporary fight against terrorism. Nazis are axiomatically evil in American culture; if the terrorists that the U.S. was fighting were as evil as Nazis, there could be no question that the U.S. was fighting the good fight.[2]

But this black and white concept of World War II itself depends upon the discourse of American Exceptionalism that has permeated U.S. culture since its founding. World War II was much more complicated than a simple conflict between white hats and black hats. As Coulter herself points out, the U.S. carpet-bombed German cities and killed civilians during that war, and not all those civilians were Nazis; the U.S. carpet-bombed Japanese cities as well, and those Japanese were not Nazis at all. The iconography of World War II as the greatest generation fighting the greatest fight eliminates these complexities to produce a tale of an inherently good nation fighting to defend a specifically American concept of freedom from the tyranny of evil men. This simplification is grounded in the tradition of American Exceptionalism. As Godfrey Hodgson defines it: "The core of this belief is the idea that the United States is not just the richest and most powerful of the world's more than two hundred states but is also politically and morally exceptional" (10). In fact, America is morally exceptional specifically because of its politics: "'[O]nly in America,' it was claimed, did men believe that government must always have the consent of the governed; only in America did a political culture of rights predominate" (Hodgson 12). World War II becomes a battle to protect the world from the oppression of Nazis; more specifically, to protect the rights and freedoms of the world from the oppression of German fascism, the opposite of the American "culture of rights." This campaign is not conceived of as an offensive one—to impose American freedoms on an unwilling population would itself be a violation of the concept of individual sovereignty that forms the backbone of this exceptionalist formulation—but a defensive one. Pearl Harbor is important in this characterization of World War II because it proves that the U.S. only entered the war as a defensive measure; the September 11 attacks serve the same purpose of justifying the American entry into GWOT. And the continuing prosecution of both wars is framed as a moral imperative because of the United States' special role as the defender of freedom and justice *for all*—not just Americans.

If there is any costumed hero who most embodies the ideals of American Exceptionalism, it is Captain America. Jason Dittmer has pointed out that superheroes in general not only reflect but help construct the exceptionalist discourse, but Cap's specific link to United States ideology puts him in a particularly visible role; he is what Dittmer calls a nationalist superhero (*Captain America* 10). Matthew Costello goes so far as to call him "an avatar of American ideology" (13). Captain America was not only created by the U.S. government in a super-soldier experiment; in his first years he fought for and at the orders of the U.S. government, battling Nazis at home and abroad throughout World War II. And while Cap has since distanced himself from politics, refusing to align himself with any specific government and even at two points refusing his role as American symbol entirely, he remains canonically the embodiment of American ideals, at least as defined by the editor of *Captain America* #131: "individual freedom, individual responsibility, moral sensitivity, integrity, and a willingness to fight for what is right" (qtd. in Hayton and Albright 18). Regardless of what the United States may do, Captain America always embodies and embraces the ideals at the heart of American Exceptionalism.

But Cap is not the symbol of just any vision of America; in fact, Captain America is defined by World War II, and it is his link to this war specifically that allows him such moral purity. Other superheroes have had the specifics of their origin story modified to reflect the passage of time in other versions or media; the cinematic Iron Man first builds his armor in Afghanistan, rather than Vietnam, and Spider-Man's spider is genetically, rather than radioactively, altered. But Captain America is always and forever a product of the American fight against Nazism. Because of the special status of World War II as the most moral of all American conflicts, Cap's origin in that war allows him to become a symbol of the best aspects of American culture. As Cynthia Weber points out: "World War II ... is a rich vein of past moral certainties that the United States mines at moments of its greatest moral uncertainty" (29). By being inextricably associated with that war, Captain America thus becomes the voice of a better past: he is the symbol of what America should be, regardless of what it actually is at any given moment. And as the cultural memory of World War II has evolved into the pinnacle of American heroism and moral greatness, so has Captain America; while 1940s Cap was not above shooting to kill—it was war, after all—today's Cap relies solely on his S.H.I.E.L.D., itself proof of the protective rather than aggressive nature of American power (Dittmer, "Retconning America" 29).

Given Cap's grounding in individual liberty, his response to the proposal of the Superhuman Registration Act should come as no surprise. Throughout the *Civil War* storyline, he continually views the SHRA as well as the actions of S.H.I.E.L.D.[3] through a World War II lens: for Cap, the situation is black and white, and his determination to protect individual freedoms over the needs of the state puts him squarely on the side of the angels and against the SHRA. But it is not just Cap's World War II history that leads him to this view; the plot itself forces Cap into a World War II narrative by introducing the SHRA to him through a Pearl Harbor frame. When Maria Hill, the director of S.H.I.E.L.D. at the time, first discusses the proposed SHRA with the Captain, she gives him little to no chance to respond before launching a sneak attack against him. Hill first asks Cap if he thinks other superheroes will accept the law; Cap tries to remain somewhat neutral, responding: "I don't think that's for me to *judge*" (Millar, *Civil War #1*, 21). When Cap finally does offer his opinion—that he believes the SHRA will cause a superhero civil war—Hill makes clear that she expects Cap to lead the team that will arrest super-humans who refuse to register. Cap objects, not to the law itself at this point, but only to Hill's expectation that he will become the law's primary agent; immediately a group of S.H.I.E.L.D. troops, who seem to appear from nowhere, surround Cap and raise their weapons.

The panel design here emphasizes the surprise nature of this attack. With a few exceptions, the entire confrontation up until the appearance of S.H.I.E.L.D. troops is presented in a series of panels featuring extreme close-ups of Hill and Cap; most of these panels are thin and horizontal, most of them depict Hill or Cap only, and most of them contain only one speech balloon with one line of dialogue. While the limiting of one line to a panel, paired with the alternating close-ups of Hill and Cap, would seem to lend itself to an adaptation of a cinematic shot-reverse-shot style, the actual panels are much more disorienting; angles are askew, backgrounds are stylized and unclear, and spatial relationships are not consistent. The effect is to build tension while also suggesting that something is seriously wrong. When the S.H.I.E.L.D. troops suddenly appear, they do so in the bottom panel on the page; this panel is also thin and horizontal, but it is a long shot, essentially revealing the S.H.I.E.L.D. troops who were out of frame in the previous panels. The build-up gives absolutely no warning that these troops are even in the room—they sneak up on the reader, as well as Cap—while at the same time making clear what exactly was so wrong with the situation—Captain America has been betrayed. As a result, the actions of S.H.I.E.L.D. here are visually marked as both sudden and corrupt. When Cap defends himself against S.H.I.E.L.D. forces, he is doing no more and no less than the United States after Pearl Harbor: defending himself from an unwarranted and cowardly sneak attack.

Furthermore, the coloring of these panels emphasizes that the conflict is about the nature of America itself; the palette is limited to red, white and blue throughout, as the colors of Cap's uniform seem to take over the ten-page sequence. Cap is consistently colored in blue tones mimicking the blue of his mask and uniform shoulders, while Hill is surrounded by red that reflects off her black uniform and echoes the blush of her cheeks. As a result, the two are definitively contrasted even as the flag itself seems split into its component parts. America is literally divided on the page here. In addition, the dialogue makes clear that the central question dividing America is a conceptual one; while Hill envisions a country founded on the rule of law, Cap considers America to be something above humanity's politics:

> CAP: You're asking me to arrest people who risk their lives for this country every day of the week.
> HILL: No, I'm asking you to obey the will of the American people, Captain.
> CAP: Don't play *politics* with *me*, Hill. Super heroes need to stay *above* that stuff or Washington starts telling us who the *super-villains* are.
> HILL: I thought super-villains were guys in masks who refused to obey *the law* [Millar, *Civil War #1*, 23].

With the final line, the surrounding S.H.I.E.L.D. agents are revealed in the act of cocking their weapons; the sound effect "chik-chak" litters the panel. Captain America is forced to fight to defend his own freedom as well as the freedom of others because Hill and S.H.I.E.L.D. have left him no choice, and their attempt to impose their own will on him by forcing him to enforce their law indicates both to Cap and to the reader the totalitarianism at the heart of their policy. Furthermore, the fact that Hill is trying to arrest Cap for breaking a law that *isn't even actually a law yet*—for simply *expressing his reservations about the law*—proves her willingness to sacrifice the rights of the individual for the wishes of the state. Once the law is passed, Cap justifies his continued resistance to the SHRA through the American Exceptionalist doctrine of the freedom of the individual. When he explains his rebellion to his sometime girlfriend Sharon Carter, he even quotes Ben Franklin and Thomas Paine to defend his actions, saying: "Those who expect to reap the *blessings* of freedom must undergo the fatigue of *supporting* it" (Brubaker 15). He thus explicitly links his determination to protect individual freedoms to that of the founding fathers. Cap's decision to fight against the American government is itself justified through an appeal to an overarching concept of the greatness of the ideal of "America" itself. If *Civil War* is an analogy for policy debates after September 11, both Captain America's origins in World War II and his reliance on the doctrine of American Exceptionalism tie his resistance to the SHRA (and by analogy, real-world resistance to the PATRIOT act) to a World War II approach to the policy of the War on Terror.

However, the attempt to view the War on Terror through World War II cannot last, for Captain America or for American society. The World War II model for GWOT proved to be temporary; despite its seeming ubiquity immediately after September 11, the parallels between the two wars were too weak to remain stable. After all, the GWOT is not a war against a nation-state, nor is it fought through conventional armies; Osama bin Laden may have been the poster child for global terrorism, but the war was not won through his death, and terrorism is not localized in the same way that Nazism was localized in Hitler. Captain America cannot punch terrorism, and World War II methods prove ineffective in his battle against the SHRA. As a result, Cap is forced to compromise his morality, perhaps most obviously in his brief admission of the Punisher to his anti–SHRA force, the Secret Avengers.

The Punisher character began his Marvel career as a villain, not a hero, and since his debut has oscillated between the two roles. A Vietnam veteran, he returns home from war only to see his entire family slaughtered by the mafia; as a result, he dedicates himself to the eradication of criminals. But what makes the Punisher an antihero is that he does not simply arrest these criminals—he executes them. As a result, the character has been written as everything from simply determined to completely psychotic, and most Marvel superheroes consider him a menace. When the Punisher appears in the Secret Avengers' headquarters, Cap's teammates certainly do not welcome him; one essentially compares the Punisher to Hannibal Lecter, and another asks: "*Please* tell me we aren't so far gone that we're signing up *the Punisher*?" (Millar, *Civil War #5*, 18). But the Punisher convinces Cap to accept his help, arguing specifically that Cap's World War II methods are ineffective in the present; he tells Cap: "No disrespect, sir. But they're not fighting *your war*, and *your ways* won't work anymore" (Fraction 2). By allowing a cold-blooded murderer onto his team, one whom Marvel has consistently coded as morally ambiguous, Cap abandons his World War II framework and thus loses the unquestionability of the rightness of his cause.[4] He is no longer fighting a just and certain war; as he eventually tells Iron Man during the climactic battle of the crossover, he is now "fighting dirty" (Millar, *Civil War #7*, 14). The black and white moral framework of the myth of World War II does not fit the War on Terror, and the murkiness of this war's ethics undermine the grounding of Captain America's strength in the image of America as a shining city on a hill.

Ironically, the Punisher proves to be a problem for the Secret Avengers not because he is too morally flexible, but because he is too morally rigid. As the civil war nears its climax, Cap is approached by a group of super-villains who offer their help, pointing out that the SHRA hurts them as much as anyone. When the Punisher overhears this conversation, he immediately breaks into the meeting and shoots the super-villains dead. His own moral code will not allow a criminal to go unpunished, regardless of the consequences. The Punisher truly sees the world in black and white terms, unlike Cap, whose world view, as the Punisher himself remarks, is red, white and blue (Fraction 3).[5] The Punisher thus demonstrates the dangers of adhering to this morally certain position during the Civil War/GWOT. If Captain America wants to win the war, he must compromise his moral code, even though doing so undermines his own belief in inherent American superiority; if he maintains his moral code, refusing to admit any ambiguity, he risks becoming the Punisher, a psychotic murderer. Spider-Man points out the similarity between the two characters, saying: "Cap's probably the reason [the Punisher] went to Vietnam. Same guy, different war" (Millar, *Civil War #6*, 14). Cap's moral absoluteness is only appropriate within a nostalgic framework of the Greatest Generation; moved to the Cold War, moved to the War on Terror, it becomes a sign of mental illness.

In the end, Captain America is not beaten by pro-registration forces: he capitulates, surrendering himself unconditionally. He does so not because he is suddenly convinced of the rightness of the SHRA's cause but because he has lost faith in the rightness of his own. When Cap is on the verge of delivering the decisive blow to Iron Man in the superheroes' final battle, he is swarmed by a group of non-powered civilians—again appearing out of nowhere—who force him to recognize the devastation this battle, and this war, have caused the very people Cap is supposedly protecting. The first panel on the page shows a close-up of Cap raising his shield to strike; the next panel, twice the size of the first, shows Cap suddenly mobbed by what looks to be a fireman, two security guards, and three other civilians in unidentifiable blue uniforms. Cap is attacked by the legitimate keepers of the peace.[6] When Cap asks them to let him go, explaining that he does not want to hurt them, one of the civilians responds: "It's a little late for that, man!" (Millar, *Civil War #7*, 19). Turning the page reveals a half-page panel showing an overhead view of several city blocks; at least nine fires have broken out, and rubble litters the streets in the aftermath of the battle. Cap surrenders because these ordinary humans force him to realize the very real cost of the ideological war he has been fighting. This war is not a war of good versus evil; it is a war of people versus people. Without the moral high ground—without his black-and-white, red-white-and-blue framework—Cap cannot continue his fight. The GWOT literally cannot be fought using a World War II approach—the World War II approach precludes the kind of war the GWOT has to be. These non-super people remind both readers and Captain America that the SHRA supporters have a legitimate grievance; as Travis Langley puts it: "In fictional worlds where heroes sometimes go rogue, get possessed, turn insane, or turn out to be villains, people are right to be wary" (430). Iron Man's forces are not Nazis, and the GWOT is not World War II; times have changed, and global politics are no longer as simple as good versus evil.

Of course, World War II itself wasn't really World War II; that is, the World War II of popular memory was not the World War II of historical reality. War is never a simple battle of good versus evil, and the glorification of World War II requires a forgetting of its details. But Captain America has not forgotten those details, and even as he founds his refusal of the SHRA in his 1940s morality, he critiques the law by referencing that forgotten history. In a brief peace talk with Iron Man, he specifically references Japanese Internment to illustrate how easily governments can infringe on the rights of individual citizens; Cap tells Iron Man:

> Governments change, administrations come and go. I had to become *Nomad* and later *the Captain* when certain politicians decided they didn't like the way I operated. The registration act takes away any freedom we have, any *autonomy*. You don't know who could get elected. How public sentiment might change. I'm old enough to remember Japanese-Americans being put in *camps* because they were judged potential threats to national security[7] [Gage 13].

Cap here separates the ideals of America—individual freedom and autonomy—from the reality of America—the United States government and the democratic election process. In the process, while he remains firmly within a discourse of American Exceptionalism, he turns that discourse against the United States generally and the memory of World War II specifically. He thus produces an aporia in the World War II rhetorical approach to the War on Terror, deconstructing the foundation of his own moral superiority. Cap reminds us that whatever the ideal, the reality of America has never been above reproach, even during the greatest war the U.S. ever fought; furthermore, that the beliefs of American Exceptionalism have themselves been the justification for some of the least ethical acts in American history. Captain America thus asks the question of how this legacy of American Exceptionalism, and its specific manifestation in the nostalgic memory of World War II, might lead American policy in the GWOT into fascism itself, as he actually rejects the democratic ideal of government. In the end, not only does the use of a nostalgic ideal of World War II as a blueprint for the GWOT undermine that nostalgic ideal, it emphasizes the inherent contradictions within American Exceptionalism.

Unsurprisingly, then, the World War II narrative of the War on Terror did not remain dominant for long in American culture. The realities of the GWOT led to the popularity of a new frame: that of the Cold War. This transition from Greatest Generation nostalgia to Baby Boomer nostalgia began at least as early as 2003, when Bush's State of the Union address moved from a rhetoric of sacrifice to one of containment. The end of the speech culminates with a conflation of Nazis, Soviets, and terrorists:

> Today, the gravest danger in the war on terror, the gravest danger facing America and the world, is outlaw regimes that seek and possess nuclear, chemical, and biological weapons.... Throughout the 20th century, small groups of men seized control of great nations, built armies and arsenals, and set out to dominate the weak and intimidate the world.... In each case, the ambitions of Hit-

lerism, militarism and communism were defeated by the will of free peoples, by the strength of great alliances and by the might of the United States of America.... Once again, this nation and our friends are all that stand between a world at peace, and a world of chaos and constant alarm. Once again, we are called to defend the safety of our people and the hopes of all mankind. And we accept this responsibility [Bush].

Bush describes Hitlerism, militarism, and communism as variations of the same recurring threat to global freedom; he defines American actions as defensive while also being a uniquely American responsibility; and he grounds the danger of this threat specifically in weapons of mass destruction. The speech thus moves the narrative of American Exceptionalism from World War II into the Cold War, combining Exceptionalism's primary concerns of individual and state freedom and the uniqueness of the American position in the world with World War II's concern with good versus evil, while adding the *realpolitik* threat of global apocalypse.[8]

The Cold War does seem a more apt comparison for the GWOT: neither the Cold War nor the GWOT are limited to specific national boundaries or territories, neither are fought through conventional means, and both are significantly longer-term. Furthermore, both require moral and ethical compromises: the threat of annihilation is so large that the U.S. cannot afford to be too picky in its choice of allies, and both the Cold War and the War on Terror have seen the U.S. partner with nations whose domestic politics stray very far from its own enthronement of freedom and democracy. Furthermore, the Cold War enemy seems a much better parallel to the terrorist threat than Nazis do; while Nazis are certainly remembered as both evil and un–American, Cold War communists were more than un–American, they were alien: devious, hiding in plain sight, using guerrilla tactics, showing no concern for the value of human life or loyalty to anything or anyone except their ideology. If the threat of global communism is taken to be at least as dire as the threat of Nazism, then the differences between World War II and the Cold War are not so drastic—both were black and white battles of good against evil, but as the stakes of the Cold War—global nuclear apocalypse—were so high, they demanded a less limited response. Equating the threat of terrorism with the threat of communism thus justifies moral compromises that a World War II narrative excludes. Finally, the comparison of the GWOT to the Cold War is a comforting one; the Cold War may have required a more realistic and less idealistic approach to foreign policy, but that strategy worked: the Cold War is over, and the U.S. won. Using a Cold War model suggests that the outcome of the GWOT is a similarly inevitable American victory.

In this Cold War imaginary, the September 11 attack ceases to be compared to Pearl Harbor and becomes an echo of the atomic bombs dropped on Hiroshima and Nagasaki in 1945. This analogy does seem at least as appropriate: both attacks were on civilian populations; both attacks came as a surprise, but were not entirely unpredictable; both attacks were shocking in their destruction; and both attacks are commonly seen as a turning point, after which nothing would ever be the same.[9] A quick look at *Civil War* would suggest that this reading is the preferred one, at least for the destruction of Stamford that leads to the SHRA; while Captain America is the victim of a S.H.I.E.L.D. sneak attack mimicking Pearl Harbor, the town of Stamford is destroyed in what seems unquestionably an atomic explosion. The villain Nitro, whose self-detonation causes the leveling of Stamford, may not literally be an atomic bomb, but his explosion is drawn to resemble atomic imagery. The page in question is divided into four panels horizontally. The second panel shows Nitro's explosion as several waves of force radiating out from an orange fireball, while the third panel depicts black silhouettes outlined by the explosion—a direct reference to the atomic shadows cast by the bombs at Hiroshima and Nagasaki. The fourth and final panel on the page—an image that will reappear several times throughout the event, in several comic series—shows from above a rounded fireball that unquestionably mimics the mushroom cloud of an atomic explosion (Millar, *Civil War #1*, 7). Thus the inciting incident of the Civil War—an incident that the crossover locates as an analogue to the September 11 attacks through repeated imagery of post–Nitro Stamford evocative of the Pile at Ground Zero—is visually positioned as an atomic explosion. This analogy also seems appropriate for the narrative; just as the atomic bombings were the result of a battle between the heroic United States and nefarious Japan which resulted in civilian casualties, the Stamford explosion is the result of a battle between superheroes and super-villains which spills over onto the town's population.

However, there is a major problem with this analogy for U.S. culture: it can put the victims of September 11 into the positions of the Japanese, not the Americans. To consider September 11 through atomic eyes is to see the America of 1945—the American greatest generation—as analogous to al Qaeda.[10] So from the outset, this nostalgic framework brings with it unresolved questions about American responsibility for mass death. These questions haunt Iron Man's approach to the superhero civil war. While not as obviously located in time as Captain America, Iron Man is the Marvel Universe's premiere Cold Warrior; he gained his superhero status as a direct result of the Vietnam War, and many of his most iconic enemies were at one time or another specifically associated with communist nations. Paul Fellman points out how Tony Stark's Iron Man armor is even "made from the same material as the famous 'curtain' which Stalin had erected across Eastern Europe" (11). As a cold warrior, Iron Man naturally views the Civil War through his own history. He chooses to support the SHRA because he believes it is necessary, as well as right; not only does he feel personally implicated by the threat super-humans present to the civilian population, but without the SHRA he predicts a future where super-humans are hunted, imprisoned and exterminated. He thus supports the act specifically to prevent global apocalypse. However, just as the U.S. bombed the Japanese in order to save them, Iron Man finds himself hunting his fellow superheroes in order to save them from being hunted and destroying cities to keep them from being destroyed.

The actions Iron Man takes as the head of the pro-registration forces follow a Cold War framework: he allies himself with even the worst criminals in the pursuit of global peace, recruiting scores of Marvel super-villains into the forces tasked with hunting down the Secret Avengers. He justifies his decision through the logic that in such straits, the ends justify the means, echoing the Cold War argument that alliances with anti-democratic, and therefore un–American, regimes were justified if those regimes would fight against the greater evil of communism. However, that Cold War logic crumbles when the enemy is not defined as evil. In the nostalgic imaginary of the Cold War, the U.S. was justified in its decision to pursue atomic and then nuclear weaponry, in its alliances with tyrannical third-world dictatorships, and in its limitation of civil rights at home because of the severity of the threat posed by global communism—communists were not only as evil as Nazis, they were exponentially more dangerous because they had the bomb. But the enemy Iron Man is fighting consists of *heroes*, Captain America being only the most obviously heroic of the Secret Avengers. By loosing super-villains on the good guys, Iron Man comes perilously close to becoming a villain himself. For instance, midway through the conflict, Spider-Man, who has been supporting the SHRA, has a crisis of conscience when he discovers the extremes to which Iron Man has gone to fight this war.[11] Spider-Man flees to the Secret Avengers, but S.H.I.E.L.D. sends troops after him: not just any troops, but the super-villains Jester and Jack O'Lantern. The two villains proceed not only to subdue Spider-Man but to beat him nearly to death, while exchanging the following dialogue:

> JACK: This gig seemed like such a *bum deal* at first. Working for S.H.I.E.L.D., forced to do what they said—
>
> JESTER: But when word from the top says kick the crap outta *Spider-Man*.... Well, what can we *do*? We're only *obeying orders*, right? [Millar, Civil War #5, 12].

The two are only stopped from killing Spider-Man by a reminder from S.H.I.E.L.D. that they will be punished for going so far, and their obvious glee at being able to beat up fan-favorite Spider-Man under government sanction permanently undermines any claims Iron Man and the pro–SHRA forces might have to the moral high ground.[12] If the SHRA supporters are on their face the bad guys, then either the Secret Avengers must be the good guys, or the good-versus-evil paradigm itself is flawed. *Civil War* thus leads its readers to question the demonization not only of the Secret Avengers, but of Cold War communists, and finally of GWOT terrorists as well.

In fact, eventually Iron Man even loses the justification that he is only trying to control super-human WMDs, as his very determination to avoid catastrophe causes that catastrophe. While he claims to support the SHRA because of the danger posed by unregistered superheroes, the only death that occurs after the SHRA's passage is a direct result of his own secret weapons program. Along with the scientists Reed Richards (Mr. Fantastic of the Fantastic Four) and Hank Pym (Ant-Man, aka Yellow Jacket), Iron Man has cloned Thor, the late Norse god of thunder.[13] During a major battle in which the two forces at first seem evenly matched, Maria Hill deploys the engineered super-human of mass destruction, "codename Lightning," and the Thor clone appears (Millar, *Civil War #3*, 23). However, this Thor clone seems to have internalized the logic of the Cold War; rather than simply try to incapacitate Cap's forces, he kills the superhero Goliath and nearly kills several other Secret Avengers (Millar, *Civil War #4*, 9–11). Iron Man may have cloned one of the most powerful super-humans in the Marvel universe only as a deterrent, but he is unable to control his new weapon; like the U.S., he becomes the only actor to ever unleash a weapon of mass destruction in war.

This problem is only exacerbated in the aftermath of the Civil War, when Iron Man first gains full control of S.H.I.E.L.D. and then loses that control to Norman Osborn, the villain known as the Green Goblin. While director of S.H.I.E.L.D., Iron Man has cemented the loyalty of a dangerously unstable and nearly all-powerful hero known as the Sentry; Iron Man reasons that the Sentry is too dangerous not to control. But when Iron Man eventually is removed from power and replaced by Osborn, the Sentry remains under Osborn's control; during the events of the Siege crossover, Osborn sends the Sentry to eradicate Asgard, the home of Thor and the Norse gods. Thus Iron Man's adherence to a super-human form of deterrence theory ends up escalating, rather than limiting, the proliferation of WMDs, suggesting that had the U.S. not built so many nuclear weapons during the Cold War, they would not be such a danger now, when they are no longer in trusted hands. Iron Man's belief in his own predictions for the future leads those predictions to become self-fulfilling prophesies, and his inability to see the conflict between himself and Captain America outside of a Cold War framework of mutually assured destruction destroys the civil liberties of the heroes of the Marvel universe while in no way solving the essential problem of the existence of super-humans of mass destruction. In the process, Iron Man reminds us that while the Cold War may have extinguished the Soviet threat, the threat of nuclear catastrophe has only grown. Iraq may have turned out not to have WMDs, but Iran and North Korea still threaten to pursue their nuclear agendas. And after all, to repurpose Langley's phrase, in real worlds where nation-states sometimes go rogue, get possessed, turn insane, or turn out to be villains, people are right to be wary.

Svetlana Boym has described nostalgia as a desire for a past that never was; she writes: "Modern nostalgia is a mourning for the impossibility of mythical return, for the loss of an enchanted world with clear borders and values.... The nostalgic is looking for a spiritual addressee. Encountering silence, he looks for memorable signs, desperately misreading them" (8). In *Civil War*, both Captain America and Iron Man misread the signs left in the wake of Stamford, reading them through their 20th century preconceptions. They thus replicate the misreadings of American culture, which in an attempt to make sense of global terrorism has turned to nostalgic imaginaries of idyllic times that never existed. Neither World War II nor the Cold War are appropriate frameworks for the War on Terror. In fact, the word "war" itself seems inappropriate and even arbitrary, given the nature of the threat; as Simon Dalby argues: "[G]eopolitical scripts might have been otherwise; the events could have been specified as a disaster, an act of madness or perhaps most obviously a crime, an act that required careful police work internationally and in the United States" (qtd. in Dittmer, "Captain America's Empire" 638). Using these nostalgic frameworks blinds us to the realities of the actual conflict: that terrorists have no nation; that military action is inadequate; that not all terrorists are evil; that American foreign policies bear part of the responsibility for nurturing terrorism in the first place; and that the United States is not inevitably destined to emerge victorious. Until American society takes the problem of global terrorism for what it is, uninflected by false memories of what never was, it is doomed to the continual, oneiric loop of forever watching New York be destroyed by civil war.

Notes

1. In mainstream comics, a crossover is a storyline that crosses over more than one comic series; *Civil War*, a major crossover event, took place in several of Marvel's ongoing monthly titles as well as the *Civil War* limited series itself.
2. See Cynthia Weber's *Imagining America at War* for a more in-depth discussion of the World War II nostalgic frame for the post–September 11 period.
3. S.H.I.E.L.D., or the Strategic Hazard Intervention, Espionage and Logistics Directorate, is the main military force of the United Nations in the Marvel Universe. S.H.I.E.L.D. is primarily responsible for enforcing the SHRA during the Civil War; why a UN agency would have the jurisdiction to enforce a U.S. law is never explained.
4. In fact, the Punisher's association with Vietnam suggest that Captain America is specifically replacing a good war, World War II framework with a dirty, Cold War one.
5. This concept is reflected in the characters' uniforms, which are color-coded accordingly.
6. This point is particularly relevant given the post-9/11 canonization of emergency workers in the United States, in comic books particularly.
7. Nomad and the Captain are other identities Steve Rogers, the man behind the Captain America mask, has taken on in moments where he was particularly alienated from the U.S. government. He became Nomad, the man without a country, after discovering high-level government corruption during the Watergate era; he took on the title of the Captain when the U.S. military demanded he follow their orders or step down from the role of Captain America.
8. For a detailed account of how American conservatives have attempted to define the Cold War through the "good war" mentality of World War II, see Jon Weiner's *How We Forgot the Cold War: A Historical Journey Across America*.

9. See Aaron DeRosa's "September 11 and Cold War Nostalgia" in *Portraying 9/11: Essays on Representations in Comics, Literature, Film and Theatre* for a detailed reading of the conflation of the 1945 atomic bombings and the 2001 attacks in American literary culture.

10. While the atomic culture of the U.S. certainly includes images of American victims of bombings, most obviously in Civil Defense films like *Duck and Cover* and *Survival Under Atomic Attack* as well as mass-market films ranging from *On the Beach* to *The Terminator*, these images themselves are always grounded in the reality that the only nation to ever drop an atomic weapon on a population center is the United States.

11. Specifically, he discovers the enormous prison Iron Man and his allies have constructed to permanently house any hero who refuses registration. This prison is an allegory for the Guantanamo Bay detention camp, where combatants captures in the GWOT are held by the U.S.; it is also positioned as a kind of concentration camp within the comics.

12. Spider-Man is also immediately rescued through the timely appearance of the Punisher, who shoots both villains before taking the unconscious hero to the Secret Avengers base, where he first joins the anti–SHRA forces.

13. Images from Thor's destruction during the final *Civil War* battle seem to suggest he is some kind of cyborg, as he contains robotic parts; however, he is usually referred to in the series as a clone.

Works Cited

Boym, Svetlana. *The Future of Nostalgia*. New York: Basic Books, 2001. Print.
Brubaker, Ed (writer), Mike Perkins (artist), and Frank D'Armata (colorist). "The Drums of War." *Captain America* #22 (Sept. 2007), Marvel Comics. Web. 15 July 2014.
Bush, George W. "Text of President Bush's 2002 State of the Union Address." *Washington Post* 29 Jan. 2002. Web. 15 July 2014.
_____. "Text of President Bush's 2003 State of the Union Address." *Washington Post* 28 Jan. 2003. Web. 10 Apr. 2014.
Costello, Matthew J. *Secret Identity Crisis: Comic Books and the Unmasking of Cold War America*. New York: Continuum, 2009. Print.
Coulter, Ann. "This Is War." *National Review* 13 Sept. 2001. Web. 16 Apr. 2014.
DeRosa, Aaron. "September 11 and Cold War Nostalgia." *Portraying 9/11: Essays on Representations in Comics, Literature, Film and Theatre*. Ed. Véronique Bragard, Christophe Dony, and Warren Rosenberg. Jefferson, NC: McFarland, 2011. 58–72. Print.
Dittmer, Jason. *Captain America and the Nationalist Superhero: Metaphors, Narratives, and Geopolitics*. Philadelphia: Temple University Press, 2013. Print.
_____. "Captain America's Empire: Reflections on Identity, Popular Culture, and Post–9/11 Geopolitics." *Annals of the Association of American Geographers* 95.3 (2005): 626–43. Print.
_____. "Retconning America: Captain America in the Wake of World War II and the McCarthy Hearings." *The Amazing Transforming Superhero! Essays on the Revision of Characters in Comic Books, Film and Television*. Ed. Terrence R. Wandtke. Jefferson, NC: McFarland, 2007. 33–51. Print.
Fellman, Paul. "Iron Man: America's Cold War Champion and Charm against the Communist Menace." *Voces Novae* 1.3 (2009): 11–21. Print.
Fraction, Matt (writer), Ariel Olivetti (artist), and Dean White (colorist). "Dead Soldiers." *Punisher War Journal* #2 (Jan. 2007), Marvel Comics. Web. 15 July 2014.
Gage, Christos N. (writer), Jeremy Haun (penciller), Mark Morales (inker), and Morry Hollowell (colorist). "Rubicon." *Iron Man/Captain America: Casualties of War* (Dec. 2006), Marvel Comics. Web. 15 July 2014.
Hayton, Christopher J., and David L. Albright. "O Captain! My Captain!" *Captain America and the Struggle of the Superhero*. Ed. Robert G. Weiner. Jefferson, NC: McFarland, 2009. 15–23. Print.
Hodgson, Godfrey. *The Myth of American Exceptionalism*. New Haven: Yale University Press, 2009. Print.
Langley, Travis. "Freedom versus Security: The Basic Human Dilemma from 9/11 to Marvel's *Civil War*." *International Journal of Comic Art* 11.1 (2009): 426–35. Print.
Millar, Mark (writer), Steve McNiven (penciller), Dexter Vines (inker), and Morry Hollowell (colorist). *Civil War* #1–7 (May 2006–Feb. 2007), Marvel Comics. Web. 15 July 2014.
Reynolds, Amy, and Brooke Barnett. "'America Under Attack': CNN's Verbal and Visual Framing of September 11." *Media Representations of September 11*. Ed. Steven Chermak, Frankie Y. Bailey, and Michelle Brown. Westport, CT: Praeger, 2003. 85–102. Print.
"Special Report." *ABC News*. ABC, 11 Sept. 2001. Television.
Weber, Cynthia. *Imagining America at War: Morality, Politics, and Film*. New York: Routledge, 2006. Print.
Weiner, Jon. *How We Forgot the Cold War: A Historical Journey Across America*. Berkeley: University of California Press, 2012. Print.

Part IV—Super-Powered, American and Marginalized: Triple Consciousness in the Marvel Universe

Battles of Family, Freedom and Femininity: Portrayals of Gender in Marvel's *Civil War*

BRANDI HODO

The portrayal of female characters in mainstream superhero comics has long been considered problematic. Many readers take issue with the exaggerated proportions and skimpy costumes of female superheroes. However, the purpose of this essay is not to criticize the over sexualized renderings of female superheroes, but to examine the roles that these women play in Marvel's *Civil War* event. Throughout the *Civil War* flagship series, women are largely absent from the action and, other than Sue Storm, do not appear in prominent roles. The starring roles of the main series are dedicated to Captain America and Iron Man. Their personal conflicts drive the action of the narrative and draw sympathy and ire from readers. To find the women of Marvel and see their stories, one must branch off into the tie-in series. It is in these tie-in issues that one can see the struggle between loyalty to one's country and to one's self. Carol Danvers, also known as Ms. Marvel, represents this struggle throughout her series. Ms. Marvel is not only a female superhero, but also a military woman. As such, she embodies the conflict between following orders and following your conscience. Focusing on the *Ms. Marvel* series, readers follow Carol Danvers' journey to find her place in a super-powered profession that sets her against former teammates, super-villains, and herself.

Following Orders or Following the Heart

Carol Danvers is one of the most visible female superheroes in the Marvel Universe, especially within the *Civil War* event and subsequent story lines. Raised as the only girl in a family of boys, she constantly strove to win her father's affections—ultimately joining the Air Force and becoming a decorated pilot. In her later adventures she gains super-powers and soon joins the Avengers as a costumed superhero. It is a profile that has often made her the focus of questions about gender and power in the Marvel Universe, a trend that continued in *Civil War*.

Writers and artists have generally portrayed Ms. Marvel as a strong female character who does not have to rely on men to reach her goals. She was introduced to readers in 1968 but would not gain super-powers until 1977, when she appeared in the first volume of *Ms.*

Marvel. Ross Murray describes her debut as strong one: "Ms. Marvel represents the emerging 'feminist' woman who has the independence to pursue her own career and lives alone" (60). Yet in a storyline that remains controversial more than thirty years after it was published, this strength and independence were severely undercut. In *Avengers* #200, Carol Danvers discovers that she is unexpectedly pregnant and gives birth in the space of three days (Layton, Michelinie, and Shooter). Her child grows to adult size in hours and—in a bizarre plot twist—turns out to be its own father. The god-like character Marcus managed to induce a pregnancy in Carol, be born, age to adulthood, and psychically compel her to leave with him in the space of a day. Of course, none of the Avengers step in to prevent her leaving and Carol is absent from the Marvel Universe for a year.

Ms. Marvel's reappearance in the *Avengers Annual* #10 makes it clear that neither her pregnancy nor her departure were of her own volition. Writer Chris Claremont addresses the controversial sendoff of Carol Danvers with a tense confrontation between her and the Avengers. When questioned about the absence of Marcus, Carol turns away from her teammates and calmly explains that Marcus is dead. Upon hearing her teammates' condolences, she smashes a glass and Thor, attempting to calm her, says, "Be not ashamed of thy womanly tears, Carol. Thou hast lost the one thou didst love" (Claremont 36). It is then that Carol angrily tells her former teammates that what happened to her was not a love story but an event that amounted to rape and slavery:

> There I was, pregnant by an unknown source, running through a nine-month term literally overnight—confused, terrified, shaken to the core of my being as a hero, a person, a woman. I turned to you for help and I got jokes.... Your concerns were for the baby, neither for how it came to be—nor of the cost to me of that conception.... You didn't doubt. You simply let me go with a smile and a wave and a bouncy bon voyage [Claremont 38].

Carol's recounting of her experience shocks her teammates, although only the Scarlet Witch seems to sympathize with the situation.

The rape, pregnancy, and kidnapping of such a powerful hero as Ms. Marvel calls into question the treatment of female heroes in the comic book genre. Narratively, the story functioned as a way to write the character out of the series. However, one must question why the writers and editors, all male, chose such a damaging and gendered way to remove Carol from the Avengers. Why not have her accept a mission or voluntarily leave the team for personal reasons? Instead the writers chose to take away her free will and make the character into a virtual sex slave. Not only did she have control of her body and her mind taken from her, but also these actions were "applauded and rewarded by all who had news" of them (Strickland n.p.). Her fellow Avengers express joy at Carol's pregnancy—no one ever questions the fact that she managed to get pregnant and deliver so quickly. The writers were asking both the characters and the readers to celebrate an incredibly damaging event.

Although, it appears that not all who read the story supported the "joyous occasion." A year after the original story, Claremont criticizes the controversial plot by presenting the events from Carol's perspective. With his reintroduction story for Ms. Marvel, Claremont gives Carol Danvers back her autonomy and provides her a chance to confront her teammates. Her speech to her former teammates not only details the horrors that she faced, but also denies her status as a victim. Carol is vehement about the fact that she will not let the experience ruin her identity as a woman or a hero. Claremont offers readers a strong woman who can come back from a terrible experience and still desires to be a hero—quite the opposite of the love struck, mind controlled character presented by the original writers Bob Layton, David Michelinie, and Jim Shooter.

Although Carol's rape and kidnapping occurred years before the *Civil War* event, the experience must be kept in mind when discussing her actions and choices during the latter event. During the Civil War, Carol is a firm supporter of the Superhuman Registration Act (SHRA). She is a soldier and knows how to follow orders. Of course, her decision to support the act puts her in opposition to many of her former colleagues. One such colleague is Julia Carpenter, also called Arachne. Julia chose to register so that she could act as a double agent and warn unregistered superheroes to flee when S.H.I.E.L.D. sets out to arrest them. Julia's duplicity is uncovered, and she is forced to flee. Although she is urged to leave the country by her partner Max, Julia reveals that she cannot without retrieving her daughter Rachel. She tells her partner, "She's my life, Max.... I screwed up and I stayed here and I fought a dumb fight and now I have to run away. But I can't run away without Rachel" (Reed, *MM* #7, 13). It is at this moment that a S.H.I.E.L.D. team, led by Carol, attempts to arrest Julia. A brutal fight ensues and Julia manages to escape.

Shortly thereafter, Carol arrives at Julia's parents' home in Colorado to search for her fugitive friend. It is revealed that she is hiding inside and holding her daughter Rachel. Julia decides to make one last stand and brings Rachel outside to confront the S.H.I.E.L.D. team. Carol incredulously asks Julia why she would involve her daughter in such a confrontation. Julia replies, "Because as much as it pains me to say it, my little girl has to grow up someday. She has to learn the difference between right and wrong. She has to learn that there are some things worth fighting for" (Reed, *MM* #8, 12). Yet another brutal fight ensues between the two women and ultimately Julia is defeated. S.H.I.E.L.D. agents then arrest Julia as her daughter screams in fear for her mother. This event troubles Carol greatly and she anguishes over her actions and questions whether following the law was worth separating a family. She expresses her desire to offer some sort of comfort to Rachel. She sobs, "But that poor little girl... God... Nobody should have to go through what she did today" (Reed, *MM* #8, 18). Carol notes that no matter what she offers Rachel, the girl will always see her as "the person who took away her mommy" (Reed, *MM* #8, 18). Her angst over her decision to arrest Julia becomes a recurring event over the next several issues of her comic book series.

A few issues later, after visiting the site of a devastating biological attack of unknown origin, Carol gets into an argument with Tony Stark about her frustrations with the war over the SHRA. Carol vents her anger that so many have died because the Avengers were not there to help and that S.H.I.E.L.D. had been employing too many of their resources to capture Captain America. In a moment of frustration Carol calls the SHRA stupid. Tony immediately retorts, "Stupid? You seemed to think the law was important enough to go to Colorado and separate Julia Carpenter from her daughter" (Reed, *MM* #13, 6). A frustrated Carol punches him and he subsequently offers her leadership of the Avengers—noting that he trusted her because she was an intelligent person who gave voice to her doubts. While this encounter ended in Carol's favor—as she is offered the chance to lead the Avengers— it is interesting to note that the incident that Tony chooses to mention is the one where Carol separated Julia Carpenter and her daughter Rachel. Tony was one of the Avengers present during Carol's pregnancy, abduction, and return. As such, he has witnessed firsthand Carol's strength and commitment to her role as a hero. One may argue that it is her ability to overcome conventionally "female" traumas that causes Tony to see her as a worthy leader. Carol has never been portrayed as the stereotypical excessively emotional victim, but as a strong leader—traditionally a more masculine trait. It is this stalwart devotion to the cause that makes her, in Tony's eyes, a viable leader for the Avengers.

In *Ms. Marvel* #13, Carol has finally accepted the leadership of the Avengers team. Her first order of business after assembling Operation: Lightning Storm, a team of S.H.I.E.L.D. agents, is to track down Julia Carpenter—who had been released from the Negative Zone during the climax of the Civil War. Carol is still wracked by guilt because of her part in Julia's arrest and Julia, as Agent Locke the team's psy-ops officer notes, is consumed by "pure cold, hard-as-a-rock hate" toward the ones who took her daughter (Reed, *MM* #13, 21). *Ms. Marvel* #14 features Carol's memories of the incident in Colorado (Reed). Her narration for three pages discusses her guilt over breaking up a family and the violent arrest of Julia Carpenter. Carol attempts to balance her responsibility as an agent of the law—knowing that Julia is a fugitive as she continues to refuse to register—and her own remorse for the broken Carpenter family. After Julia is captured, the two women come to a temporary truce and Carol assists Julia with retrieving Rachel—who has been taken by Julia's parents in an attempt to protect her from the superhero lifestyle. Ultimately Julia takes her daughter against her parents' wishes and is offered a chance to join the Canadian superhero team Omega Flight. Despite her involvement in the reunification of mother and daughter, Julia makes it clear that Carol will never earn her forgiveness.

The struggle between loyalty to one's own morals and maintaining the status quo is a frequent plot device in narratives featuring strong female characters. It is a long held belief that women are overly sentimental and, thus, unable to exert any type of authority because of the inability to view a situation objectively. The story line following the interactions of Carol and Julia conveys the struggle between loyalty to a cause and motherhood. Carol is a soldier who strives to be loyal to her country above all else. While she is interrogating Julia's partner Max, he remarks on her unwavering loyalty to the government. He questions her refusal to question orders, saying, "They say 'Hunt Captain America...' They... They say 'Hunt a Single Mother...' Your keepers say to you "Hunt them down!" and you say 'Sir! Yes, sir!'" (Reed, *MM* #8, 6). Carol angrily defends her actions and makes it clear that despite everything Julia is a fugitive.

This internal strife between being a soldier and being a friend causes Carol to doubt her position in the registration conflict. She wants to remain loyal to her country and its laws, but there is also a part of her that recognizes the pain that her friend and former teammate is going through. Carol's separation from her child was under very different, but equally traumatic circumstances. Carol's child Marcus was revealed to be her rapist and abductor. Marcus' machinations led to her leaving the Avengers behind and becoming a slave, which Carol not only blamed Marcus for, but also her teammates for not recognizing that the situation was dangerous. Carol even tells her teammates that she could no longer trust them "because when I needed you most, you betrayed me" (Claremont 37). One may argue that it is this betrayal on the part of the Avengers that influences Carol's decision to assist Julia in her hunt for her child. Carol defies orders so that she can offer Julia the support that she was denied by her fellow Avengers. It must be noted that Carol is able to make the decision to aid Julia because of her position in S.H.I.E.L.D.—a position that, as previously argued, she was able to obtain because of her more masculine attributes. Tony chose her as the leader of the Avengers because of her ability to be impartial in her decision making, as he sees that she is not easily swayed by her emotions. Thus, she may now use this power granted to her by a male-dominated hierarchy to assist her friend. Jennifer Stuller notes that female heroes tend to prize love in the form of compassion above other pursuits and this is true for Carol ("What Is a Female Superhero?" 21). The need to keep a family together outweighs the need to follow the law and may be viewed, by some readers, as a weakness for the character as Carol breaks from her normal order following facade and lets her emotions influence her actions. Stuller also notes that female heroes tend to seek redemption in their tales (*Ink Stained Amazons* 88). Carol's part in the reunification of Julia and Rachel grants her redemption from the guilt that was influencing her choices.

Julia Carpenter's actions in *Civil War* present another battle between being a hero and being a mother. The active superhero mother is rarely depicted in comic books. In his article "Supermoms? Maternity and the Monstrous-Feminine in Superhero Comics," Jeffrey Brown asserts that pregnancy and motherhood cause female characters to become "the Other," or a monstrous being (78–9). He argues that pregnancy represents a breaking of boundaries and is often not a positive event, such as Carol's forced pregnancy with Marcus ("Supermoms?" 79). Motherhood forces characters to make a choice between their mission and their child. Also, pregnancy takes away the image of the sexy hero and replaces her with a changing body that does not fit the fetishized ideal. When there are story lines featuring superhero mothers, Brown notes that they tend to fall in to four basic categories. The female-superhero-mother either gives up her heroic career to raise her child, gives up her child so that she may continue to be a hero, puts her child in danger because of her heroic adventures, or neglects her children because of her adventures ("Supermoms?" 81–82). Rarely are they portrayed as well-adjusted mothers who can separate their heroic life from their home life.

Julia represents the superhero mother who chooses to continue her mission, but manages to put her child in danger. Early in the *Civil War* conflict, she makes the choice to register and become a double agent to aid her friends and teammates. Although she believes the SHRA is wrong, and contrary to the beliefs that she holds as a hero, she is willing to make the sacrifice to support those around her. Sacrifice is the hallmark of female narratives. The need to protect, even to the detriment of one's own health or freedom is a common theme among works featuring female characters. Julia, at first, makes the decision that protecting her friends is more important than staying with her daughter and, thus, Rachel is sent to live with her grandparents. Once Julia fails in her role as a double agent, she reverts to the role of protective mother. Although she cannot protect her friends, Julia uses the full extent of her rage to protect her daughter. In *Ink Stained Amazons*, Stuller questions whether motherhood can be perceived as a heroic act or is it simply a way to make violence on a female character's part acceptable. Stuller notes that the image of "the lioness protecting her child is perhaps more palatable to a general audience than vigilantism for its own sake" (*Ink Stained Amazons* 9). Julia's continual use of violence until she is reunited with Rachel speaks to a primal instinct between mother and child. However, does the mother—daughter bond excuse Julia's actions? As Carol frequently notes, Julia has broken the law repeatedly and in a destructive fashion. Many S.H.I.E.L.D. agents are seriously injured and property damage costs are great. Yet many readers, as it seems to be the writer's intention, sympathize with Julia's plight. Yes, she is a criminal, but first she is a mother. Any action that she must take to protect her child is suddenly acceptable.

Mothering Mentorship

The mother or female mentor is often an absent figure in the superhero genre. Many heroes are orphans—through parental abandonment or tragic murders—and, thus, must create a found family. For most heroes, "their mothers are almost always either dead, alcoholic, clueless, unmentioned, insane, or otherwise emotionally unavailable and out of the picture" (Stuller, *Ink Stained Amazons* 9). Traditionally these young heroes are paired with a father figure who instructs them in the ways of crime fighting and justice— Batgirl has Batman, Buffy has Giles and the list goes on. When discussing events in the DC Comics canon, it is common to hear of the Batman Family or the Superman Family. These male characters become the surrogate father for young heroes without family of their own.

One does not, however, often read of female characters acting as mentors for young heroes, especially not on the scale of their male counterparts (Stuller, *Ink Stained Amazons* 105). Stuller notes that the few times a possible female mentor is introduced in a narrative they are not generally successful relationships (*Ink Stained Amazons* 123). This lack of female mentors and "the absence of the mother figure reinforces the idea that heroism is masculine in nature and that female knowledge all too often has no value in the formation of a superwoman" (Stuller, "What Is a Female Superhero" 22). Many comic book story lines revolve around the training of young heroes by their male teachers and those lessons tend to focus around battle techniques and strength training. Rare are the stories teaching compassion, collaboration, and balance between being a hero and a regular person—all of which Stuller maintains are defining characteristics of a female superhero. Carol Danvers, however, is given the opportunity to share her knowledge and become a mentor to a young hero because of the SHRA.

Anya Corazon, also known as Arana, is introduced to the Marvel Universe as an addition to the spider-powered set. Through magical means she gains super-powers that lead her to a life of crime fighting. Anya, like many young heroes before her, is the daughter of a single father and spends much of her time working or fighting crime. Anya is introduced into Carol Danvers' life through a series of misadventures. Carol and Wonder Man are searching Brooklyn for an unregistered superhero rumored to be operating there and, when boredom and hunger strikes, the two heroes stop at local fast food restaurant where an attempted robbery soon takes place. The heroes handle the would-be robbers and Anya, not aware of the situation, activates her powers to protect the restaurant's patrons (Reed, *MM* #6, 19–23). She manages to flee the restaurant but is soon visited by Carol and Wonder Man to discuss her registration. Unlike many characters throughout the *Civil War* event, Anya is eager to register and become a trained superhero—much to her father's initial displeasure. Mr. Corazon quickly recognizes that his daughter has an ability that she wishes to use for good and allows her to train.

It is upon her registration that Carol becomes Anya's mentor—whether she likes it or not. The enthusiastic young hero forces herself into a meeting with Iron Man and invites herself on the mission to retrieve Julia Carpenter. This first venture into being a registered superhero proves trying for Anya. She witnesses the brutal fight between Carol and Julia and is unnerved. Anya also accompanies Carol on the mission to Colorado to arrest Julia. Anya's role in the mission is to keep Julia's daughter Rachel safe from the fighting, but the little girl manages to flee to her mother. Anya is horrified to see Julia dragged away from her daughter and arrested. In the aftermath, Carol holds a crying Anya who wants an explanation for what she cannot accept in Carol's worldview.

> Carol... Is this what the good guys do now? Take kids away from their moms? Because if it this is what we do now then I don't think I want any part of it.... I don't want to be the bad guy. Carol,

I want to do what's right and this thing today? It was wrong. I don't want to take moms away from their little girls. I lost my Momma when I was little and I don't ever want anybody else to have that happen. Not... Not ever [Reed, *MM* #8, 16–17].

In her attempt to comfort Anya, Carol is forced to examine her own choices and, as previously noted, starts to have doubts about the strictness of the Registration Act.

Anya quickly overcomes her initial doubts about being a superhero and becomes a sort of sidekick for Carol. In an altercation with the Doomsday Man, Anya is injured and has a portion of her exoskeleton ripped from her face. This experience leads to Anya losing her super-powers and to her father filing a restraining order against Carol. Anya later visits Carol to talk about the experience and, once again, express her doubts about the superhero world. She leaves Carol's apartment on a negative note and Carol again wonders if Anya's criticisms of the SHRA era superhero are right. Soon, Carol is involved in a mission to locate many missing women, including Anya. The perpetrator is found to be the Puppet Master, who uses clay figurines to control women. The Puppet Master orders Anya to attack Carol but she refuses saying, "I won't. I won't kill my mother, I won't hurt Carol" (Reed, *MM* #18, 20). Carol is shocked at Anya's words, "She called me mother... Anya lost her mom when she was little. To think that she feels that way about me" (Reed, *MM* #18, 20). Anya's words spur Carol to confront the Puppet Master and when he activates a bomb in a suicidal attempt to kill both of them, Carol does not stop him.

After the encounter with the Puppet Master, Anya slowly disappears from the *Ms. Marvel* series. However, her time with Carol helps to change the way both heroes view the superhero community. Anya, for a time, has a mother-mentor, who guides her and protects her. She uses the skills that Carol teaches her to continue on her superhero journey (interestingly enough, she later adopts Julia Carpenter's costume). Carol gains a daughter-figure and is able to overcome her guilt for separating Julia Carpenter from her daughter. This experience is much different than her forced pregnancy. Anya is a chosen child, who manages to slip past Carol's defenses. Her experience with Anya also gives her the chance to train and guide her in crime fighting training. Carol has to face the fact that the training does not necessarily prepare young heroes as well as the act implies and she, once again, has to face guilt because of Anya's injury. During the encounter with the Puppet Master, Carol is shocked to hear that Anya views her not only as a mentor, but also as a mother. This realization sparks a rage in her that eventually leads to the Puppet Master's death—ironic, as Carol had previously condemned Julia's violent actions. Carol viewed Julia's various fights against the S.H.I.E.L.D. agents as legally wrong and pursued her across several states so that she could be brought to justice. Even when confronted by Julia's partner Max about the morality of her decision to pursue Julia, Carol is steadfast that the law is to be followed above all else. However, when Carol is faced with a situation where her daughter-figure is placed in danger and stripped of her own free will she decides to take the law into her own hands. Carol notes that she could have easily stopped the Puppet Master from detonating the bomb, but she chooses not to. In this situation, she becomes judge, jury, and, indirectly, executioner. It once again connects back to the protective instinct of the mother figure and the trigger of having one's young attacked. Carol saw Anya mind controlled, just as Marcus had controlled her, and her desire to protect her "daughter" won over the letter of the law.

The Warrior

Carol's issues with her emotions—battling guilt, self-doubt, and anger—continue to plague her after her partnership with Anya comes to an end. Carol, literally, fights herself and comes to recognize that her anger could damage her as a hero. However, every step forward that Carol makes, she seems to take two backwards. After the confrontation with an alternate version of herself she seems on the brink of a self-realization, but she quickly reverts back to self-doubt. She accepts leadership of the Avengers, but frequently questions whether she is strong enough to handle the role. Finally in a confrontation with a Super Skrull, Carol seems to find her center. She flies the Skrull into space where she sits and says, "I watch it die. And say what you will about me, I enjoy it.... In that instant, all the garbage that's been cranking through my head these last months, everything I've worried about, or stressed over, is gone.... I punch until my knuckles hurt and then I hit a little harder. And for the first time in forever I remember how to be a true warrior. I am so happy I could cry" (Reed, *MM* #28, 10–14). Depictions of violence and many panels of her torn costume accentuating her figure accompany her narration. It is interesting that Carol's realization comes through extreme violence. In the heat of battle, Carol does not have to be the leader or second guess her actions; she is simply a soldier with a clear enemy—no guilt, no worry, no doubt. The nurturing Carol that accompanied Anya is gone and replaced with a super-powered heavy hitter who longs for nothing else but to fight.

Subsequent story lines depict Carol in flashbacks to her time in the U.S. Air Force, and the series becomes more violent. She is depicted on the cover of *Ms. Marvel #29* as a fetishized soldier—a big gun, pouty lips, and her breasts overflowing her vest (Reed). Fight scenes alternate between panels focusing on her breasts and those focusing on her rear. The series continues in this fashion until Carol "dies" in *Ms. Marvel #37* (Reed 19). With the absence of her daughter-figure, Carol reverts into what Stuller calls "the Action Babe" (56). She is strong, violent, voluptuous, and beautiful. Innis notes, "Ms. Marvel could compete against men, but her appearance ... in no way challenged assumptions about feminine beauty" (144). In "Gender, Sexuality and Toughness," Brown discusses the function of the over-exaggerated female form in comics. He notes that, as female superheroes are just as powerful and dangerous as their male counterparts, many writers and artists compensate for these masculine traits (consciously or not) by drawing the women with voluptuous bodies (63). The portrayal of Carol as the violent beauty matches Brown's analysis perfectly. However, it is not her generous figure that allows Carol to create an image of female agency; rather it is her ability to resist the complete adoption of traditionally masculine structures of thinking and power that characterize most superheroes. Carol works within a system that looks down upon her abilities and doubts her leadership because she is female. Despite her perceived weakness, Carol is able to obtain a leadership position that allows her to aid her friends and her own agendas. Yes, like many of her male counterparts she has super strength and can easily defeat her enemies on the battlefield. However, it is her earlier depiction as a caring friend and loving mentor that connects her to Stuller's assertion that the female hero is a collaborative and redemptive one (*Ink Stained Amazons* 88). She is able to combine her strength and her leadership to accomplish what is truly important to her. Despite the later depictions of her as the violent super-woman, for a time she is the compassionate and redemptive hero that fights to reunite a family and protect her protégée.

Carol Danvers is a many-faceted character. Through the first thirty-seven issues of her self-titled series, she struggles to find her place as a hero, a friend, a mentor, and a woman. Her battles to fit the ideals of each role cause the character continuing self-doubt, but shows readers that a female superhero does not simply have to be a hero. It is possible for her to have a life, train the next generation, and retain her femininity. Carol proves to be one of the more human characters in comic books—she is flawed, but she is still a hero. Her changing characterization shows her journey as a hero—sometimes improving, sometimes doubting—but ever strong.

Works Cited

Brown, Jeffrey A. "Gender, Sexuality, and Toughness: The Bad Girls of Action Film and Comic Books." *Action Chicks: New Images of Tough Women in Popular Culture*. Ed. Sherrie Inness. New York: Palgrave Macmillian, 2004. 47–74. Print.

_____. "Supermoms? Maternity and the monstrous-feminine in superhero comics." *Journal of Graphic Novels and Comics* 2.1 (2011): 77–87. Web.

Claremont, Chris (writer), Michael Golden (penciller), and Armando Gil (inker). *Avengers Annual* #10 (Jan. 1981), Marvel Comics. Web.

Innis, Sherrie. *Tough Girls: Women Warriors and Wonder Women in Popular Culture*. Philadelphia: University of Pennsylvania Press, 1999. Print.

Knauf, Charles, Daniel Knauf, Christos N. Gage, Brian Michael Bendis (writers), Patrick Zircher, Jeremy Haun, and Alex Maleev (pencillers), and Scott Hanna and Mark Morales (inkers). *Civil War: Iron Man*. New York: Marvel, 2007. Print.

Layton, Bob (writer), David Michelinie (writer), Jim Shooter (writer), George Perez (penciller), and Dan Green (inker). *Avengers* #200 (Oct. 1980), Marvel Comics. Web.

Millar, Mark (writer), Steve McNiven (penciller), and Dexter Vines (inker). *Civil War* #1–7. New York: Marvel, 2007. Print.

Murray, Ross. "The Feminine Mystique: Feminism, Sexuality, Motherhood." *Journal of Graphic Novels and Comics* 2.1 (2011): 55–66. Web.

O'Reilly, Julie. "The Wonder Woman Precedent: Female (Super)Heroism on Trial." *The Journal of American Culture* 28.3 (2005): 273–283. Web.

Reed, Brian (writer), Roberto Delatorre (penciller), and Jimmy Palmotti (inker). *Ms. Marvel* #6 (Aug. 2006), Marvel Comics. Web.

Reed, Brian (writer), Robert Delatorre (penciller), and Jonathan Sibal (inker). *Ms. Marvel* #7–8 (Sept.-Oct. 2006), Marvel Comics. Web.

Reed, Brian (writer), Aaron Lopresti (penciller), and Jonathan Sibal (Inker). *Ms. Marvel* #13–14 (Mar.-Apr. 2007), Marvel Comics. Web.

Reed, Brian (writer), Aaron Lopresti (penciller), and Matt Ryan (inker). *Ms. Marvel* #18 (Aug. 2007), Marvel Comics. Web.

Reed, Brian (writer), Adriana Melo (penciller), and Mariah Benes (inker). *Ms. Marvel* #28–29 (June-July 2008), Marvel Comics. Web.

Strickland, Carol. "The Rape of Ms. Marvel." CarolAStrickland.com. Web. 10 May 2014.

Stuller, Jennifer. *Ink-Stained Amazons and Cinematic Warriors*. New York: I.B. Tauris, 2010. Print.

_____. "What Is a Female Superhero?" *What Is a Superhero?* Eds. Peter Coogan and Robin S. Rosenberg. Oxford: Oxford University Press, 2013. 19–24. Print.

Superdad: Luke Cage and the Heroic Fatherhood Ideal in the Contemporary Marvel Universe

Jeffrey A. Brown

The elaborate and best-selling Marvel crossover events of *Civil War*, *Secret Invasion*, *Dark Reign*, and *Avengers Vs. X-Men* explore issues of terrorism, national security, xenophobia, paranoia, and government corruption in a post–9/11 America. Large-scale battles pit superheroes against each other divided along political lines, as well as against supervillains and alien invaders, all in the service of protecting America as an ideal while simultaneously questioning what exactly that "ideal" means. The Universe-wide scale of these crossover events provides epic comic book adventure of the first order as every Marvel character and every Marvel series becomes embroiled in the action. Interwoven with these world-shattering crises was a smaller more down-to-earth, storyline at the heart of *New Avengers* (2004–2010) series written by Brian Michael Bendis, one of the prime architects of the various crossover stories. Amid all of the cataclysmic events, the leader of the New Avengers, Luke Cage, struggles to be a good husband and father. The story of Luke Cage's marriage to retired superheroine Jessica Jones, the birth of their daughter, and their struggles to be a family in the face of enormous adversity presents a very specific vision of the American family being threatened by external forces. As befits the superhero genre, spectacular paternal violence by Cage is initially presented as the solution to a family under siege. But, as the storyline develops throughout the various crossover events, violence is depicted as an inadequate way for Cage to protect his family. While issues of national security in a post–9/11 world underline the major conflicts of *Civil War*, *Secret Invasion*, *Dark Reign*, and *Avengers Vs. X-Men*, the story of Luke Cage and his family addresses competing American beliefs about masculinity and fatherhood, ultimately presenting paternal responsibility as a redeeming heroic act in and of itself.

Following the tragic events of September 11, 2001, and America's subsequent foreign and domestic War on Terror, there has been an increased cultural anxiety about the nation's fortitude and ability to protect its citizens. As critics like Susan Faludi, Michael Kimmel, and countless others have argued, these anxieties are often enunciated in public discourse in gendered terms as a crisis of masculinity. In response to this post–9/11 anxiety and the perceived crisis of masculinity, popular entertainments have reinvented heroic male characters, often by harkening back to earlier icons, such as the grittier, revamped version of James Bond performed by Daniel Craig, the return of Indiana Jones in *Indiana Jones and the Kingdom of the Crystal Skull* (2008), the return of John McClane in *Live Free or Die Hard* (2007) and *A Good Day to Die Hard* (2013), and the assorted muscular heroes of the Reagan era played by Sylvester Stallone, Arnold Schwarzenegger, and their like in the *Expendables* franchise (2010, 2012, 2014). But perhaps the most obvious parable of American remasculinization is evident in the incredible rise in the general visibility of superheroes. Frances Pheasant-Kelly notes, "[S]uperhero characters have become increasingly popular during the post–9/11 period, offering escapism and reassurance to audiences in vulnerable times" (143). Likewise, Alex Harvey argues, "after the fall of the Towers, the superhero became a figure of some focus for those seeking to express their grief, anger and fear in the wake of the attacks" (120). As this collection of essays attests, comic books since 9/11 have repeatedly used superheroes as wish-fulfilling correctives to the tragic events of the real world.[1] Likewise, blockbuster films such as *The Dark Knight* (2008), *Iron Man* (2008), *The Avengers* (2012), *Man of Steel* (2013), *Thor: The Dark World* (2013), and *Captain America: The Winter Soldier* (2014) play out a comforting scenario of powerful men saving the nation—New York in particular—from terrorists who have been metaphorically recast as super-villains or alien invaders.[2] The events of 9/11 may have instigated a fear of masculinity in crisis, but fictional superheroes have stepped in to offer reassurance that the American male is still a force to be reckoned with.

Superheroes have always been a quintessentially American fantasy of masculine empowerment, so the current cultural fascination with them is a logical means to placate widespread anxieties and feelings of emasculation. Superheroes provide a clear model of masculinity, what Anthony Easthope refers to as "super-masculine ideals" (29). Male superheroes are depicted as incredibly powerful, smart, confident, and always in control. Moreover, the illustrations, and now the cinematic costumes, emphasize the muscles and the stature of the heroes as perfect male specimens. The Clark Kent and Peter Parker side of the characters may exist, but these wimpy secret identities only stress the exceptional nature of Superman and Spider-Man. With the first appearance of Superman in 1938, the visual conventions and narrative formula of superheroes was quickly established. At its core the fantasy of mild-mannered men who gain incredible powers is a clear wish-fulfilling dream of empowerment for the traditionally young male audience. After 9/11 the superhero power fantasy no longer seems restricted just to adolescent boys. It has become a cultural fantasy of hegemonic masculinity, of American bodies either literally or figuratively armored against possible threats. Scott Bukataman points out that the superhero is "hyperbolized into pure, hypermasculine spectacle" (106). Or, as Carol A. Stabile bluntly puts it, "the superhero is first and foremost a man, because only men are understood to be protectors in U.S. culture and only men have the balls to lead" (87). The masculine ideal embodied by heroes such as Superman, Batman, Iron-Man and Captain America play out a reassuring fantasy about the eminence of American patriarchal authority that is especially reassuring in a post–9/11 world.

With the exception of *Hancock* (2008), all of the post–9/11 feature film superheroes have been white males. The predominant whiteness of these characters reflects a consistent bias within the genre over the years, and in American cultural concerns more generally. As Rebecca Wanzo argues, superheroes link Americanness with whiteness as well as masculinity: "[T]he superhero is an indelibly American invention connoting ideal citizenship through white muscular force" (93). Likewise, the perceived crisis of masculinity has been, either explicitly or implicitly, divided along racial lines. The default figure of American masculinity has always been assumed to be a white male: Davy Crockett, John Wayne,

Rambo, Superman, etc. But the masculine crisis in Post–9/11 American culture is complicated by a range of issues that intersect in varying degrees with the consequences of the War on Terror, including the economic collapse, loss of employment, lower income levels, immigration, ethnic diversity, women's movements, and the erosion of the traditional nuclear family. African American men, for example, have been presented in the media as suffering from other types of masculine crises relating to continued discriminations, lack of educational and vocational opportunities, violence, incarceration and irresponsible paternity. Many of these challenges ascribed in public discourse to black men in American culture are the result of racial stereotyping of the worst kind. In this essay, I would like to focus on the specific perception of black men as supposed "deadbeat dads."

One of the most publicly debated issues faced by African American communities in the past fifteen years has been the crisis of absent black fathers. A dominant stereotype of black men perpetuated in the media has characterized them as "deadbeat dads" who often avoid any parental responsibility for their offspring, from failing to spend time with their children to refusing to pay child support. Common headlines like "What's the Problem with Black Fathers?" (Banks) and "Who's Your Daddy? The Epidemic of Absent Black Fathers" (Screven) perpetuate the damning stereotype. Likewise, even well-intentioned projects such as Morehouse College's conference and report "Turning the Corner on Father Absence in Black America" (Morehouse), and, more recently, President Obama's "Fatherhood Initiative" reinforce the idea that black men are less than ideal fathers. A number of critics have sought to challenge this stereotype and to explore the consequences of the "absent fathers" misconception, including the collections *Black Fathers: An Invisible Presence in America* (Connor and White), *The Myth of the Missing Black Father* (Coles and Green), and *Bet on Black: African American Women Celebrate Fatherhood in the Age of Barack Obama* (Naasel). Though the statistics about black fathers and their role in their children's lives are hotly debated, a recent report by the Centers for Disease Control and Prevention (Jones and Mosher) found that black fathers are as responsible and involved in parenting as fathers in any other ethnic group, and in many categories they rank higher in parental care. The CDC report received extensive media coverage because the findings challenged the longstanding stereotype. For example, *The LA Times* reported, "Defying enduring stereotypes about black fatherhood, a federal survey of American parents shows that by most measures, black fathers who live with their children [and even those who reside separately] are just as involved as other dads who live with their kids—or more so" (Reyes). Dismantling stereotypes like the "absent black father" takes time and counter examples. The story of Luke Cage's maturation as a husband and father within the pages of *The New Avengers* offers readers a corrective to this negative stereotype as well as a specific vision of remasculinization based on paternal responsibility rather than just spectacular violence.

In many ways Luke Cage and his family are at the heart of award-winning writer Brian Michael Bendis' run on *The New Avengers*. Bendis' tenure on *The New Avengers* begins with Cage joining the team and ends with Cage, his wife, and their infant daughter leaving the Avengers. After dismantling the previous incarnation of Marvel's flagship team of heroes in his first story, "Avengers Disassembled," Bendis reconstructed the team in 2004 as *The New Avengers*. Gone, or relocated, were such iconic characters as Captain America, Iron-Man and Thor. Instead, Bendis included a mix of big name characters like Spider-Man and Wolverine alongside traditionally second tier superheroes such as Luke Cage, Spider-Woman, The Sentry, Iron-Fist, Echo ... and eventually a wide range of other heroes. After a chance team-up during a super-villain prison break, Captain America recruits Luke Cage and the others to form their own version of The Avengers. Cage, an African American character who first appeared in the Marvel Universe in 1972 as part of a blaxploitation wave in comics, is an ex-con with unbreakable skin and super strength. In the 1970s, Cage's uniform consisted of an unbuttoned yellow shirt and a silver headband; the modern Cage refuses any flamboyant superhero costumes and is clad in just jeans and a t-shirt. Though he is incredibly strong and resistant to damage, Cage is still considered a street-level hero rather than a top-powered one. Cage seemed to many fans to be an odd fit with The Avengers, whose adventures are usually on a global or even interstellar scale. But through the ensuing adventures of *Civil War*, *Secret Invasion*, *Dark Reign*, and *Avengers Vs. X-Men*, Luke Cage became an integral part of the New Avengers, and as a black character with limited powers and limited financial resources, Cage facilitated a different perspective on the post–9/11 issues addressed in the Marvel comics. Still, right from the very beginning of the series, paternity was a central theme explored through Luke Cage's life and exploits. In *New Avengers* #3 Steve Rogers (aka Captain America) asks Luke to be part of the team, in front of his visibly pregnant girlfriend Jessica Jones. Cage is surprised and says: "%!^^* like this, groups and teams and whatnot, never even occurred to me to bother with it. But … I sure wouldn't mind my little girl growing up and hearing that her Dad was an Avenger once upon a time. Wouldn't mind that at all" (Bendis, *NA #3*, 19).[3]

Luke Cage's progression as a husband, father, and superhero within Brian Michael Bendis written stories is one of the most interesting character developments in the history of Marvel Comics. The serial nature of comics and the generational changes in the core audience of young readers requires that even as the long-running characters develop each month, they cannot change too much. As Umberto Eco famously pointed out in his landmark discussion of Superman: "The stories develop in a sort of oneiric climate—of which the reader is not aware at all—where what has happened before and what has happened after appear extremely hazy" (114). In this serialized "oneiric climate," rife with reboots, reimaginings, time travel, alternate universes, and other industrial and narrative devices used to perpetually keep characters in their prime, real changes are very rare. Superman needs to remain in his late twenties, Batman needs to remain a bachelor, Iron-Man needs to remain an arrogant genius, Spider-Man needs to remain insecure and guilt-ridden, etc.… But Bendis' work entirely redefined Luke Cage as a character, from an irresponsible thug to a protective family man.

As originally crafted by Archie Goodwin in the 1970s as Marvel's attempt to capitalize on the success of blaxploitation films, Cage was, in large part, rooted in racial stereotypes about black masculinity. Michael van Dyk has argued, "One of the most embarrassing characters in comics history, Cage typified Marvel's disregard for the cultural effects their images were producing. Like the films that spawned him, Luke Cage served to reinforce the black male stereotype in America" (473). Specifically, van Dyk describes the stereotype of Cage derived from the films as "a militant, sexually insatiable ghetto tough bent on overthrowing the oppressive white system" (471). Other critics remember the original version of Luke Cage in a much more positive light. Adilifu Nama, for example, argues that despite the stereotypical elements Cage "is in many ways the most inherently political and socially profound black superhero to ever emerge, regardless of his connection to the Blaxploitation film fad" (54–55). Regardless of whether the 1970s Luke Cage was "the most embarrassing character in comics history" or "the most inherently political and socially profound black superhero," his earliest appearances did establish Cage as a hypersexual street level type of character more than as a thoughtful, intelligent, and noble hero.

Luke Cage's stereotypical past depictions are not forgotten by Brian Michael Bendis, but they are rewritten to illustrate personal development. Bendis first utilized Cage in his series *Alias* (2001–2004) that focused on Jessica Jones' noir-like exploits as a private investigator. Jessica and Luke were acquaintances as street level heroes in the seedier parts of New York. In the first issue of *Alias* Jessica uses Luke for rough sex when she feels like degrading herself. Luke Cage appears to be cast according to his Blaxploitation roots as a hypersexual black buck, and he is more than willing to have sex with Jessica (anally it is implied) when she drunkenly propositions him late at night. Jessica's internal narration makes it clear that she just wanted a dirty experience: "Lucas will feel guilty about this. He's a decent guy and a buddy and he'll feel bad about this. But that feeling will pass. Because he'll look back and remember this was the one night I let him do anything he wanted. And even though he'll know it's wrong, he'll smile to himself.... But I can't say that I care, really. I don't care what he feels like. I just want to feel something. It doesn't matter what. Pain. Humility. Anger" (11). Jessica may like Cage, but in their first scene together she treats him like a piece of meat, a black bull who can dominate and degrade a white woman looking for humiliation. Compounding Luke Cage's hypersexual reputation, a few issues later, Carol Danvers (aka Ms. Marvel) warns Jessica over lunch that Cage is "a total cape chaser ... likes to, you know, those with capes ... just ask Jessica Drew [Spider-Woman], and Tigra, and She-Hulk" (*Alias #3*, 8). Even after Luke and Jessica are married and he has become the leader of the Avengers, his prodigious sexual past is treated as a recurring joke as earlier conquests keep appearing and flirting with Cage, much to Jessica's chagrin and Luke's embarrassment.

While Bendis' depiction of Cage across various series does not ignore Cage's past characterizations as street-wise and sexually promiscuous, he does quickly develop Cage into a thoughtful, sensitive and more three dimensional character. Readers are provided with an intimate look at the development of Luke Cage through his evolving relationship with Jessica and their daughter. When Jessica tells Luke that she is pregnant with his child he is thrilled that she is going to keep it and excited to become a father even if their romantic relationship is still tenuous. During Jessica's seemingly interminable pregnancy, shown primarily in *The Pulse* (2004–2006), Bendis' second series focuses on Jessica Jones. Luke is supportive, concerned and protective. When Jessica does finally go into labor the event is treated with all the excitement that befits a superhero adventure (*The Pulse* #11 to #14) and involves all of the Avengers. Luke proposes to Jessica in issue #14 right after the baby is born with a speech that recognizes his love for his family and his desire to redress the absent father stereotype of black men:

> This is it. This is the life I want and the life I got. In fact, it's the life I never thought I'd get. An Avenger. Someone's father. And in love with you. So, that said, do we *have* to get married? Hell, no. Won't change a thing and it's just a piece of paper. But listen to this: We're two "super hero" parents and this is a biracial relationship. Don't mean to shock you with that last bit, but it's true. For some people out there that is about a million different reasons to hate us all wrapped up in one convenient package. And now we have the Avengers spotlight right up our ass. And you know I don't care what people think of me.... But I do know that now we represent something larger than who we are.... Why the hell does this girl, this perfect little baby girl, have to contend with being illegitimate on top of all the other crap that's going to come her way because of her biracial, super hero parents?? Why set her up for more? And why I got to be the cliché of being someone's baby's daddy when it ain't the case. It ain't me, I *ain't* that cliché. You're my life. So I think if we have to represent—let's represent who we are... I think we should get married [4–5].

Jessica does not accept Luke's proposal until a few months later in *The New Avengers Annual* #1. Luke is so pleased that he shouts out: "Yo! She said Yes!! WE'RE GETTIN' MARRIED!" (Bendis, *New Avengers Annual #1*, 7) embarrassing Jessica in front of all the other Avengers. The issue ends with Luke and Jessica's wedding (presided over by a minister who bears an intentional resemblance to Stan Lee), and a touching speech delivered by Jessica about how much she loves Luke despite all the craziness of their lives, and how much she loves watching him be a father.

The novelty of having a married couple with an infant daughter involved with the Avengers is often played for humor, with numerous jokes about jealousy, dirty diapers, lack of sleep, mother-in-laws and arguments over money. But the realities of being active superhero parents, particularly during the tumultuous events of storylines like *Civil War*, *Secret Invasion*, *Dark Reign* and *Avengers Vs. X-Men*, are primarily treated by Bendis as a spectacular threat to the very idea of domestic bliss. Near the start of the *Civil War* crossover event, for example, the implementation of the Superhuman Registration Act is portrayed in *New Avengers* #22 as a direct invasion and assault on the Cage family home. Moreover, writer Brian Michael Bendis uses Luke Cage's iconic position in the Marvel universe as a black hero to draw an analogy between the curtailing of civil rights in the fictional comic book world, the post–9/11 climate of unprecedented NSA surveillance of private citizens, and the Civil Rights struggles of the 1950s and 1960s. When Iron Man, the leader of the pro-registration side, comes to the Cage's apartment and tells Luke that if he does not register by midnight he will be a criminal again, and "they will come to your home and they will take you out of here." Luke replies, "Oh, is it Mississippi in the 1950s now? ... Getting pulled out of your *home* in the middle of the night for being *different* is the same now as it was then." When Iron Man disagrees, claiming, "No. This is about breaking the law," Cage reminds him that "slavery used to be a law" (Bendis, *NA #22*, 4–5). Luke then says a heartfelt goodbye to his wife and child as they leave for the safety of Canada, and awaits the arrival of the military. When they try to arrest him at midnight, Luke fights back spectacularly and makes his escape with the aid of his friends and allies Captain America, Daredevil, and The Falcon. Luke maintains his principles, and proudly fights against government oppression for being "different," but his home is destroyed and his family is temporarily torn apart. Balancing superheroic adventures and family responsibilities is clearly depicted as difficult to reconcile. To be a noble and idealistic man of action Luke is compelled to join the battle even if it means parting with his family.

The story of Luke Cage adjusting to married life and fatherhood is primarily a subplot that runs throughout Brian Michael Bendis' time writing *The New Avengers*. In the immediate aftermath of *Secret Invasion* Luke Cage's role as a father takes center stage. The Marvel-wide *Secret Invasion* event addressed American post–9/11 paranoia with a story about hundreds of shape-shifting Skrull sleeper agents that have replaced key military personnel and numerous superheroes in order to lay the ground work for taking over the Earth. Once the heroes uncover the plot they realize nobody can be trusted and infighting, betrayal, and suspicion undermine even the Earth's mightiest heroes' ability to fight back. Eventually the real heroes gain the upper hand and during the final monumental battle Jessica leaves baby Danielle in the care of kindly old Jarvis, the Avengers' long-time trusted butler, so that she can help Luke and the heroes keep the Skrulls from taking over Earth. But after defeating the bulk of the Skrull invaders, Jessica learns that Jarvis has been replaced by a Skrull agent. Luke and Jessica race back to Avenger's tower in horror to find that the Skrull-Jarvis has disappeared and taken baby Danielle as a hostage. Racked with guilt and worry, Luke and Jessica return to the New Avengers stronghold in issue #48 and inform them of the situation. "They got the baby! They got Danielle!" Luke cries. "He could be any shape or size. He could be anyone. Our baby could be dead, alive. We don't know" (Bendis, *NA #48*, 13). Their teammates try to comfort Luke and Jessica and they all set out to find the baby, enlisting the aid of the Fantastic Four and other superheroes along the way. But, despite scouring the city and roughing up every villain and remaining Skrull they can get their hands on, Skrull-Jarvis and the baby cannot be found.

Luke is so desperate to find his baby daughter in *The New Avengers* #49 that he turns to the villain Norman Osborn (aka The Green Goblin), who has become the leader of the all-powerful S.H.I.E.L.D. agency and has resources at his command after the events of *Civil War* that the outlawed heroes cannot match. Luke agrees to register his super-powers, and to work for Osborn if he can help find Danielle. While teamed with Osborn's crew of super-villains disguised as government sanctioned heroes, Luke tacitly condones the torture of Skrull prisoners until one of them finally reveals a secret meeting location where Skrull-Jarvis can be found. Luke meets with Skrull-Jarvis on his own and promises not to hurt him if he just hands over the baby. A relieved and tearful Luke holds his child, who smiles at the sight of her father. Then, to Luke's surprise, the Skrull is shot between the eyes by Osborn's assassin, Bullseye, from several buildings away. Luke reunites Danielle with the overjoyed and grateful Jessica back at the Osborn occupied Avengers' tower. "This was a major risk," Jessica says. "You sure this is the road you want to go down?" With resolve, Luke replies: "We have to—we have to do what is right for her. It's all about her. Everything we do from now on. It's *all* about her. I know we knew that in theory, but this is it. This is how it *has* to be.... I have never been so relieved about anything ever in my whole entire life. How on God's Earth would we be able to go on if we didn't get her back?" (Bendis, *NA #49*, 17). Once his family is safely out of the building, Luke grabs a magic crow-bar (yes, they exist in superhero stories), storms into Osborn's office, beats up his henchmen and declares that he will never work for a murder like him, but that he will leave Osborn unharmed because he did help find the baby.

Luke's quest to save his abducted child from alien invaders, to make a deal (and break it) with the devil incarnate if that is what it takes to ensure his daughters safety, is used by Bendis to reveal the emotional stakes that underlie the traditionally hyperbolic superhero adventures. The storyline also shifts the project of post–9/11 remasculinization from fantastic large-scale, military-like, superheroism to a more specific emphasis on remasculinization through paternal commitment. While themes of paternal responsibility are rare in comic books, it has become a dominant trope in post–9/11 Hollywood films, particularly as a message about the need to heroically protect the family (especially children) from the threat of metaphorical terrorists. For example, in *War of the Worlds* (2005), Tom Cruise's character has to keep his children safe from an alien invasion. In *Taken* (2008), Liam Neeson's displaced father has to rescue his daughter from European white-slavers. In *World War Z* (2013), Brad Pitt's character has to keep his wife and two daughters safe from a zombie apocalypse. In *Prisoners* (2013), Hugh Jackman's distraught father has to find his daughter who has been kidnapped by a sexual predator, and in *Homefront* (2013), Jason Statham's father has to protect his daughter from the local druglords that attack his family home. In these movies, and countless other film and television examples, American masculinity is redeemed through the protection of families under siege.

Most of the fathers in these films are initially depicted as inadequate in some way. They are divorced, or they are unable to support their children financially, or they are workaholics, or they are immature, or estranged from their children. In short, though they love their children they do not seem to measure up to the cultural ideal of responsible paternity. This early paternal deficiency is not equated with a lack of rugged masculinity; these men are represented as tough, working-class guys, several with military or law enforcement backgrounds. But, as with Luke Cage, this toughness alone is not enough to redeem their masculinity along paternal lines. Protective, paternal masculinity has to be realized in these narratives not only through spectacular action, but through a single-minded devotion to safeguarding their children by any means necessary. Luke's bullet proof skin and super-human strength may be great for fighting aliens but it does not keep his daughter out of harm's way. Luke's frantic search, and more importantly the dangerous bargain he strikes with Osborn to find his child, is what validates his paternal masculinity. In her discussion of *War of the Worlds* and other post–9/11 films featuring fathers who must save their children, Hannah Hamad identifies the purpose of such masculine heroics.

> These films depend upon similarly contrived scenarios that recuperate failing fatherhood through enactment of paternal protectiveness in extreme circumstances, whereupon the reconstitution of a normative familial unit is not the point of the protagonist's narrative journey, so much as the revalidation of his initially derogated fatherhood. These extreme scenarios depict the redemption of inadequate fathers, deflecting feminist critiques of masculinity, by positing the male's fulfillment of the role of father-protector as compensating for domestic and interpersonal failings [Hamad 250].

Similar to these action movies, the redemption of Luke Cage's father-protector role is the crucial point of the story. Luke's selfish desire to continue as an active superhero, thus courting danger for himself and his family, is compensated for by his devotion to saving his daughter. This is why it has to be Luke who actually gets Danielle back; he is the one in need of redemption. Jessica also has super-powers, knows Osborn, and is struggling to find the baby. But Jessica is consistently portrayed as the good mother who takes care of the baby rather than willingly jumping into whichever adventure pops up each week. Luke needs to learn the lesson Jessica has already accepted.

In "Supermoms? Maternity and the Monstrous-Feminine in Superhero Comics," I posit Jessica Jones as one of the few examples of superheroine mothers who choose to leave behind their crime fighting careers in order to safely raise their children. The choice Jessica makes to remove herself from costumed adventures is harder for Luke to come to terms with. Despite Luke's speech about having to do what is right for their baby after saving her from Skrull Jarvis, Luke continues his dangerous life as the leader of the New Avengers. On more than one occasion over the course of Bendis' run on *The New Avengers*, Jessica actually takes Danielle away from Luke in order to keep her out of harms way. At the onset of the *Civil War*, Jessica and baby Danielle flee to Canada (*NA #23*). In the middle of the ongoing conflict, after reuniting with Luke and the renegade New Avengers who are constantly on the run, Jessica takes the baby and absconds to the safety of Avengers' tower occupied by Iron Man and the other leaders of the registration movement (Bendis, *New Avengers Annual #2*, 37). And again in *New Avengers* #22 to #24 (*NA* vol. 2), Jessica and the baby go into hiding after Osborn escapes from jail and threatens to kill Danielle. Each time Jessica leaves with the baby Luke searches for her and Danielle, pleads for their return, and declares that they mean more to him than anything else. But, after hearing Luke promise to put Jessica and the baby first several times, and then always running off on some world-saving mission, Jessica questions Luke's priorities. In this construction, by forcing Jones to regularly leave him, Cage's consistent decision to prioritize super-heroics over fatherhood renders him one kind of absent father. In *New Avengers* #24, after Jessica and the baby are reunited at Avenger's mansion, Jessica explains her disappearance: "I had to. I'm sorry. Norman Osborn threatened her and nothing was more important than getting her to safety. I had to get her out of here. Nothing's more important than the baby." When Luke angrily says, "I know," Jessica replies, "I know you *think* you do." Luke asks, "What does *that* mean?" Jessica offers a lengthy explanation of why she feels that Luke has not fully put the protection of his family before his own needs yet:

> Going by actions and actions alone... The Avengers are more important to you. Being Luke Cage is more important to you... What are we doing here? With a baby? Are you really going to say with a straight face that this place is as safe as any other place in the city? Really? This place? What part makes you feel safe? The angry protestors outside? The Nazi robots? The homicidal mutant with indestructible, retractable claws? Babe, our lives are different now. This baby changes everything. Every time you or I leave the house it's not like we're just going to work ... we're not going to 9-to-5 jobs. We're going to war. We're going to fight. When people go to war, by definition, no matter who they are or where they are, there's a chance they're never coming back [Bendis, *NA #24* vol. 2, 15–16].

Jessica tells Luke she loves him and wants him to come with her and the baby away from the dangers of being an Avenger. But, even as they are discussing what this means for their family, Iron Fist interrupts and calls them to a meeting where Captain America informs them that they are going into battle with the mutant population and the fate of the Earth may hang in the balance. Luke kisses baby Danielle goodbye and goes off to battle again.

It is not until near the end of the series that Luke Cage truly comes to the realization that his superhero life is dangerous to the baby. Luke realizes that he needs to do more than just love the baby but still carry on selfishly with his life of adventure. Luke finally recognizes that being physically powerful is not enough to be a real father-protector, that beating up aliens, super-villains, and monsters is not the best way to protect his family. In *The New Avengers* #30, during a brief quiet moment amid the *Avengers vs. X-Men* crossover storyline, Daredevil, one of Luke's closest friends (who had also single handedly saved baby Danielle and her nanny from an army of Nazi robots in *New Avengers* #16), comments, "I can't believe you're trying to raise a child in all this.... This life is no place for a baby." Luke reluctantly admits he is considering quitting the New Avengers. "Something's gotta give, man. I never had something to lose before. I *thought* I did but I was kidding myself. But once you got a baby ... cliché as it is ... everything changes" (Bendis, *NA* #30 vol. 2, 2–3). Luke and Daredevil's discussion is cut short when they are attacked by religious race purifiers out to destroy mutantkind. But, as Luke fights for his life, images of Jessica and the baby race through his mind, intercut with panels of his struggle. The battle only reinforces Luke's realization that that the most important thing in the world is his family. Luke defeats the bad guy, calls his wife and walks away, determined to give up being an Avenger.

Brian Michael Bendis' final *New Avengers* story arc wraps up the popular series with Luke and his family leaving the team. The degree of Luke Cage's development from street-level thug to devoted family man is repeatedly made clear in *The New Avengers* #31. When Jessica fears that the other heroes will be angry with her for taking Luke away, Ms. Marvel tells her, "You *let* him figure it out all by himself. And though he took his sweet time getting there, congratulations that you have a man who has the ability to figure out what the big-boy, right thing to do is. Because a guy like that is few and far between." Even Cage is self-aware about how far he has come, saying, "I'm not saying I'm not going to help out. I just have to, you know, prioritize.... Damn, that sounds weird coming out of my mouth, right?"

(Bendis, *NA #31* vol. 2, 20). Of course, this is a superhero series, so some mystical threat plunges the team into danger before the Cage family can move out of Avengers' mansion, but the rest of the team forces them to leave for the sake of the baby. Jessica sends Luke back to help their former teammates one last time, and once the crisis is averted the series ends in issue #34 with the Cage family saying their goodbyes and walking off to start a new, presumably safer, life. As they are leaving, Doreen their mutant nanny (aka Squirrel-Girl), sums up the change that Luke has gone through: "It occurs to me that you went from once upon a time being in jail, to being an Avenger, to being a husband and father … it seems that both of you should be really proud of yourselves for all of this" (Bendis, *NA #34* vol. 2, 35). The events of *Civil War*, *Secret Invasion*, *Dark Reign*, *Avengers Vs. X-Men* and all the other dangers the New Avengers faced between 2004 and 2012 redefined Luke Cage as a character, and redeemed him not just as a man, but as a father.

The culmination of Brian Michael Bendis' authorship of *The New Avengers*, after such a long and tumultuous run, was celebrated with an additional one-shot comic: *The New Avengers: Finale* #1. This special issue tied-up loose ends and looked back on the amazing events of the previous years, but importantly it also gave Luke Cage the final word of the series. In reflecting on their adventures and miraculous accomplishments, Cage delivers a long speech: "I realized … even with the globe-trotting, Earth-shattering, spectacularly colorful lives we have led … there's only one thing I wanted to do this entire time … only one thing that will tell me the battle was won. That the fight was over. And that is one day I am going to go for a walk. A free man of convictions. And I said to myself, if I ever get to do that again … I'll know, on that day … we won" (Bendis, *New Avengers Finale #1*, 37–38). Throughout most of Luke's speech the accompanying images feature montages of some of their greatest battles against other heroes, against the Skrulls, and against Osborn's super-villain version of S.H.I.E.L.D. But the final two-page image is a peaceful depiction of the New Avengers in civilian clothes, smiling as they walk through a sunny park together. The focus of the celebratory image is fittingly the Cage family, with Jessica's arm around Luke as he pushes the laughing baby Danielle in a stroller. The culmination of the series is equated with the culmination of Luke Cage as a devoted father rather than just a superhero. The victory which Luke values the most is not saving the world, it is saving his family.

The epic crossover events in the Marvel universe in recent years have functioned like much of popular culture has: as a way to deal with the tragedies of 9/11, and to restructure a belief in American fortitude, perseverance, and eventual victory over external and internal threats. Central to this fantasy has been a remasculinization of the American hero. These comic books have provided comforting fantasies of superheroes that can defy the odds and save America from any and all threats. The story of Luke Cage's development from a streetwise (and promiscuous) hero-for-hire to a responsible and protective husband and a father represents a more specific form of masculinization. Cage's ascension as a superdad is more important than his ascension as a superhero. Moreover, Cage's embrace of fatherhood, even at the expense of his own exciting life as a hero, provides a counter example to the misleading stereotype of absent Black fathers. There is a recognition in the way Bendis uses Cage regarding the symbolic importance of utilizing one of the most iconic African American characters in comics as the emotional anchor to the stories. Through all of the incredible events of *Civil War*, *Secret Invasion*, *Dark Reign*, and *Avengers Vs. X-Men* the message may be that America is still tough—is still masculine. But in *The New Avengers* the message is also that to be a "real" man, a real hero, you need to be more than tough: you need to be a good father.

Notes

1. For discussions of how superhero comic books have addressed post-9/11 fears, see Treat, Lewis, Geers, and Smith and Goodrum.

2. For discussions of how superhero movies have addressed post-9/11 fears, see Muller and Pheasant-Kelly.

3. The shifting membership of the New Avengers has been featured in multiple volumes, sometimes called *New Avengers* and sometimes *The New Avengers*, which can be confusing. Citation has followed what each individual issue has included in its colophon.

Works Cited

Banks, Rick R. "What's the Problem with Black Fathers?" *Patheos*. Patheos, 29 Nov. 2011. Web. 20 Sept. 2014.

Bendis, Brian Michael (writer), Mark Bagley (penciller), and Scott Hanna (inker). *The Pulse* #4 (July 2004), Marvel Comics. Print.

Bendis, Brian Michael (writer), Olivier Coipel (penciller), and Drew Geraci, et al. (inkers). *New Avengers: Annual* #1 (Apr. 2006), Marvel Comics. Print.

Bendis, Brian Michael (writer), and Mike Deodato (artist). *New Avengers* 2 #16 (Sept. 2011), Marvel Comics. Print.

Bendis, Brian Michael (writer), and Mike Deodato (artist). *New Avengers* 2 #30 (Sept. 2012), Marvel Comics. Print.

Bendis, Brian Michael (writer), and Mike Deodato (artist). *New Avengers* 2 #34 (Nov. 2012), Marvel Comics. Print.

Bendis, Brian Michael (writer), and Mike Deodato and Will Conrad (artists) *New Avengers* 2 #24 (May 2012), Marvel Comics. Print.

Bendis, Brian Michael (writer), David Finch (penciller), and Danny Miki, Allen Martinez, and Victor Olizaba (inkers). *New Avengers* 1 #3 (Feb. 2005), Marvel Comics. Print.

Bendis, Brian Michael (writer), and Michael Gaydos (artist). *Alias* #1–28 (Nov. 2001–Jan. 2004), Marvel Comics. Print.

Bendis, Brian Michael (writer), and Michael Gaydos (artist). *New Avengers* 2 #31 (Oct. 2012), Marvel Comics. Print.

Bendis, Brian Michael (writer), Bryan Hitch and Stuart Immonen (pencillers), and Butch Guice, et al. (inkers). *New Avengers: Finale* #1 (May 2010), Marvel Comics. Print.

Bendis, Brian Michael (writer), Billy Tan (penciller), and Matt Banning (inker). *New Avengers* 1 #48–49 (Dec. 2008–Jan. 2009), Marvel Comics. Print.

Bendis, Brian Michael (writer), and Leinil Yu (artist). *New Avengers* 1 #22 (July 2006), Marvel Comics. Print.

Brown, Jeffrey A. *Black Superheroes: Milestone Comics and Their Fans*. Jackson: University of Mississippi Press, 2000. Print.

_____. "Supermoms? Maternity and the Monstrous-Feminine in Superhero Comics." *Journal of Graphic Novels and Comics* 2.1 (2011): 75–87. Print.

Bukatman, Scott. "X-Bodies: The Torment of the Mutant Superhero." *Uncontrollable Bodies: Testimonies of Identity and Culture*. Ed. Rodney Sappington and Tyler Stallings. Seattle: Bay Press, 1994. 92–129. Print.

Coles, Roberta, and Charles Green, eds. *The Myth of the Missing Black Father*. New York: Columbia University Press, 2009. Print.

Connor, Michael E., and Joseph White, eds. *Black Fathers: An Invisible Presence in America*. New York: Routledge, 2006. Print.

Easthope, Antony. *What a Man's Gotta Do: The Masculine Myth in Popular Culture*. New York: Routledge, 1990.

Eco, Umberto. *The Role of the Reader: Explorations in the Semiotics of Texts*. Bloomington: Indiana University Press, 1979. Print.

Faludi, Susan. *The Terror Dream: Myth and Misogyny in an Insecure America*. New York: Picador, 2008. Print.

Geers, Jeff. "'The Great Machine Doesn't Wear a Cape!' American Cultural Anxiety and the Post-9/11 Superhero." *Comic Books and American Cultural History: An Anthology*. Matthew Pustz, ed. New York: Bloomsbury Academic Press, 2012. 250–62. Print.

Hamad, Hannah. "Extreme Parenting: Recuperating Fatherhood in Steven Spielberg's *War of the Worlds*." *Feminism at the Movies: Understanding Gender in Contemporary Popular Cinema*. Hilary Radner and Rebecca Stringer, eds. New York: Routledge, 2011. 241–54. Print.

Jones, Jo and William D. Mosher. "Fathers' Involvement with Their Children: United States, 2006–2010." *National Health Statistics Report* 71 (2013): 1–22. Web. 21 Sept. 2014.

Kimmel, Michael. *Angry White Men: American Masculinity at the End of an Era*. New York: Nation Books, 2013. Print.

Lewis, A. David. "The Militarism of American Superheroes After 9/11." *Comic Books and American Cultural History: An Anthology*. Matthew Pustz, ed. New York: Bloomsbury Academic Press, 2012. 223–36. Print.

Morehouse Research Institute and the Institute for American Values. *Turning the Corner on Father Absence in Black America*. New York: Institute for American Values Press, 1999. Print.

Muller, Christine. "Power, Choice, and September 11 in *The Dark Knight*." *The 21st Century Superhero: Essays on Gender, Genre and Globalization in Film*. Richard J. Gray II and Betty Kaklamanidou, eds. Jefferson, NC: McFarland, 2011. 46–60. Print.

Nama, Adilifu. *Superblack: American Popular Culture and Black Superheroes*. Austin: University of Texas Press, 2011. Print.

Naasel, Kenrya Rankin. *Bet on Black: African American Women Celebrate Fatherhood in the Age of Barack Obama*. New York: Kifani Press, 2013. Print.

Pheasant-Kelly, Frances. *Fantasy Film Post 9/11*. New York: Palgrave Macmillan, 2013. Print.

Reyes, Emily Albert. "Survey Finds Dads Defy Stereotype About Black Fatherhood." latimes.com. *The Los Angeles Times*. 20 Dec. 2013. Web. 20 Sept. 2014.

Screven, Nadaysha. "Who's Your Daddy: The Epidemic of Absent Black Fathers." Oldschool1003.com. Interactive One. 12 June 2013. Web. 20 Sept. 2014.

Smith, Phillip, and Michael Goodrum. "'We have experienced a tragedy that words cannot properly describe': Representations of Trauma in Post–9/11 Superhero Comics." *Literature Compass* 8.8 (2011): 487–98. Print.

Stabile, Carol A. "'Sweetheart, This Ain't Gender Studies': Sexism and Superheroes." *Communication and Critical/Cultural Studies* 6.1 (2009): 86–92. Print.

Treat, Shaun. "How American Learned to Stop Worrying and Cynically Enjoy! The Post–9/11 Superhero Zeitgeist." *Communication and Critical/Cultural Studies* 6, no. 1 (March 2009): 103–109.

Van Dyk, Michael. "What's Going On? Black Identity in the Marvel Age." *International Journal of Comic Art* 8.1 (2006): 466–90. Print.

Wanzo, Rebecca. "The Superhero: Meditations on Surveillance, Salvation and Desire." *Communication and Critical/Cultural Studies* 6.1 (2009): 93–97. Print.

Part V—Character(s) Revealed Through Trauma

Between Two Towers: The Struggle for the Soul of Spider-Man

Daniel J. O'Rourke

What is a hero? Newspaper reports would tell us that an athlete performing an extraordinary feat on a playing field or an individual overcoming personal obstacles would possess "heroic" qualities. More often, we think of a hero as someone who selflessly serves others. She might do so at some risk to her own physical, financial, or social-well being. Unfortunately, we tend to overlook everyday heroes such as parents, firefighters, or nurses to focus on more dramatic tales of risk or rescue. Difficult times can create circumstances that call seemingly ordinary people to perform extraordinary acts. These heroic feats then fire the imaginations of artists to record tales and create images of heroism in art, music, and literature. Such tributes can raise spirits and inspire viewers/listeners/readers in the community to find a bit of bravery in themselves. This art preserves the best of our humanity and stands to define our hopes for future generations.

In the twentieth century, the superhero narrative captured the attention of young people around the world. It first achieved mass appeal in the golden era of comic books in the United States (1938–1945). The story of the superhero was initially somewhat linear: An individual with incredible powers helps average citizens fight for "Truth, Justice, and the American Way." The paradox of this heroic myth was that the super-powered advocate was a vigilante acting outside the framework of a civil society. These caped crusaders were neither deputized nor authorized to act on behalf of the public. This narrative followed the tradition of the American cowboy taking justice into his gun hand when the courts and officers of the law failed to bring justice to powerless citizens. Yet few narrative forms were serialized as often or explored in as many ways as the characters of the simple comic book. As comic books continued decade after decade, readers grew older and more sophisticated (Wright 280). Eventually, portraits of costumed avengers became more nuanced and complex. In 1962, a landmark hero was created in the character of Spider-Man.

The world had changed since the golden era of comics in the 1940s. Soldiers who read comic books overseas returned home to create the next generation of readers. In the 1960s, eighteen-year-old "Baby Boomers" now faced a Cold War environment with the threat and promise of the nuclear age represented by the hope of new sources of energy versus the destructive power of the atomic bomb. The black and white world of the previous generation had been transformed into the psychedelic pastels of the modern world. Heroes also changed to reflect this new generation of readers. Square-chinned twenty-somethings of the Big Band era took a back seat to the silver age heroes of rock 'n' roll. No character represented this era better than "your friendly, neighborhood Spider-Man."

Peter Parker was a slight, bright teenager who was bullied by more aggressive athletes in his high school. He was bitten by a radioactive spider while on a science field trip and transformed into a being with the proportionate strength and agility of a spider. Yet, as readers of this volume will recall, this did not make him a superhero. Parker's first instinct was to use his abilities to acquire wealth to support himself and his family. A fateful choice would change his destiny. After one performance exhibiting his new talents, Parker did not help police stop a robber. Later, that same man would kill Peter's Uncle Ben. Peter Parker was now driven by a sense of guilt to accept the mantra: "With great power comes great responsibility." Suddenly, comic book writers were portraying the acquisition of super-human powers not only as a blessing, but also, a curse.

Spider-Man was a living duality: human/super-human, celebrity/nerd, hero/menace. He was the perfect hero for the comic books of the 1960s and 1970s. A teenage boy who was not a sidekick, but a hero making life and death decisions all the while trying to lead a "normal" life in his now secret identity of Peter Parker. The war in Vietnam and the battle for Civil Rights called into question laws, traditions, and the role of government in our lives. A generation of young people was questioning the role of women in society and the moral norms of American culture. Stan Lee and Steve Ditko created a young hero who struggled with his sometime super-powered demons while readers were trying to cope with the chaos and confusion of a changing society. Peter Parker represented readers struggling with all the issues of young life while Spider-Man protected us from extraordinary threat of super-villains. Parker/Spider-Man was one of us and showed us that heroism rested not only in the great battles but also in the seemingly small moral choices in our daily lives.

Readers grew up with Spider-Man. We reveled together in victory and commiserated in loss. Perhaps no character suffered as many triumphs and tragedies as the Web Slinger. The death of loved ones, finding love, graduating, marrying the girl of his dreams, and the day-to-day struggles of finding a job while protecting the people and city he loved. Spider-Man gave us hope and inspired a bit of courage in readers to do the right thing. It is little wonder then that when another unprecedented moment occurred in American history, readers would turn again to Peter Parker/Spider-Man for advice in making the right choices.

Marvel's Civil War

In 2006, Marvel presented a "major event" in its *Civil War* series. The core of the story was an examination of the issues facing readers in a 21st-century, post–9/11 America. Timeless dialectics of democracy such as "Freedom versus Security" and "Privacy or Protection" were being re-presented in the new age of terrorism. Five years after the attack, America was still at war and struggling with the moral questions of torturing prisoners, incarcerating "enemy combatants" without trial, weapons of mass destruction, and spying on foreigners and American citizens via cell phones and the Internet. In the Marvel Universe, the duality of superheroes—illegal vigilantes fighting for justice—became a metaphor for legal/moral issues of waging a war on terrorism. Marvel's *Civil War* begins when a group of young, inexperienced heroes confront a group of super-villains in an effort to win ratings for their reality television show. More than 800 people are killed as a consequence of the battle including many students at a nearby grade school (Millar, *CW #1*, 10). Public outrage calls for a new "Superhuman Registration Act" (SHRA) that will require all superheroes to register with the government and surrender their secret identities. The sides are drawn in the characterizations of two towering Marvel heroes: Iron Man and Captain America. Tony Stark/Iron Man, a former munitions dealer and Secretary of Defense, takes the pragmatic view that a new era calls for new laws and this legislation is the best that heroes could hope for. Steve Rogers/Captain America, the super soldier of World War II, argues for tradition and independence. To some new readers, this portrait might seem inconsistent with the red, white, and blue image of Captain America. However, longtime Cap fans know that the reawakened Cap had his own struggles with authority and change in the 1960s and 1970s. At one point in the era of Watergate, Steve Rogers cast off his shield and became Nomad, the "Man without a Country" (Engelhart *CA #180*). This is the libertarian Captain America who later opposes the SHRA.

At the center of the moral drama, Marvel once again places Spider-Man. It is a logical choice, as the teenage Peter Parker had looked up to both Iron Man and Captain America as role models in his formative years as a superhero. Prior to the outbreak of Marvel's *Civil War*, a bond is formed between Peter Parker and Tony Stark in the Spider-Man series. Peter suffers a near-death experience and undergoes a transformative metamorphosis embracing the totem of the spider (Straczynski *SM #527*). Parker's body lies dormant for several days because Spider-Man has shed his skin to be born anew. The Avengers rally around Peter's wife, Mary Jane, and Aunt May, fearing that Parker may be dead. Stark assumes the role of benevolent protector housing the Parkers and the giving Peter a job at Stark Industries upon his return. But something more is happening; Stark designs a new ultra-tech uniform for Spider-Man. The billionaire industrialist has anticipated the coming Civil War and seeks Parker's allegiance in a "blood oath" of loyalty. Peter, appreciative of the support Stark has shown his family, declares: "Whatever it takes, whatever it costs, in time or in blood—I'm there. You've got your blood oath" (Straczynski, *ASM #529*, 22). Clearly, Peter has no idea what is about to unfold.

Tony Stark is called to Washington to testify before a Senate Committee on Superheroes. The Committee does not know that Stark is currently Iron Man but he is called as an expert witness because he invented the armor and previously donned the suit. Parker accompanies Stark to Washington as his aide. Charges are lobbed back and forth: the collateral damage of superhero battles ($200 billion), the number of times superheroes saved the planet (47), senators ask, "Doctors, pilots, and taxi drivers must register with government, why not superheroes?" (Straczynski, *ASM #530*, 8–9). In a moment of passion, Peter responds that most superheroes "have lives, and families, and loved ones who would be at terrible risk to the very same bad guys if their identities were revealed.... Most superheroes never asked for these powers. Never wanted them" (Straczynski, *ASM #530*, 10). These are key distinctions between Spider-Man and the two chief protagonists of the *Civil War* narrative. Captain America did volunteer to become the super soldier in World War II and Tony Stark invented the Iron Man suit to save his life from terrorists. Neither Stark nor Rogers have families and both have surrendered their secret identities at various times in the careers. Only Spider-Man is an accidental hero who accepts his fate at great risk to himself and his loved ones. Thus, it makes sense that he would become the moral marker in the battle for security or freedom in the *Civil War* series.

From the outset, questions of privacy, trust, and security are at the center of the *Civil War* series. While Peter and Mary Jane are staying with Stark, Tony secretly listens to their conversations to determine if the young hero can be trusted (Straczynski *ASM #528*, 22–23). Later, in the heat of battle, Iron Man asks Spider-Man to employ his Spider-Sense to detect any trouble. Peter realizes that he never told Tony about this power and that there must be secret monitors in the new Stark-designed costume (Straczynski, *ASM #534*, 6). Stark makes his case more overt when he asks Peter to accept the SHRA and publically reveal his secret identity: "We live in a time when everyone has had to make sacrifices of their privacy. Wiretaps, increased surveillance, random searches at airports" (Straczynski, *ASM #532*, 15). Indeed, Americans have grown to accept changes in airport security as a consequence of 9/11. But it is the unseen listening that worries many U.S. citizens. Foreign Intelligence Surveillance Courts (FISA) were established in 2001 to expedite investigations that might prevent another terrorist attack. If information from suspected threats could save lives, most citizens would support targeted investigations. But the American Civil Liberties Union (ACLU) reports that of the 33,900 requests that were made, only 11 were denied ("Watching the Watchers" 20). It seems unlikely that investigators would be that precise in identifying potential threats. In 2008, the FISA Amendment Act extended government surveillance to include analysis of domestic phone calls if one of the callers was foreign ("Watching the Watchers" 20). The net grew wider still in 2013 when *The Guardian* newspaper published government documents revealing that Verizon, one of the nation's largest mobile phone carriers, had released significant records to the National Security Agency (NSA) and continues to do so in an "ongoing daily basis" (Greenwald). It would seem that the potential of the unseen enemy could be far worse than the enemy you can see.

Ironically, Captain America is the first hero confronted with the potential consequences of the imminent SHRA. He is conferring with Maria Hill, acting head of S.H.I.E.L.D., when the director interrogates him about his intentions and willingness to track down other heroes who break the coming law. Cap tells the Director of S.H.I.E.L.D., "Don't play *politics* with *me*, Hill. Super heroes need to stay *above* that stuff or Washington starts telling us who the *super-villains* are" (Millar, *CW #1*, 30). When the law passes, Captain America tries to recruit Spider-Man to his cause. He states, "I respect you Peter, and I know you. I know your *heart*. I know that you hate doing what you are doing.... We could use you on our side." Spider-Man can only respond, "I'm legal. I'm registered.... I just hope to God that I'm also right" (Straczynski, *ASM #534*, 32). It is clear standing in the shadow of Captain America that Peter Parker has doubts about the path he has chosen.

Tony Stark, however, has no such doubts. He refers to the superhero accident that killed hundreds as "What alcoholics call a *moment of clarity*. Becoming public employees makes *perfect sense* if it helps people sleep a little easier" (Millar, *CW #1*, 25). Spider-Man expresses his concerns over surrendering his secret identity but is assured by Sue Storm, the Invisible Woman, that it is no big deal. He responds, "Yeah, well ... not until the day that I come home and find my wife impaled on an *Octopus arm* and the woman who raised me begging for her *life*" (Millar, *CW #1*, 26). Nonetheless, Peter honors his "blood oath" to Stark and reveals his secret identity in a nationally telecast press conference in an effort to "earn back a little public trust" (Millar, *CW #2*, 36). In typical Spider-Man fashion, Peter Parker becomes an instant celebrity praised by the public and adored by the media. Then, as Parker and his wife make their way through an adoring mob to enter their apartment, one "fan" accuses Parker of betraying Captain America and attempts to shoot Peter and Mary Jane (Straczynski, *ASM #533*, 28).

The divide is now set. Either a hero is "with us" and registered, or "against us" and violating the law. Stark invokes memories of 1950s anti–Communist McCarthyism when he declares in a press conference, "I have determined the identities of 137 heroes. Those names are on the list I have in my hand right here" (Straczynski, *ASM #533*, 24). When asked by a member of the press how non-registered heroes will be treated, he responds that anyone "on this list who has not come forward to register, or who gives aid and comfort to those who refuse—will be hunted down, arrested, and imprisoned, without exception.... We will use whatever means necessary" (Straczynski, *ASM #533*, 24). One seminal moment in the storyline illustrates this point. A band of renegade heroes led by Captain America are lured to a chemical plant by a false alarm. Iron Man and his followers confront the non-registered heroes in an effort to make one final appeal to have them submit to the new law. Tensions quickly rise and a confrontation ensues. Suddenly, Thor comes to the rescue of the registered heroes. Bill Foster/Goliath confronts Thor and is killed by a massive bolt of lightning (Millar, *CW #4*, 11). Foster is the first fatality of the Civil War. It is soon learned that Tony Stark, Henry Pym, and Reed Richards cloned the God of Thunder to be a secret weapon in this war of superheroes.

Suddenly, Peter Parker finds himself in a most familiar and yet uncomfortable situation. Parker became a superhero because of a poor decision he made that cost the life of his Uncle Ben. Now, a seemingly older and wiser Spider-Man has chosen to side with a group of heroes who killed one of their own. Peter tries to comfort Henry Pym, a friend of Bill Foster and co-creator of the cloned Thor. As they talk he is left with a haunting question: "Do you ever wonder if we picked the right side here, Hank?" (Millar, *CW #4*, 17). Other heroes notice the seeming change in Parker and begin to question his loyalty to the cause. A critical doubt has been sown in Spider-Man. The legal certitude of the law is losing ground to the immorality of its advocates.

The grey area of security darkens when it is discovered that Stark Industries and the Fantastic Four Incorporated have garnered two billion dollars in no-bid government contracts to build a prison in the Negative Zone (Straczynski, *ASM #535*, 2–9). Memories of corporate profiteering and the incarceration of "enemy combatants" without trial are reflected in Peter's anguished challenge to Stark: "Following the *law* means these people get a *trial* before you send them away *to be imprisoned for the rest of their lives*" (Straczynski, *ASM #535*, 11). Stark replies in an agitated manner: "You can't put an atomic bomb on probation.... This place is not on American soil. American laws don't touch here. Once nonregistrants come here. They're legal nonentities. Occupants. Prisoners" (Straczynski, *ASM #535*, 11). The full consequences of the SHRA finally become apparent. Nonregistered Superheroes are now defined as rogue "Weapons of Mass Destruction." Heroes who have risked their lives to save American citizens are now political prisoners of the government denied due process. This is the breaking point. That night, Peter tells Mary Jane and Aunt May, "I've made a terrible mistake.... God, help me, I realize I've been on the wrong side" (Straczynski, *ASM #535*, 39).

Peter Parker's private confession to his family foreshadows a second appearance on television. This time Spider-Man interrupts a newscast to announce his change of heart: "Hello, people of New York, I've ... well, I've got a confession to make. I was wrong. I made a mistake" (Straczynski, *ASM #536*, 29). Spider-Man removes his mask a second time and speaks directly to the audience. He speaks of the concept of justice being destroyed and due process being denied. Finally, he states, "Some people say that the most important thing in the world is that we should be safe. But I was brought up to believe that some things are *worth* dying for. If the cost of silence is the soul of the country ... then the price is too high" (Straczynski, *ASM #536*, 31). The conversion is complete and the final battle of Civil War is set: Spider-Man will fight a losing battle at the side of Captain America.

Conclusion

The consequences of the *Civil War* series were dramatic in the Marvel Universe. Readers witnessed the deaths of Bill Foster and Steve Rogers, resentment and mistrust among the community of heroes pitted one against the another, but again, few suffered as much as Peter Parker. There were multiple attempts made on his life, one that resulted in grave injury to Aunt May. Most fans know that comic book stories are not written in stone and can be amended—witness the resurrection of Captain America (Brubaker *CA #25*). Yet such stories require even more suspension of disbelief and a little loss of faith that anything really matters in the comic book canon. The infamous story line of "One More Day?" costs Peter Parker the love of his life and the promise of an unborn daughter to restore the health of Aunt May and his secret identity (Straczynski *ASM #544–545*). However, since that time, this narrative has also been rewritten.

The loss of faith in leaders and the government is quite another matter. In the 1970s, the power of the National Security Agency (NSA) was abused by President Nixon to spy on American citizens perceived as "enemies" of the administration. Congressional sanctions were enacted that placed strict controls on the NSA that remained in place until 9/11. In the aftermath of the terrorist attack, a new policy of government surveillance was approved that expanded gradually to enable spying not only on suspected foreign terrorists, but world leaders, and every American citizen ("United States of Secrets [Part 1]"). Enemy combatants were tortured and imprisoned at Guantanamo Bay without hope of trial or parole. The attack of September 11 alerted Americans to a new kind of threat. Our shores might be safe from foreign invasion but a small cell of terrorists could attack anywhere and use unconventional weapons such as airplanes, bombs, or cyberattacks on citizens, corporations, or military installations. We learned that day that the enemy you cannot see (or hear) might be as dangerous as a physical army or navy. Unfortunately, in the real world, one cannot simply rewrite history in a subsequent edition of the daily news.

More than 250 years ago, Benjamin Franklin wrote: "Those who would give up essential Liberty, to purchase a little temporary Safety, deserve neither Liberty nor Safety" (Lemay 625). It is doubtful that even a scientist as brilliant as Franklin could have imagined the weapons of modern warfare or a tool as great as the Internet, but he did know something about fear and the costs of democracy. In 2013, President Obama spoke at the National Defense University and sounded a similar theme: "And yet, as our fight enters a new phase, America's legitimate claim of self-defense cannot be the end of the discussion. To say a military tactic is legal, or even effective, is not to say it is wise or moral in every instance. For the same human progress that gives us the technology to strike half a world away also demands the discipline to constrain power—or risk abusing it" (Obama).

The writers of Marvel's *Civil War* might not be as eloquent as Franklin or Obama, but their work did give us pause to look back and reflect. Tragedies such as 9/11 can lead to swift and decisive actions by political leaders to satisfy the public's immediate demand for justice and retribution. Emergency powers can be granted to leaders and laws will be passed quickly to meet the needs of a crisis. In such times, it can take great courage to look past the fear and confusion of the moment to question the long-term consequences of such actions.

Comic books are artistic renderings that can provide readers insight into complex issues as reflections of our popular culture. In comic books, superheroes die and are resurrected, plot lines are written and rewritten; narrative mistakes are made and forgiven by readers. In Marvel's *Civil War*, Peter Parker reminds us that "if the cost of silence is the soul of the country ... then the price is too high" (Straczynski, *SM #536*, 31). Democracy is costly. Americans are reminded of this fact when news of our nation's longest war in Afghanistan occasionally creeps onto the front page of our newspapers. And we are reminded when we recall the illegal activities and spying conducted by our government in the name of national security. Democracy is hard. It requires engagement, activity, information, and dissent when it is called for. James Madison wrote in the Federalist Papers that "if men were angels, no government would be necessary" (Shane 208). Democracy can be messy. It can be loud, boisterous, contentious, and colorful. (Perhaps more like a comic book than first imagined.) Mistakes can be made with the best of intentions in moments of crisis. Citizens and leaders of democratic nations are challenged to recognize and admit these errors in our quest to form "a more perfect Union." As Spider-Man reminds us in Marvel's *Civil War*, democracy requires a little heroism and the willingness to admit our mistakes.

Works Cited

Brubaker, Ed (writer), Steve Epting (artist), and Joe Caramagna (letterer). "Death of Captain America." *Captain America* #25 (March 2007), Marvel Comics. Print.

Engelhart, Steve (author), Sal Buscema (artist), and Vince Colleta (inker). "Nomad." Captain America #180 (Dec. 1974), Marvel Comics. Web. 4 Nov. 2014.

Greenwald, Glenn. "NSA collecting phone records of millions of Verizon customers daily." The Guardian.com. Guardian News and Media Limited, 6 June 2013. Web. 12 May 2014.

Lemay, J. A. Leo. *The Life of Benjamin Franklin*. Vol. 3. Philadelphia: University of Pennsylvania Press, 2008. Print.

Millar, Mark (writer), and Steve McNiven (penciller). *Civil War* #1–7 (May 2006–Feb. 2007), Marvel Comics. Print.

Obama, Barack. "Remarks by the President at the National Defense University." whitehouse.gov. The White House, 23 May 2013. Web. 8 August 2014.

Shane, Peter M. *Madison's Nightmare: How Executive Power Threatens American Democracy*. Chicago: University of Chicago Press, 2009. Print.

Straczynski, J. Michael (writer), Mike Deodato (penciller), and Joe Pimentel (inker). "The Other." *Amazing Spider-Man* #527–528 (Dec. 2005–Jan. 2006), Marvel Comics. Print.

Straczynski, J. Michael (writer), Ron Garney (penciller), and Bill Reinhold (inker). "Mr. Parker Goes to Washington." *Amazing Spider-Man* #529 (Feb. 2006), Marvel Comics. Print.

Straczynski, J. Michael (writer), Ron Garney (penciller), and Bill Reinhold (inker). "The War at Home." *Amazing Spider-Man* #532–536 (May–Nov. 2006), Marvel Comics. Print.

Straczynski, J. Michael (writer), Tyler Kirkham (penciller), and Jay Leisten (inker). "Mr. Parker Goes to Washington." *Amazing Spider-Man* #530 (March 2006), Marvel Comics. Print.

Straczynski, J. Michael (writer), Tyler Kirkham (penciller), and Sal Regala (inker). "Mr. Parker Goes to Washington." *Amazing Spider-Man* #531 (April 2006), Marvel Comics. Print.

Straczynski, J. Michael (writer), Joe Quesada (penciller), and Danny Miki (inker). "One More Day." *Amazing Spider-Man* #544 (Sept. 2007), Marvel Comics. Print.

Straczynski, J. Michael, Joe Quesada (writers), Joe Quesada (penciller), and Danny Miko (inker). "One More Day." *Amazing Spider-Man* #545 (Dec. 2007), Marvel Comics. Print.

"United States of Secrets (Part 1)." *Frontline*. Public Broadcasting System. 13 May 2014. Television.

"Watching the Watchers." *Stand* (Winter 2014): 18–23. Print.

Wright, Bradford W. *Comic Book Nation: The Transformation of Youth Culture in America*. Baltimore: John Hopkins University Press, 2003. Print.

Captain America in the 21st Century: The Battle for the Ideology of the American Dream

John McGuire

On the morning of March 7, 2007, the superhero Captain America, leader of the Avengers and defender of the American Dream, was murdered on the steps of a New York City courthouse. The crime sent shock waves throughout the fictional Marvel Universe and also made headlines in the real world of the comic books' readers. His readers had little reason to be worried. Since *The Death of Superman* in 1992, superhero deaths have become a comic book convention that had been quickly followed by the convention of superhero resurrection. In fact, Captain America himself had "died" as recently as 2001. Readers knew that Captain America would return to the Marvel Universe. Only time and a somewhat ingenious plot twist was needed to bring him back.[1]

Without the inside knowledge of his pending resurrection, news programs in the real world reported his death as something to be mourned. CBS reported his death on their website: "Captain America, the stars-and-stripes-wearing crime fighter, was gunned down by a sniper as he left a courthouse today. He was 66[qm] (Morgan). The BBC reported that Captain America's death had angered his 93-year-old co-creator Joe Simon: "It's a hell of a time for him to go, we really need him now" ("Comic Hero"). MSNBC reported that Captain America had been shot dead and suggested that the death of Captain America might be because he was not able to tell stories about modern day America as he had in the past (Tucker). The *New York Times* quoted Marvel comics publisher Dab Buckley on the Captain's fate: "He is very dead right now" (Gustines).

Bryan Robinson, writing for ABC News, quotes an angry comic book fan, 34-year-old commercial production director Ken Feliu: "I'm definitely pissed off.... I mean, why did they have to kill him off? ... He's supposed to represent all our ideals, everything we're supposed to aspire to and they couldn't leave him intact?" Robinson puts Captain America's death in context of not only what was happening in the Marvel Universe, but where this superhero narrative interacted with reality, summarizing the *Civil War* storyline and drawing connections to American society. He notes that Iron-man, Captain America's long time friend and ally, supports the registration and "secretly orchestrated a campaign that created circumstances to scare and mislead the public and government officials into supporting the act and all the programs that it entailed" (Robinson). Robinson lets the American mainstream public in on the truth that only Marvel's readers had known up until then: this is all about the Iraq war, the Patriot Act, and domestic surveillance. This is all about the very much *non*-fictional United States of America and its reality after September 11, 2001. The Captain America narrative within the *Civil War* limited series of 2006–2007 and the *Captain America* comic of 2007–2008 were both engaged in a discourse about what had happened to American society. This paper is an attempt to explore that discourse using the concepts of hegemony and ideology to see at what level these superhero comics were able to take part in the social debates and discussions of an American society in crisis, a crisis that began with the 9/11 attacks six years before the death of Captain America.

The catastrophe of September 11, 2001, fundamentally affected American society. The sense of triumph that America had carried since the defeat of its longstanding nemesis, the Soviet Union and Communism in the late 20th century (a triumph that had led an optimistic Francis Fukuyama, in 1992, to declare the end of history) ended the day of the terrorist attacks. A point of social crisis and shock, 9/11 became the source for America's aggressive actions on the world stage. A thick black line of causality is drawn from the September 11, 2001, to the invasions of Afghanistan and Iraq. The abuses at Guantanamo Bay and Abu Ghraib are born in the shadow of that day.

Domestically the PATRIOT Act and the creation of the Department of Homeland Security were the direct responses by the Bush Administration to 9/11. However, the reduction in civil rights and the creation of a new federal department does not fully illustrate the changes to day-to-day life that the attacks caused. Ideologically, American society became concerned with its own safety and security. In the wake of 9/11, President George W. Bush achieved immense popularity (Footman 5). The Bush Administration articulated these fears of terrorism in such a way as to make "security" a goal for the American people and to usher in the hegemony of the Right. Americans had to live with a new mantra, "With us or against us."[2] They lived under the cloud of daily reports of color-coded terror alerts telling them how likely another attack would be, effectively maintaining each day the fear of reliving the attacks. For America, post 9/11, "security" became a new measure of collective success.

Hegemony

To be able to explore the relationship between the Captain America narrative and American society post 9/11, it is necessary to use a sociological tool of analysis that can bring into focus the ideological power structures and the ideology of American society itself. The theory that best suits this task is Antonio Gramsci's Marxist concept of hegemony as radicalised by Ernesto Laclau and Chantal Mouffe.

Gramsci's theory of hegemony is the process that enables an economically dominant class to create and preserve a cultural dominance over the other classes in a society (R. Williams 108–110). The dominant class is able to do this by use of a shared ideology or world view that encompasses the totality of a society (the cultural, the economic, and the social). This ideology ensures that rule of the dominant class does not rely on coercion, but is consented to by the other groups in society. As a process, hegemony needs intellectuals in service of the dominant class. They have the task to manage and negotiate the shared ideology, ensuring that the ideology can adapt to the threats and crises that challenge it and the dominant class' rule. One of the sites for this ongoing negotiation and management by intellectuals of the shared ideology is the media of which popular cultural texts such as superhero comics are a part.

Gramsci's original work on hegemony, while having a revolutionary goal itself, explains how a national ideology works in the favour of the dominant class. It explains what the ideology must contain: the hegemonic principle of the dominant class. It also contains other elements such as a shared outlook and world view, patriotism, and the myths about the nature of the society. Gramsci's work was later radicalised by Laclau and Mouffe, who questioned the privileged position of the proletariat and bourgeoisie as the only classes that could truly be hegemonic and thus allowed hegemonic struggles in society to be seen independently from the class struggle. This, in turn, allowed for recognition of multiple struggles in a democratic space. This changed the way hegemony could be conceived and the multiple spaces within a society where it could be contested. Laclau and Mouffe also expanded on the details Gramsci proposed about the ideology at the heart of hegemony. Using ideas drawn from semiotics, Laclau and Mouffe presented the ideology as a floating signifier that is a combination of ideological elements that are connected via a process of articulation within the culture. Within each hegemonic ideology, these constituted ideological elements form nodal points where meaning is somewhat defined, although still open to articulation. These nodal points allow for the identification of the hegemonic ideology, its analysis, and its use as a tool of sociological analysis to explore the ideological content of other discourses in relation to hegemony.

The American Dream

In regard to American society, the identification of the ideology is made easier by its cultural self-sufficiency (Crockatt 5). By cultural self-sufficiency, Richard Crockatt means that American society consumes its own cultural products and for the most part is uninterested in the cultural products of other nations (although from time to time exceptions will be made). By ignoring other nation's cultural products, America is not exposed to the other nation's ideologies, which are embedded in those foreign cultural products. At the core of America's ideology is its belief in its own superiority and its uniqueness, a celebration of competition and success; in short, a manifest destiny. These elements are brought together in the concept of the American Dream. The American Dream has the potential to work ideologically in the support of hegemony in American society. Within its logic is the justification of the position of those groups who are at the top of the social hierarchy. Their success must, by necessity, be the result of their own hard work. The American Dream suggests that there is something inherently superior about the United States that is lacking in the other nations of the world. It gives the other classes in American society a process of merit for their own advancement—success in America is not about birth, but effort. The American Dream may be a myth, but Americans still believe in it and American popular culture continues to reproduce it (Samuel 1–7).

Scholarship considering the American Dream has shown that Americans have an intimate understanding of the American Dream (see Cullen, as well as Samuel). For non–Americans, the Dream is harder to grasp. The American Dream is an ideology that exists on many levels in American society, from personal American Dreams of individuals to a national ideology that explains the United States' place in the world. According to Jennifer L. Hochschild, the American Dream is "the promise that all Americans have a reasonable chance to achieve success as they define it—material or otherwise—through their own efforts, and to attain virtue and fulfilment through success" (xi). Within the frame of

Hochschild's definition are the key constituted ideological components of the American Dream: Success as the goal; Hard Work as the process; and Virtue as both a goal and necessary by-product of the process. In addition to these three named components within Hochschild's definition there are other ideological components which are unnamed but are also constituted elements of the ideology: Equality in that the Dream is open to all Americans; American Exceptionalism in that the American Dream is only possible within the United States, which suggests that American society is superior to other societies; Patriotism, which is the collective celebration of that superiority; and Freedom as an important condition in American society that can be perceived as both an ideological part of the creation of the American Dream, a condition for its efficacy, and a product of the American Dream as well. Freedom is an extremely open signifier within the American Dream (in that it verges upon having no clear referent). It has been used to justify contradictory points in American history from the freedom to own slaves to the freedom to not be a slave (Cullen 84).

These elements are not the only ideological components that can be included in the ideology of the American Dream or that can be articulated to it. When the American Dream is used within hegemony these ideological components become the nodal points of the hegemonic ideology and can have additional elements and concepts articulated to them. The nodal points are articulated in specific ways within a hegemonic ideology, defined in ways that serve the hegemonic purpose. For example, the concept of Success is a nodal point that can be defined in different ways within the American Dream, including but not limited to financial wealth and non-material concepts of happiness. The past articulations of these ideological components work to somewhat fix the meaning of these floating signifiers, influencing the potential articulations. For example, within the history of the American Dream, wealth as a goal has had a very strong history of articulation and can easily emerge within the ideology with little effort in articulation.

Two different versions of the American Dream became hegemonic ideologies of two different hegemonic groups in American society from 2001 to 2008. The first is the hegemony of the Right that emerged directly after the 9/11 terrorist attacks and is personified in President George W. Bush and his administration. Referred to in this paper as the *American Dream of Security*, it is articulated in Bush's speech to the joint session of congress on September 20, 2001 (Bush). Positioning the Bush administration as the hegemonic group, the American Dream of Security presents Security and the safety of the American people as the principle articulation of success, the privileged nodal point.

The second version of the American Dream is the *American Dream of Hope* that emerged in 2007 and 2008 as part of Barack Obama's successful presidential campaign. This hegemony of the Left articulated the American Dream in a very different way. The Obama campaign addressed a perception that the equation of Hard Work equaling Success in the American Dream was broken under the Bush Administration. Obama promised policy changes to re-establish the American Dream, but also offered a more direct expression of the reality of the American Dream. As an African American man brought up in single parent family, his success in reaching the heights of the Illinois state senate, U.S. Senate, and the Democrat nomination for president showed that the American Dream did still exist. In essence the American people, in electing Barack Obama as President in November 2008, claimed this version of the American Dream true for themselves.

Security versus Freedom in Civil War

The Bush Administration was able to secure a second term in the 2004 presidential elections; however, by January 2007, President Bush's approval rating had dropped to only 37 percent. Throughout the final two years of the Bush Administration, Bush's approval would never best 38 percent and would drop as low as 25 percent (Gallup). At the same time as President Bush became increasingly unpopular, so did the Iraq war. From early 2005, there was a clear shift in public opinion against the war in Iraq. A Pew Research Center's report on January 2005 showed that Americans had started to change their views and more Americans were starting to see military intervention in Iraq as a mistake (Pew "Additional Findings"). By October 2006 the majority of Americans surveyed had turned against the war with 58 percent stating that the war was going not too well or not at all well (Pew "Iraq Looms"). Through the rest of the Bush Administration's second term, the American public saw the Bush Administration's decision to invade Iraq as wrong (Pew "Less Optimism").

Pollster John Zogby's analysis of American society supports the data from the Pew Research Centre that the Iraq War was a major factor in the loss of support of the Bush Administration. Zogby makes the point that the Iraq war was not the only factor in the swing against the Right in American society; instead Zogby points to the effect the natural disaster of Hurricane Katrina had on the Bush Administration. Zogby believes that "historians will ultimately treat Hurricane Katrina as a more significant moment in American history than 9/11" (Zogby 59).

Hurricane Katrina hit the city of New Orleans and the surrounding areas on August 29, 2005, causing at least 1833 deaths, the displacement of over a million people, and over $80 billion in property damage, making it one of the biggest disasters in American history (Powell 863–64). The Bush Administration was widely blamed for the Federal Emergency Management Agency (FEMA) not doing enough to protect people from the hurricane or to help them in the wake of the disaster. In the wake of the hurricane, images of what appeared to be a third world country in the midst of disaster, rather than a major city in the United States, were unimaginable to many Americans. For many Americans this systematic failure was compounded by the fact that, after 9/11, America should have been prepared for this sort of disaster (Simmons 478).

Zogby states that Hurricane Katrina taught the American people that their government could not protect them from natural disaster and it would not be able to succour them when disaster hit (Zogby 58). In the months after Hurricane Katrina, President Bush's disapproval rating hit 60 percent for the first time in his presidency (Gallup). Zogby's point about the American people no longer believing that the American government could protect them and Simmons point that in a post 9/11 world Americans were shocked that the government failed in New Orleans touches on the nodal point of Security as Success in the American Dream of Security. The ideology that had justified the invasions of Afghanistan and Iraq and the Hard Work had cost not just American lives and resources but also a moral cost in the support of torture and abuse of prisoners and unlawful combatants. This ideology was, according to shifting American opinion, proven false by the failure of FEMA in New Orleans. The Security as Success ideology had promised that Americans would achieve Security as Success if American society engaged in the Hard Work of the military action of the War on Terror and the Hard Work of believing in the American Dream of Security. American Society had engaged in both tasks, but Hurricane Katrina had shown them that the hegemony of the Right had not made them safe. Once Hurricane Katrina showed that Security had failed, the ideology of the American Dream of Security was damaged and lost its hegemonic position. While the crisis of 9/11 had enabled the Right to assemble hegemony in American society, the articulations of Hurricane Katrina struck a blow to that hegemony and to the project that the Bush Administration and the Right had born from that hegemony, the War in Iraq. At the end of 2006, the contest for hegemony was more open in America than it had been since the September 11 attacks.

In the Captain America narrative of 2006, after Hurricane Katrina, the nodal point of Success as Security is directly challenged and positioned into opposition with another ideological component of the American Dream, Freedom. The narrative is played out in *Captain America* and in the limited series, *Civil War*, which runs from May 2006 to February 2007, with associated crossover issues throughout Marvel's monthly comics. *Civil War* follows on from the previous event titles—*Secret War* (Bendis and Dell'Otto) and *House of M* (Bendis and Coipel)—to create a meta-narrative about power and governance that runs throughout many of the Marvel comics. The *Civil War* section of the meta-narrative ends with the assassination of Captain America in *Captain America #25* in March 2007 (Brubaker).

Civil War begins with a 9/11-like crisis when a young superhero team, the New Warriors ambush super-villains while filming a reality television show which results in the villain Nitro, a human bomb, exploding and killing over 600 innocent people in the suburb of Stamford. From this a political movement is created in American society that sees superheroes as dangerous. In response, the President proposes legislation that superheroes must register with the government. From the outset, Captain America opposes this idea, on the basis of principle rather than practicality as he is already registered with S.H.I.E.L.D. and the United States government. He states that superheroes need to stay above politics and that registration will mean that it will be Washington telling them who the super-villains are (Millar, *CW* #1, 23). On the opposite side is Ironman who assumes leadership of the pro-registration forces. Iron Man is motivated by the political will of the American people, personified in the relatives of the victims of the Stanford disaster (Millar, *CW* #1, 13–15).

In *Captain America #22*, the ideological nodal points of Security and Success are articulated in a way that critiques and challenges the American Dream of Security. Captain America's lover, Sharon Carter/Agent 13, tries to convince him to give up his opposition to superhero registration in a conversation about the ideological basis of American society.

> SHARON: And because it's against the law. And the rule of law is what this country is founded on.
> CAPTAIN AMERICA: No ... it was founded on breaking the law. Because the law was wrong.
> SHARON: That's semantics, Steve, you know what I mean ...
> CAPTAIN AMERICA: It's not semantics, Sharon. It's the heart of the issue. The registration act is another step towards government control. And while I love my country, I don't trust many politicians. Not when they are having their strings pulled by corporate donors. And not when they are willing to trade freedom for security.
> SHARON: Now you're going to quote Benjamin Franklin at me? Give me a break.
> CAPTAIN AMERICA: How about Thomas Paine? "Those who expect to reap the blessings of freedom must undergo the fatigue of supporting it" [Brubaker 14–15].

The narrative attempts to find authority for its articulation of the incompatibility of Freedom and Security as Success in the American Dream through appeals to the ideas of the founding fathers, Benjamin Franklin and Thomas Paine. The articulation continues in *Civil War* when the pro-registration forces are forced to escalate their actions further and further from a position of morality. The goals of the pro-registration side evolve from just superheroes registering their real identities with the government. Superheroes are put into government sanctioned and run teams, one for each American state, and are trained by other superheroes in their abilities. Those superheroes who oppose registration are hunted down by pro-registration superheroes, military personal called cape-killers, and even super-villains who have been injected with nanotechnology that can be used to punish them.[3]

Once captured, anti-registration superheroes are placed in a special prison in the negative zone (named "42" because it was the 42nd idea, out of 100, developed by Reed Richards, Tony Stark, and Henry Pym after the tragedy at Stamford in order to keep their world from falling apart). In *Civil War* #4, it is revealed that the pro-registration side has cloned missing superhero Thor and inserted him into a battle with the combined anti-registration forces. Here he murders African American superhero Goliath. After these escalations, Spider-Man regrets his support for registration, for which he revealed his real identity on television, and joins the rebels. Reed Richard's wife, the Invisible Woman, also leaves, calling the pro-registration side fascist.

In the final battle between pro- and anti-registration forces, Captain America and Iron Man engage in combat. Just as Captain America is about to win the battle, he is tackled by a group of American emergency workers, including police officers and firemen (Millar, *CW* #7, 13–21). It is at this point that Captain America realises that the American people of the Marvel Universe want the Registration act and that they have made the choice for Security over Freedom. In effect, Captain America admits the defeat of his ideological stance and, in tears, agrees to be arrested. On the comic book stands the following month is *Captain America* #25, in which the character of Captain America is assassinated while in hand cuffs on the steps of an America court house, a metaphorical death of the American Dream during the Bush Administration. *Civil War* ends with the superhero community still divided, the rebels now working underground, and the pro-registration superheroes receiving the admiration and support of society.

Civil War and the associated issues of *Captain America* contest the importance of the privileged nodal point of Security as Success by counterposing the importance of an articulation of Freedom. This is a direct contest of the American Dream of Security as a hegemonic ideology and the hegemony of the Right. However, the timeframe of the publishing of *Civil War* tempers this ideological challenge. Published in May 2006, nine months after Hurricane Katrina, *Civil War* enters an ideological contest with the American Dream of Security after it had been discredited by the failure of the Bush Administration in the aftermath of Hurricane Katrina. Rather than attempting to confront the American Dream of Security in a hegemonic contest, *Civil War* and the *Captain America* comics are attempting to put the ideology and the hegemony of the Right into a historical context. *Civil War* is an examination of why America chose Security over Freedom. In revisiting this recent history of American society, the comic is caught in explaining the discredited former hegemonic ideology. This is itself an important part of the process of ideologically moving beyond the moment. At the time that it was published, American society was in a sort of hegemonic vacuum. The Bush Administration was still in a position of political power, but the political Right were no longer able to exert ideological power as they had between September 11, 2001, and August 29, 2005. In an attempt to move beyond this ideology and build a new national ideology, *Civil War* takes on the task of explaining ideologically what happened between 2001 and 2005. This understanding is a necessary part of a broader social mission of building a new consensus. In essence, *Civil War* is part of the new intellectual effort to construct a new social ideology after the failure of the hegemony of the Right. This is possible with the more open field of articulation and hegemony available in 2006.

Bucky Barnes and the New Captain America, the New American Dream

Whereas *Civil War* attempted to explain how America had come to the moment of crisis post–9/11 and Hurricane Katrina, the *Captain America* narrative after the death of Steve Rogers went beyond explaining hegemony. Instead it became part of the intellectual process of the creation of an ideology of the renewed American Dream intended to address the crisis. This ideology was personified in the election of Barack Obama on November 4, 2008.

The end of the Bush years had found American society dealing with significant social issues. The American public had largely lost faith in government by 2007, with only 31 percent believing "they could trust the government in Washington to do the right thing always or most of the time" (Pew "In 2007"). By 2008 the majority of the American people saw the original decision by the Bush Administration to go to war in Iraq as a mistake and wanted America to reduce its role in the broader world both militarily and in regard to international goals like reducing the spread of weapons of mass destruction (Pew "Even as" 1–13). The American public were concerned about the economy. In 2007, 44 percent of respondents to a Pew survey stated that they did not have enough to make ends meet, up from 35 percent in 2003. More Americans agreed that the rich were getting richer and the poor getting poorer in the American economy in 2007, 73 percent up from 65 percent in 2003 (Pew "Trends in"). By December 2008 public pessimism had risen to 92 percent for the future of the national economy and 61 percent for their personal finances (Pew "Job Worries" 1). The American public had even started to lose faith in themselves (Pew "Trends in"). This description of American society fits Gramsci's concept of organic crisis: "If the ruling class has lost its consensus, i.e. is no longer 'leading' but only 'dominant,' exercising coercive force alone, this means precisely that the great masses have become detached from their traditional ideologies, and no longer believe what they used to believe" (Gramsci 275–276). There could be an argument that the Bush Administration and Congress were not ruling by coercive force alone, but that American society still accepted the legitimacy of their political power.

While the structural causes of these issues were still to be resolved, the ideological solution was presented by the Obama campaign through his ability to articulate his concept of change to the American Dream as the national ideology. He was able to at once create and to lead a new American Dream that, due to the contradictory notion of national ideology (Security vs. Freedom), also seemed to have always existed throughout American history. The hope that Obama's campaign stirred within Americans drew heavily on a renewal of the American Dream. This made change seem exciting but not radical or revolutionary, in fact a conservative throwback to the ideas of a more successful America of the past. As a modern presidential election, the emphasis of Obama's campaign was not so much on policy, but on vision of a reconstitution of community, with the American Dream as the core value of American society.

Obama contrasted the Bush-articulated American Dream as a failure to value the whole community that had excluded many Americans (see Rowland), with his own more communitarian American Dream (Jenkins and Cos 197). While there was a strong theme of change within Obama's rhetoric that positioned the American people as the agents of this change, the ideas of change were drawn not outside of the American ideology, but conservatively from ideas of America's past. Obama articulated that America's solutions were within itself, the American people, and the American ideology of the Dream. His campaign drew on his ideas of the American Dream, which he clearly stated in accepting the Democratic nomination of president: "It is that promise that has always set this country apart—that through hard work and sacrifice, each of us can pursue our individual dreams but still come together as one American family, to ensure that the next generation can pursue their dreams as well" (qtd. in Jenkins and Cos 189).

As Keith B. Jenkins and Grant Cos make clear, the reconstitution of the American community and the renewal of the American Dream were not revolutionary ideas for a Presidential candidate. At a moment when Americans might have started to look for revolutionary change outside of their political system and ideology, Obama returned Americans back to faith in the political system with the ideological strength of the renewed American Dream. While the election of an African American president is indeed change, it was on the back of a rearticulated new American Dream that sat comfortably within the paradigm of the established ideology, rearticulated but within the confines of the "narrative parameters of the American Dream myth" (Jenkins and Cos 198). In his speeches to the American public, Obama used the authority of his own experiences to reassert the concept of access to success of others, at times referring to them as groups of Americans and other times as individuals. It was Obama's ability to show that the problems of America "were undercutting that dream for ordinary Americans and then his ability to show that the ultimate solution to those problems lay in a return to the basic values of the American Dream that energized his message" (Rowland 205).

Essentially, the American Dream of Hope was just a renewal in belief in the American Dream more broadly. Obama's articulation of the American Dream of Hope was intentionally open and broad to allow inclusion of peoples' personal American Dreams. Material and non-material Success were included in the American Dream of Hope. Obama articulated Individual Success and specifically a Collective Success that could be handed on to the American children. The nodal points of the American Dream of Hope are much more open than those of the American Dream of Security. However, there are few specific articulations around the concept of the American Dream of Hope that Obama does clearly articulate. Firstly, Obama's campaign speeches insisted that the ideology is valuable and real. Secondly, Obama articulated that the American Dream equation of Hard Work equalling Success was broken under the Bush Administration. Obama suggested that the American people were already providing the Hard Work of the promise. The last articulation was Obama's own personification of the American Dream, which is closely related to it in reality and to the evidence of the reality that Obama's election would give the American society. The solution to the 2007 crisis of leadership and ideology, of an American people who doubted their leaders, their ideology, and even themselves, was the charismatic leader Barack Obama, who answered these issues in both himself and the American Dream of Hope.

At the same time that the Obama campaign was emerging in American society, Ed Brubaker was exploring a narrative in *Captain America* that can be seen as part of the renewal of the American Dream after the failure of the Bush presidency. The death of Captain America at the end of *Civil War* created the space for Bucky Barnes, Steve Roger's former sidekick, to take on the role of Captain America. This Bucky-Captain America (often jokingly called "Bucky Cap" by figures like Spider-Man) was like the American Dream of Hope, in a way a call back to the legacy and ideology of the Steve Rogers Captain America, but also a new Captain America with new concerns, weapons, and a new costume.

The link between Brubaker's narrative of Bucky's transformation and the real world American society is strengthened by the similarities of the issues and concerns faced by the fictional American public of the Marvel Universe. The real economic crisis of American society is a major plot point in the story, though with fictional villains and outcomes. The Red Skull stars as the arch-nemesis throughout the Captain America comic of this time frame. Through his control of an international company, the Kronas Corporation, he is able to push America into financial crisis. Kronas crashes the stock market by doubling the price of petrol and uses its subsidiary, Peggy Day Finances, to foreclose on thousands of American mortgages in *Captain America* #34 (Brubaker 2–3). This mirrors the real world subprime mortgage crisis and the Federal National Mortgage Association known as Fannie Mae. The economic crisis leads to protests on the streets of Washington, which are further made violent by Kronas drugging the protesters. Within the narrative, the fictitious American politicians make decisions not in the interest of American society, but in the interest of the Kronas Corporation, from which they receive political donations. Here, *Captain America* narrativizes the American lack of faith in the political class as real-world politicians are unable to act against corporate interests (and hearkens back to the conversation between Captain America and Sharon Carter).

The representation of country within *Captain America* reflects the views and conflicts within American society discussed earlier. In *Captain America*, the economic crisis occurs and the American people lose faith in their political leaders and are forced onto the streets to protest. It also shares the same viewpoint as Barack Obama that the reason for the crisis in American society is that the American Dream has been broken; the equation of Hard Work Equalling Success has been damaged; the rich are getting richer while the poor get poorer. While Barack Obama put the blame on the Bush Administration, *Captain America* puts blame on American politicians, corporations, and the Red Skull (an embodiment of fascist anti–Americanism).

The solution in the comic book to the crisis in America is the renewal of the Captain America identity, which works metaphorically as renewal of the American Dream, detailing the process. In his early experiences as Captain America, Bucky faces two representations of "Captain America" that stand in opposition to him. The first is the shadow of the dead Captain America, Steve Rogers. Bucky fears that he cannot meet the legacy of Rogers and fears to even try. However, he is also prepared to defend his idea of this Captain America. He gets involved in a bar fight when a thug accuses the dead Rogers of being a traitor, because he didn't follow public opinion about superhero registration, to which Bucky makes the point that the American public once thought slavery was right as well (Brubaker, *CA* #26, 18–22). Bucky's relationship with this idea of Captain America is not antagonistic. Bucky's admiration for Rogers and his mission are clear within the comic and in the end, when Bucky adopts his own Captain America identity, it is seen to be in honour of Rogers and as a progression forward with the concept. Like Obama, Bucky draws on the legacy of the past.

The other Captain America that Bucky contends with is the Captain America of the 1950s. This is an interesting character in the history of Captain America. Functionally, the character was retconned in 1972 to explain two Captain American comics that were published in the 1950s subtitled "Captain America—Commie Smasher." *Captain America* #156 explains that these stories were not about the Steve Rogers who was frozen in the arctic at the end of World War II, but about a school teacher named William Burnside who assumes the role of Captain America, has reconstructive surgery to look like Rogers, and takes a version of the super soldier serum with a new version of Bucky. However, this version of the serum drives the faux Captain America insane and, rather than fighting communism, he starts to see the enemies of America everywhere and has to be put in suspended animation (see Englehart). In 2008, *Captain America* #38 makes it clear who these enemies were in a flash back showing the 1950s-era Captain America beating up African American men. So while the reuse of the Burnside Captain America explains two rarely seen *Captain America* comics, it is also a device to explain and show that the American Dream and American society has changed over time. This is further reinforced when Burnside is seen to support the new and villainous presidential candidate for the Third Wing party when he states, "Because no one has the courage to do what must be done ... to make the American future the Dream it was meant to be" (Brubaker, CA #39, 12). Burnside communicates throughout the story arc that America in 2008 is not his America, but it could become his America, in that he could remake it. The 1950s Captain America is representative of a particular American ideology of the past—valorizing Hard Work but closed and rigid—and the idea that this conservative ideology should become dominant today. Bucky's Captain America, though, is open and flexible. He, like Obama, adopts the values of the past but marries them to pragmatism and inclusiveness.

The fact that this narrative includes multiple representations of the superhero that compete for authority echoes the same process of articulation within the concept of hegemony. It is at this point that this superhero narrative separates itself from the sort of comics that replicate hegemony. Some comics have attempted to reproduce, or critique, or challenge, or contest hegemony. Brubaker's Captain America differs in that it *explores and explains the process of hegemony and articulation* at a time in which the field of articulation is open within American society.

For Bucky, the struggle for hegemony over the identity and authority of Captain America is reasonably simple. Bucky has a physical confrontation with the Captain America of the 1950s and defeats him. The fictional American society accepts Bucky as the new Captain America when he saves both Presidential candidates at the first presidential debate in issue #42.

In past situations where Captain America has been replaced by a new character (such as the 1950s Captain America and the 1980s replacement of Steve Rogers with a more Right Wing Captain America in John Walker) the Captain America uniform did not change. As far as citizens of Marvel's fictional America knew, this was the same Captain America and a continuation of the same idea and identity. With Bucky's assumption of the Captain America idea, it is clear that this is a new man under the Captain America mask and a new type of Captain America. Bucky does not just adopt the same costume that Steve Rogers wore; instead Bucky takes elements of the Captain America ideal and then adds other elements that are representative of himself and the society that he comes from. The new Captain America wears a red, white, blue and black costume that instead of being made with chainmail is made of a smooth metallic material and with a different stars and stripes design. Bucky also adds a gun and knife to his weapons as well as the use of his bionic arm. This action itself marks Bucky's Captain America as something new and yet makes claims on the historical Captain America idea. Bucky adopts the shield and the heroic mission of Steve Rogers, teaming up with Steve's best friend, the Falcon, and working to save the life of Steve's girlfriend Sharon Carter.

Bucky's transformation into the new Captain America is metaphoric and complex. In one way he is indeed a new Captain America, but yet he retains elements of the original. Within the context of Obama's mantra of "being the change" (borrowed from Gandhi) and his promise of renewal of the American Dream, *Captain America* is complementary to the Obama campaign. Taking into account the articulation of the messages of the Obama campaign on the causes for America's crisis, the Bush administration's broken American Dream, and the similar narrative in *Captain America* in regard to the crisis and the villains, it is clear that this narrative is ideologically supportive of Barack Obama and his project. The ability of Obama to personify the American Dream and the concept of Bucky finally personifying the identity of Captain America help bring the two ideas even closer together

Conclusion

There is little doubt about whether it is possible for comic books to make representations of hegemonic ideology (see Dorfman and Mattelart). There has been some concern about the ability of superheroes to subvert dominant ideology. Williams has made the point that superheroes were more likely to reinforce hegemonic ideology (J. Williams 134–36). On the other hand, studies by Matthew J. Costello and Jason Dittmer have shown that superhero comics can be part of the process of construction of ideology. Dittmer's work has focused on the superhero subgenre of the nationalistic superhero (specifically Captain America) and its role in "legitimising, contesting and reworking a state's foreign policies" (Dittmer 3). Dittmer makes the point that nationalistic superheroes are not the only or the most important part of the construction or reproduction of national identity and ideology, nor are they just the reflection of the values of society or the result of economic policy. Nationalistic superhero narratives have a complex role that involves the reproduction of national identity and ideology, and also the negotiation and contest of those ideological concepts. Costello argues that superhero comic books do not just map this national identity, but actually reconstruct this identity (Costello 18).

The meta-narrative of the Marvel Universe, which explores America's reaction to 9/11 and security becoming dominant over liberty, is a detailed and rich commentary. However, its ability to impact hegemony is limited by its timeline. *Civil War*, which shows the victory of security over liberty, is published in 2006 and 2007. While this meta-narrative engages in the debate about the primary values in American society, its authoritative conclusion (which is detailed later in the Marvel limited series *Siege*, from 2010) occurs after the presidential election, reducing its claim to intellectual leadership. This meta-narrative is more about putting the recent history of the American Dream of Security into an historical context. This contributes to the ideological movement forward, but not in as direct a way as Brubaker's fable of the new Captain America.

The commentary on America's ideological crisis is much clearer in *Captain America*. This can be attributed to the nationalistic elements that Captain America necessarily presents, but it is also due to a difference in style in the writing of both comics. Brubaker's

Captain America presents meanings and ideas that are much easier to see at first glance (phrases like getting "our country back," which connect with the Tea Party politics that were emerging as the story played out, come to mind). The use of capitalist villains and the direct commentary on the relationship between corporations and American politicians is overt and works to enhance the metaphor of the birth of a new Captain America as the process of articulation of the American Dream personified in Obama. The setting of the final victory of the new Captain America—at the fictional 2008 Presidential debate in which Captain America is accepted by the American public—helps to make the commentary on America's way forward extremely clear. What makes Brubaker's narrative so ideologically powerful is its time frame. The production of a comic from start to finish takes around four months, with many storylines plotted out well before that in consultations with editorial committees and other writers of the company, a process that does affect comic books' ability to provide hegemonic leadership. *Captain America*, however, did fit within the timeframe of the presidential election. The issue that ends with the acceptance of Bucky in the role of Captain America and by the American community at the presidential debate is published in September 2008, two months before the presidential election in November. This gives *Captain America* a strong case for providing intellectual leadership and ideological leadership to the American public.

Notes

1. For the earlier deaths of Superman and Captain America, see *Superman* #75 (vol. 2), written by Dan Jurgens, and the story "Relics," in *Captain America* #50 (vol. 3), written by Brian David-Marshall. Many other popular characters have died and been resurrected: DC's Green Arrow, Martian Manhunter, Robin (Jason Todd), Green Lantern (Hal Jordan), and the Flash, and Marvel's Bucky, Jean Grey, Iron Man, and the Punisher, among others.

2. Of course, the rest of the world also had to live with the mantra, as George W. Bush used various versions of the phrase as a talking point behind a series of podiums, including at the United Nations. See "Bush says...."

3. It is the essence of the Foucaultian vision of the post-modern condition, a system perfectly designed to discipline and punish (or to "discipline and surveil," as the title of Foucault's famous work would be more accurately translated). See Foucault.

Works Cited

Bendis, Brian Michael (writer), and Olivier Coipel (penciller). *House of M* #1–8 (June–Nov. 2005), Marvel Comics. Web.
Bendis, Brian Michael (writer), and Gabrielle Del'Otto (painter). *Secret War* #1–5 (Feb.–Dec. 2005), Marvel Comics. Web.
Brubaker, Ed (writer), Mike Perkins (art), and Frank D'Armata (color art). *Captain America* #22 (Sept. 2006), Marvel Comics. Web.
Brubaker, Ed (writer), Steve Epting (art), and Frank D'Armata (color art). *Captain America* #25–26 (Mar. 2007), Marvel Comics. Web.
Brubaker, Ed (writer), Steve Epting (penciller), and Butch Guice (inker). *Captain America* #34 (Jan. 2008), Marvel Comics. Web.
"Bush says it is time for action." CNN.com. Cable News Network LP. 6 Nov. 2001. Web. 12 Dec. 2014.
Bush, George. Presidential Address to a Joint Session of Congress. The Capitol Building, Washington, D.C. 20 Sept. 2001. Video. C-Span.com. National Cable Satellite Corporation. 20 Sept. 2001. Web. 12 Dec. 2014.
"Comic hero Captain America dies." BBCNEWS.com. BBC. 8 Mar. 2007. Web. 12 Dec. 2014.
Costello, Matthew J. *Secret Identity Crisis: Comic Books and the Unmasking of Cold War America*. London: Bloomsbury Academic, 2009.

Crockatt, Richard. *After 9/11: Cultural Dimensions of American Global Power*. New York: Routledge, 2007.
Cullen, Jim. *The American Dream: A Short History of an Idea That Shaped a Nation*. London: Oxford University Press, 2003.
David-Marshall, Brian (writer), and Igor Kordey (artist). "Relics." Captain America #50 (Feb. 2002), Marvel Comics. 49–59. Web.
Dittmer, Jason. *Captain America and the Nationalist Superhero: Metaphors, Narratives, and Geopolitics*. Philadelphia: Temple University Press, 2012.
Dorfman, Ariel, and Armand Mattelart. *How to Read Donald Duck: Imperialist Ideology in the Disney Comic*. Trans. David Kunzle. New York: International, 1991.
Englehart, Steve (writer), Sal Buscema (artist), and Frank McLaughlin (inker). Captain America and the Falcon #156 (Dec. 1972), Marvel Comics. Web.
Footman, Tim. *The Noughties: A Decade That Changed the World 2000–2009*. London: Crimson, 2009.
Foucault, Michel. *Discipline and Punish: The Birth of the Prison*. Trans. Alan Sheridan. New York: Vintage, 1995.
Fukuyama, Francis. *The End of History and the Last Man*. New York: Free Press, 1992.
Gallup. "Presidential Approval Ratings—George W. Bush." Gallup.com. Gallup, Inc. n.d. Web. 12 Dec. 2014.
Gramsci, Antonio. *Selections from the Prison Notebooks of Antonio Gramsci*. Trans. Quintin Hoare and Geoffrey Nowell Smith. New York: International, 1971.
Gustines, George Gene. "Captain America Is Dead; American Hero Since 1941." NYT.com. The New York Times Company. 7 Mar. 2007. Web. 12 Dec. 2014.
Hochschild, Jennifer L. *Facing Up to the American Dream: Race, Class, and the Soul of the Nation*. Princeton: Princeton University Press, 1995.
Jenkins, Keith B., and Grant Cos. "A Time for Change and a Candidate's Voice: Pragmatism and the Rhetoric of Inclusion in Barack Obama's 2008 Presidential Campaign." *American Behavioral Scientist* 54.3 (2010): 184–202. Print.
Jurgens, Dan (writer and penciller), and Brett Breeding (inker). "Doomsday." Superman #75 (Jan. 1993), DC Comics. Print.
Laclau, Ernesto, and Chantal Mouffe. *Hegemony and Socialist Strategy: Towards a Radical Democratic Politics*. New York: Verso, 2001.
Millar, Mark (writer), and Steve McNiven (penciller). Civil War #1–7 (May 2006–Feb. 2007), Marvel Comics. Print.
Morgan, David. "Captain America Killed Outside Courthouse." CBSNews.com. CBS Interactive, Inc. 7 Mar. 2007. Web. 12 Dec. 2014.
Pew Research Center. "Additional Findings and Analyses." PewResearchCenter.com. Pew Research Center. 13 Jan. 2005. Web. 12 Dec. 2014.
_____. "Even as Optimism About Iraq Surges: Declining public Support for Global Engagement." PewResearchCenter.com. Pew Research Center. 24 Sept. 2008. Web. 12 Dec. 2014.
_____. "In 2007, Mood Just Beginning to Sour, Democrats Better Regarded." PewResearchCenter.com. Pew Research Center. 20 Dec. 2011. Web. 12 Dec. 2014.
_____. "Iraq Looms Large in Nationalized Election." PewResearchCenter.com. Pew Research Center. 5 Oct. 2006. Web. 12 Dec. 2014.
_____. "Job Worries Mount, 73 percent Spending Less on Holidays: Psychology of Bad Times Fueling Consumer Cutbacks." PewResearchCenter.com. Pew Research Center. 11 Dec. 2008. Web. 12 Dec. 2014.
_____. "Less Optimism About Iraq." PewResearchCenter.com. Pew Research Center. 1 May 2008. Web. 12 Dec. 2014.
_____. "Trends in Political Values and Core Attitudes: 1987–2007." PewResearchCenter.com. Pew Research Center. 22 Mar. 2007. Web 12 Dec. 2014.
Powell, Lawrence N. "What Does American History Tell Us About Katrina and Vice Versa?" *The Journal of American History* 94.3 (2007): 863–876. Print
Rowland, Robert C. "The Fierce Urgency of Now: Barack Obama and the 2008 Presidential Election." *American Behavioral Scientist* 54.3 (2010): 203–221. Print
Samuel, Lawrence. *The American Dream: A Cultural History*. Syracuse: Syracuse University Press, 2012.
Simmons, Lakisha Michelle. "Justice Mocked: Violence and Accountability in New Orleans." *American Quarterly* 61.3 (2009): 477–498. Print
Tucker, Neely. "End of American Heroes?" Interview by Amy Robach. Today.com. NBC Universal. 8 Mar. 2007. Web. 12 Dec. 2014. Originally aired on MSNBC on 7 Mar. 2007.
Williams, Raymond. *Marxism and Literature*. London: Oxford University Press, 1977.
Williams, Jeff. "Comics: A Tool of Subversion?" *Journal of Criminal Justice and Popular Culture* 2.6 (1994): 129–146. Print
Zogby, John. *The Way We'll Be: The Zogby Report on the Transformation of the American Dream*. New York: Random House, 2008.

Part VI—Graphic Narrative and Cultural Resonance

Visual Form and Meaning Making in Marvel's *Civil War*

Joseph J. Darowski

A Collaborative Medium

When analyzing comic books the narrative itself often takes precedence in the discussion. A narrative analysis is a perfectly valid approach, but as with any medium, a close look at *how* the story is told can also be rewarding. A more formalist approach to Marvel's *Civil War* mini-series highlights the way in which the art, with pencils by Steve McNiven, inks by Dexter Vines, Mark Morales, Steve McNiven, John Dell, and Tim Townsend, and colors by Morry Hollowell, enhance, enrich, and clarify many of the themes in the story Mark Millar is writing. This interpretive lens does not negate the many insights that can be gained from analyzing the narrative, but does highlight an area of comic books studies that sometimes receives too little focus.

Writing for Sequart, an organization devoted to the study of popular culture and comic books, Forrest Helvie highlighted the problem: "[I]t still confounds me to no end that someone will take the time to write a review about a comic book or graphic novel and utterly fail to address the artwork. Sadly, it happens all too often" ("Don't Ignore … Part 1"). While Helvie is explicitly addressing online reviews of comic books and graphic novels, his point also stands for more academic criticism. While deconstructing narratives does lend insights, every storytelling medium also benefits from analysis of the form. Comic books are no exception to this rule, and indeed more work is needed in this area. As Bradford W. Wright notes, "Few enduring expressions of American popular culture are so instantly recognizable and still so poorly understood as comic books…. They communicate narratives through a unique combination of text and sequential illustration that works within its own aesthetic vocabulary" (xiii). Particularly when it comes to comic books, more studies that combine analysis of the art with the story itself can deepen our appreciation of both. As Randy Duncan and Matthew J. Smith point out, in comic books "all aspects of the narrative are represented by pictorial and linguistic images encapsulated in a sequence of juxtaposed panels and pages" (4). To separate the narrative from the art does a disservice to both.

Every working definition of comic books must include the fact that art is key to the storytelling. Whether it is Shirrel Rhoades' simple definition of "sequential panels of four-color art and written dialogue that tell an original story" (2) or Scott McCloud's headier and more theoretical conclusion that comic books are "juxtaposed pictorial and other images in deliberate sequence, intended to convey information and/or produce an aesthetic response in the viewer" (9), no definition of comic books can possibly exclude the art as a key component. Proper analysis of comic books and graphic novels requires more acknowledgment and criticism of the art itself.

When discussing the art, the penciller is, of course, of key importance. But the work of the inker and especially the colorist has also been undervalued. In fact, it was only in June 2014 that DC Comics, "responding to strong industry opinion," began to give colorists cover credits on issues to which they contributed (Ching). Many other publishers had been giving cover credit for some years, but for most of the history of the industry the colorist has been less-acknowledged despite the key role they play in the finished product. In 2006, Morry Hollowell, the colorist for *Civil War*, discussed the fact that colorists were beginning to receive more recognition: "I have my name on the cover of my books. But this really should be standard practice for comic companies now. Especially since coloring has reached a point where we're on equal ground with inkers. A colorist can really make or break a book these days" (Offenberger). Whether a work has been produced by a single creator or is the product of collaboration, the art is key to interpreting the piece. Marvel's *Civil War* mini-series, one of the most successful comic book events in recent history, is the product of the collaboration of several talented creators.

Speaking of the collaborative process that is necessary to produce a mainstream comic book, which will include writers, pencillers, inkers, colorists, and editors, McNiven explained that "having a good relationship with each member of the team is crucial in making good comics" (Northcott). Furthermore, speaking of his frequent collaborations with Mark Millar, he added,

> The number one thing is that I think he's a fantastic writer. If I had no confidence in his abilities as a writer I wouldn't work with him. When I go to conventions I am asked a lot about my favorite characters and, while I do have them, I explain that I do not chase them but the writers that make them great. That's how it has always been with me—chasing down writers I think are the best the industry has to offer and trying my best to tell their stories as well as I can. And I scored big time when Mark thought it would be fun to work together! [Northcott].

McNiven describes Millar's storytelling as "very cinematic" and he tries to reflect that style in his art (CBR). In terms of his process, McNiven has said that he reads an entire scene before beginning to conceptualize it, hoping to get "the overall feel of it" and then do small simple thumbnail sketches to begin planning layouts and positioning (Leong). Morry Hollowell had colored McNiven's pencils regularly prior to *Civil War*. As with any collaboration, familiarity aided Hollowell's work:

> I think our stuff is really good together, but that also has to do with how long we've worked with each other. When I start working on someone new it takes me a while to adapt to their art. So I'd have to say my stuff would just naturally be better on [McNiven's pencils] because I've worked with his art so long [Wiltfong].

The combination of Mark Millar's script, Steven McNiven's pencils, and Hollowell's colors made for some of the most striking moments in Marvel's *Civil War*. Dexter Vines provided most of the inks on McNiven's pencils, and his contribution to the final look of the series is also significant. Understanding how the artistic style is situated within the tradition of superhero comic books is necessary for a full appreciation of this series. A close reading of a single image will demonstrate how the artistic choices made by these co-creators enhance the themes of the narrative.

Artistic Style

There can be as many artistic styles found in comic books as exist in any other medium, but the superhero genre has generally attracted a particular style. As Rikk Mulligan notes, "Graphic novels or comic books are a medium or mode of visual storytelling; some make a point of depicting reality with as much fidelity as possible, but far more blend reality and fantasy" (41). The superhero genre has traditionally featured art that walks this line, settling for a heightened reality as the standard look to mainstream fare from Marvel and DC Comics. However, with the wealth of titles that have been published across the decades there are clearly examples that tend toward more strictly realistic and those that fully embrace outright fantasy. The more realistic styles can include heavy (sometimes distracting) photo-referencing for backgrounds and character faces, while the more fantastic can feature extreme stylistic exaggerations of forms. The best marriage of narrative and artistic style will see the artists' choices match and enhance the tone, themes, and goals of the narrative.

Scott McCloud addresses this issue, explaining that "one's choice of styles can have consequences far beyond the mere 'look' of a story" (45). For example, the brightly colored cartoon style of *Life with Archie* comic books reflects the general tone of that series, but when the publisher produced a much darker and macabre zombie storyline titled *Afterlife with Archie* a much darker color palate was employed and the art style was much more angular. Another example of how artistic style adds to the storytelling is Ed Brubaker and Sean Phillip's series *Criminal: Last of the Innocents*. The storyline is about what David Brothers called "poisonous nostalgia" or "the gulf of years and mistakes that sit between The Way Things Are and the Way Things Used to Be." To visually demonstrate this, the modern day setting in the series is drawn in a heavily inked, noir style while the nostalgic past is drawn in the style of classic Archie comic books. The style and tone established by the art simultaneously matches and deepens the thematic heft of the story itself.

Throughout the history of the industry there have been several styles that have been dominant within the superhero genre at different times. For example, Jack Kirby's blocky art defined Marvel Comic books in the 1960s, a style McCloud called "a middle ground of iconic forms with a sense of real about them bolstered by a powerful design sense" (55). In the 1990s, the sketchy, heavily crosshatched styles of Rob Liefeld and Jim Lee were the iconic styles. Douglas Wolk calls McNiven's style in *Civil War* the "look of superhero comics, circa 2007" (53). Certainly there were other styles on display, Humberto Ramos was employing a much more exaggerated and distorted illustration style in the Wolverine tie-in issues to *Civil War*, but McNiven's tight style was definitive for the era. McNiven's art is more realistic than Kirby's, but cleaner and less-crosshatched than Lee or Liefeld's art of the 1990s. Surprisingly, McNiven was fairly new to superhero comic books at the time his style became so defining for the era. In the midst of the popular *Civil War* storyline, McNiven admitted,

> I've only been drawing superhero comics for three years, comics of any kind for five, so I don't have a bag of styles to choose from. Just one and I make it up as I go along. It's all about the storytelling anyway. Styles come and go. Often faster that you can master them, but good storytelling never goes out of style [CBR].

Perhaps because of his relative inexperience, when talking with fans and interviewers he would recommend that they look into more established comic book artists for insights into the process of creating comic books, including Will Eisner, Jack Kirby, Frank Miller, Gil Kane, Jim Steranko, Alex Toth, rather than follow his lead (Leong).

Despite his own reservations, McNiven's work on the series was highly praised at the time, and it holds up well. Notably, the series experienced delays in schedule and shipping because McNiven fell behind and Marvel felt it was worthwhile to allow McNiven to complete the entire series rather than have fill-in artists complete any issues. Millar expected Marvel to have a fill-in artist complete the fifth issue of the series, but was very pleased when the decision was made to delay the series (and the dozens of tie-in issues) so that McNiven could complete all of the art in the series (Weiland).

Marvel editor C.B. Cebulski noted, "I for one, as a fan, am happy that they delayed it because a series of this caliber, I would not want a fill-in artist" (Yukcevic). Writer Brian Michael Bendis also approved of the decision, noting that when he rereads a previous Marvel event mini-series, *The Infinity Gauntlet*, his "heart kinda sinks" when the art changes from George Perez to Ron Lim in issue #4 because Perez was unable to complete the issue on schedule (Yukcevic). Cebulski, Bendis, and others at Marvel made the point that keeping McNiven on the book despite having to juggle publishing schedules and force fans to wait would be worth it particularly when it came to collected editions of the series. This was the best decision not only for the sake of consistency in the series, but because McNiven's style was such an ideal match for ideas and concepts being explored in *Civil War*.

McNiven's art, though clearly not photo-realistic, is less cartoonish or iconic, instead opting for a more lifelike and realistic representation (McCloud 52–53). The more realistic pencils of McNiven serve a story that is clearly inspired by events of the real world. Millar was attempting to explore how a real world with superheroes would function, and Millar clearly used contemporary events to shape the series. An article in *The New York Times* by George Gene Gustines published a few months before the first issue of *Civil War* hit the stands opens with a lead that seemed more suited to the front page than to a feature page:

> Embedded reporters on the front lines of war. The search for weapons of mass destruction. An attack on civil liberties. Sounds like a job for [...] Spider-Man? America's current real-world political issues will wind themselves into the lives of the heroes of Marvel Comics in "Civil War" [Gustines].

The promotion and content of the series make it clear that contemporary sociopolitical issues were being commented on within the story, and the more realistic art helps to ground the series within that context. Obviously there are still fantastic elements to the art. Inhuman feats, garish costumes, god-like musculature, and improbable battles abound, but while accepting those elements as the reality of the superhero genre McNiven's pencils ground all of it with a more realistic atmosphere.

Aiding in establishing the atmosphere of the *Civil War* are Morry Hollowell's colors. While superhero comic books are stereotypically bright fare with primary colors abounding, much of *Civil War* has a much more muted color scheme. In fact, the opening scene, in which the New Warriors attack a group of super-villains which leads to the tragedy at an elementary school, is colored with the traditional highly-saturated hues for which mainstream superhero comic books are known. However, turning the page to the first double-page spread of the series, featuring Iron Man and Captain America in front of rubble, reveals much darker tones that will pervade much of the remaining series. Dominant use of grays and deep reds evoke very different reactions, more somber emotions, than the greens and yellows that had been prominent in the previous sequence (Millar, *CW #1*, 1–9). This doesn't only change the mood of this particular scene, it helps to situate the series. *Civil War* was viewed as a change for Marvel and for superhero comics, deliberately bringing the Marvel Universe into conversation with real-world issues. Forrest Helvie explains that "more muted or cooler color palettes," such as what would be used for most of *Civil War*, "can lend themselves to more realistic settings" ("Don't Ignore ... Part 2"). Much like McNiven's style, the colors chosen in the series ground this storyline in a more realistic setting than is seen in many previous Marvel comic books.

The use of darker hues and more grays has additional symbolic significance for the series. There is a tradition within superhero comics that the superheroes wear brightly hued primary colors while the super-villains wear darkly hued secondary colors. This can be seen in many of the early Marvel comic books. Spider-Man wears red and blue and battles the Lizard who has green skin. When the Fantastic Four adopt costumes they are bright blue and they battle Dr. Doom and the Mole Man who both wear green. The X-Men wear blue and yellow uniforms and battle a series of villains who wear purple (Magneto, the Vanisher, even the Blob wears purple shorts). In a series that is built around the conceit of heroes battling heroes, the colors are all moved to a darker hue because there is no obvious good guy. The characters still wear their traditional costumes, which often feature primary colors, but the actions of everyone involved in this confrontation remove them from the classic heroic pedestal, and they now are shown in a darker light. The fact that both the pro- and anti-registration sides are given this more muted coloring plays into one of the themes Millar deliberately explored in the series:

> It's really lazy writing to make everything black and white.... I'm a politics buff and I really hate seeing America divided into red and blue states because I know people in red states who have blue opinions. And we're all very complex. No one person can really even be described as a liberal or a conservative.... People are more complex than you think and I wanted to do the same thing with superheroes [Richards].

Millar hoped to reveal that there are shades of gray in everyone, and the Holloway's choices help to visually shore up that theme while the narrative plays out for the reader.

In addition to grounding the superhero genre, McNiven's clean and appealing art style and Holloway's deliberate coloring made a complex and multi-faceted story more accessible. David Wallace notes that McNiven's art delivered an "undeniably pretty and detailed look" at a "challenging and relevant story." Addressing the story, he adds that it obviously suits the political climate of 2006:

> [T]he fact that I'm not quite sure exactly what Millar is trying to say politically is perhaps one of the highest compliments that I can pay to his writing, as he adopts a decidedly un-preachy writing style which leaves neither side coming off as whiter-than-white, despite the fact that the methods of the pro-registration heroes are so clearly questionable [Wallace].

A storyline with such moral ambiguity can be off-putting, yet McNiven and his artistic collaborators give the story a clean, and inviting appearance. This almost seems like a disconnect between theme and presentation. The morality of the story is undeniably murky, but the art is crisp and easy to digest. But that disconnect serves the story well. In both the art and the narrative, both sides appear inviting. That was one of the goals of the series—to not have one side be the outright villain—and the art does not paint either side as heroes or villains.

A Close Reading

Having discussed some of the ways McNiven's art and Holloway's coloring are significant for the series as a whole, a close reading of one single image can more specifically highlight their contributions. By considering their choices and exploring how significant aspects of the entire series are encapsulated in one image, the impact of the art on the narrative can be better understood.

The first double page spread of *Civil War*, taking place on pages eight and nine of the first issue (Millar), foreshadows the "rift between those supporting heightened security (such as Iron Man) and those supporting civil liberties (such as Captain America)" (Howe 425). In the foreground, Iron Man and Captain America stand, heads turned to take in a horrific scene of devastation that follows the ill-fated battle between the New Warriors and group of second- and third-tier villains. Across the bottom of the page, a black banner has white text in all-capital letters declaring, "CIVIL WAR PART ONE OF SEVEN." Placing the title here makes the aftermath of the New Warriors' battle the inciting incident of the series, not the fight itself. It is this scene of destruction that will set Iron Man and Captain America down contradictory paths.

Because Marvel has published the original script written by Millar, we can analyze what choices McNiven made with his pencils, which were inked by Dexter Vines. The coloring by Morry Hollowell adds to the pages' impact as well. The final script by Millar from which McNiven would have penciled the scene describes the two-page spread in a paragraph:

> PAGE EIGHT AND NINE
> 1/ Cut to just a few hours later and a double-page spread where, most prominently, we see Captain America and Iron Man standing in full-figure shots in the ruins of this place. It looks like a Hiroshima picture with burned bones everywhere. The place is in darkness and we see lots of Avengers and X-Men helping out here with the rescue effort, everyone wearing oxygen masks and working with the official rescue workers. Cap and Iron Man are just surveying the quite awesome damage here. I see this as a full-figure shot of Iron Man and Cap (one on each page) but you're the boy, Steve McNiven. Your call [Millar, *Civil War Script Book*, 10].

As is explicit in the script, significant leeway was given to McNiven to interpret the scene. Regarding what it is like to work from a Millar script, McNiven explained:

> To me the script is best when it's almost like a movie script, with as much direction, dialogue and such as the writer wants to put in. Tell me the shots, the background info, how the characters feel, what they are saying, all that stuff will go towards a better understanding for me as to the kind of the story the writer is going for [Northcott].

In this particular image, some of the staging comes directly from Millar's description. Captain America and Iron Man are in full-figure shots, one on each page. In the background, superheroes and rescue workers are engaged in rescue activities. But, the posing and additional elements of the mise-en-scène are chosen by McNiven and do reflect the themes which will come to define the series.

First, let us address the fact that this is a two-page spread. Comic books rely on panels to separate the action on a page, with the exception of a two-page spread, in which a single image encompasses all of the available space. In this instance, there is a banner at the bottom of the page announcing the title of the series. Two-page spreads can be powerful. In pages with panels separated by gutters the reader becomes a "willing and conscious collaborator" in the storytelling, filling in the beats between the panels and supplying closure that links the events (McCloud 65). Not so with a two-page spread.

This type of spread invites readers to pause and take in the art. Notably, this spread has no text, the art is telling the entire story. There are only two other double-page spreads in the entire *Civil War* mini-series. One, from the fifth issue, features the massive jail in the negative zone that Mr. Fantastic and Iron Man have built. This spread includes a single word balloon, "Nobody wants to put you in jail" (Millar, *CW* #5, 21–22). The word balloon is tiny, the speaker unseen, as the image the vastness of the jail that the pro-registration side has built. (It is a moment of naïve and painful irony, as if such prisons are built for any other reason than to imprison people just like Daredevil). The third and final two-page spread in the series occurs near the end of the sixth issue and sets up the final battle that will occupy the majority of the final issue. The spread features Iron Man and Captain America facing off with the respective super-powered individuals who have joined each side of the debate (Millar, *CW* #6, 21–22). All three of the spreads play to different strengths that this sort of narrative pause can provide. The first image allows the reader to take in a tragedy, the second reveals the scale of the prison, and the third is overflowing with characters and the tension is palpable as the inevitable battle is about to begin.

In the first two-page spread of the series, firemen and costumed superheroes are seen in the background, clearing wreckage, covering human remains, and attempting to resuscitate a child. Captain America stands over a tattered American flag, the symbol the country and ideals for which he dons a costume and fights. Members of multiple teams of the superhero community are clearly seen in the background, including the Thing of the Fantastic Four, Iceman of the X-Men, and Cage of the Avengers among others. Some are clearing debris, others carrying bodies, though it is unclear if they are dead or wounded.

The sky in the top third of the image features the setting sun and is red in the center of the image and fades to gray at the edges. The bottom two thirds of the image feature wreckage, rubble, and skeletons. It is colored a dark gray with black cracks and shadows adding depth. In short, this is colored as a hellscape, which is exactly what the image is meant to evoke. This is the superheroes' hell.

Much of the imagery in the scene is evocative of images from 9/11. In a series meant to parallel post–9/11 America, the Marvel universe experiences its own massively-scaled tragedy. Notably, the horizon-line of the scene features girders jutting up into the sky reminiscent to many of the famous images of the World Trade Center after its collapse. Additionally, Captain America is standing over a tattered American flag. This, combined with the destruction in the background and the firemen within the scene, can remind viewers of the famous photograph of firemen raising an American flag onto a broken flagpole during rescue efforts following 9/11. However, in that photograph the flag was remarkably whole; McNiven's flag is burned and ragged, with only some of the field of blue and stars and a red and a white stripe remaining.

This mise-en-scène sets the thematic stage for the story to follow. Captain America's positioning just above a tattered American flag is significant. As Mark Millar explained, the mini-series is "a story where a guy wrapped in the American flag is in chains as the people swap freedom for security" (qtd. in Johnson 183). The ideals the flag symbolizes are at least partially destroyed within the narrative. While the reader would not have known which side Captain America would represent in the story or its ultimate conclusion, Millar and McNiven are visually representing the themes.

Iron Man and Captain America face one another, other superheroes and first responders in the background. Iron Man and Captain America will become the symbolic faces of the pro-registration and anti-registration sides. They will become responsible for the very same destruction they are surveying.

Also, the presence of the firemen in this image is a foreshadowing of the conclusion of the series. In the final battle Captain America is preparing to hit a prone Iron Man when he is tackled by a fireman, a police officer, two EMTs, and other civilians. Their actions cause Captain America to realize how much destruction the battle has caused. Captain America removes his mask, and as Steve Rogers, surrenders and orders his anti-registration side to stand down.

McNiven, Vines, and Holloway greatly added to the story that Mark Millar wrote. Their contributions are worthy of even more consideration and study than this chapter has provided, and the same is true of comic book art in general. Comic books are a unique medium, and failing to properly examine the artistic side does a disservice to the co-creators of the stories, our understanding of the narratives, and our appreciation of the art form.

Works Cited

Brothers, David. "'Criminal: The Last of the Innocent' Mixes Murder with Nostalgia in a Brubaker Master Class." Comics Alliance.com. Townsquare Media, 1 June 2011. Web. 12 July 2014.
CBR News Team. "Catching Up with 'Civil War's' Steve McNiven." CBR.com. Comic Book Resources, 22 Nov. 2006. Web. 14 May 2006.
Ching, Albert. "Breaking: DC Comics Implements New Creator Payment Plan." CBR.com. Comic Book Resource, 24 June 2014. Web. 24 June 2014.
Duncan, Randy, and Matthew J. Smith. *The Power of Comics: History, Form, & Culture.* New York: Continuum, 2009.
Gustines, George Gene. "The Battle Outside Raging, Superheroes Dive in." NYT.com. The New York Times Company, 20 Feb. 2006. Web. 13 June 2014.
Helvie, Forrest. "Don't Ignore the Art: Reviewing and Commenting on Comics Part 1." *Sequart.* Sequart Organization. 14 July 2014. Web. 14 July 2014
_____. "Don't Ignore the Art: Reviewing and Commenting on Comics Part 2." *Sequart.* Sequart Organization. 15 July 2014. Web. 15 July 2014
Howe, Sean. *Marvel Comics: The Untold Story.* New York: HarperCollins, 2012. Print.
Johnson, Jeffrey. *Super-History: Comic Book Superheroes and American Society, 1938 to the Present.* Jefferson, NC: McFarland, 2012. Print.
Leong, Tim. "Steve McNiven Interview on Civil War." *Comic Foundry.* Comic Foundry, 4 May 2006. Web. 10 May 2014.
McCloud, Scott. *Understanding Comics: The Invisible Art.* Northampton, MA: Kitchen Sink Press, 1993. Print.
Millar, Mark. "Civil War Script Book." *A Marvel Comics Event: Civil War."* Ed. Mark D. Beazley. New York: Marvel Comics. 2007. Print. The *Script Book* is not paginated, so page numbers have been provided, beginning with the traditional summary and credits page as 1.
Millar, Mark (writer), Steve McNiven (penciller), Dexter Vines (inker), and Morry Hollowell (colorist). *Civil War #1–7* (May 2006–Feb. 2007), Marvel Comics. Web. 12 Dec. 2014.
Mulligan, Rikk. "The Reality/Fantasy Narrative and the Graphic Novel." *Critical Insights: The Graphic Novel.* Ed. Gary Hoppenstand. Ipswich, MA: Salem Press, 2014.
Northcott, Blake. "Interview: MARVEL Artist Steve McNiven." *Man Cave Daily.* CBS Local, 15 Nov. 2013. Web. 12 May 2014.
Offenberger, Rik. "Morry Hollowell: The Color of War." *First Comic News.* First Comic News, 15 June 2006. Web. 28 Mar. 2014.
Rhoades, Shirrel. *A Complete History of American Comic Books.* New York: Peter Lang, 2008. Print.
Richards, Dave. "Our Marvels at War: Millar Talks 'Civil War.'" *CBR.* Comic Book Resources, 12 Apr. 2006. Web. 14 May 2006.
Wallace, David. "Civil War: Failing to Register?" *Comics Bulletin.* Comics Bulletin, n.d. Web. 10 May 2014.
Weiland, Jonah. "Millar & McNiven Respond to 'Civil War' Delay News." *CBR.* Comic Book Resources. 16 Aug. 2006. Web. 12 July 2014.

Wiltfong, David. "Q&A with Civil War Colorist Morry Hollowell." *The Walt Disney Company*. Marvel.com. 31 May 2007. Web. 7 Apr. 2014.

Wright, Bradford W. *Comic Book Nation: The Transformation of Youth Culture in America*. Baltimore: Johns Hopkins University Pres, 2001. Print.

Yukcevic, Fillip. "Toronto FanExpo 2006: Marvel Civil War Confidential." *IGN*. Ziff Davis, 5 Sept. 2006. Web. 28 May 2014.

When Flaw Meets Form Meets Function: Narration, Crossover Comic Events and a New Art Experience

KEVIN MICHAEL SCOTT

Like most Americans, I could think of little else other than the falling Towers for weeks after 9/11. The tragedy was so large, so unexpected, so unimaginable, that we struggled to find a way to comprehend it. This was true, as well, in both popular and high culture. The discomfort faced by comedians like David Letterman, Jon Stewart, and the *Saturday Night Live* crew in the immediate aftermath—*how to bring humor to a situation like this?*—presaged the difficulties to come in the fine arts. Ten years after the attack, *New York Times* literary critic Michiko Kakutani reviewed the creative work that had arisen both from the events of 9/11 and from the American response to them. While there had been some high points, art had been "outdone by reality"—the results were, in a word, disappointing.

Kakutani's article highlights "how resistant 9/11 remains to artistic treatment." Early creative responses were largely memorializing, and some of these were powerful, such as the "Tribute in Light" at the World Trade Center site, but art such as this, which is largely cathartic rather than challenging, does not move the culture, or any necessary conversations, forward. Kakutani surveys a variety of genres, and with a few exceptions that largely approach the topic peripherally, post–9/11 art has been either "sentimental" and "heavy-handed" or "obvious" and "shrill." Although she does highlight the proliferation of superhero films, which she seems to find unsatisfying entries, she does not include in her survey comic books or graphic novels.

But comics did respond to 9/11. Soon after the attacks, several companies, including Marvel, published memorial comics or series.[1] As time passed, writers and artists began focusing more on the attacks' impact on culture than on the tragedy itself, with series like Brian K. Vaughn's *Ex Machina* and Garth Ennis' *The Boys* providing thoughtful and dark, if not fatalistic, takes on American culture.[2]

Marvel's *Civil War*, though, has advantages that none of the other works share, either within comics or in other art forms. First, built into *Civil War* is a particular conception about how art is supposed to work on its viewer. Most of the art spawned by 9/11 has a clear argument, theses such as "We are strong and will survive," "Torture is an easy but immoral answer," or "The hatefulness directed toward Muslims in America is an abandonment of our values." *Civil War*, on the other hand, presents art as a meditation, an intensive and thoughtful exploration of its subject rather than some ideological puzzle to be solved. The tagline "Whose Side Are You On?" alludes to the fact that fans would be asked to choose a position on the Superhuman Registration Act (SHRA). The law, passed in the wake of a fictional tragedy mirroring 9/11, requires all super-powered individuals to register with the government, including surrendering their secret identities. The "correct" response to this law is not clear in the series, and serious discussions of what to do took place both among the characters and within the fan community. For all of the reasonable complaints that have been leveled at *Civil War* (primarily concerning whether or not plot inconsistencies or its allegedly reductionist approach to American politics undercuts its effectiveness), the series does not stack the deck in favor of one position over another. If positioning Captain America, a figure who brings disproportionate fan affection with him, with the anti-registration "rebels" seems to place narrative weight on that side of the argument, beginning the story by laying responsibility for the death of hundreds of school children at the feet of heroes more than balances the scale.

The emphasis on a discernable argument is largely why most of the art inspired by 9/11 has failed to have an impact upon the culture or to inspire the kind of conversation that great public art is supposed to attain. While Americans have tilted firmly toward one particular political opinion or another several times in the years since the attacks, uncertainty is by far the most common state of being the culture has faced. The reason why "freedom versus security"—the debate in national values that often places a variety of civil rights and civil liberties in opposition to each other—has presented such an ongoing philosophical problem is simply because the answer is not easy. While pundits like to quote Benjamin Franklin's saying about how the person who gives up freedom for security deserves neither, not even Franklin, whose words have been taken completely out of context, believed it to be true.[3] His—*and our*—feelings on the issue have been diverse and often contradictory.

Comics, and Marvel Comics in particular, are uniquely and particularly situated to make the kind of art that addresses 9/11 and the response to it, taking into account the breadth and multiplicity of American culture, and Marvel's advantage is formal. Moreover, the much-derided comic "event" is the specific form where such art can be most powerful. There is a burgeoning body of comics-oriented narratology, and most of it is quite good.[4] This scholarship, however, tends to examine the workings of narration in the comics at the panel-to-panel level or the story level, focusing on the interplay between word and image or on the meanings of the spaces between panels, for example. My interest here takes several steps back and exams the large-scale narration of comics, specifically, the kind of narration available only to comics companies that create their own "universes."

It's a Big Marvel Universe

One story lies at the heart of all of the formal aspects of Marvel Comics that provides the Marvel Universe such artistic potential. In May 1940, Jim Hammond, the Human Torch, had a typical adventure in *Marvel Mystery Comics* #7.[5] It was a notable day for him, as he was formally hired as a New York City policeman on special assignment, and he used his new authority to take down the corrupt politician and mobster, Roglo. At the end of the story, the Torch sees the police station in an uproar, and the captain tells him, "It's a riot call!—The Submariner is wrecking the city!" To which the Torch responds, "Submariner? Who's he?" (Burgos 12).

Betrayed by a justice system that failed to trust his good intentions, Namor, the Sub-Mariner, has vowed vengeance on New York and proceeds to commandeer the Statue of Liberty, sink a ferry, wreck an elevated train, and rip off the top of the Empire State Building (Everett 21–30). Over the next three issues, the Torch and Sub-Mariner fight to a stalemate (Burgos, Everett, and Compton). What makes the moment so important is that it is the first time characters—created by different writers and artists and appearing in their own, separate series—were seen as existing in the same fictional universe. It is difficult, as a comics historian, to overstate the impact of this quiet revolution.

By demonstrating that all of its characters exist in a shared universe, Timely Comics (which would later become Marvel) expanded not just the story-telling possibilities but also the required imaginative participation of the readers by vastly expanding the subtext of which the reader must be in command in order to make meaning. In stories dedicated solely to, say, the Human Torch, the reader identifies with the hero, an android who desperately wants to be a part of establishment culture—a policeman—and simply accepts that construction of identity as he proceeds on his adventures. Something similar happens with stories dedicated to Sub-Mariner, who resents the arrogance and violence with which the surface world treats his Atlantean kingdom. Despite the fact Sub-Mariner regularly commits violence against land dwellers, readers are encouraged to understand and root for him as an anti-hero with a legitimate complaint. In a crossover event, then, readers must bring their understanding of the characters' values and experiences into their interpretive strategies. Simply seeing a "Human Torch versus Sub-Mariner" title on the splash page requires readers to ask questions, to foreground what has been previously accepted, and to bring their own values to the story in ways much more necessary than in the single-character storylines.

From the beginning, Timely/Marvel has made the shared universe nature of their stories more important to its success than any other company. While Superman and Batman appeared on covers together as early as 1941 with *World's Best Comics* #1, the comic was an anthology and the pair would not appear in the same story until 1952, with *Superman* #76. Timely's crossovers sold incredibly well and encouraged more such interaction between characters by Timely and its competitors (Howe 22). Other comic companies followed suit. These companies had discovered a secret: a shared universe makes a fictional universe more like the reader's universe. Although other art forms exist in a version of this (such as when one artist references another's work), the density of the imaginative field that a shared universe creates has not been effectively matched by any other art form.[6]

Continuity: Why Namor Is Still So Angry

While the *Civil War* storyline progressed, writer Ed Brubaker reintroduced Captain America's young World War II partner, Bucky, to the Marvel Universe. In *Winter Soldier: Winter Kills* #1, as Bucky wanders the New York streets, he sees signs and graffiti calling Captain America a traitor for fighting the SHRA, and he muses, "It's like someone knocked the wind out of America" (5). Stan Lee wrote the original story of Bucky's demise in 1964, a tragedy designed to give the surviving Captain America a backstory to fuel the kind of angst that characterized Marvel heroes of the 1960s (Lee, "Captain America," 7). Like many such events, Bucky's death was "retconned"—given a retroactive continuity—to allow his return. In this case, the reader discovered he had actually been rescued by Soviet scientists, who brainwashed him and used his training with Captain America to make him a Soviet assassin. He was placed in suspended animation between assassinations, allowing him to reappear in the 20th century as a young man (Brubaker *CA #8–14*). In trying to find a reference point to describe how 21st-century New Yorkers are dealing with the superhero civil war in a way that makes sense to his World War II–era consciousness, Bucky remarks that this is "the way it must've felt to this city in 1940, when the Torch fought Namor and they blew up and drowned half the Bowery" (6). Sixty-two years after the original story, the events are still relevant.

Like a shared universe, this sort of continuity produces rich ground for art. Almost all of the important characters in the Marvel Universe have decades of story behind them. Such a history could be seen as a limitation (which it often is), and added to the needs of the corporations behind Marvel and DC (the other comic company with a vast shared universe and decades of continuity) to avoid permanent damage to an important—and *high-earning*—character, this would seem to minimize artistic possibility. It often does. However, placed in service to a complex and ongoing story, as opposed to the kind of villain-of-the-week approach that largely faded out by the 1980s, these decades of backstory, combined with the shared universe, create a massive diegesis, a simulacrum of the world in which the readers exist that, due to the time and breadth of its construction, dwarfs that which is available in other art forms.

In explaining the cultural power of Marvel and DC, critic Douglas Wolk argues that readers help construct this diegetic richness:

> [Their] dominance is also related to what's interesting about the costumed-hero thing in the first place, which is what particular characters and their histories mean, and how that meaning has piled up, page by page, over the decades. Within each of the two big stories of superhero comics, the interaction of familiar characters over time is a ritualized enactment of the ideas their readers and creators have about culture and morality or, in some cases, a testing ground for them [92].

To readers, then, comic book characters are complex moral, cultural, and ideological constructs, evolving over time. To put the argument in Saussure's terms, characters, with their immense backstories and cultural representations, are the language of comics (langue), and individual storylines are the specific utterances (parole). And since, as Bakhtin argued in his expansion of Saussure, language is inextricable from ideology, when writers and artists construct their stories, pitching this character into battle with that one (such as the Torch and the Sub-Mariner), they present not merely a "slam-bang" adventure, but an interaction between ideologies deeply embedded in the reader's world and individual psyche.[7]

There is neither a precedent nor an equal to Marvel's dedication to continuity. Although DC's shared universe actually begins earlier than Marvel's, in 1938, nevertheless DC has initiated several universe-wide retcons that have allowed the company to simplify its diegesis, with the goal of minimizing the knowledge necessary for full interaction with the stories and thereby making the comics friendlier for new readers. While Marvel has also regularly retconned individual characters, overall continuity even for these characters has been seen as nearly sacred (the marriage, family, and public identity of Spider-Man is a prime example of both phenomena). Writer and artist Alex Ross was hired by Marvel to co-plot and provide art for Captain America after *Civil War* and the end of Ed Brubaker's run, and part of the draw for him was exactly this corporate trait: "Well, continuity really,

really matters with Marvel. The various efforts that have happened with their characters haven't been retconned continually and, generally, you can treat most of what Kirby, Lee and Ditko did [in the 1960s] as canon. That's very important" (Weiland). In discussing the responsibility of writing the main series of an intensely complicated comic event such as *Civil War*, Mark Millar explained that each draft has to be vetted by continuity editors: "But you can't moan about continuity when you've agreed to write an inter-company crossover. You either respect it or you bugger off and do your creator-owned book" (Millar, *CWSB* 115).

Winter Soldier: Winter Kills is a "one-shot," a common comics strategy designed to tell a good story that does not fit neatly into an ongoing series but fills out the diegesis of the Marvel Universe. The purpose of this comic is to round out the character of Bucky (who will take the place of Captain America after his post–*Civil War* assassination). Bucky wanders New York, reminiscing about his World War II experiences and how they inform—or fail to inform—his current situation. At the end, he stands at the grave of Jack Monroe, a man who had been obsessed with the adventures of Captain America and Bucky during World War II and, for a short period after the war, had acted as a new Bucky when the original team disappeared. It is a difficult moment for Bucky; he is struggling to process the public condemnation of his mentor at the same time as he comes to terms with his sudden, post-brainwashing emergence into 21st-century America. It is a complex story of an identity struggling for coherence, and it requires understanding of both the decades of continuity and the shared universe for a reader fully to appreciate it.

As Bucky mourns Jack Monroe, who wanted to be him and who died badly because of it, Namor arrives and they visit another grave, that of "Toro" Raymond, the Human Torch's sidekick. Namor is stiff, arrogant, and unpleasant, but also generous and even kind in his own way, just as he was in the comics of the 1940s. Bucky, who was there, says, "Good to know not **everything** has changed" (37). Bucky visits the grave to reconnect to a time he sees as simpler and better, a time that for him feels quite recent. Namor visits the grave because, for him, much time has passed (nearly all of Marvel's history), and it connects him to the first time he felt the sting of bigotry and to the Torch, the first surface man he came to trust. While the story is constructed to be coherent to the reader who is not immersed in the Marvel Universe, such immersion renders a merely poignant story deeply moving and redolent of the many cultural and social changes in six decades of American history.

Mythos and the Bagel

Soon after their first fight, Timely decided to pit Sub-Mariner and the Human Torch against each other again, and in an even bigger brawl. In November 1941, with World War II dominating the public discourse (and a month before Pearl Harbor), Timely presented "The Human Torch Battles the Sub-Mariner as the World Faces Destruction." The splash page presents the Sub-Mariner, Mussolini, Hitler, and Death as the four horsemen of the apocalypse (Burgos and Everett 1). After a naval battle between the Russians, Germans, and British destroys his home city of Atlantis, he first vows to end the war, by force, and is then manipulated by a femme fatale, Rathia, into believing that the only way to make the world safe is to conquer it. The battle extends across the globe and includes several other major characters in Marvel's expanding shared universe, and it ends apocalyptically, with Sub-Mariner flooding Manhattan with a tsunami (53). The battle breaks the "spell" of manipulation binding Sub-Mariner, and the Human Torch saves his life while helping him stop Rathia and end the war, forever earning the Sub-Mariner's respect (56–60).

In the year before Pearl Harbor, comics were full of images of large-scale war. Although public attitudes were still largely anti-war, the comics seemed to know what was coming. Captain America's arch-enemy was the Red Skull, whose secret identity was George Maxon, an industrialist working to overthrow the U.S. government and sell arms to the Germans (Simon). When Namor floods Manhattan, then, the comics are entering into a painful conversation with an American culture that is deeply ambivalent—expecting but wanting to avoid war. The images of Manhattan being destroyed created an intertext between comics and the news coming from Europe. In the DC Universe, if Batman's Gotham or Superman's Metropolis are damaged or destroyed, a layer of fantasy distances the reader. There is an Olympian aspect to characters such as these. Their cities are not places the reader can visit. But in their battles, the Torch and the Sub-Mariner lay waste to a host of places where many readers *live*.

Critics of comics have long discussed the genre as a mythology of American culture. Richard Reynolds argued in 1992 that superheroes are a "modern mythology," that they are symbols of the core values—or *mythos*—guiding American society. Variations on the argument have continued, notably including *Supergods*, by Grant Morrison, one of the most successful comic book writers of recent decades. Such conversations, though, tend to focus on such superheroes as Batman and Superman, who live in fantastical cities and seldom engage in the quotidian tasks of life. Of course, Marvel characters also represent core values or aspirations of American culture. The most famous is the guilt-ridden Peter Parker's guiding philosophy: "With great power there must also come—great responsibility" (Lee, "Spider-Man!" 11).[8] But Marvel's characters have always been firmly planted in specific, real-world locations, usually New York, largely because this is where most of the writers and artists lived at the dawn of the industry and because this affords more opportunity for crossover events.

Marvel has always made the corporeality of its universe central to its storytelling.[9] In discussing the differences between Marvel and DC with non-comics readers, I have often used two examples, the first being that a person who lives in New York could use a recent Marvel comic to know where to find a good bagel. In 2010, after years of using this illustration, I read *Amazing Spider-Man Annual #37*, in which Spider-Man tells Captain America that the reason he is so often seen near the *Daily Bugle* (where his alter ego, Peter Parker works as a photographer) is that "there's just a … really good bagel place around here" (Kesel). Studious readers of Spider-Man comics know that the *Daily Bugle* is at 39th Street and 2nd Avenue, in the Murray Hill neighborhood in midtown Manhattan.[10] Comic book critic and historian Peter Sanderson has even published *The Marvel Comics Guide to New York City* in 2007, detailing the intensive connection between the Marvel Universe and the city.

The corporeality of the Marvel Universe is not determined solely by its connection to a physical New York or any other location. In addition to placing their characters in known environments, Marvel stories include the kinds of activities and concerns that readers share. Stan Lee described this as the goal of the creators of many of Marvel's characters in the 1960s:

> I would guess it's because we tried to make our characters as human and empathetic as possible. Instead of merely emphasizing their super feats, we attempted to make their personal life and personal problems as realistic and as interesting as possible. We wanted to make them seem like

real people whom the reader would like to spend time with and want to know better [Stan Lee Interview].

This effort is the source of what I term *Mythos and the Bagel*, the unique phenomenon in Marvel comics of combining the mythic qualities of the superhero concept with the novelistic qualities that theorists like Bakhtin have identified.

The second example I would offer in my discussions of the differences between the DC and Marvel universes was a question. Can you imagine Superman, Batman, Wonder Woman, and Aquaman sitting around in a diner, drinking coffee and complaining about the quality of the French fries? To the comics reader, the image is a bit profane. Between 1994 and 1996, the brilliant, satirical animated series, *The Tick*, parodied exactly this situation regularly, and it was the very ridiculousness of the image that gave these scenes much of their humor. In the Marvel Universe, however, such situations happen regularly. *Civil War* series editor Tom Brevoort explains, "Even superheroes need to eat every once in a while" (Millar, *CWSB* 79). (Not seeing Superman or Batman eat is part of a strategy for heightening the sense that they are *different* from us.) Indeed, such quotidian moments are used as important plot devices. After rejecting his father's power and violence, Peter Parker's friend, Harry Osborn, opens a coffee shop. The overarching story is mythic: a brilliant, hyper-successful father—Norman Osborn—slowly loses his sanity and grows dissatisfied with mere business success, becoming the super-villain, Green Goblin, and aiming his obsessive madness at a pure-hearted hero, Spider-Man. The son is torn between his loyalties to his father and his friend. The actual expression of the story, however, is family drama—hurt feelings and epithets; the son's struggling café is an open rebuke to the father. It is small, local, and personal.

Even more notably, in the heart of *Civil War*, when half of Marvel's most important characters have been rendered fugitives, Captain America, Hercules, Daredevil, and Goliath meet at a diner to discuss the war and their coming to terms with accepting new secret identities. The trauma of the scene is undercut by the humor. Captain America is now a security guard. The Greek god Hercules is an IT specialist. And in an example of the subtle way Marvel writers often address the American legacy of race, Bill Foster, the African American scientist whose original hero name was Black Goliath (now just *Goliath*), is not amused to find that his new identity is a racial cliché: "Rockwell Dodsworth ... community outreach worker" (Millar, *CW* #3, 8–9). Other than coffee, the reader is not privy to what they are eating, but the scene is nearly a pantomime of the concept, mythos and the bagel. The hero whose costume is the American Flag discusses civil liberties with companions who similarly see themselves in this context as sentinels of liberty; but, while they sip, Steve Rogers's biggest concern is that he is missing a chance to fulfill an engagement with the Make a Wish Foundation and play baseball with a dying child.

Collaboration, Creative Conflict, and Contested Art

The 1940 and 1941 battles between the Human Torch and the Sub-Mariner not only brought together characters who had previously only existed in separate diegeses, it brought together creators who had previously been imagining those separate worlds, worlds that functioned somewhat differently and conveyed divergent views of the social order. Carl Burgos's Human Torch, like many characters, was a version of Superman in that he was different by nature (an android), and he was created by a Jewish artist who changed his name (from Max Finkelstein).[11] Like Superman, the Torch was also eager to be accepted into respectable society (being a policeman is being part of the establishment). Bill Everett's Sub-Mariner addressed some of the same themes, but from the opposite direction. Namor was born in an environment where his people had already been badly harmed by the arrogance and bigotry of "white people," and his response is to reject and to attack. Each character represented its creator's relationship with the world. Burgos left school early, eager to make his name, while Everett, at 21, had already been struggling with alcohol for ten years and would be fired from multiple jobs (Howe 12–13). The difference in their writing and drawing styles added an energy to their collaboration that extended beyond the success of their own work, and "The Human Torch Battles the Sub-Mariner as the World Faces Destruction" was a massive hit for the company (Howe 22).

Since "The Human Torch Battles the Sub-Mariner as the World Faces Destruction," crossover events have grown increasingly complex. While Mark Millar wrote the title series of the *Civil War* event, two-dozen writers, dozens more artists, and several editors were involved in the creation of the nearly one hundred tie-in issues covering twenty-nine different titles. The unprecedented scale of the project for Marvel was so large, according to Millar, and would affect so much of the Marvel Universe that such an event could only be done "once in a generation" (*CWSB* 15). The consideration of the freedom-versus-security debate in *Civil War* initiated a four-year examination of linked themes—such as race and ethnicity, unexamined government power, and preemptive action, among others—in the crossover events *Secret Invasion*, *Dark Reign*, and *The Siege* (which is generally seen as the culmination of a four-year story arc).

The writers and editors of Marvel knew from the beginning of the creative process that *Civil War* would be intense, complex, and fraught with conflicts. Millar explained that, because the series uses characters already established in other books, constant negotiation was necessary: "I've made this ten times harder by trying to give every character a piece in this and there's always somebody's favorite either getting under-used or not done the way they want them. It's a huge undertaking and very political even in the office because you are borrowing characters from other writers" (*CWSB* 171). Because *Civil War* would be so clearly political, writers were required to work with characters taking a political stand who had not been particularly political in the past, and the stands taken by the characters were determined by the needs of the story and the history of those characters rather than by the preferences (political or otherwise) of the writers. In the years since *Civil War*, a few writers have openly discussed the discomfort and even the open disagreement they had with the development of important characters and the story in general.

According to Brevoort, Dan Slott (*She-Hulk*) and Brian Reed (*Ms. Marvel*) were writing characters whose political choices went against the values of the writers, but each worked within the crossover's continuity to tell stories that reflected their own values (Millar, *CWSB* 139). In the light-hearted *She-Hulk*, Jennifer Walters, who received a blood transfusion from her cousin, the Hulk, can control her change back and forth into her heroic (large, green) form, and her day job is as a lawyer. Her belief in the law leads her to accept, support, and fight for the SHRA. However, in issues #14–18, she is drafted into S.H.I.E.L.D., forced into dangerous service, has sex with Tony Stark (Iron Man), and rebels when she finds out that Stark has betrayed her cousin. With the power of the SHRA and S.H.I.E.L.D. behind him, Stark responds to her rebellion by stripping her of her powers.

Similarly, in *Ms. Marvel* (at the time, the most prominent female character in the Marvel Universe), the main character, Carol Danvers, had a long history in the military before becoming a superhero. She immediately accepts the SHRA, but Reed uses her pro-registration stance to highlight the inevitable realities of the policy, placing Ms. Marvel in the position of having to pull an anti-registration hero, Arachne, away from the reaching arms of the woman's daughter (15–16). Certainly, such a scene is the height of melodrama, but it is also highly effective and remains one of the most memorable moments of the crossover event. While the tension between the writers' political values and those of their characters could have created resentment at being forced to write stories supportive of an opposing political philosophy, given the emotional sense of ownership that comes with writing a character, both writers used the tension to tell stories not covered in the main series but that furthered the political allegory at the heart of that story. In *She-Hulk*, Slott explores the ways that government power tends to want to extend itself, to see itself as both a means to an end and the end itself. In *Ms. Marvel*, Reed highlights the human cost of government decisions, especially those that involve identifying a particular class of people as problematic. Both are themes suggested by the main series, but *Civil War* simply did not have space to explore them.

In the media promotion leading up to *Civil War*, Joe Quesada, Marvel Comics' editor in chief, argued that *Civil War* is "the first real comic event of its kind that doesn't really have a villain" (Quesada). This sentiment was echoed during and after the publication of the series. Brevoort said that Marvel Comics' general rule is to remain "non-partisan" and that the series has no "bad guy" (Millar, *CWSB* 41, 65). Millar acknowledged that the enterprise was influenced by contemporary politics, but that his approach was to shake up the traditional binaries: "It's really lazy writing to make everything black and white. I'm a politics buff and I really hate seeing America divided into red and blue states because I know people in red states who have blue opinions. And we're all very complex.... I wanted to do the same thing with super heroes" (Millar, *CWSB* 93).

This mixing up and complicating of expected political formulations had an impact on both the creators and readers of the series. In a humorous but pointed moment in "The Road to Civil War," Tony Stark and Peter Parker fly to Washington, D.C., to argue against the passage of the SHRA. Stark explains to Parker that they need to win the argument because all of the other options are "downright ugly." What follows is a generic convention related to the "Dear Reader" asides common to Victorian literature; two editors of the *Amazing Spider-Man* (presumably Michael O'Connor and Axel Alonzo) metafictionally argue the merits of the SHRA in narrative captions colored yellow and green:

> EDITOR'S NOTE [yellow]. Some of us at Marvel disagree with this statement, and feel that many of those options are perfectly reasonable.
> EDITOR'S NOTE [green]. Okay, but the rest of us don't feel that way.
> EDITOR'S NOTE [yellow]. Who asked you?
> EDITOR'S NOTE [green]. Look, we've already been through this—
> EDITOR'S NOTE [yellow]. You're not listening— [Straczinski, *ASM* #530, 2–3].

The interchange cleverly highlights the unsolvable nature of the conflict, both in American culture and in the fictional Marvel Universe. Internet forums and chat rooms tended to see Captain America's commitment to personal civil liberties as on the political left and Iron Man's support for government regulation as conservative, despite the fact that such positions would normally be ascribed to the opposite political camps (Brevoort has compared the SHRA to gun control legislation—to his mind, a reasonable effort by the government to regulate dangers to average citizens. See Millar, *CWSB* 81).

Millar has acknowledged that, to his mind, *Civil War* is evenhanded but that the argument leans toward Iron Man's position, supporting the SHRA (*CWSB* 169). He is correct in this. However, after the first emotional beat of the tragedy at Stamford, where poorly trained and motivated young heroes initiate a conflict with super-villains that leads to an explosion killing over 600 civilians, including most of an elementary school, the great majority of the affecting emotional moments support the "freedom fighter" group of anti–SHRA heroes. In the final violent moment of the series, though, as Captain America is poised to deliver a potential death stroke to Iron Man, he is tackled by a host of "first responders"—police, EMTs, and firefighters—who bust through his commitment to the cause, reminding him that the people support Iron Man and that his fight is, at that very moment, endangering the lives of citizens he claims to protect. It is a powerful and almost irrefutable admission of the "real" world outside of the Marvel Universe, an admission that actual U.S. citizens would never allow super-powered individuals to take on the role of de facto government without any accountability to American citizens, just as they would not accept a terrorist attack without a response.

Millar and Brevoort also acknowledge that many readers and most of the writers of the tie-in issues reacted against the SHRA and cast Tony Stark (and, to a lesser extent, Reed Richards) as a villain of the moustache-twirling variety. Millar explained, "What the other guys did in the tie-in books demonized them a little, but I think that made it interesting as Tony's victory at the end was much more of a curveball" (*CWSB* 171). The key here is that, though *Civil War* was the main series, designed to lead the entire Marvel Universe for about eight months and to earn the most money in sales, writers of other titles felt free, even given editorial leadership, to write *against* the main storyline. Brevoort addressed the public perception of Tony Stark as the villain of the story: "I think that many of the people who feel he's coming off that way are those who were reading the assorted tie-ins. But this was the compromise I made, good or bad—to let each writer try to address the issues of *Civil War* in their own way, telling the truth as they saw it" (*CWSB* 103).

No writer felt that desire more than J. Michael Straczinski, the writer of both *Amazing Spider-Man* and *Fantastic Four*. Straczinski, well known for his left-of-center politics,[12] had to deal with both Peter Parker and Reed Richards supporting registration. Millar uses Spider-Man as the moral touchstone of the Marvel Universe, a much beloved character who bears his "great power/great responsibility" as a cross. In *ASM*, the ongoing story highlights Tony Stark manipulating, deceiving, and spying on Peter Parker, even, potentially, in his and his wife's bedroom (*ASM* #529, 1). In one notable episode, the same fight—following Spider-Man's decision to switch sides to anti-registration—is portrayed differently in *Civil War* #5 and *ASM* #535. Millar depicts Spider-Man as equally responsible and as throwing the first illustrated punch (some wreckage suggests the fight had already started), while Straczinski shows Iron Man blindsiding Spider-Man as he attempts to remove his family to safety (*CW* #5, 5–8; *ASM* #535, 20–21). It is an important moment, suggesting both that the tie-in stories are vital in filling out the story for sheer narrative coherence and complexity, but also for representing the difficulty of coming to terms with the kinds of conflicts between fundamental American values that continues to characterize post-9/11 culture. The overall story, like Walt Whitman's persona, is a "Kosmos." *Civil War* contains multitudes. One writer may have an identifiable position on how these contending values should be balanced, but the overall story—the crossover event—is less about one value or another than it is about the nature of the social and political struggle.

Similarly, in *Fantastic Four*, Straczinski follows the dictates of the crossover imperative, in that Reed Richards supports registration, but his construction of Richards resists the clear commitment present in Millar's *Civil War*. Reed and Sue Richards are likely the most famous married couple in the Marvel Universe, and in the main series, Richards tells her that the government's actions, and their participation is revolutionizing, "the most exciting thing we've ever worked on," and "an amazing opportunity." Richards, whose historical characterization is of the man of science sometimes blind to personal hurts, further argues that his complex mathematical projections show that only something like the SHRA can stave off an otherwise inevitable meta-human "apocalypse" (Millar, *CW* #2, 6–7). In Straczinski's construction of the Fantastic Four, however, Richards's wife, Sue, operates as the author's ideological stand in, and she casts Richards's argument in a very different light. Straczinski's Richards depends on a pro-registration argument that is a simple appeal to authority—it is the law. Twice, in issues #538 and #540, Sue accuses her husband of using the Nazi argument of "just following orders" and doing the equivalent of capturing their friends and herding "them into cattle cars for train rides to places like Auschwitz and Treblinka" (*FF* #538, 2; *FF* #540, 5–6). In response, Richards looks distraught and frustrated, clenches his fist (though without "pointing" it at his wife), and later admits to her that he is motivated as well by the fear of losing everything he has built, which would include his powerful business empire and the powerful social standing he enjoys as a leader of the establishment (*FF* #540, 6–10). With these developments, Strazcinski's deconstruction of the character—and the pro-registration argument—is largely complete.

One of the more notable efforts of the *Civil War* event was the limited-run series, *Civil War: Front Line*, a take on the events from the perspectives of two, non-super-powered reporters. Millar acknowledged that most of the tie-ins tended to be more or less anti–SHRA (*CWSB* 169), but an exception is *CWFL*. Writer Paul Jenkins presents a Richards who is much more emotional than the way he is represented in other books. He is deeply concerned for Robbie Baldwin, the young hero whose carelessness catalyzed the tragedy at Stamford and who is now injured, imprisoned, and demonized. In *CWFL* #3, Richards has a reflective discussion with a reporter about the SHRA in which he thoughtfully responds to challenging questions. Although he takes a utilitarian approach to social management, it is also clear that he takes this approach based on a deep respect for human life—a value based on emotions. Richards here is much more attractive, possibly even "heroic." Working against the grain, Jenkins's series shows another—avowedly liberal—reporter having her positions upended and coming to dismiss most of Captain America's arguments and begrudgingly respect Tony Stark for his actions (Jenkins).[13]

More than any other figure, the characterization of Reed Richards in *Civil War* led to howls of anguish and anger within the comic book community.[14] The most common argument is that "Reed wouldn't act this way." Indeed, in an earlier story, Richards testifies before Congress against a proto–SHRA (Simonson 12–14). In an interview, Straczinski argued that *Civil War* forced a change in the characterization of Richards: "I'm all for crossovers if they benefit the individual books. But it was feeling more and more like the individual characters were being bent towards the event in ways I didn't think were appropriate. I mean to make Reed Richards a bad guy in *Civil War* ... I just never bought into that" (Starczinski).

To many fans, these varying representations of "Richards" create an unacceptable tension. However, it could also be argued there is no real tension. Such prescriptive understandings of character (as communicated by Straczinski and many fans) are unrealistic both in the Marvel Universe and in the real one. Is it unreasonable to believe that one character could behave very differently in different contexts, that he could be more defensive and ineloquent arguing with his wife than chatting with a reporter? The characters have decades of backstory in which Richards's obsessive focus on scientific research has torn at their marriage. (Moreover, in the 1990 story, Richards is arguing against passage of an SHRA-type bill. In *Civil War*, the SHRA is a fait accompli. This would sensibly change his approach.) Read more holistically, the various incarnations of "Richards" suggest nothing more than the complexity of the subject and the emotional and intellectual difficulty in coming to terms with something like the SHRA.

Civil War also speaks to the power of the crossover event as a form of art that can employ tools inaccessible to any other art form. The crossover event brings more voices collaboratively into play, voices that are simultaneously collective and individually coherent. Coupled with the sheer density and scope of the Marvel Universe's diegesis, the crossover has the ability to replicate and comment on the complexities and contradictions of the lived world *in like kind*. The varying constructions of Reed Richards tie together the ideas of Saussure and Bakhtin in interesting ways. If, as I suggested earlier, comic book characters are the *langue* and story arcs the *parole*, then a crossover event functions as the kind of utterance that Bakhtin considers a novel, but *moreso* (heteroglossic, but with super-powers). The centrifugal and centripetal forces that Bakhtin identifies—those that push against and toward centralized authority, be it literary or political—are at play in *Civil War* in that the comic event is "multilanguaged," "conflict-ridden," and "tension-filled" (Bakhtin, "Discourse" 272–74). Despite the desire (the "orientation toward unity") of many fans and even comic creators to find a clean answer to the cultural and political trials of post–9/11 America, *Civil War* is characterized by its "deepening of dialogic essence, its increased scope and greater precision. Fewer and fewer neutral, hard elements ('rock bottom truths') remain that are not drawn into dialogue. Dialogue moves into the deepest molecular and, ultimately, subatomic levels" (Bakhtin, "Discourse" 274, 300).

Given the number of authors involved in *Civil War*, the dialogue available here is made a bit more literal. Brevoort echoed these ideas in his discussion of editing the series and its tie-ins.

> What some readers look at as inconsistencies between titles, I look at as the ordinary cost of doing business when you've got this many people writing stories about the same characters and situations in a short span of time.... It may not have worked for you—each reader takes whatever he wants from the work. But in my experience, placing order above storytelling is a recipe for mediocre comic books [Millar, *CWSB* 177].

The writers of the event used the latitude Brevoort provided to do more than merely argue individual points of political or literary contention. Individual writers brought in concerns that need not have been addressed for a more purely political story, but which, in the context of Marvel's massive diegesis, deepen and complicate the story. *Wolverine* examines the ways corporations use 9/11-like events to seize more social and political authority (Guggenheim). *She-Hulk* shows how legal identity became much more fluid once the War on Terror began (Slott). *Civil War: X-Men* explores how American culture retreats into old ways of understanding ethnicity, placing suspicious people on reservations (Hine). Most poignantly, in depicting the burial of the still massive Goliath, *Black Panther* reveals how, when a nation is in crisis, the already marginalized suffer most (Hudlin). And there is a host of other stories that both intersect and run parallel to the unfolding *Civil War* crisis. Each of these strands enters into dialogue with the overarching political story and, to borrow again from Bakhtin, the result is open and unfinalizable (Bakhtin, "Toward a Methodology" 170).

Civil War succeeded as art (and as commerce) for largely the same reasons so many critics and readers found it unsatisfying. Built upon the often conflicting ideas of its creators, its dialogic voice matches that of the culture of its readers. *Civil War* was a meditation on the American response to 9/11 rather than a focused, monologic argument about it. Its artistic purpose was to reveal rather than to proscribe. The controversial ending—Captain America distraught, becoming aware of the destruction his fight has caused, ending his rebellion, and surrendering to authorities—does not represent a clear victory for Tony Stark and the government. Cap surrenders to *citizens* first, who are themselves grappling with a man who represents a suddenly uncertain idea about civil liberties in a compromised age. It is a visual symbol of struggle that neatly captures the American condition after 9/11 and stakes a claim about comics as art.

Notes

1. Among others, Marvel published *Heroes*, in honor of first responders. Dark Horse, Chaos, and Image published *9–11: Artists Respond, Volume One*, and DC Comics followed up with *9–11: The World's Finest Comic Book Writers and Artists Tell Stories to Remember, Volume Two*.

2. It is notable that Vaughn's and Ennis's series connect superheroes to fictionalized versions of the events of 9/11 and are both deconstructions of the superhero concept, suggesting a link between the confidence and certainty of superheroes (and the culture that loves them) with the events and aftermath of 9/11. The idea that there is more than a whiff of fascism behind every superhero's mask is not new and is also significantly the subject of *Civil War*.

3. A search of the quotation on Google Books will result in dozens of books about terrorism and national security making hay with the saying, generally for anti-government arguments, while Franklin's original use of words was as a member of the colonial-era Pennsylvania Assembly. He wrote to the colonial governor to advocate for the assembly's *power to tax* the Penn family to promote security on the frontier. His was not an anti-government power message. See Morgan 100–102, as well as Wittes.

4. For a few examples, see Groensteen, Cohn, and Postema. All such work, most of it recent, grows out of the two foundational works by Scott McCloud and Will Eisner.

5. The form was still so new the editors called it a "Picture Action Story" (Burgos 12).

6. Notably, the other narratives that exist in a shared universe borrow either directly or indirectly from comics. The comic book-based movies, the "Whedon-verse" created by director/producer Joss Whedon, and the "Doctor Who Universe," or "Whoniverse," of the 21st century draw upon the same dynamic, as did television's *The X-Files* at the end of the 20th century.

Television has a long tradition of spin offs, of course, but none have created the cultural density *within* their respective fictional universes that these "nerd"-focused fictions have. Moreover, a number of these universes have crossed media. Comics set in the shared universes of the X-Files, Joss Whedon's creations, and the "Whoniverse" have all introduced stories that are understood to be canon—or "officially" part of the universes' continuities.

7. Most of Bakhtin's work assumes the ideological nature of language and its functions, but for one example see Bakhtin, "Discourse in the Novel."

8. The quotation comes, originally, from a narrative caption. In later interpretations of Spider-Man's story, such as in the Sam Raimi-directed movies or the *Ultimate Spider-Man* comics, the phrase comes from Peter Parker's Uncle Ben, a retcon that heightens Peter's feelings of guilt for Uncle Ben's death.

9. It is my view that Marvel depicts its characters *en route* more than does DC. The reason for this, I suspect, is that since Marvel characters are moving through the "real world," watching them move through areas that are either seen or at least understood to be real enhances the sympathetic experience between reader and character.

10. A 1972 story in *Amazing Spider Man* #105 shows a protest outside of the *Bugle*, but at an intersection of Madison in the East 50s (the precise number is not shown), but the site in Murray Hill is generally considered to be the location (Lee, "The Spider Slayer," 5; Sanderson 36–39).

11. Such choices were common. Stanley Martin Lieber signed his early work as Stan Lee, though he has maintained that was to protect his eventual career as a serious author. He has since legally changed his name to Stan Lee.

12. Straczinski's work consistently supports liberal values, but his public conversation through interviews and such sources as his Twitter feed ("@straczinski") makes this perfectly clear.

13. The politics of the SHRA are, surprisingly, often misunderstood both by the creators and the fans. This is, I suspect, because both groups are pre-disposed to side with the "rebels" and the status quo of their free agency. We want our heroes to be heroes, and given that the comics world is largely left-of center, that which attacks heroes must be conservative.

14. A simple Internet search of "Reed Richards *Civil War*" results in extensive evidence of the power of this controversy, which has not ended. Eight years after its conclusion, comic critics and fans are still arguing about the event and Richards's role in it (see Cronin, and the comment section to the webpage).

Works Cited

Bakhtin, M. M. "Discourse in the Novel." *The Dialogic Imagination: Four Essays*. Austin: University of Texas Press, 1981. 259–422. Print.

_____. "Toward a Methodology for the Human Sciences." *Speech Genres and Other Late Essays*. Austin: University of Texas Press, 1986. 159–72.

Brubaker, Ed (writer), Steve Epting (penciller), and Steve Epting and Mike Perkins (finishes). "The Winter Soldier." *Captain America* #8–14 (July 2005–Feb. 2006), Marvel. Web. 27 Dec. 2014.

Brubaker, Ed (writer), Lee Weeks, Stefano Gaudiano, and Rick Hoberg (artists). *Winter Soldier: Winter Kills* #1 (27 Dec. 2006), Marvel. Web. 28 Dec. 2014.

Burgos, Carl (writer and artist). "The Human Torch." *Marvel Mystery Comics* #7 (May 1940), Timely Comics. Web. 27 Dec. 2014.

Burgos, Carl, and Bill Everett (writers and artists). "The Human Torch Battle the Sub-Mariner as the World Faces Destruction." *The Human Torch* #5 (Fall 19401), Timely Comics. Digital.

Burgos, Carl, Bill Everett, John Compton (writers), Carl Burgos and Bill Everett (artists). "The Human Torch versus the Sub-Mariner in the Battle of the Century." *Marvel Mystery Comics* #9. (May 1940), Timely Comics. Web. 27 Dec. 2014.

Cohn, Neil. *The Visual Language of Comics: Introduction to the Structure and Cognition of Sequential Images*. London: Bloomsbury, 2013. Print.

Cronin, Brian. "The Abandoned an' Forsaked—So Why Did Reed Richards Support the Superhuman Registration Act." CBR.com. Comic Book Resources. 4 Jan. 2015. Web. 6 Jan. 2015.

Eisner, Will. *Comics and Sequential Art*. Tamarac: Poorhouse Press, 1985. Print.

Ennis, Garth (writer), Darick Robertson, Russ Braun, Peter Snejbjerg, John McCrea (pencillers and inkers), and Rodney Ramos (inker). *The Boys* #1–72 (May 2007–Nov. 2012), Dynamite. Print. The first six issues of The Boys were originally published by Wildstorm, a DC Comics imprint, which cancelled the series in January 2007. Dynamite acquired the rights, republished the previous work, and continued the series in May 2007.

Everett, Bill (writer and artist). "Prince Namor, the Sub-Mariner." *Marvel Mystery Comics* #7 (May 1940), Timely Comics. Web. 27 Dec. 2014.

Groensteen, Thierry. *Comics and Narration*. Trans. Ann Miller. Jackson: University Press of Mississippi, 2013. Print.

_____. *The System of Comics*. Trans. Bart Beaty and Nick Nguyen. Jackson: University Press of Mississippi, 2007. Print.

Guggenheim, Marc (writer), Humberto Ramos (penciller), and Carlos Cuevas (inker). "Payback." *Wolverine* #45–47 (Nov. 2006–Jan. 2007), Marvel. Web. 29 Dec. 2014.

Hine, David (writer), Yanick Paquette (penciller), and Serge LaPointe (inker). *Civil War: X-Men* #1–2 (Sept. 2006–Oct. 2006), Marvel. Web. 29 Dec. 2014.

Howe, Sean. *Marvel Comics: The Untold Story*. New York: Harper, 2012. Print.

Hudlin, Reginald (writer), Koi Turnbull (penciller), Don Ho, Sal Regla, and Jeff De Los Santos (inkers). "War Crimes: Part One." *Black Panther* #23 (Feb. 2007), Marvel. Web. 29 Dec. 2014.

Jenkins, Paul (writer), Ramon Bachs (penciller), and Johns Lucas (inker). *Civil War: Front Line* #1–11. (7 June 2006–28 Feb. 2007), Marvel. Web. 29 Dec. 2014.

Kakutani, Michiko. "Outdone by Reality." NYT.com. The New York Times Company, 1 Sept. 2011. Web. 26 Dec. 2104.

Kesel, Karl (writer), and Paulo Siqueira (artist). "The Spider and the Shield." *Amazing Spider-Man Annual* #37 (26 May 2010), Marvel. Web. 29 Dec. 2014.

Lee, Stan. Interview by Lucy Blodgett. "Stan Lee Interview: The Comic Book Creator on Adventures, Women & Which Superhero Has the Highest Value to Humanity." TheHuffingtonPost.com. TheHuffingtonPost.com, Inc. 28 Apr. 2012. Web 15 Dec. 2014.

Lee, Stan (writer), and Jack Kirby (artist). "Captain America Joins the Avengers." *The Avengers* #4 (10 Mar. 1964), Marvel. Web 28 Dec. 2014.

Lee , Stan (writer), and Steve Ditko (artist). "Spider-Man!" *Amazing Fantasy* #15 (10 Aug. 1962), Marvel. Web. 28 Dec. 2014.

Lee, Stan (writer), Gil Kane (penciller), and Frank Giacuia (inker). "The Spider Slayer!" *Amazing Spider-Man* #105. (10 Feb. 1972), Marvel. Web. 28 Dec. 2014.

McCloud, Scott. *Understanding Comics: The Invisible Art*. Northampton, MA: Kitchen Sink Press, 1993. Print.

Millar, Mark (writer), Steve McNiven (penciller), and Dexter Vines (inker). *Civil War* #1–7 (May 2006–Feb. 2007), Marvel Comics. Web. 25 Dec. 2014.

Millar, Mark (writer), Steve McNiven (penciller), and Dexter Vines (inker). *Civil War: Script Book*. New York: Marvel, 2007.

Morgan, Edmund S. *Benjamin Franklin*. New Haven: Yale UP, 2002. Print.

Morrison, Grant. *Supergods: What Masked Vigilantes, Miraculous Mutants, and a Sun God from Smallville Can Teach Us About Being Human*. New York: Spiegel and Grau, 2012. Print.

Postema, Barbara. *Narrative Structure in Comics: Making Sense of Fragments*. Rochester: Rochester Institute of Technology Press, 2013. Print.

Quesada, Joe, and Paul Lenkins. "Marvel Characters Split in 'Civil War' Series." *Talk of the Nation*. NPR.com. National Public Radio, 6 May 2006. Web. 24 Dec. 2014.

Reed, Brian (writer), Roberto Delatorre (penciller), and Jonathan Sibal (inker). "For the Best." *Ms. Marvel* #8 (18 Oct. 2006), Marvel. Web. 12 Dec. 2014.

Reynolds, Richard. *Super Heroes: A Modern Mythology*. Jackson: University Press of Mississippi, 1992. Print.

Sanderson, Peter. *The Marvel Comics Guide to New York City*. New York: Pocket Books, 2007. Print.

Saussure, Ferdinand de. *Course in General Linguistics*. Trans. Wade Baskin. Eds. Perry Meisel and Haun Saussy. New York: Columbia University Press, 2011. Ebook.

Simon, Joe (writer), and Jack Kirby (artist). "Captain America and the Riddle of the Red Skull." *Captain America* #1 (March 1940), Marvel. Web. 28 Dec. 2014.

Simonson, Walter (writer), Ron Lim (penciller), and Mike DeCarlo (inker). "Dark Congress!" *Fantastic Four* #336 (Jan. 1990), Marvel. Web. 21 Dec. 2014.

Slott, Dan (writer), Rick Burchett (penciller), and Cliff Rathburn (inker). *She-Hulk* #14–18 (20 Dec. 2006–23 May 2007), Marvel. Web. 21 Dec. 2014.

Straczinski, J. Michael (writer), Ron Garney (penciller), and Bill Reinhold (inker). *Amazing Spider-Man* #529–535 (Feb. 2006–Sept. 2006), Marvel. Web. 21 Dec. 2014.

Straczinski, J. Michael. Interview by Bill Graham. "J. Michael Straczinski Talks Studio JMS, Joe's Comics, EPIDEMIC, VLAD DRACULA, His Desire to Work With Neil Gaiman, and More." Collider.com, LLC. 21 Apr. 2012. Web. 1 Jan. 2015.

Straczinski, J. Michael (writer), Mike McKone (penciller), Any Lanning, Kris Justice, and Cam Smith (inkers). "Street Fighting." *Fantastic Four* #538 (28 June 2006), Marvel. Web. 21 Dec. 2014.

Straczinski, J. Michael (writer), Mike McKone (penciller), Any Lanning and Cam Smith (inkers). "Some Words Can Never Be Taken Back." *Fantastic Four* #540 (4 Oct. 2006), Marvel. Web. 24 Dec. 2014.

Vaughn, Brian K (writer), Chris Sprouse (penciller), Tom Feister, Jim Clark, and Tony Harris (inkers). *Ex Machina* #1–50 (Aug. 2004– Aug. 2010), Wildstorm. Print.

Weiland, Jonah. "WWC: Alex Ross Talks 'The Return' to Marvel." CBR.com. Comic Book Resources. 11 Aug. 2007. Web. 27 Dec. 2014.

Wittes, Benjamin. "What Ben Franklin Really Said." Lawfare.com. The Lawfare Institute. 15 July 2011. Web. 25 Dec. 2014.

Wolk, Douglas. *Reading Comics: How Graphic Novels Work and What They Mean*. Cambridge: De Capo Press, 2007. Print.

Part VII—Teaching the Trouble: Pedagogy and *Civil War*

Teaching Ethics When Hero Battles Hero

MARK D. WHITE

In a comics industry dominated by line-wide, universe-altering crossover events with little in-story motivation, Marvel Comics' *Civil War* storyline stands apart for its boldly philosophical and political foundation. This was not a story of the Earth's heroes banding together to face an intergalactic or supernatural menace, or a thinly veiled excuse to have one superhero team fight another. *Civil War* grew out of an idea, drawn from the real world and seeded in the comics months ahead of the event itself, an idea that divided heroes on the intellectual battlefield as well as the physical one. As a result, it provided the opportunity for Marvel's writers to cast various heroes in different ideological positions and have them debate their positions in a way that closely responds to ethical and political arguments in the world outside the comics—and provides educators with an excellent tool for teaching about these topics.

One of the most prominent themes in the book is the ethical dispute between Iron Man and Captain America over super-human registration following a tragedy caused by irresponsible young heroes. Iron Man exemplifies *utilitarianism*, which leads him to support registration because he thinks it will lead to the greatest good for the greatest number of people, while Captain America symbolizes *deontology*, which leads him to emphasize the principles (such as liberty) that would be violated by registration. In between the two stood Spider-Man, who begins the storyline as Iron Man's protégé and pawn but gradually moves to Captain America's side, which allows each hero to argue his case to Spidey, and through him to the reader as well.

In this essay I will discuss how and why *Civil War* provides an excellent platform to teach moral philosophy. I will start by summarizing the basic ethical conflict between Iron Man and Captain America. We will see how the comics highlight not only the main features and contrasts between their moral philosophies, but also the nuances and limitations of each one, especially the need for judgment to put simple ethical rules into action in specific choice situations. Second, I will pull back and discuss why *Civil War*—and, by extension, superhero comics in general—are an excellent way to teach principles of moral philosophy. With its stark contrast (no pun intended) between Iron Man's and Captain America's positions, as well as its balanced presentation of them, *Civil War* allows writers and teachers to explain utilitarianism and deontology using clear examples drawn from an entertaining graphic narrative. This is further enhanced by Spider-Man, who acts as a needle moving between the two extremes of the moral "gauge" and represents the reader or student, caught between two moral philosophies, neither of which settles the question of superhero registration on its own.

Ethics 101: Iron Man versus Captain America

While Captain America and Iron Man have rarely seen eye-to-eye on big issues, *Civil War* served as an extended debate (with fights!) over fundamental views on moral philosophy. In this section, I'll briefly survey the ethical views of both and how they came into conflict over the issue of superhero registration during the events of *Civil War*.

Utilitarianism and Deontology

Iron Man exemplifies the school of ethics known as *utilitarianism*, developed in its modern form by philosophers Jeremy Bentham and John Stuart Mill.[1] Utilitarianism maintains that the morally right action is the one that promotes the greatest happiness of the greatest number of people—or, in other words, the action that increases aggregate *utility* by the greatest amount. In Bentham's conception, utility comes down to pleasure versus pain, and the action that results in greatest surplus of pleasure over pain, or "when the tendency it has to augment the happiness of the community is greater than any it has to diminish it," is the best action to take (Bentham 3).

Technically, utilitarianism is a type of *consequentialism*, which judges the morality of actions by their consequences. Utilitarianism specifies that the relevant consequence is the total utility created, although the definition of *utility* varies among philosophers, ranging from pleasure to satisfaction to well-being, with some (such as Mill) claiming different types of utility.[2] But for most purposes—especially when contrasting utilitarianism with deontology as done in *Civil War*—it is sufficient to associate utility with a general concept of "the good" and say that utilitarianism endorses those actions that maximize the good in society.

Furthermore, the fact that everyone's utility counts equally in the sum total that is to be maximized reflects one of utilitarianism's basic foundations: equality of status among persons. Each person's utility, regardless of class, race, gender, or religion, is added up with everyone else's—a radical idea in Bentham and Mill's day, and still a radical idea in much of the world today. However, this egalitarian aspect of utilitarianism also has a negative side: even though each person's utility counts just as much as anyone else's, it also counts just as little as anyone else's when compared to the sum total of utility. Under utilitarianism, a certain degree of harm to one group of persons is justified if it results in a greater benefit to another group, regardless of any rights or consideration we may think persons in the first group are owed by virtue of being persons. As a result, there is the possibility that some people will be used as a means to promoting the end of maximizing total utility, implying that persons are mere "receptacles" of utility and not valuable in and of themselves.

The phrase "ends justifies the means" is used often to criticize utilitarian thinking, especially in superhero comics in which the unspoken code is that innocents are never to be harmed, even if it means letting the villain escape (hence the popularity of hostage-taking). In a story fifteen years before *Civil War*, Captain America criticizes Iron Man for the extreme actions he has taken to defeat a foe, to which Iron Man replied, "I knew you could never understand that—you don't believe that the ends justify the means" (Gruenwald 17). In a later story, after Iron Man uses a villain's mind-altering technology to erase the world's knowledge of his secret identity, Captain America tells him, "your ends didn't justify your means as neatly as you say" (Busiek, Stern, and Waid 38). As we will see when we discuss *Civil War* in detail, Iron Man takes pride in doing what he believes needs to be done to reach the desired outcome, has the confidence that he can do it well, and is rarely willing to acknowledge limitations on that based on nonconsequentialist considerations of right and wrong.

Captain America does recognize such limitations, though; there are certain actions, such as dishonesty, treachery, and harm to innocents, in which he will not engage even if it means that the end goal is compromised. This reflects the moral philosophy known as *deontology*, which maintains that actions should be judged by their intrinsic nature, not by their consequences—or, in more moderate versions of deontology, not exclusively by their consequences.[3] In deontology, the ends do not always justify the means because the ends are not all that matters—the means themselves must also be judged to be ethical. Depending on the specific version of deontology, this judgment may be based on rights, duties, or some other property of actions, often based on respect for persons. Valuable ends can and should be promoted, but not at any cost; means must be selected that respect persons as valuable individuals and consider their rights at the same time.

The most well-known deontologist, Immanuel Kant, based his concept of ethics on the essential dignity of persons as beings capable of autonomous moral action.[4] In this spirit, he devised his *categorical imperative*, a rule that could be used to assess whether a plan of action was consistent with "the moral law." One of the forms of the categorical imperative speaks directly to means/end thinking: "act in such a way that you treat humanity, whether in your own person or in the person of another, always at the same time as an end and never simply as a means" (Kant 429). Note the precision in Kant's wording: we are not forbidden from using people, but we must be careful how we do it, always making sure to treat people as valuable ends in themselves and not just as tools to our own ends. Because of its emphasis on intrinsic properties of action themselves rather than their consequences, deontology is often described as focusing on the "right" whereas utilitarianism stresses "the good"—not an entirely accurate or precise characterization, but nonetheless it's a useful contrast of the two positions.[5]

Even though utilitarianism and deontology can be described in simple terms, neither can be put into action in actual, specific moral dilemmas within the crucial faculty of *judgment*. For instance, despite the apparently basic arithmetic behind utilitarianism—add up the utilities for each options and choose the one with the largest sum—that is just the final step, and it takes a tremendous amount of nonqualitative judgments to get there. For example, there is no obvious and clear way to assign utility values to different outcomes. It is one thing to say that building a new playground will make nearby children and their parents happier, and another thing entirely to say how much happier, or compare that increase in happiness with that resulting from the construction of a new skating rink. In a story just before *Civil War* begins, Iron Man defeats a foe by stopping his heart before reviving him, and an angry Captain America shouts, "You could have handled the situation without stopping the man's heart! I can think of at least four ways—" Iron Man interrupts: "—and I can think of seven. But this one was the most expedient." Cap responds, "Expedient, Tony? Or interesting?" (Knauf and Knauf, *IIM #7*, 15).

Captain America is not questioning Iron Man's skill or competence, but rather how he assesses the value of the options at hand and weighs them using his judgment (influenced by his bravado). Furthermore, most moral dilemmas are fraught with uncertainty and risk, and the utilitarian must assess not only the utility for each possible outcome of each action but also the likelihood of each outcome—none of which can be computed with certainty. Of course, even a genius like Iron Man cannot calculate every possible outcome and its probability, so only the most significant and likely outcomes will be included, but this decision too demands judgment before a final choice can be made.

Even though deontology avoids the problem of estimating utilities and probabilities, relying on principles or rules defining right and wrong, judgment is nonetheless essential when applying these simple rules to complex situations. For example, several principles may come into conflict, such as when you are called to help a loved one at a time when you have already promised your help to a friend. In the world of superheroes, the villain will often put the superhero's loved one in mortal danger at the same time that the hero must rush to save a bus full of schoolchildren, and the hero must decide whom to save. Also, adhering to a principle may come at a very high cost, and even though consequences normally don't affect deontological decision-making directly, that cost may be in the form of another principle that will be abandoned. (We will see exactly this problem at the end of *Civil War*.) No matter how important a principle is to someone, there is likely some cost that, when it becomes high enough, will affect that choice, such as the ticking-bomb scenario used in moral debates about torture.[6] Given the qualitative nature of deontological decision-making, judgment is more thoroughly enmeshed in it, as opposed to utilitarianism in which the role of judgment is preliminary—but no less essential—to the final step of maximization.

Captain America, Iron Man and Civil War

Although Iron Man and Captain America had debated their respective ethical viewpoints through decades of Marvel Comics stories, their differences take center stage in *Civil War*, a storyline that spans seven issues of its own miniseries plus nearly a hundred tie-in issues in most of Marvel's major titles. The motivating incident parallels the attacks on September 11, 2001, absent the element of terrorism: irresponsible behavior on the part of a group of teenaged heroes known as the New Warriors results in the death of hundreds of people (including many schoolchildren) in Stamford, Connecticut. Following a major catastrophe involving the Hulk, the Stamford disaster prompts legislative action to register the nation's super-powered heroes, resulting in the passage of the Superhuman Registration Act (SHRA). The SHRA requires all heroes to reveal their identities to the U.S. government and submit to training in the hope of preventing similar incidents in the future while establishing a mechanism to hold them accountable. As a result, the *Civil War* storyline combines the American domestic response to 9/11 (specifically the PATRIOT Act) with the recurring discussion of gun control following tragic mass shootings.

True to his characterization as a futurist, Iron Man had predicted registration would happen; before the incident in Stamford, he showed other heroes an early draft of the SHRA and said, "I'm telling you: this is happening. Right now.... An environment of fear has been created where this can not only exist but will pass" (Bendis, *CWTC* 28). He tries to convince Congress to reject the bill, but once it passes, Iron Man becomes the public face of SHRA and leads a team of heroes to enforce it. His logic is consistently utilitarian: before the

SHRA was passed he felt that the best thing to do was to oppose it, but once it is passed, he accepts it and works to maximize utility within that new status quo. As he tells Captain America, "It was coming anyway. I always thought it was inevitable, though I did try to delay it. But after Stamford there was no stopping it" (Gage 14).

Iron Man's primary goal is to protect innocent people and his fellow heroes (particularly against the threat of their identities being released).[7] Because of his struggle with alcoholism, he is particularly sensitive to the threat of the power wielded by superheroes and the lack of accountability or responsibility when innocent people are hurt and their property is devastated. As he tells Captain America during the Civil War, "You know how dangerous a drunk is behind the wheel of a car? Imagine one piloting the world's most sophisticated battle armor" (Gage 15). In a storyline that leads up to *Civil War*, a villain takes control of Iron Man's mind and uses his armor to kill hundreds of innocent people. Even though Iron Man knows he is not responsible, the incident reminds him of the danger of such powerful weaponry falling into the wrong hands; as he tells a friend, "Every super hero is a potential gun ... and the last time I checked, guns required registration" (Knauf and Knauf, *IIM #12*, 24).

Iron Man's actions in *Civil War* also reflect his utilitarianism, including the decision to take charge of registration in the first place. As a futurist, engineer, and genius, he feels he is uniquely qualified to take charge, saying after the war ends, "I knew that I would be put in the position of taking charge of things. Because if not me, who? Who else was there? No one. So I sucked it up" (Bendis 10). At the same time, he poses the question, "Do you really think I'd let anyone else guard my friends' secret identities?" (Millar, *CW #7*, 28). He also asks his best friend Happy Hogan (soon before his tragic death), "Can you imagine some C-plus-average public-sector schlub in the Department of Redundancy Department riding herd on people like Cap?" (Knauf and Knauf *IIM #13*, 17). He feels a responsibility to do what he thinks will lead to the best outcome for all, regardless of how he is seen by his fellow heroes (many of whom vilify him). More controversial than his presumption of leadership are his actions in support of SHRA, including enlisting captured super-villains to help capture unregistered heroes and building a prison in another dimension to detain them indefinitely—actions which exemplify the "ends justify the means" reasoning that characterizes utilitarianism.

Captain America, on the other hand, primarily emphasizes the danger posed by registration for the principles of liberty and autonomy. As he tells a reporter, "If you know me at all, you'll know I'm a simple man at heart. I believe in the fundamental freedoms accorded us by our Constitution... I saw the possibility of a registration act as a basic violation of our rights as Americans" (Jenkins 9). He states repeatedly throughout *Civil War* that heroes need to stay above politics, "or Washington starts telling us who the super-villains are" (Millar, *CW #1*, 23).[8] He also questions the motivation of those in power, telling a friend that "while I love my country, I don't trust many politicians. Not when they're having their strings pulled by corporate donors. And not when they're willing to trade freedom for security" (Brubaker 14). Captain America puts it in succinct deontological terms when he proclaims, "What they're doing is wrong. Plain and simple" (Brubaker 12). To be sure, Captain America also has utilitarian reasons to oppose registration, such as the well-being of heroes who need to keep their identities secret to protect their loved ones, but he puts even this in terms of the principle of autonomy, making it an issue of choice first and welfare second. And while he sees the need for accountability and training, he believes this should be done independently by the superhero community in an atmosphere of autonomous responsibility (as the Avengers had done for years with their procedures of court-martial).

Captain America criticizes Iron Man in particular for having too much confidence in his own judgment, especially considering his history of mistakes (whether sober or intoxicated): "You've always thought you knew best by virtue of your genius. And once you decide, that's it" (Gage 21). As explained above, even a futurist genius such as Iron Man cannot consider every possible contingency, computing its utility as well as its likelihood, to arrive at a "perfect" answer. This should inspire a certain amount of humility that Iron Man famously lacks; he does, however, regret his mistakes, such as creating a clone of Thor that ends up killing a fellow hero, Goliath. Deontology, on the other hand, requires no such computation of utilities and probabilities, relying instead on qualitative categorizations of right and wrong, allowing Captain America to tell Iron Man, "What's right is what's right. If you believe it, you stand up for it" (Gage 24). Steadfast adherence to what is decided to be "right," however, can also imply a lack of humility, but as we will soon see, Captain America does not suffer this flaw as much as his fellow Avenger.

Most pointedly, Captain America criticizes Iron Man for sacrificing principles he should have maintained as a hero, telling him after the war ended, "We maintained the principles we swore to defend and protect. You sold your principles.... I know what freedom is. I know what it feels like to fight for it and I know what it costs to have it. You know compromise" (Bendis, *Avengers Prime* #1, 21–22). But Captain America finds cause to compromise the principles he is fighting for when the costs of fighting become too high. During the climactic battle at the end of *Civil War* that wreaks havoc and destruction on New York City, Captain America is about to deliver a crushing defeat to Iron Man when a small group of civilians pulls him away and points out the tremendous damage the heroes are doing to the city. After this epiphany, Captain America stops fighting and asks his comrades to do the same, having realized that not only was the cost of the battle too high, but it is being incurred by the people they are trying to protect. He shows humility in revising his judgment when he becomes aware of new facts and circumstances, something he explains to reporters after the end of *Civil War*: "I believe what I did was right.... I now realize that while my intentions were correct and honorable, I could as easily have come to the table as Tony Stark or Reed Richards.... For that, I wish to apologize to the country I love" (Jenkins 9). By surrendering, Captain America does not give up his principles, but instead accepts that another principle—protecting innocents from immediate danger—has become more important, or, that the costs to others have simply become too high.

Using Civil War *as a Teaching Tool (with Help from a Friendly Neighborhood Spider-Man)*

As I summarized, *Civil War* provides a clearly delineated and well-motivated contrast between utilitarianism and deontology, all within an exciting graphic narrative that does not lack in traditional superheroic action. It contains explicit statements of each main character's ethical position, standard criticisms from the opposing hero, with much of the nuance of real-world ethical decision-making, including the difficulties with putting the simple moral systems into action using judgment.

One thing that distinguishes the Marvel Comics superheroes created (or recreated) in the 1960s from their counterparts at DC Comics is the consistency of their characterization, both in terms of personality traits and the specifics of their moral characters. Since his creation, Iron Man has been portrayed as a confident engineer, inventor, and futurist, traits that naturally lend themselves to a utilitarian approach to solving problems. This naturally contrasts with Captain America's military background and his adherence to duty and principle, and this disagreement results in many arguments and debates over the years, starting long before *Civil War*.[9] This consistency of characterization, maintained for over fifty years by as many writers and editors, not only makes their adventures a fulfilling experience for readers, but also makes them useful avatars for classical philosophical positions—perhaps even more so than people in the real world, who are often inconsistent in their ethical behavior (even though their lives are "written" throughout by a single "author"). Their debates over the years are paradigmatic examples of the contrasts between utilitarian and deontology, and *Civil War* is the most ambitious and expansive example of this. Not only is each character's ethical position well depicted, but their counterarguments reflect the same ones used in introductory philosophy courses, often in the same language, such as ends justifying the means (or not).

At the same time, the portrayal of Iron Man's and Captain America's ethical positions are not without nuance, which also reflects the complexity of ethics in the real world. While the two heroes exemplify their respective schools of moral philosophy, the textbook representations of them do not exhaust the depth of their ethical perspectives. Iron Man, the utilitarian, is primarily concerned with assuring the best outcome, but he is not ignorant of issues of liberty and justice. This is shown in a later story when Captain America is put in charge of global security and questions whether his fellow Avenger should keep his armor, and the following exchange ensues:

> CAPTAIN AMERICA: I'm not convinced letting you keep that armor is in the best interests of the country, Iron Man. I haven't made up my mind.
> IRON MAN: There will never be an appropriate time to tell me that I can't have what is rightfully mine.
> CAPTAIN AMERICA: Well, look who's all for civil rights all of a sudden.
> IRON MAN: That has nothing to do with anything—
> CAPTAIN AMERICA: Fine.
> IRON MAN: So, what you're saying is these inalienable rights that you were willing to die for—freedom of power, all that... all of that goes out the window now that you're in charge! [Bendis, *Avengers Prime* #31, 3–4].

By the same token, Captain America's concern for safety as well as liberty reflected in his surrender at the end of *Civil War* is not a new innovation. In a much earlier story, after Captain America defeats an unbalanced recipient of his super soldier serum, he expresses concern over safety; in unspoken narration, he remembers the way he became Captain America, and realizes that "no one knew anything about Steve Rogers—least of all himself. There had been no security checks on him, before entrusting him with his power. What if he had had the fatal flaw, that would have driven him to super-patriotism, madness, and mayhem?" (Englehart 20). Even though both Captain America's and Iron Man's moral positions have been written consistently for decades, they have been written simplistically, and instead reflect the complicated ethical codes of real people, few of whom are purely utilitarians or deontologists.

Through these examples, *Civil War* demonstrates that no textbook presentation of moral philosophy is complex enough to apply to ethical dilemmas in the real world (or fictional ones). Utilitarianism and deontology are often taught in terms of simple rules and guidelines, such as "promote the good" and "respect the rights of others," but as we saw above these are useless in practical decision-making contexts without using judgment based on context and circumstances. In *Civil War*, judgment is illustrated when the heroes tackle moral dilemmas in their respective stands on registration by balancing principles and outcomes to arrive at decisions that reflect who they are as persons. As explained above, both Iron Man and Captain America find reason to question their judgment and consider changes in circumstances or priorities, unable to follow simple rules or formulae. Also, it shows how two heroes who share the same basic commitment to justice and service can interpret and implement them in different ways; as many people do, Iron Man and Captain America believe in the same goals and principles, but they still disagree about the details of how to further them.

We get another perspective on the moral disagreement between Iron Man and Captain America through the eyes of Spider-Man, the point-of-view character that vacillates between the two older heroes in an ethical tug-of-war.[10] Starting out as an ally of Iron Man—including accompanying his alter ego Tony Stark when he spoke against registration before Congress—Spider-Man agrees to back registration out of loyalty (a deontological concept) in addition to being swayed by his utilitarian arguments. Because of his close relationship with his Aunt May and his wife Mary Jane (*MJ*), Spider-Man has strong reasons to be concerned about his identity becoming public, and when Iron Man asks him to unmask on national television, he initially refuses based on the danger to his loved ones. But Iron Man turns this concern into an argument for unmasking: "If you don't unmask, you'll be just like the other powers who defy the law. Wanted criminals. Hunted. Jailed. Not just you, but MJ and your aunt, because they'd be considered accomplices. If you turn against the law, I can't have you with me. I won't be able to protect you ... or your family" (Straczynski, *ASM # 532*, 10–11). Here, we see the perverse side of the incomplete nature of utilitarian reasoning: Iron Man can select which aspects of Spider-Man's situation to highlight in order to manipulate him into choosing one action over another. This may be seen as a criticism of utilitarianism, but a deontologist could do the same thing by highlighting certain principles, duties, or rights above others. While he's not a deontologist, we see Iron Man do this also when he invokes the duty to obey the law to Spider-Man—a strategy chosen to achieve Iron Man's goal of furthering registration.

When Spider-Man is forced to confront Captain America for the first time during *Civil War*, he maintains that fidelity to the law is the most important principle to consider. Afterwards, Spider-Man finds Captain America's shield and webs it to the side of a building, thinking to himself,

> When he finds it, I hope he understands. I hope he gets the message—that the shield represents the country, and the laws of the country decide who's right. Even the laws we don't like. Even the ones that suck. Cap thinks in terms of right and wrong, but this isn't a matter of right and wrong, moral or immoral. It's legal vs. illegal. At least, that's what I tell myself in the middle of the night, when I wonder what the hell I'm doing here. I'm legal. I'm registered. I'm authorized. And as I feel this whole situation starting to unravel around me—I just hope to God that I'm also right [Straczynski, *ASM #534*, 23].

We also see in this passage that already Spider-Man has doubts regarding his alliance with Iron Man and his support for registration, especially once he discovers some of the actions Iron Man has taken, such as the secret prison and Iron Man's profiteering from the conflict.

The creation of the Thor clone and the resulting death of Goliath is the deciding factor that leads to Spider-Man abandoning Iron Man and joining Captain America's resistance. As he tells his aunt and wife, "I've made a terrible, terrible mistake. There's going to be a price for both that mistake and any attempt I make to fix it. But I have to do what I think is right, and right now—God help me, I realize I've been on the wrong side" (Straczynski, *ASM #535*, 19). After he makes amends with Captain America, Spider-Man thinks to himself, "It feels good to be on the right side again" (Straczynski, *ASM #537*, 15).

True to his character, Captain America makes deontological arguments of principle to convince Spider-Man to join the resistance, such as this one about conviction: "This nation was founded on one principle above all else: the requirement that we stand up for what we believe, no matter the odds or the consequences" (Straczynski, *ASM #537*, 14). Also, in one of the most stirring speeches Captain America has ever delivered, he follows a passage from Mark Twain with the following:

> Doesn't matter what the press says. Doesn't matter what the politicians or the mobs say. Doesn't matter if the whole country decides that something wrong is something right. This nation was founded on one principle above all else: the requirement that we stand up for what we believe, no matter the odds or the consequences. When the mob and the press and the whole world tell you to move, your job is to plant yourself like a tree beside the river of truth, and tell the whole world—"no, you move" [Straczynski, *ASM #537*, 12–13].

Despite this rousing call to determination and principle, at the end of *Civil War* Captain America does surrender when he realizes the costs of fighting for his principles have become too high and the well-being of those he is sworn to protect is endangered. When he orders his allies to stand down, it is Spider-Man who tells him, "We were winning back there." Captain America replies, "Everything except the argument" (Millar, *CW #7*, 21). Through this, we see Spider-Man struggle to reconcile his deontological tendencies with considerations of consequence, as most of us find ourselves doing from time to time.

Over the course of the *Civil War* storyline, in the main title as well as his own book, Spider-Man serves as the fulcrum in a conflict between the moral philosophy of utilitarianism and deontology, demonstrating the contrasts between the two schools and, more usefully, the shortcomings of each one. While he sides with Iron Man, Spider-Man sees how the best intentions can lead to morally questionable action, as well as the complicated nature of utilitarian decision-making that requires judgment to sort through. After joining with Captain America, he learns how standing up for principle can bring tremendous costs that ultimately may take precedence, as well as how principles can conflict, also requiring judgment to find the right balance. Given Spider-Man's historical role as the "every kid" figure in Marvel Comics, it is appropriate for him to serve as the point-of-view character for the moral debate between Iron Man and Captain America, providing another way for readers to see the various aspects and nuances of utilitarianism and deontology.

Conclusion

Civil War is an engaging, exciting, and well-paced storyline that deals with real-world ethical and political issues in the context of a straightforward narrative, and as such it makes an excellent tool for teaching those concepts. The creators rely on the well-established ethical positions of Iron Man and Captain America to drive the story, which allows readers, including educators and students, to see moral philosophy at work in story contexts that are fantastical but still grounded in reality. In general, *Civil War* demonstrates that fictional characters, because of their simplicity and consistency relative to people in the real-world, can prove useful to convey ethical concepts, provided they are placed in compelling situations in which they have opportunity to interact with other characters with different moral codes and where the consequences of their decisions are shown. *Civil War* portrays both sides of one of the most significant and essential debates in moral philosophy with balance and nuance—something on which I think even Captain America and Iron Man can agree.

Notes

1. Both Bentham's *The Principles of Morals and Legislation* and John Stuart Mill's *Utilitarianism* are widely available as e-texts online. For an excellent discussion of the pros and cons of utilitarianism, see J.J.C. Smart and Bernard Williams, *Utilitarianism: For and Against*.
2. For more on the varieties of consequentialism, see Walter Sinnott-Armstrong's entry, "Consequentialism," in the online *Stanford Encyclopedia of Philosophy*.
3. For more on deontology, see Larry Armstrong and Michael S. Moore's entry, "Deontological Ethics," in the online *Stanford Encyclopedia of Philosophy*.
4. The basic elements of Kant's moral philosophy are found in his *Grounding for the Metaphysics of Morals*; for an approachable overview, see Sullivan's *An Introduction to Kant's Ethics*.
5. For example, in 1930 the deontological philosopher W.D. Ross wrote a book titled *The Right and the Good*, setting deontology (focusing on the "right") against consequentialism (focusing on the "good").
6. This is the point of *threshold deontology*, which recommends acting according to your principles unless the cost reaches a certain level (or threshold), after which consequentialist considerations take over. Michael S. Moore raises this possibility in the context of torture in his chapter "Torture and the Balance of Evils" (669–736).
7. For more on Iron Man's motivation regarding the SHRA and the Civil War, see Mark D. White, "Did Iron Man Kill Captain America?" in *Iron Man and Philosophy: Facing the Stark Reality* (64–79).
8. Captain America has a long history of conflicts with American politicians and policy; see Mark D. White, *The Virtues of Captain America*, ch. 6.
9. Notable arguments appeared in the *Operation: Galactic Storm* storyline in *The Avengers*, *Iron Man/Captain America Annual*, and *Iron Man* before CW.
10. For more on Spider-Man's journey through *Civil War*, see *Amazing Spider-Man* #529–538.

Works Cited

Armstrong, Larry, and Michael S. Moore. "Deontological Ethics." *Stanford Encyclopedia of Philosophy*. Stanford Encyclopedia of Philosophy, 2012. Web. 12 Dec. 2012.
Bendis, Brian Michael (writer), Alan Davis (penciller), and Mark Farmer (inker). *Avengers Prime* #1 (June 2010), Marvel Comics. Web.
Bendis, Brian Michael (writer), Alex Maleev (artist), and Jose Villarrubia (color artist). *Civil War: The Confession* #1 (May 2007), Marvel Comics. Web.
Bentham, Jeremy. *The Principles of Morals and Legislation*. Buffalo: Prometheus, 1988. Print.
Brubaker, Ed (writer), Mike Perkins (art), and Frank D'Armata (color artist). *Captain America* #22 (Sept. 2006), Marvel Comics. Web.
Busiek, Kurt, Roger Stern, Mark Waid (writers), Patrick Zircher (penciller), and Randy Emberlin (inker). *Iron Man and Captain America Annual* 1 #1 (Jan. 1998), Marvel Comics. Print.
Englehart, Steve (writer), Sal Buscema (artist), and Frank McLaughlin (inker). *Captain America* #156 (Dec. 1972), Marvel Comics. Web.
Gage, Christos (writer), Jeremy Haun (penciller), and Mark Morales (inker). *Iron Man/Captain America: Casualties of War* #1 (Dec. 2006), Marvel Comics. Web.
Gruenwald, Mark (writer), Rik Levins (penciller), and Danny Bulanadi (inker). *Captain American* 1 #401 (June 1992), Marvel Comics. Web.
Jenkins, Paul (writer), Roman Bachs (penciller), and John Lucas (inker). *Frontline* #11 (Feb. 2007), Marvel Comics. Web.
Kant, Immanuel. *Grounding for the Metaphysics of Morals*. Edited by James W. Ellington. Indianapolis: Hackett, 1993. Print.

Knauf, Daniel, Charles Knauf (writers), Patrick Zircher (penciller), and Scott Hanna (inker). *The Invincible Iron Man* #7–13 (June–Nov. 2006), Marvel Comics. Web.
Mill, John Stuart. *Utilitarianism*. Buffalo: Prometheus, 1987. Print.
Millar, Mark (writer), and Steve McNiven (penciller). *Civil War* #1–7 (May 2006–Feb. 2007), Marvel Comics. Web.
Moore, Michael S. *Placing Blame: A Theory of the Criminal Law*. Oxford: Oxford University Press, 1997. Print.
Ross, W. D. *The Right and the Good*. Oxford: Oxford University Press, 2003. Print.
Sinnott-Armstrong, Walter. "Consequentialism." *Stanford Encyclopedia of Philosophy*. Stanford Encyclopedia of Philosophy, 2014. Web. 31 August 2014.
Smart, J. J. C., and Bernard Williams. *Utilitarianism: For and Against*. Cambridge: Cambridge University Press, 1973. Print.
Straczynski, J. Michael (writer), Ron Garney (penciller), and Bill Reinhold (inker). *The Amazing Spider-Man* #532–538 (May 2006–Feb. 2007), Marvel Comics. Web.
Sullivan, Roger J. *An Introduction to Kant's Ethics*. Cambridge: Cambridge University Press, 1994. Print.
White, Mark D., ed. *Iron Man and Philosophy: Facing the Stark Reality*. Hoboken, NJ: John Wiley & Sons, 2010. Print.
_____. *The Virtues of Captain America: Modern-Day Lessons on Character from a World War II Superhero*. Hoboken, NJ: John Wiley & Sons, 2014. Print.

Illustrating *Pedagogy of the Oppressed*: A Freirian Approach to Teaching Marvel's *Civil War*

SENECA VAUGHT

Some have suggested that in a crowded curriculum, history students should be devoting more time to working with primary sources, monographs, and writing. Entertaining lectures, films, and even discussions detract from much neglected exposure to the "tools of the trade." Do students really have time to read comics in class? Can our students effectively engage serious themes and problems of American history—socioeconomic inequality, national security, and justice—through a format that was not designed by social studies educators for this purpose?

Critical pedagogy acknowledges the previous concerns but also engages the prospects of these exercises not just for knowledge's sake but to empower students to address social injustice and inequality on their own terms. In his seminal work, *Pedagogy of the Oppressed*, the Brazilian educational theorist Paulo Freire asserted education should develop teachers and students simultaneously through a model of critical reflection and action (Freire 80). Educational models are all encompassing, from the attitudes teachers harbor toward their students to the selection of some texts and the omission of others. As Ira Shor has written, education *is* politics: "In sum, the subject matter, the learning process, the classroom discourse, the cafeteria menu, the governance structure, and the environment of school teach students what kind of people to be and what kind of society to build" (15). In order to fully engage students for critical consciousness, educators should attempt to make the content relevant to the everyday interests and generational curiosities of the students.

Comics have long presented such a venue of interaction and act as somewhat of a leveling media. They are a form of cultural commentary that can be readily engaged by a wide-swath of the public regardless of social, economic, and educational background. Given the rise in the popularity of comics in the last decade, it would seem that Marvel Comics would be a good way to engage public interest in a variety of social issues, but is Marvel's *Civil War* Series appropriate for the history classroom?

In this essay, I argue history teachers can use Marvel's *Civil War* series to engage difficult questions about race, equality, security, and justice in the survey American history course. *Civil War* provides a useful case study for the application of Paulo Freire's theory in the classroom. Students often know more about the Marvel crossover event than they do about the history that informed it, and many feel more comfortable engaging controversial and historical themes via familiar comic book characters. Educators, if they are willing, can use this opportunity to provide a broader historical and critical framework for central themes in these works.

Using comics as a text in a history course certainly comes with some disadvantages, but teachers can effectively engage critical perspectives on race, socioeconomic equality, national security, and other themes that are often difficult to breach using more conventional approaches. Adopting the *Civil War* series in an American history course provides an interesting conversational focus of a variety of historical themes (e.g., Japanese internment, the Double "V" Campaign, the rise of Jim Crow, and so forth). This essay addresses strategies to address these themes from a Freirian perspective—bringing together popular culture and academic inquiry to raise critical consciousness.

Critical Assessment of Common Objections to the Graphic Novel

Critical pedagogy and graphic novels can be complementary tools in challenging dominant social constructions of power. According to Freire, the role of humanization and education is to enable the oppressed to liberate not only themselves but also their oppressors (Freire 43–44). The superhero genre is a useful tool to engage students on the possibilities of creativity, transforming ideas about what is into what could be. This is a very difficult process and is often inimical to the current approach to teaching history—rote memorization of facts or regurgitation of accepted interpretation. Unlike critical thinking, which emphasizes merely coming to terms with popular misconceptions, Freire and critical pedagogues are interested in the process of humanization, liberation, and preventing the oppressed from becoming oppressors once they achieve power themselves (45). As in *Civil War*, evil is not inherent but is transmutable based on the decisions one makes from moment to moment.

As the "Queen of the Humanities," the discipline of history has often attempted to emphasize the master narrative and isolate other marginal voices, in effect becoming powerful tools of propaganda and manipulation (in support of the status quo). Freire argues, "Propaganda, management, manipulation—all arms of domination—cannot be instruments of [the people's] rehumanization" (68). One of the most important processes of history is to allow students to narrate and interpret the past and the circumstances stemming from those experiences on their own terms (69). This addresses Freire's concern that the oppressed have been destroyed because they have been reduced to "things" (68).

Employing graphic novels is but one of many approaches that reverses the power dynamics of this process in a history class. Gretchen Schwarz has written that graphic novels can assist instructors in presenting alternative views of history, giving voice to minorities and others that are not always considered effectively in the mainstream narrative. Furthermore, she notes that graphic novels written by those outside of the mainstream historical profession may often present harsh truths for those accustomed to mainstream interpretations (Schwarz). These views, although marginal, present valid perspectives that enrich the overall understanding of the historical process and the persistence of structured inequalities. By democratizing the medium in the process of historical reading and imagination, the reader is invited to explore the meaning of the text on its most rudimentary level. Readers are provided the opportunity to ask questions that teach-back and challenge their roles as voiceless masses to amplify individual concerns, social needs, and—most importantly—the dynamics of power.

Some of the skepticism some historians harbor toward graphic novels/comics as an effective pedagogical medium may be cultural. The graphic form is much more widely adopted in Japan and Europe as serious literature ("Using Comics"). Despite several important works that have addressed the numerous possibilities for integrating comics and graphic novels into the history classroom, American educators remain somewhat skeptical.

Lila Christensen explores how graphic novels are useful not only to explore issues of social justice and conflict with intelligence and humor but also to meet the fundamental needs of the reader. Graphic novels are useful to engage readers with limited language proficiency and operative reading difficulties (227–28). Maryanne Rhett also argues that graphic novels can provide intellectually stimulating subject matter for undergraduate courses because of their brevity and attentiveness to central themes ("The Graphic Novel"). Furthermore, Alicia Decker and Mauricio Castro provide ample evidence that graphic novels can speak to a variety of past and contemporary themes across geographic regions (178–82). These works are the beginning of a new wave of scholarship engaging the educational possibilities of the genre and debunking past misconceptions and criticisms (Phelps).

Fictionalized history can be a powerful tool for engaging interpreting the past. As Christensen has argued, many historians will not hesitate to incorporate literary fiction in that class but are skeptical of the uses of the graphic novel ("The Graphic Novel"). This is unfortunate. There is a plethora of important fictionalized historical narratives that invoke the superhero to interpret serious historical themes. A text that readily comes to mind is *V for Vendetta*, addressing the dilemma of privacy and inequality in Thatcherite Britain, but there are also other works that interpret past events in the graphic form, such as Eisner's *The Plot*, a debunking of *Protocols of the Elders of Zion* using primary sources, and Joe Sacco's *Palestine* and *The Fixer*, about the Bosnian War.

Some would argue that in an already crowded curriculum there is no room to add the graphic novel. Teachers struggle to pack in content and sacrifice a tremendous amount of detail in order to cover the ever-expanding amount of material in the survey American history course. On the other hand, the graphic novel is a useful mechanism to get teachers to think about the scope of historical inquiry and what they can gain by zooming in and paying attention to particular details. The framing of the visual image in comics compels the reader to focus squarely on the caption and to see the sequential development between events. This perhaps is one of the most important skills that historians develop but it often develops in isolation from the "assigned" historical reading. Students come away not really understanding or thinking about how writers decide what to include or omit and how important these skills are to historical interpretation. In Marvel's *Civil War*, as in other comics, students grapple with the spaces between events and practice the same kind of thinking that historians use when confronted with two historical documents.

One of the key strengths of graphic novels, according to Scott McCloud, is "amplification through simplification" (30). In other words, graphic novels can deeply investigate large ideas by investing them in the lives of individual characters and situations more familiar to student-readers. A critic who focuses on how many simple facts a comic addresses misses the point of the medium. As this relates to graphic novels in history courses, by committing to cover less in terms of scope, graphic novels may allow students to dig into deeper content and detail, engaging the parallels that are one of the most important benefits of history. One of the interesting ways that this skill of historical analysis is paralleled in the *Civil War* series is in the use of the tie-ins. Tie-ins are quite analogous to how different schools of historians work to think and process similar if not identical events in their consequences.

For example, addressing the work of Jim Crow (commonly referred to as racial segregation), few historians really gave adequate thought to how the practice that had become a central institution in much of American life developed and had a story of its own. In 1955, C. Vann Woodward published the *Strange Career of Jim Crow* in the midst of the civil rights movement and raised some very important questions on the history of this racial architecture. Woodward's history, a prequel of sorts, gave rise to other new histories on racial segregation that have come to transform the way that we think not only about the history of the practice but of its central impact on American life.

Lendol Calder, prominent among the voices arguing for a new approach to teaching history that avoids dependence on lecturing, posits that "uncoverage" may be a powerful pedagogy to confront the current crises of history education that emphasizes doing over knowing (148). Signature pedagogy, long used in the case method of law schools, provides hypothetical situations with changing facts that have particular relevance to the history student. Instead of only emphasizing the facts, there is an emphasis on the role of interpretation and identifying key components of the past by interchanging key points of data and raising new questions.

Similarly, addressing the *Civil War* prequels ("The Road to Civil War" storyline occurring mostly in *The Amazing Spider-Man* and *The Fantastic Four*) and their relationship to the tent pole series can help students understand how the historical imagination works. Injustice does not simply appear but has a history that develops in an often-innocuous process that unfolds with far-reaching and unintended consequences. The ability of historians to describe those processes and how they evolve is central to good historical thinking and critical pedagogy.

Students may feel overwhelmed by the central discussion of injustice and its impact, and the effect can be paralyzing on their desire to learn and to act. The same characteristic that educators mistake for apathy in the class may stem from the sheer volume of information that students are exposed to. Integrating comics, with their familiar characters, superheroes, and villains, is one way to urge students to present their ideas, critiques, and opinions. Introducing small episodes indicative of larger, complex problems can build student confidence.

Finally, the medium of comics is an irreverent engagement of the status quo that is empowering to read and discuss. Comics emerged alongside the history of graffiti as a valid historical commentary on power relations (Roger Sabin, qtd. in Martin 171), but have generally been seen by scholars as marginal to the reifying prose of academic discourse. Proponents of this view fail to understand that comics are one of many sources that can convey the zeitgeist of a particular era (Wheeler). Indeed, popular comic characters can themselves convey meanings about the cultural, political and economic pulse of the decade. In this manner, comics can also be used in the present as a mode of reflective inquiry. By critically engaging the meaning of comics in the present and juxtaposing them with the past, readers can get a deeper understanding of where they are in the continuum of history.

For example, the role of Captain America in *Civil War* reveals cues on contemporary America a bit different than the Captain America Jack Kirby popularized during the 1960s. Similarly understanding the context for Marvel creations like the X-Men, Black Panther,

Doctor Strange, Falcon, and Prowler (Wheeler) all lend themselves to a critical reading of historical engagement and the often invisible forces of structured inequality and racial injustice.

Lastly, the ability of graphic novels to present complex concepts in an approachable format (Cohen) is often dismissed as a "dumbing down" of literary value rather than an augmenting of visual rhetoric. This interpretation of the role of comics is also rather limited. Elaine Martin has written that comics can be very useful in developing "innovative, thought-provoking, and entertaining new relationships between texts and images" (170).

The Parallel Goals of the Marvel Civil War Series and Social Studies Educators

As discussed above, if properly considered and implemented, graphic novels can be excellent tools in history classes. Their non-linear, ambiguous interpretation of historical events easily lends itself to use in world history classes, seminars, or a variety of other humanities-based courses (see Cromer and Clark, as well as Rhett, "Leagues").

Civil War is also especially useful in addressing certain themes because Marvel Comics has an overlooked educational side. "Educational" not in the sense of teaching to certain standards or criteria but rather engaging the readership to consider broader themes of oneself as an individual and an American citizen. Marvel Comics has had a long history of dealing with dual identity of readers in two realms: the real world and as citizens of the Marvel Universe (for an example, see the comments by series editor, Tom Brevoort in Millar, *CWSB*, 19). As readers associate with certain characters in the series, they work out their own anxieties and expectations.

As previously discussed, some historians see the use of graphic novels in general and this one in particular as a poor substitute for time that could be spent on primary sources. While it is certainly a valid concern that students should spend more time engaging first-hand materials and learning to interpret documents for their historical value, few of these advocates have fully considered the use of comic books themselves as a primary source. The history of the Marvel universe has documented many of the emotional impulses of the nation through major developments that are considered in nearly every survey in American history. Themes such as World War II, Vietnam, the civil rights revolution, and presidential challenges have been common themes throughout the company's history. Careful readers have understood how many past issues were statements about the contemporary issues of the time.

Captain America, Iron Man, and Spider-Man mean different things to different generations, but *Civil War* presents an opportunity to engage how the historical evolution of these characters present conflicting perspectives on themes that have been central to American identity and discourse on social justice over the last fifty years. Mark Millar addresses the indirect way comics speak to social and political concerns in the *Civil War: Script Book*:

> The Golden Age Superman isn't about immigrants needing a hope figure in the middle of the Depression. It's about Superman fighting Luthor and mad robots. The undercurrents are there with all these stories and it gives them a little depth. Children and adults will, even subconsciously, be able to identify this as the world they're living and hopefully what's essentially a fan boy beat 'em up on some level will also have a little more resonance [Millar 91].

Despite the DC Comics reference, Millar's point is easily understood across multiple generations, between educators and students. The stories that comics convey are simultaneously universal and specific. Universal, in that they resonate with readers because they present scenarios that individuals can identify with, such as Peter Parker's lack of confidence. Specific, in that they respond to events the reader may see in contemporary newspapers or in their own neighborhoods.

In addition to this role, comics also have a great deal to teach us about power, politics, and history. The tendency in history classrooms is often to attempt to hide one's political ideology and to present the straight facts. However, as Freire argues, attempts to teach history this way are insincere at best and a dishonest form of propaganda in the worst cases. Political perspectives and biases do not cease in the history classroom any more than they do in the pages of Marvel Comics. Millar argues that these biases are often "contradictory" and need to be considered in the light:

> I'm a politics buff and I really hate seeing America divided into red and blue states because I know people in red states who have blue opinions. And we're all very complex. No person can really even be described as a liberal or conservative.... People are more complex than you think and I wanted to do the same thing with superheroes [Millar 93].

It can be useful for students to clearly understand multiple perspectives of a political issue and what better venue to present the political tensions of American history than through superheroes.

The Marvel Universe is no stranger to issues of social or economic inequality. In this series, as in previous storylines, the narrative focuses on class disparities and provides deeper characterization to particular heroes who have strong historical relationships with Marvel's readership. In a *Civil War* tie-in, *Captain America/Iron Man: Casualties of War*, class conflict is evidenced in the fight between Iron Man (Tony Stark), a rich kid, and Captain America, "a blue-collar kid from the Bronx" (Millar 89; also see Brevoort's comments on the same page). The ideological rift between these two characters illustrates how different perspectives are maintained from different vantage points and social realities—not just as a matter of a personal preference (Millar 89).

The mechanics of comic creation in itself yields useful insight for history students. As mentioned previously, the process of editing *Civil War* and the tie-ins is quite similar to the process of writing good narrative history. Tom Brevoort, series editor of *Civil War*, was responsible for working with other editors to make sure that the many stories connected to *Civil War* fit together properly (in Millar 175). He explains, "What some readers look at as inconsistencies between titles, I look at as the ordinary cost of doing business when you've got this many people writing stories about the same characters and situations in a short time span" (Millar 177). Historical interpretation is a process that involves similar concerns. Considering this parallel is useful: we want to get students to engage with the idea that historical knowledge is the result of multiple stories, sometimes conflicting and contradictory. It is a negotiated truth. History—not the past but the *story we tell about the past*—becomes the compromise of a myriad of perspectives and not the summation of a single talking head or a single subject position.

In the widely acclaimed *Lies My Teacher Told Me*, James Loewen warns teachers that learning about history is often spoiled by instructors and texts that are overzealous to make neat and tidy conclusions (2–7). Students, however, are much more interested in the unresolved and open-ended questions than typical history pedagogy—with its grand narrative bias—often presents. *Civil War* highlights some of these historical complexities in stunning graphical fashion. According to Brevoort, there are no clear winners and losers in the series. "The only real way for Cap and his guys to 'win' in a macro sense would be to change popular opinion to such a degree that the registration legislation was repealed. But really, Cap's day-to-day goal was simply to continue to defend the country and battle evil, and aid other like-minded individuals in doing so" (Millar 205).

Civil War raises important historical questions about racial equality, national security, and social justice that complement themes in the survey American history course. One particular historical episode that is alluded to in the series is the question of national security. Is it right for Americans to violate the civil liberties and privacy of "certain people" who are different for the security of the broader public. Franklin Delano Roosevelt faced this issue in 1942 when he signed Executive Order 9066, which led to the internment of more than 100,000 Japanese Americans.

Students looking back often make the mistake of identifying the moral questions of that decision but leave that dilemma frozen in the past as if this question had been resolved. In doing so, students and teachers fail to engage the gravity of this theme's recurrence throughout American history and in contemporary debates such as the decision by Presidents Bush and Obama to house detainees at Guantánamo Bay. The fictional Superhuman Registration Act (SHRA) is a useful template for problematizing and critically working through such policies. Tom Brevoort is much more modest in his discussion of the historical significance of the SHRA, comparing it to gun legislation (Millar 53), though it is, nonetheless, another important point of comparison.[1]

A number of themes in *Civil War*—especially the role of S.H.I.E.L.D. Commander Maria Hill in registering heroes—evoke the hotly contested role of J. Edgar Hoover at the Federal Bureau of Investigation (FBI) through multiple generations of American history. Hoover, charged with making the nation safe, in many instances used the FBI as his own personal police force to surveil, harass, and interrogate those with unpopular political beliefs. There is a wealth of documents about the FBI's activities available under the Freedom of Information Act (see Churchill and Vander Wall) and a graphic novel on the life of Hoover (Geary) that can serve as useful complementary readings and primary sources, along with *Civil War*, in a unit of curriculum on the history of civil liberties.

The *Black Panther* tie-in to *Civil War* provides an interesting take on the complex and multifaceted racial narrative of African Americans and questions of patriotism and allegiance. T'Challa, the King of the fictional African nation of Wakanda, is married to Ororo Monroe (Storm), an American mutant of African descent. The two characters often engage in complex dialogue that illustrates deep contradictions of national allegiance and racial subtext (Hudlin 2–12). T'Challa feels bound by his duty to his new wife and his old friends, especially Captain America, while facing simmering issues in his native Wakanda. This compact storyline couples well with themes from African American history during the World War II era, giving students a sense of how African Americans were fighting a war on two fronts to preserve democracy at home in the Double "V" Campaign (see Rawn Jr. for an excellent account). The role of Ororo in *Black Panther* also effectively engages issues of racial segregation and its legacy, in that the questions raised about the decision to separate mutants from non-mutants is a recurring theme in the Marvel Universe that has strong parallels with the crisis of racial inequality in the United States.

As Ora McWilliams has argued, comics have struggled to differentiate between character and caricature as it relates to race (66). The story of Captain America, for example, has developed from engaging offensive caricatures to directly engaging racial questions in ways that some history textbooks from the same period have failed to, for example, the testing of the serum on black soldiers as a parallel to the Tuskegee experiment (McWilliams 66; Morales).

In *Civil War*, the issue is not only that superheroes are different and seen as dangerous but more squarely the question that this raises about what divides the superheroes and villains. The series raises critical pedagogical questions about who is marginalized and why, who has the power to decide, and what should be done about it. Sometimes students can be uncomfortable discussing such issues of race, class, and inequality. Students tend to be particularly fearful about discussing issues of race because no one wants to be categorized as a racist for saying something that he or she may not fully understand. One of the benefits of using comics is that it allows the tension normally associated with these discussions to be relaxed a bit. After students are able to see the relationship between fictional characters, they are then much more willing to discuss how these issues played out in history examining the lives of real people.

Civil War also effectively engages the paradoxes of democracy. For example the juxtaposition of the dialogue between Captain America and Maria Hill illustrates differing views about what it means to live in a free democratic society (Millar 28). Captain America's perspective emphasizes "freedom from" while Maria Hill's interpretation emphasizes the "freedom to" (for a discussion of the important differences, see Kaufman and Martinez). These conflicting views allow us to more critically examine the transfer of autonomy and individualism for the public good. This is far too often portrayed as an issue of liberals versus conservatives in the mainstream media, but these questions are much more convoluted and contradicting, as both characters see themselves as serving a philosophy in support of the average American.

One particular reason that *Civil War* is so useful is that it does not insist immediately on identifying who is right. Rather it allows the reader to follow the series to its logical conclusion, from a variety of perspectives. Marvel's editor-in-chief, Joe Quesada, argues that this was part of the purpose of the series.

> [In] *Civil War*, the government is doing its job. It's acting responsibly. It's the citizens of America in the Marvel U who are asking for something to be done and the government answers the call by coming up with the only solution that is truly feasible to them. The Super Hero Registration Act is something that really seems like the only alternative seeing as how people are now living in fear of anyone with superpowers.... What makes *Civil War* truly unique and like no other big event in the history of comics, is that there is no real villain. Like sometimes happens in real life, the villain is sometimes the person who has the opposite belief to yours" [Millar 40].

Civil War effectively engages central concepts of the dynamics of power that are essential in a critical pedagogy. One example of this difficulty in the history classroom is getting students to understand the rise of the Black Power movement.

While it is useful to historicize the experience of racial and socioeconomic inequality in the United States to better understand the dynamics of power, it can also useful to leverage *Civil War* not merely as an allegory of 21st-century issues of civil liberties but as a methodology for approaching such issues generally. Black nationalism is a very complex issue that cannot be quickly summarized, but it is a historical development that, like the fictional SHRA, almost encourages strong reactions. Students often fall prey to distortions and popular misconceptions, equating the Black Panther Party with the Ku Klux Klan or appeals to support black-owned businesses with a brand of reverse discrimination.

Black Power, as it was articulated most popularly in 1964, was a direct response to the lack of progress in the African American Civil Rights Movement. It is important for students to consider that of the many forms of Black Power that were at work during the era, the media tended to cover varieties that emphasized controversial rhetoric (Joseph 1003–1006). "Black Power," however, could mean many things to different political actors. When Martin Luther King, Jr., endorsed Black Power in 1968, he was not endorsing black superiority, but the consolidation of their political and economic resources to bring about change that the federal government and state governments were unwilling to enact.

A comics event such as *Civil War* promotes more than just a specific discussion of Bush- and Obama-era responses to terrorism. Rather, the series' refusal to identify a clear "good guy" or "bad guy"—especially in a medium dedicated to them—promotes a mode of thinking and academic engagement that encourages a multi-perspective approach to the consideration of such historical moments as the African American Civil Rights Movement generally and Black Power in particular.

Examples of Core Questions and Assignments

Historians have long faced the challenge in discussing social movements like the African American Civil Rights Movement. Often in an attempt to paint the broader impact of the movement, historians omit explaining how the transpiring events came to affect individuals. Graphic novels, however, are able to quickly and effectively zoom in on injustice to caricature developments on a *macro*, *meso*, and *micro* scale. The following sample assignments use graphic novels to achieve several objectives that engage these themes:

1. *Students should be able to explain the process of the historical thinking through an interpretive lens.* Students often struggle with identifying bias in historical narrative, but the interpretive biases of the graphic artist are immediately visible and then can be discussed in contrast with narrative sources. Graphic images present one way of juxtaposing visual perspective against historical biases.
2. *Students should be able to identify and narrate the ways in which the instructor is working out his/her own understanding of the past.* Critical pedagogy emphasizes making the context of power inside the classroom and outside of the classroom visible (see Burbules and Berk). These following assignments explicitly state that there are advantages and disadvantages to approaching the subject in particular ways and reveal the positionality of analysis instead of encouraging students to assume the omniscience of the instructor or the source.

Sample Assignment 1

One way to introduce and better understand the dynamics of power in history is to juxtapose historical documents with fictional characters whom you may feel more comfortable discussing than real historical figures or themes. Historically, the Marvel Universe has engaged in this practice. The writers did not hesitate to integrate contemporary social questions and historical interpretations into the fictional drama. In this assignment we will explore some of these themes and experiment with interesting mash-up questions ("What would happen if....?"). What would happen if Guantanamo detainees were to be held with captives from Manzanar and 42, the prison in the Negative Zone? Based on the exchange in the Senate Hearing with Tony Stark (Straczynski 7–12), what would happen if Spider-Man were interviewed by Senator Joseph McCarthy? What types of discussions could be had? What types of documents could we use to support our projections?

Sample Assignment 2

After reading *Major Problems in American History*, Chapter 12–13: "We Can Do Better" and "The Sixties," identify a comic strip, graphic novel, or cartoon illustrating an actual event from the modern American civil rights struggle (Cobbs-Hoffman, Blum, and Gjerde). Find a comic strip, graphic novel, or cartoon on the web that illustrates a parallel theme similar to one addressed during the modern American civil rights struggle.[2] How does this graphic document help you engage the meaning of the civil rights movement in ways that the reading from the text could not? How does this graphic document help you engage aspects of the civil rights movement in ways that the reading from the text could not? What are some drawbacks of learning civil rights history in this format?

Sample Assignment 3

We are going to pair a historical graphic novel and revisit the *Civil War* tie-ins in order to see how historical interpretations are integrated into a variety of contexts outside of the classroom. I would like for you to summarize the historical interpretation of any one of the following topics based on the sources you select: (1) the impact of racial segregation in the post–World War II era, (2) the significance of Emmett Till, (3) FBI surveillance of the New Left, (4) the role of African Americans in the Double "V" Campaign, (4) the internment of Japanese Americans, and (5) the rise of the Black Panther Party.

Sample Assignment 4

Please select a 25-page passage from one of the following: (1) *The Road to Civil War*, (2) *Civil War*, (3) *Black Panther: Civil War*, (4) *Wolverine: Civil War*. Make a list of any unfamiliar terms or phrases that you encounter. After you are finished reading, use a web search to identify unfamiliar terms, people, and places from your list. Be prepared to share your list with other classmates. What themes do you see emerging? What time periods seem to be emphasized the most? What do you think this tells us about how the authors interpret the past? The instructor? Yourself?

On a fundamental level this is exactly the same process that students would encounter reading a historical text. For some reason, students feel much more comfortable engaging the illustrated text, but teaching them to parse the illustrated pages of graphic novels develops similar cognitive skills that they would require when reading a historical document. Importantly, 21st-century students engage content and multimedia formats much more readily than the printed word. It is equally important for students to develop skills to make sense of the constant barrage of visual documents they receive.

The proliferation of comics and digital cartoon strips on the Internet makes it quite easy for students to search and find some interesting material. I have them cut and paste the actual image into the post with a link to the source so that the rest of the class can see it and reply. I can then engage key concepts of race and power stemming from the cartoons and not the students themselves. I feel that this allows me to really critically engage the dynamics of power without having students feel like they are being personally attacked. I then use an example from *Civil War* to segue back into the reading.

Typically, students understand and articulate the limitations of graphic representations. Importantly, they begin to see how knowledge is constructed and the role of power in determining what the history is and how it is presented. By the end of the course they are able to discuss the drawbacks of learning using pictures, comics, and cartoons but also equally capable of identifying the subjective aspects of historical writing. Engaging the challenges of history as a social science and as a part of the humanities, they are more capable of developing meaningful interpretations of their own.

Conclusion

Critics say that graphic novels are not appropriate for the history classroom and that they are a corrupting influence in higher education, distracting our students from broader themes of critical thinking and reading. These attitudes harken back to comments by Frederic Wertham in 1954 that assumed comic books were perverting youth and causing delinquency.[3] Instead of creating juvenile delinquents, critics argue that teachers seeking to deploy comics in the classroom are delinquent in their pedagogy. As the above arguments have demonstrated, this is most certainly not true. As described here, using *Civil War* demonstrates an approach that moves away from a deficit model that consolidates the power of the expert over the possibilities of dialogue and, rather, engages the possibilities of transformative teaching for social change using a participatory approach.

Perhaps one of the reservations that academics have to engaging these documents for their historical word is that it places them on a grounding in which their advantage is not as pronounced. Students have exhibited great enthusiasm in engaging comics and graphic novels as a source and can easily outpace the ability of their instructors to address their questions. However, such is the emphasis of critical pedagogy. The appropriate role of the teacher is not to deposit information into the minds of the student but rather to develop relationships that are co-intentional, encouraging ideas to flows both ways between the instructor and student.

One of my concerns in crafting lessons plans for engaged citizenship is getting students to see the parallels between the past and the present. We can easily identify injustices in the past, but the more interesting question is whether and how effectively are we engaging these issues in the present.

The resistance to works such as *Civil War* stems from much more then assumptions of their pedagogical effectiveness but rather is concerned with the cultural production of knowledge. Historians, like other academics, are loath to relinquish the reins of expertise. This approach is wrongheaded. If the historical discipline is to maintain its relevance going forward, it will have to engage its role in actively preserving and interpreting the past but also in engaging and empowering those in the present. Adopting pedagogies that incorporate comics is one of the many ways in which our understanding and teaching of the past can empower students in the present.

The end game is not to get students simply to develop a love for comics (as happy a result as that would be) but to develop a critical awareness of power and how it operates in the world. Similarly, the goal of critical pedagogy has never been to win the argument in a strictly intellectual sense. Simply acknowledging the fact of inequality is insufficient. Critical pedagogues do not make the singular goal the mere acknowledgement of fact or exposure of misconception. It is not enough for students only to reflect critically; they must also locate themselves in that process and realize their own potential to be complicit in the process or to transform their circumstances. At the end of *Civil War*, all the main characters undertake to transform the new status quo, each thinking they could imagine a safer and more just future. Similarly, critical pedagogues, critical race theorists, critical multiculturalists, anti-racist educators and so on are fundamentally concerned with transformation of not only the mind but also our own status quo.

Notes

1. Brevoort's comparison is useful but limited by its inaccuracy. He assumes that there are federal registration laws for owning and for carrying guns, but no such federal laws exist. Indeed, such laws are handled by states and there are an incredibly broad set of approaches (and underlying ideologies) regarding how individual states handle the issue. For instance, in April of 2014, Georgia's governor, Nathan Deal, signed into state law legislation popularly called the "Guns Everywhere Bill," allowing the carrying of weapons into churches and schools, among other places (see Copeland and Richards). One Georgia congressman, Paul Broun, Jr., argued that the right to carry guns, so broadly defined, was "god given" (Ashtari).

2. There are a host of resources on the World Wide Web for incorporating historical cartoons and comics into lesson plans. One excellent resource is the Opper Project at Ohio State University. The recently published *March* (Lewis and Aydin) illustrates civil rights themes and comes with a teacher's guide that parallels well themes from Marvel Comics *Civil War*. For readers more interested in periodization, see the *Big Book of the 70s* (Vankin), Marvel's *Combat Zone: True Tales of GIs in Iraq* (Zinsmeister), and the graphic novel of the *9/11 Commission*, and lastly Julian Bond and T.G. Lewis' *Vietnam* comic book, reprinted in eds. Alana Murray's and Deborah Menkart's edited collection *Putting the Movement Back into Civil Rights Teaching*, pp. 160–179.

3. For more on Fredric Wertham and his assault on comics, see Bart Beaty's *Frederic Wertham and the Critique of Mass Culture*.

Works Cited

Ashtari, Shadee. "Georgia Republican Says New 'Guns Everywhere' Law a 'God-Given' Right." Huffington Post.com. The Huffington Post.com, Inc., 2 July 2014. Web. 12 Dec. 2014.
Beaty, Bart. *Fredric Wertham and the Critique of Mass Culture*. Jackson: University Press of Mississippi, 2005. Print.
Burbules, Nicholas, and Rupert Berk. "Critical Thinking and Critical Pedagogy." *Critical Theories in Education: Changing Terrains of Knowledge and Politics*. Ed. Thomas S. Popkewitz and Lynn Fendler. New York: Routledge, 1999. 45–66. N.pag. University of Illinois Faculty Pages—Burbules. Web. 14 May 2014.
Calder, Lendol. "Uncoverage: Toward a Signature Pedagogy for the History Survey." *The Journal of American History* 92.4 (2006): 1358–1370. JSTOR. Web. 22 July 2014.
Christensen, Lila L. "Graphic Global Conflict: Graphic Novels in the High School Social Studies Classroom." *The Social Studies* 97.6 (2006): 227–230. Print.
Cobbs-Hoffman, Elizabeth, Edward J. Blum, and Jon Gjerde, eds. *Major Problems in American History, Volume II: Since 1865*, 3d ed. Boston: Wadsworth, 2011. Print.
Copeland, Larry, and Doug Richards. "Ga. governor sign 'guns everywhere' into law." *U.S.A Today*. Gannett Satellite Information Network, Inc., 23 Apr. 2014. Web. 12 Dec. 2014.
Churchill, Ward, and Jim Vander Wall. *The Cointelpro Papers: Documents from the FBI's Secret Wars Against Dissent in the United States*. Cambridge: South End Press, 2002. Print.
Cohen, Lisa. "But This Book Has Pictures! The Case for Graphic Novels in an AP Classroom." *AP Central CollegeBoard*. N.pag. 2014. Web. 24 Apr. 2014.

Cromer, Michael, and Penney Clark. "Getting Graphic with the Past: Graphic Novels and the Teaching of History." *Theory and Research in Social Education* 35.4 (2007): 574–591. Print.
Decker, Alicia, and Mauricio Castro. "Teaching History with Comics Books: A Case Study of Violence, War, and the Graphic Novel." *The History Teacher* 45.2 (2012): 169–188. Print.
Eisner, Will, and Umberto Eco. *The Plot: The Secret Story of the Protocols of the Elders of Zion*. New York: W.W. Norton, 2005. Print.
Freire, Paulo. *Pedagogy of the Oppressed*. New York: Continuum, 2000. Print.
Gage, Christos. *Iron Man Captain America: Casualties of War #1*. Marvel Comics, 2007. Print.
Geary, Rick. *J. Edgar Hoover: A Graphic Biography*. New York: Hill and Wang, 2008. Print.
Hudlin, Reginald (writer), Koi Turnbull (penciller) and Don Ho, Sal Regla, and Jeff De Los Soantos (inkers). *Black Panther #23* (Feb. 2007), Marvel Comics. Print.
Joseph, Peniel E. "The Black Power Movement, Democracy, and America in the King Years." *American Historical Review* 114.4 (2009): 1001–1016. Print.
Kaufman, Cynthia, and Elizabeth Martinez. *Ideas for Action: Relevant Theory for Radical Change*. Cambridge: South End Press, 2003. Print.
Lewis, John, Andrew Aydin (writers) and Nate Powell (artist). *March: Book One*. Marietta: Top Shelf Productions, 2013. Print.
Loewen, James W. *Lies My Teacher Told Me: Everything Your American History Textbook Got Wrong, Revised and Updated Edition*, rev. ed. New York: New Press, 2008. Print.
Martin, Elaine. "Graphic Novels or Novel Graphics? The Evolution of an Iconoclastic Genre." *The Comparatist* 35.1 (2011): 170–181. *Project MU.S.E.* Web. 24 April 2014.
McWilliams, Ora. "Not Just Another Racist Honkey: A History of Racial Representation in Captain America and Related Publications." *Captain America and the Struggle of the Superhero: Critical Essays*. Ed. Robert G. Weiner. Jefferson: McFarland, 2009. Print.
McCloud, Scott. *Understanding Comics: The Invisible Art*. New York: HarperPerennial, 1994. Print.
Millar, Mark, and Steve McNiven. *Civil War: Script Book*. New York: Marvel, 2007. Print. The *Script Book* is not paginated, so page numbers have been provided, beginning with the traditional summary and credits page as 1.
Morales, Robert (writer), and Kyle Baker (artist). *Truth: Red, White & Black*. New York: Marvel Comics, 2004. Print.
Murray, Alana, and Deborah Menkart, eds. *Putting the Movement Back into Civil Rights Teaching*. Washington, D.C: Teaching for Change and PRRAC, 2004. Print.
Phelps, Valarie. "Pedagogy of Graphic Novels." *WKU TopSCHOLAR*. Western Kentucky University, April 2011. Web. 6 May 2014.
Rawn, Jr., James. *The Double V: How Wars, Protest, and Harry Truman Desegregated America's Military*. New York: Bloomsbury Press, 2013. Print.
Rhett, Maryanne. "The Graphic Novel and the World History Classroom." *World History Connected* 4.2 (2007): n. pag. *World History Connected*. Web. 5 May 2014.
Sacco, Joe. *Footnotes in Gaza*. New York: Metropolitan, 2009. Print.
_____. *Palestine*. Seattle: Fantagraphics Books, 2001. Print.
_____. *Safe Area Gorazde: The War in Eastern Bosnia 1992-1995*. Seattle: Fantagraphics, 2002. Print.
Schwarz, Gretchen. "Graphic Novels for Multiple Literacies." *Journal of Adolescent and Adult Literacies* 46.3 (Nov. 2002): 262–265. *Reading Online*. Web. 6 May 2014.
Shor, Ira. *Empowering Education: Critical Teaching for Social Change*. Chicago: University of Chicago Press, 1992. Print.
Straczynski, J. Michael (writer), Tyler Kirkham (penciller), and Jay Leisten (inker). *The Amazing Spider-Man* #530 (March 2006), Marvel Comics. Web.
Syma, Carrye Kay, and Robert G. Weiner. *Graphic Novels and Comics in the Classroom: Essays on the Educational Power of Sequential Art*. Jefferson: McFarland, 2013. Print.
"Using Comics and Graphic Novels in the Classroom. *The Council Chronicle* (Sept. 2005). NCTE. Web. 28 Apr. 2014.
Vankin, Jonathan (writer), and Andrew Robinson, et al. (artists). *The Big Book of the 70's*. New York: Paradox Press, 2000.
Wertham, Fredric. *Seduction of the Innocent*. New York: Rinehart, 1954. Print.
Wheeler, Andrew. "Zeitgeist '60: 10 Comic Book Characters That Embody the '60s." *Comics Alliance*. 20 Feb. 2014. Web. 24 Apr. 2014.
Woodward, C. Vann. *The Strange Career of Jim Crow*, comm. ed. New York: Oxford University Press, 2001. Print.
Zinsmeister, Karl (writer), and Dan Jurgens (penciller). *Combat Zone: True Tales of GIs in Iraq*. New York: Marvel, 2005.

Afterword: Why *Civil War* Matters, Why This Book Matters

Marc DiPaolo

Civil War changed my life. It guided me in emotionally and intellectually processing terrifying, history-making current events in a way that mainstream news organizations had entirely failed to do. It helped me come to grips with the American political landscape: what was working, what wasn't, and what I wanted to do about it. Finally, it helped me discover and nurture the social justice activist lurking inside me when I had previously spent my formative years scornfully/admiringly regarding social justice activists as "better people than me."

I say that "*Civil War* changed my life" knowing full well that many of you will not relate to the sentiment. The idea that a work of serious literature could change the person reading it seems quaint in these jaded times, when no one seems likely to admit to any form of art moving them to even the slightest emotional feeling. How much more unlikely would it be for someone to admit that a superhero funnybook could shake them to their emotional, intellectual, and ideological core? I say this knowing that my reading of *Civil War* is not the same as others' readings, that my context reading it was personal and specific, that I read primarily the issues written by Mark Millar, J. Michael Straczynski, and Brian Michael Bendis, and that my fan affinity for Spider-Man has always been so keenly felt that it facilitated a particularly gut-wrenching emotional reaction to the events of the story. So I'm not expecting anyone else to have read the story in the way that I did or to have reacted to it as I did. So, in order for my reaction to *Civil War* to make sense, I have to explain to you why I feel fiction is powerful and why this particular event comic series resonated with me so strongly.

Fiction can be very powerful. As a college professor, I've met many students over the years that have chosen their vocational major because they were inspired by a film or television show they watched during their formative years. I've known young people who have joined the FBI because of their love of Dana Scully, studied forensics after a full-on immersion in various *CSI* shows, made their own independent film because of *Clerks*, became vocal majors thanks to *Glee*, or become a marine biologist because of *Jaws*. Indeed, I believe a small part of my desire to pursue a doctoral degree stemmed from my lasting childhood affection for Doctor Doom, Doctor Strange, Doctor Octopus, and the Time Lord known as the Doctor. So fiction can inspire normal, everyday children to dream of growing up to be one kind of person or another during the relative tranquility of peacetime.

During wartime, fiction has the potential to be even more powerful in the way it can channel the heightened emotional states of civilians and military personnel alike.

The fiction produced in response to 9/11 had a *particularly* powerful affect on me and on friends of mine. *Battlestar Galactica, 24,* and *Civil War* were evocative war on terror allegories that reflected and shaped public opinions and anxieties in very real, palpable ways. The show *24* briefly convinced me that torture was not only an acceptable form of interrogation, but it was the only way to go. The persuasive, tightly constructed narrative bullied me into believing that any reticence on my part to sanction the U.S. torture program was treasonous. Around the same time, a friend of mine switched political allegiances from Democrat to Republican and converted from atheist to Roman Catholic in part because of how emotionally involving he found the abortion episode of *Battlestar Galactica*. "The Muslims are breeding and we are not, so we better ban birth control," he told me in a very reasonable and logical voice. He condemned me for not nodding in assent. That was the last conversation I had with him. Another friend who grew up watching 1980s action movies often told me during our college years that he hoped to become a sniper one day, like Tom Berenger. He enlisted after 9/11 to defend Americans from the Taliban and fulfill his lifelong dream of becoming a sniper. These possibly radical, anecdotal examples notwithstanding, the period immediately following 9/11 was incredibly traumatic for most Americans, especially following on the heels of the economically stable, militarily painless (what Kosovo War?), culturally trivial 1990s.

I have written elsewhere (in autobiographical essays for the books *Generation X Professors Speak* and *Unruly Catholics from Dante to Madonna*) that my Reagan-era suburban childhood and Opus Dei sympathetic parish priest helped condition me to uncritically embrace a zealous love for the Republican Party during my teenage years. After all, the party celebrated the same "family values" that Italian-Americans such as myself embraced, most notably an end to the "marriage penalty tax" that Dan Quayle campaigned against. While conservative comics fans often complain of political correctness in comics, I found that, as a center-right thinker, there were very few comics that offended my sensibilities outside of the occasional "very special issue." Spider-Man never discussed politics in terms that offended me, but I assumed he leaned center-right like I did. I was a nerdy teen bullied in public school who learned to hate the "proles" I grew up beside, just as Peter Parker was a nerdy teen bullied in public school who learned to hate the proles he grew up beside. I had dreams of being recognized for my genius as he did, only I wanted to become a famous author/filmmaker and Peter wanted to be a trailblazing scientist. We shared ambition, a mordant sense of humor, and even—depending on how he was drawn—a physical appearance. Like virtually every other die-hard Spider-Man fan or long-term Spider-Man comics writer, I felt that I was Spider-Man and that I owned Spider-Man.

Over the years, my instinctual, elitist embracing of an Ayn Rand–style philosophy— an instinctual, elitist tendency shared by both Peter Parker and his co-creator, Steve Ditko— was mitigated by a liberal arts college education, a realization that the Republican Party was pretty damn ruthless in refusing to recognize the legitimacy of *any* Democrat president (no matter how conservative), and the dawning understanding that there is a lot of poverty and human suffering in the world that could—and should—be mitigated by the wealthy and influential. I learned, as Peter learned from his blue-collar, left-leaning uncle, that "with great power comes great responsibility."[1] But this was a lesson I have needed to learn time and again. Peter has needed to learn it time and again as well. Just as I was on the verge of leaving my right-wing past behind for good, 9/11 frightened me into briefly reinvesting in the party and its view of homeland security, military might, and the safety of the American people.

It took a very long time for Ground Zero to be reclaimed and renewed after the Twin Towers fell. During that extended period of seeming inactivity at the site of the attack, every time I went past the gaping hole in the ground that used to be the World Trade Center, I wondered when the next attack would be and if the collateral damage would include the entirety of my borough and everyone I knew. After 9/11, Muslim service station owners across New York City taped "Wanted: Dead or Alive" posters of Osama bin Laden upon their glass front doors to reassure their patrons that (a) they didn't *really* look like bin Laden and, therefore, weren't him and (b) they weren't on his side. I felt bad for them and understood why they were scared of falling victim to a racially and religiously motivated attack. I was worried about much the same kind of attack coming from folks who looked kind of like them.

I was angry and I was scared, and I was even elated when George W. Bush promised that those who brought the Towers down would soon be hearing from the United States. I was elated, even though I knew this was the alcoholic buffoon who had conspired to steal the presidency from the rightfully elected president of the United States, Al Gore. I was elated even though I was so angry at how the 2000 recount went down, and at the role the Supreme Court played in his installation in the White House, that I permanently severed all of my lifelong ties with the Republican Party. And yet, here I was, cheering Bush's vow to seek revenge on those who had killed my fellow New Yorkers. I wore an American flag on my lapel for the first time. Before then, I had been too cool to wear such a pin. The news coverage of Bush and the war on terror was uniformly positive. The Democratic Party and Tony Blair threw their full support behind his agenda, and America was "united." The supposedly liberal NPR would spend the next several years offering its covert support for the wars in Iraq and Afghanistan as well, until those wars started to go on for too long and it became "safe" for NPR to criticize them for being "poorly planned" and for having "no exit strategy in place from the outset."

During this period, a handful of Hollywood actors, activist stand-up comedians, documentary filmmakers, and out-of-the-mainstream journalists seemed a little worried about the excesses of the Bush Administration pushing the Iraq War, creating torture and surveillance programs, and accusing anyone politically to the left of Rush Limbaugh of high treason. The 2005 relaunch of *Doctor Who* written by Russell T. Davies mocked George W. Bush, Tony Blair, and Fox News mercilessly in episode after episode. The criticisms seemed more than apt, but the show was irritatingly grotesque and the criticisms were blunted for me by their being made by an outsider, and not by an American who lived in New York during 9/11 as I did.

Thankfully, Marvel stepped up to the plate.

First, Mark Waid wrote the Fantastic Four story *Authoritative Action* (2004), which seemed refreshingly critical of the Iraq War. And then there was *Civil War*. Spider-Man was behaving like I had been behaving of late. The reformed conservative is given an invitation to become rich, famous, and respected by becoming a member of Tony Stark's inner circle and joining in the effort to quell Captain America's rebellion. He convinces himself he is doing his bit to protect America in the aftermath of 9/11 ... um ... Stamford by briefly suspending civil liberties until the crisis passes, not knowing that the crisis will never pass, and further encroachments upon civil liberties were on the way. When he finally realizes he is on the wrong side, largely because of his discovery of what was going on at Gitmo ...

um ... the Negative Zone ... he switches sides. In being tempted to join Dick Cheney on his voyage to the dark side, Spider-Man is doing what I was doing, and what James Kirk would later do in *Star Trek into Darkness*. The good news is that Spider-Man grows as a person and admits his mistake. In *Amazing Spider-Man* #537, after Spider-Man rejects Tony Stark's definitions of freedom and safety, Falcon observes, "I mean, it takes a lot of courage to change your mind about something after going so far down the road. Saying 'I was wrong' has to be the hardest sentence in the English language" (Straczynski 20).

Reading this story made it clear to me that I had made the same mistake that Peter Parker had. I had joined Bush's side as Spider-Man had joined Iron Man's, and Spider-Man's defection to Captain America's side made me realize that I needed to make this second move as well. I needed to join the small, ragtag band of liberals that still had the gumption to stand up to homegrown tyranny when it was dangerously unpopular for them to do so. At the height of Bush's popularity, most of the press and the Democrats had rolled over and agreed to Bush's entire agenda, so there wasn't much of an opposition to join. Still, I was inspired by Spider-Man to sign on with what remained of the Democratic wing of the Democratic Party, as well as ally with the disaffected independents and some of the saner libertarians to work toward creating a loyal, patriotic opposition to Bush's misguided efforts to harm the nation in the name of defending it. So I saw myself as defecting to the oft-maligned Captain America, Michael Moore, George Clooney, and Dixie Chicks contingent. Saying "I was wrong" was very hard indeed, but I was glad I did admit my mistake to myself and correct my course. I was also glad to know that Falcon would support me in this decision, if he were real.

I think it is important to note that, in the final analysis, Spider-Man pays a high price for his mistake. His aunt is almost killed, his privacy is destroyed, and his liberty is in jeopardy. The only way he can undo some of the damage he's done to his own life is to make a deal with Satan to change the course of history with black magic. As a result of this demonic pact, Spider-Man's civilian identity becomes secret from the public once again and Aunt May's life is saved, *but* Peter's marriage to Mary Jane is wiped from existence and May forgets that her nephew is Spider-Man. Consequently, Peter loses his two closest confidants, is essentially estranged from both of them in the new course of history, and is left fundamentally alone for years. These are high costs indeed, and they further cement the point that it may well be wiser to make a deal with Satan than to get into bed with the Republican Party. (If you can avoid dealing with either, then that would be even wiser.) I didn't suffer as much as Peter did, but I bear the guilt of knowing I tacitly approved of far too many evil laws for a longer period than I should have, and I have to live with that mistake.

While my lifelong liberal friends found this political and spiritual journey of mine irritating because they saw through the Republican Noise Machine from the beginning, and weren't fooled for a minute, my conservative friends were horrified that I had decided to jump ship and join the legions of foolish young people in voting for that black man for president. Well, I'm not a superhero. I'm a flawed, regular guy. Spider-Man woke me up, and made me rethink my entire worldview. The experience I've just described to you was so life-altering that it inspired me to write a book about it that was half autobiography, half monograph study of political propaganda in superhero narratives. It is called *War, Politics and Superheroes: Ethics and Propaganda in Comics and Film*. I put my heart and soul into that one.

Over the years, I've occasionally assigned *Civil War* as reading in interdisciplinary honors classes to students of mine who were six years old when 9/11 happened. They grew up in Oklahoma, the reddest state, raised by conservative parents who were not inclined toward affection for President Obama. Their *Civil War* is not my *Civil War*. First of all, the way Marvel collected the story into trade paperbacks makes little sense. The miniseries on its own lacks the richness it has when the Bendis and Straczynski issues are added in. The artwork is too busy for non-comics readers to follow. There are too many characters that laymen have never heard of cluttering up the narrative. Still, the students generally love it after they've hacked their way through it. Occasionally, a liberal student sees it as a cool precursor to *The Hunger Games* in its populist opposition to domestic tyranny and empire building. More frequently, conservative students tell me they embrace it because they see Captain America as a Tea Party Republican standing up to Iron Man's Barack Obama in opposition to the Affordable Care Act and gun control initiatives symbolized by the Superhuman Registration Act. While I wish these students were better at understanding my reading than they are, I am proud of them the first time they come up with this reading because it means I have taught them to interpret political allegory on their own, in ways that don't always parrot what I do. The teacher learns from the students. In the cases of both the liberal and conservative students, they tend to see in the narrative a worldview that already mirrors their own, which means *Civil War* is not likely to get them to switch parties the way it got me to. Well, no matter. It still got all of them to think in terms of social commentary, political allegory, and the role of grassroots activism in the political process.

My students' most common reading of *Civil War* recently surfaced in an October 20, 2014, *Slate* editorial by Jamelle Bouie, "Marvel's Civil War Is a Far-Right Paranoid Fantasy—and a Mess. Can the Movies Fix It?" The internet post was written in light of the breaking news that *Civil War* would become the basis for the plot of the third *Captain America* film and would star Chris Evans as Steve Rogers and Robert Downey, Jr., as Tony Stark. Bouie's reading of *Civil War* involves viewing superhuman registration as akin to common-sense gun-control laws—a reading that turns Stamford into the Sandy Hook school shootings, Tony Stark into Barack Obama, and Steve Rogers into a libertarian NRA member. As Boule observes, "[Rather] than borrow from real world gun registration, it borrows from the loony anti-registration fears of gun fanatics, who imagine that registration and background checks are the beginning of a slippery slope to jackbooted thugs and a fascistic New World Order. Marvel could have given a sensible treatment of registration. Instead, it gave us a superhero version of NRA paranoid fantasies." This reading is intelligent and valid, and a far cry from seeing Stark as Dick Cheney and Rogers as Michael Moore, which was how I always viewed the story. In many ways, I find Bouie's interpretation interesting. I don't like the brevity of the piece, its dismissive take on one of my favorite comics, and Bouie's clear lack of knowledge of the story's original historical context.

My friend Bill Murphy, a visiting assistant professor of history at SUNY Oswego, contacted me when the article came out and suggested that I write a response to the piece in *Slate* that would be more informed and help broadcast my reading to the public. "Gun control wasn't an issue in 2006. Republicans who staunchly opposed gun control were in charge of the government, and the issue was dormant until Sandy Hook rekindled public debate about it. So it isn't fair to dismiss *Civil War* on those terms just because it happens to fit a current debate it wasn't written to comment upon."

"Maybe you should write the rebuttal," I joked. But he was right. Newspapers and web sites were starting to engage in more serious commentary on superhero movies, and it made sense for me to try to get my writing and my perspectives out into the news. The problem, of course, is that the news isn't very deep or intelligent and it isn't a great forum for professors to express their ideas.

As a case in point, I held out some measure of hope that a journalist might find my book online and interview me the weekend of the release of *Captain America: The Winter Soldier*. The film was so darn political, there were bound to be news stories about its allegorical dismantling of the NSA and its showcasing of Captain America's classic, *Civil-War*–style opposition to tyranny and martial law disguised as homeland security. It turns out I was right. Rhys Blakely of *The London Times* sought me out for an interview to ask me what my feelings were about the film. I told him I was delighted to see a thematic adaptation of *Civil War* on the screen, updated in a way that foregrounds the revelations of whistleblower Edward Snowden about the NSA surveillance program and increasing concern over the use of predator drone strikes and surveillance. I said, "While I'm surprised and delighted at how liberal the film is, my most progressive friends think it isn't subversive enough and promotes stealth conservatism in a seemingly liberal exterior package. I know exactly where they are coming from and respectfully disagree. We have much the same friendly debates about President Obama."

I thought that was a fun quote for the article, but it wasn't what he was looking for, clearly. "Hmmm..." he said.

This moment was one of several hints during the interview that Blakely's editorial supervisors did not like the film precisely because it was anti-establishment and were hoping that my quotes would be less enthusiastic. When I discussed how Captain America has a history of being political, Blakely prodded me by saying, "But this is a news story. We need to be current. Have you heard that Vladimir Putin likes this movie?"

"Um ... no. Why do we have to drag him into this? I bet a lot of people interested in civil rights and social justice and freedom like this movie. What does he have to do with anything?"

"Do you think the global market makes it easier for Hollywood to make films that criticize America because they can recoup profits overseas that they lose domestically?"

"Sure," I said. "If that means filmmakers will no longer live in fear of offending a small percentage of really conservative, my-country-right-or-wrong folks and superhero fans can get more intelligent, progressive messages in movies, then that's very good news. And those folks can watch *Duck Dynasty* if they want something marketed to them."

The article was published on April 12, 2014, with the headline: "No More U.S. Superheroes: Subversive Hollywood Makes Putin's Day." The article was brief and read much like the headline suggested it would. This is the part of the piece that I appeared in:

> Marc DiPaolo, the author of *War, Politics and Superheroes*, suggests that lucrative foreign markets have given superheroes new licence to explore anti–U.S. themes. "Hollywood doesn't have to worry about a backlash from the American market," he said....
>
> It has been suggested that Vladimir Putin, the Russian president, might enjoy the movie, which could also be interpreted as a rebuke to NATO and the UN.

I posted the article on Facebook and one of my students, Joe Jenen, wrote me right away. "Are you okay?" he asked. "I read your quote in that article and it was weird. It didn't sound like you. Are you back in the right-wing corner, or something?"

"No," I said. "I was just totally misquoted. That's Britain's liberal media at work, taking my progressive sentiments and turning them on their head. The way they plugged me into that article's overall hysterical argument, they made it sound like I think that Marvel's very apt depiction of the NSA is tantamount to anti–Americanism. So *Captain America 2* is weakening our country, leaving it ripe for Putin to take over, apparently."

"Oh, good. I was worried you really thought that for a minute."

"And now the rest of the world will think I think that. If anybody reads the article, or gives a damn who I am or what I think. Still. It is the principle of the thing."

"Well ... you were quoted in the *London Times*! That's cool."

"Um ... yay? I guess? Hooray?"

Annoyed at the article I wound up stuck in, I scoured the Internet looking for better stories about the film and stumbled upon three fantastic articles on the *Sequart* blog about the film. "Ah! You see! *Sequart* knows how it is done, *London Times*." So I wrote to the editors at *Sequart* and asked to become a columnist.

And what is the upshot of all of these autobiographical anecdotes and why am I foisting them upon you as an afterword to an academic anthology? A legitimate question.

While my tenure as a journalist at *The Staten Island Advance* was short-lived, I never behaved the way Rhys Blakely did. He knew he was misrepresenting me and did it anyway because he had the story written in his head before he interviewed me. I left the occupation precisely because I saw it becoming more and more sensationalistic and more of a blight on society than an educator of it. The kind of writing Blakely churned out on deadline was not journalism. It was not social commentary. It was bullshit.

Enter this book.

When Kevin Scott told he was beginning work on this project and invited me to participate, I was enthusiastic about the news. I'd already written a lot about *Civil War*, but I was eager to see what others had to say. Now that I see the end result of the collective labor, I'm delighted to see so many brilliant, reasonable, well-researched articles on the best mainstream superhero event story ever published. It is a culturally important tale and one that warrants serious study.

Here's the important bit. Scholars such as those who have contributed to this volume and publishers like McFarland are doing an enormous public service. We have no real news service to speak of any more, and so little serious cultural and political commentary is being written about the pressing issues of our time. Scholarship such as this has a real potential to reach hardcore fans and even some casual fans. McFarland anthologies and monographs can be brought to the people at less cost than the $120 cover price of most academic books and boast far more accessible writing styles than most academic books contain. Indeed, I first encountered McFarland at various horror and science fiction conventions I attended in New York, New Jersey, and Virginia during the 1990s. I bought their excellent volumes on *Godzilla* and *Doctor Who* years before I entered academia or even knew what an academic book was. I read those books at high school age and I loved them. I didn't know I was accessing forbidden, elitist knowledge. Now that McFarland sells still more affordable versions of their books in electronic format and superhero scholarship akin to these articles appear on websites like *Sequart* and get tweeted, the reach of superhero studies scholarship is beginning to seem limitless. Superhero stories are important and they deserve to be interpreted by intelligent commentators.

So, if you are reading this book as a fan, as a scholar, or as a student, I congratulate you for thinking seriously about these women and men in pajamas who mean so much to contemporary Americans.

If you are a fellow scholar and/or a contributor to this book, I have a message for you.

We cannot rely on journalists to do their jobs any more. If we want smart readings of comics, smart social commentary, and smart political science reaching mainstream audiences, it is up to academics to produce it, because almost no one else will outside of a small handful of indie filmmakers and activist comedians. Thanks for being part of one of the most important conversations of our time. Thanks for being part of this book. Don't stop now. There's a lot more work to be done.

See you in the trenches.

Note

1. The phrase "With great power comes great responsibility" did not originate with Uncle Ben. It first appeared in the final panel of narration in Spider-Man's first story, in *Amazing Fantasy* #15 (and was worded slightly differently. See Lee). Soon thereafter, due to regular restagings, it became associated with Uncle Ben. The concept has been around for centuries, but this specific phrase has, due to Spider-Man's angst and popularity, entered the popular imagination, and is widely used without any reference to Spider-Man, most recently in an International Monetary Fund working paper about mortgage insurance titled, *With Great Power Comes Great Responsibility: Macroprudential Tools at Work in Canada* (see Krznar and Morsink). Great power, indeed.

Works Cited

Blakely, Rhys. "No More U.S. Superheroes: Subversive Hollywood Makes Putin's Day." The Times.com. Times Newspapers Limited, 12 Apr. 2014. Web. 7 Dec. 2014.
Bouie, Jamelle. "Marvel's *Civil War* Is a Far-Right Paranoid Fantasy—and a Mess. Can the Movies Fix It?" Slate.com. The Slate Group, 20 Oct. 2014. Web. 7 Dec. 2014.
Krznar, Ivo, and James Morsink. *With Great Power Comes Great Responsibility: Macroprudential Tools at Work in Canada*. International Monetary Fund, 2014. Web.
Lee, Stan (writer), and Steve Ditko (artist). "Spider-Man!" *Amazing Fantasy* #15 (Aug. 1962), Marvel Comics. 1–11. Web.
Straczynski, J. Michael (writer), Ron Garney (penciller), and Bill Reinhold (inker). *Amazing Spider-Man* #537 (Jan. 2007), Marvel Comics. Web.

Marc DiPaolo is an associate professor of English and film at Oklahoma City University. He is the author, most recently, of *War, Politics and Superheroes* (McFarland, 2011). He has edited and co-edited multiple collections, including *Godly Heretics: Essays on Alternative Christianity in Literature and Popular Culture* (McFarland, 2013), *Unruly Catholics from Dante to Madonna: Faith, Heresy, and Politics in Cultural Studies* (Scarecrow, 2013), and *Devised and Directed by Mike Leigh* (with Bryan Cardinale-Powell, Bloomsbury Academic, 2013).

About the Contributors

Mark **Bousquet** is the author of several books for children (the *Adventures of the Five* series) and adults (the *Gunfighter Gothic* series), as well as numerous works of scholarship, including *Atomic Reactions: Marvel Comics on Film*.

Jeffrey A. **Brown** is a professor in the Department of Popular Culture at Bowling Green State University. He is the author of three books with the University of Mississippi Press: *Black Superheroes: Milestone Comics and Their Fans* (2001), *Dangerous Curves: Gender, Fetishism and the Modern Action Heroine* (2011), and *Beyond Bombshells: The New Action Heroine in Popular Culture* (2015).

Scott **Cleary** is an associate professor of English at Iona College in New Rochelle, New York. He has published on Alexander Pope, Christopher Smart, Benjamin Franklin and Thomas Paine. He is also the director of the Institute for Thomas Paine Studies at Iona.

Joseph J. **Darowski** is a member of the editorial review board of *The Journal of Popular Culture* and the editor of *The Ages of Superman* (McFarland, 2012) as well as subsequent volumes in that series on Wonder Woman, the X-Men, the Avengers, Iron Man, and the Hulk. He is the author of *X-Men and the Mutant Metaphor: Race and Gender in the Comics* (Rowman & Littlefield, 2014).

Ryan M. **Davidson** is an attorney in private practice in Lancaster County, Pennsylvania, where he focuses on criminal defense and landlord-tenant disputes. He graduated from Notre Dame Law School, *cum laude*, and earned a B.A. in philosophy and history from Covenant College, *cum laude*. He is also the co-author, along with James E. Daily, JD, of *The Law of Superheroes* (Gotham, 2012).

Brenna Clarke **Gray** teaches in the Department of English at Douglas College. Her most recent publication is an essay on Scott Pilgrim and multicultural identity, co-written with Peter Wilkins, for *Representing Multiculturalism in Comics and Graphic Novels* (Routledge, 2015).

Brandi **Hodo** is an instructor at the University of Alabama. She teaches courses in composition and world literature. Her primary research interests focus on the intersections of popular culture, race and gender.

Travis **Langley** is a professor of psychology who teaches on mental illness, crime and media including comics at Henderson State University. He presents analyses of comic book storylines and characters at conventions and universities throughout the world. PsychologyToday.com carries his blog "Beyond Heroes and Villains."

Karl E. **Martin** is a professor of literature in the Department of Literature, Journalism and Modern Languages at Point Loma Nazarene University. Martin has contributed to the following collections: *Sexual Ideology in the Works of Alan Moore* (McFarland, 2012), *Dark Faith: New Essays on Flannery O'Connor's The Violent Bear It Away* (University of Notre Dame Press, 2012), and *Reel Histories: Studies in American Film* (Press Americana, 2008).

Kathleen **McClancy** is an assistant professor of film and media studies in the Department of English at Texas State University. Previous publications include "The Iconography of Violence: Television, Vietnam, and the Soldier Hero" in *Film & History* and "The Rehabilitation of Rambo: Trauma, Victimization, and the Vietnam Veteran" in *The Journal of Popular Culture*. She is also the primary organizer and co-chair of the Comics Arts Conference.

John **McGuire** is a sociologist at the University of Western Sydney, Australia. His research interests include national ideologies and the political, social, religious and cultural content of popular culture. A lifelong comic book fan, his work has focused on American comic books and superheroes.

Daniel J. **O'Rourke** is an associate professor at Ashland University. His research interests include the rhetoric of popular culture and the rhetoric of sport. In 2003, he co-edited *Case Studies in Sport Communication* with Robert S. Brown (Praeger, 2003). He has also written on subjects as diverse as Spider-Man, Theodore Roosevelt, and irony after 9/11.

Kevin Michael **Scott** is an associate professor and coordinator of English education at Albany State University. He is the author of several articles about 19th-century American culture and the coauthor (with Carmen Sarracino) of *The Porning of America: The Rise of Porn Culture, What It Means, and Where We Go from Here* (Beacon, 2008).

Anthony Petros **Spanakos** is an associate professor in the Department of Political Science and Law at Montclair State University. He was Fulbright visiting professor at the University of Brasilia (2002) and the Institute for Advanced Study of Administration in Venezuela (2008), and a visiting fellow at the East Asia Institute in Singapore (2009). He is co-editor of the Conceptualising Comparative Politics series published by Routledge.

David **Sweeney** is a lecturer in the Glasgow School of Art's Forum for Critical Inquiry. His primary research field is contemporary popular culture and he has published articles on the director Mike Leigh, the Marvel Cinematic Universe and the novels of Michael Marshal Smith.

Seneca **Vaught** is an assistant professor of history and interdisciplinary studies at Kennesaw State University who combines his expertise in race, policy and technology to address contemporary problems. He has interned at TransAfrica Forum and is a senior fellow of information and technology at the Africana Cultures and Policy Studies Institute. He has published articles on race, critical pedagogy and policy.

Mark D. **White** is a professor in and chair of the Department of Philosophy at the College of Staten Island/CUNY. He is the author of four books, including *The Virtues of Captain America: Modern Day Lessons on Character from a World War II Superhero* (John Wiley & Sons, 2014). He has published more than 40 articles and essays on in the intersections of economics, philosophy and law, and is a frequent editor and contributor to the Blackwell Philosophy and Pop Culture series.

Daniel Davis **Wood** is an instructor in American literature, history and politics at the Ecole d'Humanite, Switzerland. He received a Ph.D. from the University of Melbourne, Australia, with a dissertation on the legal and political implications of the frontier novels of James Fenimore Cooper and their legacy in artifacts of American popular culture. He regularly writes literary criticism online at danieldaviswood.com.

Index

ABC News 5, 109, 150
absent black father stereotype 132, 134–39
Abu Ghraib 151
Adams, John 90
Afghanistan 8, 62, 82, 86, 149, 151, 154, 215
Afterlife with Archie 167
Agamben, Giorgio 87n4
al Qaeda 71, 116
A.L.A. Schechter Poultry Corp. v. U.S. 16
Alias (comics) 134
All-Star Squadron 38
Allan, Chantal 58, 61, 66n7
Allen, Danielle 79
Alonzo, Axel 182
Alpha Flight 58–65
Alphona, Adrian 48, 56
American Civil Liberties Union (ACLU) 146
American Dream 7, 150–62
American exceptionalism 110–15, 153
Anderson, Benedict 99
Anonymous (hacker community) 56
Ant-Man 31
Aquaman 180
Arachne (Julia Carpenter) 123–27, 182
Arana (Anya Corazon) 126–28
Aristotle 87n4
Arkansas National Guard 79
Armstrong, Larry 198n3
Asgard 32–33
Asimov, Isaac 104
Astonishing X-Men 50; see also X-Men
Astro City 72
Aunt May (May Parker) 96n4, 100, 145, 148, 196, 216
Aurora 65
The Authority 54–55
Avatar Press 55
The Avengers 1, 42, 58, 63, 81–82, 122–24, 128, 130, 132–35, 137, 145, 150, 171, 194–95; *Avengers Disassembled* 37; *Avengers: The Initiative* 14; *New Avengers: The Illuminati* 12, 20, 38–39, 43, 81; *Kree Skrull War* 1, 39, 41

Bakhtin, Mikhail 177, 185–86, 186n7
Baldwin, Robbie *see* Speedball
Banner, Bruce *see* The Hulk
Barnes, Bucky (James Barnes, the Winter Soldier, or Captain America) 7, 29, 31, 101, 157, 159–60, 162n1, 176–78; Jack Monroe 178
Barthes, Roland 53, 56
Bateman, John 27, 30, 32
Batgirl 126
Batman 1, 5, 126, 131, 176, 179–80; *Death in the Family* 1; *Knightfall* 1
Battlestar 94
Battlestar Galactica 214
BBC News 150
Beaty, Bart 59–60, 66n9, 211n3
Bell, John 60
Bendis, Brian Michael 12–13, 29, 39–45, 46n7, 46n15, 59, 62–64, 66n8, 82–83, 91, 95, 103–06, 130, 132–39, 155, 168, 192–95, 213, 217
Bentham, Jeremy 1, 190, 198n1
Benton, Bond 27–28
Berenger, Tom 214
The Bible 102
Big Book of the 70s 211n2
Big Brother 51
bin Laden, Osama 112, 215
Black Bolt 12, 39, 42, 44, 81–82, 88n17, 104
Black Panther (T'Challa) 39, 41, 81–83, 88n17, 88n19, 104, 106n3, 185, 203, 206
Black Panther Party 207, 209
Black Summer 52, 55
Blair, Tony 215

Blake, Donald 31, 33, 34n2
Blakely, Rhys 218–19
The Blob 169
Bloom, Harold 49
Blum, Edward J. 209
Bond, James 130
Bond, Julian 211n2
Bouazizi, Mohamed 87
Bouie, Jamelle 217
Bousquet, Mark 6, 37–47
Boym, Svetlana 118
The Boys 174
Bradley, Elijah *see* Patriot
Brecht, Bertolt 56
Brevoort, Tom 7n3, 69, 90, 180–83, 185, 204–06, 211n1
Brodie, Mike 52
Brothers, David 167
Broun, Paul, Jr. 211n1
Brown, Jeffrey A. 7, 125, 128, 130–41
Brown vs. Board of Education 79
Brubaker, Ed 29, 75, 101, 104, 112, 148, 155, 159–62, 176–77, 193
Buchanan v. Warley 15
Bucky *see* Barnes, Bucky
Buffy the Vampire Slayer (TV) 48, 51, 126
Bukataman, Scott 131
Bullseye 30, 136
Burgos, Carl 176, 178, 180–81, 186n5
Burke, Edmund 88n16
Burns, Abigail Beryl 54–55
Burnside, William (Captain America) 160
Bush, George W. 4, 27, 37, 43, 51, 61–62, 109, 114–15, 151, 153–59, 161, 162n2, 206, 208, 215–16
Busiek, Kurt 74, 87n5, 191
Byrne, John 45n4, 59–60

Cable 103
Cage, Danielle 135–39
Cage, Luke 7, 13–14, 17, 20–22, 29–30, 80, 130, 132–39, 171

Calder, Lendol 203
Campbell, Joseph 74
Canada 6, 58–66, 67n4–7
Captain America (Steve Rogers) 1–2, 4–7, 21, 23n5, 26–30, 32, 39–40, 42, 45, 46n18, 51, 53, 58, 60, 66n10, 69, 73–74, 75n1, 77–81, 84, 90, 92–94, 98–106, 108–16, 118, 118n7, 121, 123–24, 131–33, 135, 138, 145–51, 155–57, 159–62, 168, 170–72, 175–80, 182–84, 186, 189–98, 198n7–9, 203–07, 215–19; *see also* Bucky; Falcon; John Walker; William Burnside
Captain Canuck 60, 66n3
Captured Ghosts 56
Carlson, Tucker 62
Carpenter, Julia *see* Arachne
Carpenter, Rachel 123–27
Carter, Sharon 101, 112, 155, 161
Cassady, Jon 48–49
Castle, Frank *see* Punisher
Castro, Mauricio 202
Cavuto, Neil 62
CBS News 150
Cebulski, C. B. 168
Center for Disease Control (CDC) 132
Chaos Comics 186n1
Chaos War 65, 66n2
Cheney, Dick 216–17
Cheung, Jimmy 39
Chrétien, Jean 61
Christensen, Lila 202
CIA (Central Intelligence Agency) 65
civil liberties 1, 4, 27, 45, 69, 71, 206
civil rights 23n8, 45, 73, 88n20, 94–95, 108, 116, 135, 144, 151, 175, 195, 203–06, 208–09, 211n2, 218
Civil War (1861–65) 18, 73–74, 97n5
Claremont, Chris 72, 122
Clark, Penny 204
Cleary, Scott 6, 90–97
Clerks 213
Clinton, Bill 71
Clinton, Hilary 62
Clooney, George 216
CNN (The Cable News Network) 62
Cobbs-Hoffman, Elizabeth 209
Cohen, Lisa 204
The Cold War 2, 53, 100, 108–09, 113–19
The Collective (Michael Pointer) 58, 63–66
Combat Zone: True Tales of GIs in Iraq 211n2
Comic Arts Conference 75n1

The Commerce Clause 15–18, 20
communism 115–16, 151, 160
Congress 12, 15–20, 24n9, 31, 37, 38, 45, 72, 93, 105, 148, 153, 157, 184, 192, 196
Congressional Record 37–38
consequentialism 190–91
The Constitution 6, 11, 15, 17, 21, 23n6, 28, 32, 34
continuity 38–39, 69
Coogan, Peter 74
Corazon, Anya *see* Arana
Cos, Grant 158
Costello, Matthew 110, 161
Coulter, Anne 62–63, 109
Craig, Daniel 130
Criminal: Last of the Innocents 167
Crisis on Infinite Earths 1
Crockatt, Richard 152
Crockett, Davy 131
Cromer, Michael 204
crossover comic events 1, 46n16–17, 50–51, 108, 118n1, 130, 139, 174, 176, 178–79, 181–85, 189, 200
Cruise, Tom 136
CSI 213
CSIS (Canadian Security Intelligence Service) 65

The Daily Bugle 179
Dalby, Simon 118
Daredevil (Matt Murdoch) 14, 30, 135, 171, 180
Dark Horse Comics 186n1
The Dark Knight 87n5
Dark Reign 5, 130, 133, 135, 139, 181
Darowski, Joseph J. 7, 165–173
Davidson, Ryan, M. 6, 11–25, 34n5
Davies, Russell T. 215
Dawson's Creek 48
DC Comics 23n1, 48, 55–56, 72, 126, 162n1, 177, 179–80, 186n9, 194, 205
Deal, Nathan 211n1
Decker, Alicia 202
DeFalco, Tom 59
de la Durantaye, Leland 87n4
Deleuze, Gilles 49
Dell, John 165
deontology 189–97, 198n3, 198n5–6
Department of Homeland Security 4, 51
DiPaolo, Marc 7, 213–20
Ditko, Steve 38, 45n3, 144, 178, 214
Dittmer, Jason 7n4, 27, 58, 60, 66n3, 110–11, 161

Dixie Chicks 4, 216
Doctor Doom 30, 104, 169, 213
Doctor Manhattan 23n5
Doctor Octopus 30, 213
Doctor Strange 12, 26, 39–42, 44–45, 46n22, 81–82, 104, 204, 213
Doctor Who 186n6, 213, 215, 219
Doctorow, Cory 51–52, 54; *Homeland* 52; *Little Brother* 51–54
Dodd, Christopher 109
Dolby, Thomas 43
Doomsday Man 127
Dostoyevsky, Fyodor 79
Downey, Robert, Jr. 217
Drew, Jessica *see* Spider-Woman
Duck Dynasty 218
Duncan, Randy 165

Eaglesham, Dale 59
The East (film) 52–53
Easthope, Anthony 131
Echo 132
Eckford, Elizabeth 79
Eco, Umberto 133
Edwardson, Ryan 59
Eisenhower, Dwight D. 19
Eisner, Will 168, 186n4, 202
Ellis, Warren 48–49, 52, 54–56
Ellison, Ralph 79–80; *Invisible Man* 79; *Three Days Before the Shooting* 80
Ennis, Garth 48, 174, 186n2
Evans, Chris 217
Everett, Bill 176, 178, 181
Ex Machina 174

Facebook 218
Falcon 4, 103, 135, 161, 204, 216
Faludi, Susan 130
Fannie Mae 159
Fanon, Frantz 80, 88n12
The Fantastic Four 1, 12, 29–31, 39, 43, 72, 81–84, 92, 136, 147, 171, 183–84, 203, 215; *The Galactus Trilogy* 1
fascism 66, 84, 108, 110, 114, 186n2
Federal Bureau of Investigation (FBI) 206, 209, 213
Federal Emergency Management Agency (FEMA) 154
federalism 15
Federalist Papers 149
Feingold, Russ 37–38, 45
Fellman, Paul 116
Filiu, Ken 150
First Eng. Evangelical Lutheran Church v. Los Angeles 15
Flag-Smasher 53, 55
Flash 162n1
Floyd, Sally 93, 105

Foreign Intelligence Surveillance Courts (FISA) 146
Foucault, Michel 106n2
Fourth World Saga 1
Fox News 5, 58, 62, 215
Frankfurter, Felix 24n9
Franklin, Ben 112, 148, 156, 175, 186n3
freedom versus security conflict 6, 11, 22, 45, 69–73, 90–91, 93, 95, 144, 154, 156–58, 161, 175, 181, 195
Freire, Paulo 7, 200–201, 205
Fromm, Erich 6, 70–74
Front Line 88n15, 96, 97n5, 105
Fukuyama, Francis 151
Fury, Nick 31, 42, 101

G-7 Nations 55
Gage, Christos 114, 193–94
Galactus 1, 30
Gallup, Inc. 154
Gandhi, Mohandas Karamchand 161
Gellner, Ernest 99
German Great Depression 70
Giant Man (Henry Pym) 34n2, 45, 117, 147, 156
Gillen, Keiron 54–55
Gitmo *see* Guantanamo Bay
Gjerde, Jon 209
Glee 213
Godzilla 219
Goliath (Dr. Bill Foster or Black Goliath) 29, 31, 78, 83, 88n20, 95, 147–48, 156, 180, 185, 194, 197
Goodwin, Archie 133
Gore, Al 215
Gramsci, Antonio 151–52, 157
Gray, Brenna 6, 58–68
Green Arrow 162n1
Green Goblin (Norman Osborn) 23, 104, 117, 136–38, 180
Green Lantern (Hal Jordan) 162n1
Grey, Jean 162n1
Grimm, Ben *see* The Thing
Gruenwald, Mark 38, 191
Guantanamo Bay detention camp 1, 4, 14, 71, 119n11, 148, 151, 206, 209, 215
Guardian 53, 59, 63–65, 66n1
The Guardian (newspaper) 53, 146
gun-control 182, 192–93, 206, 211n1, 217
Gun Free School Zones Act of 1990 16
Gustines, Gene 168
GWOT (Global War on Terror) *see* War on Terror

Hamad, Hannah 137
Hamilton, Alexander 1
Hammond, Jim *see* The Human Torch
Happy Hogan 193
Hardt, Michael 84
Harvey, Alex 131
Hayes, Molly 53, 56
Hegel, Georg Wilhelm Friedrich 80
hegemony 54–55, 151–53, 155–57, 160, 163
Helvie, Forrest 165, 169
Hercules 87n8, 180
Hill, Maria 30, 78, 81, 95, 101–02, 111–12, 117, 146, 206–07
Hiroshima 115–16, 170
Hitch, Bryan 54
Hitler, Adolf 84, 109, 112, 115, 178
Hitman 48–49
Hochschild, Jennifer L. 152
Hodgson, Godfrey 110
Hodo, Brandi 7
Hollowell, Morry 165–66, 168–70, 172
Holmes v. U.S. 18
Hoover, J. Edgar 206
Horney, Karen 70
House of M 37, 63
Howard the Duck 21
Howe, Sean 59
The Hulk (Bruce Banner) 23, 28–29, 31–33, 41, 44, 100, 192
Human Torch (Johnny Storm) 29, 43, 83; Jim Hammond 175–81
The Hunger Games 217
Hurricane Katrina 154–57, 163

Iceman 171
Idle No More movement 66n11
The Illuminati 6, 37–44, 45n5, 46n7, 46n14, 46n17, 81, 91, 104, 106
Image Comics 55, 186n1
Immortus, Marcus 123–25
The Incredibles 72
India 86
Indiana Jones 130
The Inhumans 12, 39, 88n17
The Initiative 17–20, 63, 103, 105
Inness, Sherrie 128
The Insurrection Act 19, 24n10
Internal Revenue Service 21
Invisible Woman (Sue Storm) 29–30, 41, 43, 78–79, 83–84, 87n7–8, 121, 146, 156, 184–85
Iran 86, 118
Iran-Contra scandal 72
Iraq 8, 27, 58–59, 61–62, 86, 118, 151, 154–55, 157, 211n2, 215

Iron Fist 132, 138
Iron Man (Tony Stark) 2, 6–7, 12–14, 17, 20–23, 26–29, 31–33, 34n3, 39–46, 46n8, 46n15, 50, 54, 63–65, 67, 77–78, 81–84, 86, 88, 90–96, 98, 102–06, 108–10, 113–14, 116–19, 121, 123–24, 126, 131, 135, 137, 145–47, 156, 162n1, 168, 170–72, 181–84, 186, 189–98, 204–05, 209, 215–17
Islam 4, 62, 85–87, 174, 214–15

Jack O'Lantern 117
Jackman, Hugh 136
Jackson, Robert 24n9
James Barnes *see* Bucky
Jarvis, Edwin 135–37
Jaws 213
Jenen, Joe 218
Jenkins, Keith B. 158
Jenkins, Paul 88n15, 93, 105, 158, 184, 193–94
Jennings, Peter 109
Jester 117
Jim Crow 201, 203, 213
Jobs, Steve 46n20
John Warner National Defense Authorization Act for Fiscal Year 2007 24n10
Johnny Canuck 60
Jones, Gerard 56
Jones, J. G. 49–50
Jones, Jessica 13–14, 17, 130, 133–39
Justice League of America 49
Justice Society of America 72
Juvenal (Decimas Iunias Iuvenalis) 72

Kakutani, Michiko 174
Kane, Gil 168
Kant, Immanuel 191, 198n4
Keith, Toby 4
Kelly, Walt 86
Kerouac, Jack 52–53
Kimmel, Michael 130
King, Martin Luther, Jr. 208
King, Rodney 19
Kingdom Come 73
Kingpin 30, 105
Kirby, Jack 38, 45n3, 100, 167–68, 178
Kirk, James 216
Klock, Geoff 49–50, 55
Knauf, Charles 191, 193
Knauf, Daniel 191, 193
Kree 1, 39–40, 45n6, 50, 104
Ku Klux Klan 207

Langley, Travis 6, 7n4, 27–28, 30, 69–76, 114, 118
Larsen, Soren 60, 66n3

Leclau, Ernesto 151–52
Lecter, Hannibal 113
Lee, Jim 167
Lee, Stan 38, 45n3, 100, 135, 144, 176, 178–80, 186n11
Legion of Superheroes 49; *The Great Darkness Saga* 1
Letterman, David 174
Lewis, John 211n2
Lewis, T. G. 211n2
liberty versus security conflict *see* freedom versus security
Liefeld, Rob 167
Life with Archie 167
Lim, Ron 168
Limbaugh, Rush 215
Linklater, Richard 56
Lizard 169
Loewen, James 205
London Times 219
Los Angeles Riots (1992) 19
Lukin, Aleksander 31

Madison, James 149
Magneto 169
Major Maple Leaf 59, 63
Major Problems in American History 209
Maleev, Alex 39
Manifest Destiny 65, 152
March 211n2
Marcus *see* Marcus Immortus
Martian Manhunter 162n1
Martin, Elaine 204
Martin, Karl E. 6, 98–107
Marvel Boy (Noh-Varr) 49–50
Marvel Comics (Marvel Worldwide, Inc.) 1, 7n5, 22, 23n1, 41, 55, 63, 69, 72, 133, 175, 177, 182, 186n1, 192, 194, 200; Marvel editors 11, 38, 69, 205; Timely Comics 176, 178
The Marvel Encyclopedia 59
Marvel Girl (Rachel Summers) 78, 88n14
Marvel Knights 50
Marvel Universe 2, 6–7, 19, 28, 30, 33–34, 39, 45n5–6, 48, 57–58, 77, 92, 96, 99, 121, 130, 139, 144, 150, 159, 161, 169, 177–80, 182–83, 185, 186n9, 204, 208
Marxism 53, 84, 151
Maximus 40
Maxon, George 179
McCann, Jim 98
McCarthy, Joseph 209
McClancy, Kathleen 6, 108–19
McClane, John 131
McCloud, Scott 165–66, 186n4, 202
McCrea, John 48
McGuire, John 150–63
McNiven, Steve 4, 46n7, 165–72

McWilliams, Ora 206–07
Meaney, Patrick 56
Microsoft Corporation 52
Midas 50
Mill, John Stuart 190, 198n1
Millar, Mark 4, 8n3, 12, 14, 26, 28–32, 34n4, 38, 40–45, 46n15, 53, 55, 63, 69–71, 73, 77, 80–84, 90, 101, 103, 11–13, 117, 145–47, 155–56, 165–66, 168–72, 178, 180–85, 193, 197, 204–07, 213
Miller, Frank 87n5, 168
Minoru, Nico 48, 56
Mister Fantastic (Reed Richards) 12, 21, 28, 31, 39–45, 46n13, 63, 72, 81–84, 92, 95, 104, 106n1, 117, 147, 156, 171, 183–85, 186n14
MLA Handbook 6
Mole Man 30, 169
Moon Knight 52
Moore, Alan 23n5, 55, 72, 87n5
Moore, Michael (documentarian) 216–17
Moore, Michael S. 198n3, 198n6
Morales, Mark 46n7, 165
Morales, Robert 207
Morehouse College 132
Morrison, Grant 49–51; *Supergods* 179
Mouffe, Chantal 151–52
The Movement 56
Ms. Marvel (Carol Danvers) 7, 13–14, 23n5, 34n5, 63, 121–29, 134, 138, 181–82; pregnancy 122
Ms. Marvel (Kamala Khan) 4
Mulligan, Rikk 167
Murdoch, Rupert 52
Murdock, Matt *see* Daredevil
Murphy, Bill 217
Murray, Ross 122
Mussolini, Benito 84, 178
Mutant Registration Act 34n4, 72
mutants 34n4, 46n10–11, 72–73, 88n17, 206

Nagasaki 115–116
Nama, Adilifu 133
Namor 12, 29, 39–44, 46n12, 81–83, 104–05, 176–81
National Defense Authorization Act for Fiscal Year 2008 24n10
Nat'l Fed. of Ind. Bus. v. Sebelius (NFIB) 12, 16–17
National Public Radio (NPR) 5, 215
National Review 109
National Rifle Association (NRA) 217
National Security Agency (NSA) 1, 135, 146, 148, 218–19

nationalism 99, 104
natural rights 95
Nazi Germany 53, 70, 73, 99, 109–10, 112, 114–16, 138, 184
Neeson, Liam 136
Negative Zone *see* Project 42
Negri, Antonio 84
Nelvana of the North 60
The New Avengers 13, 45, 45n5, 46n7, 58, 62–63, 130, 132–33, 135–39, 140n3
The New Deal 16
The New Warriors 29, 31, 34, 41–42, 155, 168, 170
New X-Men 50–51, 54; *see also* X-Men
New York Times 38, 150, 168
newspaper coverage 7n2
Nicieza, Fabian 103
9/11 *see* September 11, 2001
9/11 Commission 45; graphic novel 211n2; *Report* 37–38
9/11 Memorial Museum 3, 7
Nitro 41–43, 45, 115–16, 155
Nixon, Richard 148
Noble, David W. 99–100, 103
Noh-Varr *see* Marvel Boy
Nolan, Christopher 96n2
Nomad *see* Captain America
Northstar 65

Obama, Barack 4, 85, 90, 132, 148, 153, 157–63, 206, 208, 217–18; administration 21
Occupy Movement 56, 66n11, 85
O'Connor, Michael 182
O'Hagan, Sean 53
Oklahoma 32
Olson, Jake 31, 34n2
Omega Flight 58, 62–65, 124
On the Road 52
Opper Project 211n2
Opus Dei 214
O'Rourke, Daniel J. 7, 143–49
Orwell, George 51
Osborn, Harry 180
Osborn, Norman *see* Green Goblin

Paine, Thomas 6, 90–96, 112, 156; *Common Sense* 91–95; *Rights of Man* 93–94
Pak, Greg 59
Pakistan 4, 86
Palmiotti, Jimmy 50
Pannenberg, Wolfhart 39, 41, 43–44, 45n2
Park51 4
Parker, Ben *see* Uncle Ben
Parker, Mary Jane 145–46, 196, 216
Parker, May *see* Aunt May
Parker, Peter *see* Spider-Man

Patient Protection and Affordable Care Act (ACA or "Obamacare") 6, 11–12, 20–22, 217
Patriot (Elijah Bradley) 56
PATRIOT Act *see* USA PATRIOT Act
Pearl Harbor 109–11, 115, 178–79
Peaslee, Robert Moses 7n4
Penny, Laurie 54
Pentagon 37
Perez, George 168
Pew Research Center 62, 154, 157
Peyer, Tom 55
Pheasant-Kelly, Francis 131
Phillips, Sean 167
Phoenix 1
Pitt, Brad 136
Planetary 48–49
Plex 50
Pointer, Michael *see* The Collective
Posse Comitatus Act 19
The President of the United States 19–20
privacy 1, 4, 27–29, 41, 69, 71, 94, 108, 144–46, 202, 206, 216
Prodigy 91
Project 42 1, 14, 28, 92–93, 105, 119n11, 147, 156, 171, 209, 216
Protocols of the Elders of Zion 202
Prowler 204
Puck 59
Puck II 59, 65
The Pulse 134
Punisher (Frank Castle) 2, 91, 96n3, 112–13, 118n4, 119n12, 162n1
Puppet Master 127
Putin, Vladimir 218–19
Pym, Henry *see* Giant Man

al Qaeda 71, 116
Quayle, Dan 214
Quesada, Joe 8n3, 14, 38, 44, 50, 182, 207
Quire, Quentin 54

race 4, 15, 19, 180–81, 190, 200–01, 206–11; "absent black father" 7
Raimi, Sam 186n8
Rambo, John 132
Ramos, Humberto 167
Rancière, Jacques 80–81, 83–84
Rand, Ayn 214
Reagan, Ronald 72, 131, 214
The Reconstruction Acts 18
Red Peril (character) 54, 56
Red Skull 5, 53, 159, 179
Reed, Brian 181
Rehnquist, William 15

Reinstein, Josef 99
retcon (retroactive continuity) 38–39, 45n2, 72, 160, 177–78, 186n8
The Return of Captain Invincible 72
Reynolds, Richard 48, 179
Rhett, Maryanne 202, 204
Rhoades, Shirrel 165
Richards, Reed *see* Mr. Fantastic
Roach, Kent 42
Roberts, John 17
Robin (Jason Todd) 162n1
Robinson, Bryan 150
Roosevelt, Franklin Delano 206
Rosenfield, Sophia 91
Ross, Alex 38, 87n5, 177
Ross, W. D. 198n5
Rostker v. Goldberg 18
Rousseau, Jean-Jacques 88n16
Runaways 48–56

Sabin, Roger 203
Sacco, Joe 202
Saga 52
Salazar, António de Oliveira 84
Sanderson, Peter 38, 179
Sandy Hook Elementary School shootings 217
Sasquatch 59, 63–64
Saturday Night Live 174
Saussure, Ferdinand de 177, 185
Scalia, Antonin 17
Scarlet Witch 122
Schad v. Borough of Mt. Ephraim 15
Schwarz, Gretchen 201
Schwarzenegger, Arnold 131
Scott, Kevin Michael 2, 3–9, 88n20–21, 174–88, 219
Scully, Dana 213
Secret Avengers 112–13, 116–17
Secret Invasion 5, 24n12, 37, 46n17, 130, 133, 135, 139, 181
Selective Draft Law Cases 18
Sensenbrenner, Jim 37, 45
Sentry 117, 133
September 11, 2001 (9/11) 1, 3, 6–8, 11, 27, 37–38, 42–43, 51–52, 56, 58–62, 64–66, 66n6, 69–71, 77, 80, 84–86, 93, 108–09, 112, 115–16, 118n2, 118n6, 119n9, 130–33, 135–37, 139, 140n1–2, 144, 146, 148, 151, 153–55, 157, 161–62, 171, 174–75, 183, 185–86, 186n2, 192, 214–16
Sequart 165, 219
Shaman 59, 63
Sharpe, Miriam 42, 82, 88n10
Sharzer, Greg 53
She-Hulk (Jennifer Walters) 134, 181–82, 185

S.H.I.E.L.D. 12–14, 17–18, 20, 23n3–4, 24n12, 29, 31, 34n1, 50, 58, 63–65, 81, 91, 95–96, 101, 105–06, 111–12, 115, 117, 118n3, 123–25, 127, 136, 139, 146, 155, 181, 206
Shuster, Joe 66n4
Siege 5, 11, 117, 161, 181
Simone, Gail 56
Sinnott-Armstrong, Walter 198n2
Skrulls 1, 19, 24n12, 39–41, 45n6, 46n17, 51, 73, 104, 128, 135–37, 139; *see also* Secret Invasion
Slott, Dan 181
Smallwood, Marrina 65
Smith, Matthew J. 165
Snowbird 65
Snowden, Edward 218
social contract 88n16
Socrates 88n9
Spanakos, Anthony Petros 6, 77–89
Speedball (Robbie Baldwin) 93, 105, 184
Spider-Girl (Anya Corazon) 14, 26
Spider-Man (Peter Parker) 1, 5, 7, 11, 28, 30, 33, 34n1, 42, 44, 54–55, 71, 90–93, 95–96, 96n4, 100, 102, 105, 110, 113, 117, 119n12, 131–33, 143–49, 156, 159, 168–69, 177, 179–80, 182–83, 186n8, 189, 194, 196–97, 198n10, 203–05, 212–16, 220n1; *Clone Saga* 1; *Death of Gwen Stacy* 1
Spider-Woman (Jessica Drew) 134
Squadron Supreme 73
Stabile, Carol A. 131
Stallone, Sylvester 131
Stamford, Connecticut 42, 78, 80, 83, 92, 105, 108, 115–16, 155, 184, 192–93, 215, 217
Star Trek into Darkness 216
The Staten Island Advance 219
Statham, Jason 136
Steranko, Jim 168
Stern, Roger 191
Stewart, Jon 174
Storm (Ororo Monroe) 206
Straczynski, J. Michael 29, 32–33, 90, 92, 102, 105, 106n1, 145–49, 196–97, 209, 213, 216–17
Strange, Stephen *see* Doctor Strange
Stuller, Jennifer 124–26, 128
Sub-Mariner *see* Namor
Superhero deaths 1, 4–5, 8n2, 38, 62, 65, 74, 83, 148, 150–51, 156–57, 159, 162n3, 177, 197

Superhuman Registration Act (SHRA) 2, 6, 11–23, 24n10, 26, 28–34, 42–45, 46n19, 64, 70–73, 77–79, 83, 87, 90–96, 98, 100–01, 103–08, 111–17, 118n3, 119n11, 123–27, 135, 137, 145–47, 150–56, 159, 169, 171–72, 175–76, 181–85, 187, 189–90, 192–93, 196, 206–07, 217
Superman 1, 4–5, 23n5, 56, 66n4, 126, 131–33, 176, 179–81; *Death of Superman* 1, 150, 162n1; slogan 143
Supreme Court 12, 15–18, 79
Sweeney, David 6, 48–57

tagline *see* "Whose Side Are You On?"
Taliban 71, 214
Talisman 63–65
T'Challa *see* Black Panther
Tea Party 4, 85, 162, 217
teaching *Civil War* 189–212
Teen Titans 49, 53
terrorism 1, 5–6, 11, 37–38, 40, 42, 45, 47, 51, 58, 61–62, 65–66, 71, 77, 86–87, 105, 108–09, 112–15, 117–18, 130–32, 136, 144–46, 148, 151, 153–54, 183, 185, 186n3, 192, 208, 214–15
Thanos 30
The Thing (Ben Grimm) 43, 84, 171
Thinker 92, 96
Thirteenth Amendment 18
Thomas, Roy 38
Thor 2, 4, 28, 32–33, 34n3, 122, 132, 156; clone 31, 34n2, 83, 95, 105, 109, 117, 119n13, 147, 194, 197; *see also* Donald Blake
Thoreau, Henry David 101
The Tick 180
Tigra 134
Till, Emmett 209
Toro (Thomas Raymond) 178
Toth, Alex 168
Tower Commission 72
Townsend, Tim 165
Trudeau, Pierre 59
Twain, Mark 53, 102, 197
24 214
Twin Towers *see* World Trade Center

Uncanny X-Men 59, 72
Uncle Ben 144, 147, 186n8, 214, 220n1, 186n8
Undercliff Cottage, LLC v. FHRE, LLC 23n7
United Nations 13–14, 42, 118n3
United States v. Butler 16
United States v. Morrison 16–17
United States v. Lopez 15–17
Urich, Ben 105
USA Patriot Act 1, 4, 7, 11, 23n2, 27, 37–38, 45, 45n1, 69, 71, 108, 112, 151, 192
USAgent 58, 63, 65, 66n10
utilitarianism 184, 189–97, 198n1

V for Vendetta 202
van Dyke, Michael 133
The Vanisher 169
Vankin, Jonathan 211n2
Vaughn, Brian K. 48, 52, 56, 174, 186n2
Vaught, Seneca 7, 200–12
Veloso, Francisco 27, 30, 32
Verizon 146
Vietnam 211n2
Vietnam War 97n5, 110, 112–13, 116, 118n4, 144, 204, 211n2
Vindicator 59, 65
Vines, Dexter 165, 170, 172
Violence Against Women Act of 1994 16
Vulture 30

Waid, Mark 191, 215
Wakanda 39, 206
Walker, John (Captain America) 160
Wallace, David 169
Walters, Jennifer *see* She-Hulk
Wanzo, Rebecca 27, 131
"War on Terror" 51, 58, 61, 108–09, 112–15, 118, 130, 132, 154, 185, 214–15
War Powers Clause 18, 20, 24n10
The Warden 50–51
Washington Times 62
The Watcher (Uatu) 45, 46n21
Watchmen 23n5, 55, 72, 87n5
Wayne, John 131
Weber, Cynthia 110, 188n2
Weber, Max 82, 87n1
Weiner, Robert G. 1–2, 6, 7n4

Wells, Zeb 48, 55
Wertham, Frederic 210, 211n3
West Coast Avengers 45n4
Whedon, Joss 48, 50, 186n6
White, Mark D. 7, 7n4, 189–99, 198n7–8
Whitman, Walt 183
"Whose Side Are You On?" 5, 26, 86, 90, 175
Wiccan 51
Wickard v. Filburn 16
Wildstorm Comics 48, 55
Williams, Freddie, II 56
Williams, Jeff 161
Winter Soldier (James Barnes) *see* Bucky
Wired 90
Wolk, Douglas 167, 177
Wolverine (Weapon X) 58–60, 66n5, 66n8, 132, 167, 185
Wonder Man 126
Wonder Woman 180
Wong 45
Wood, Daniel Davis 6
Woodward, C. Vann 203
World Trade Center 3, 37, 43, 86, 171, 174, 215
World War I 3, 70
World War II 5–6, 73, 99–100, 104, 109–14, 118n4, 118n8, 176–78, 204, 206, 209
Wozniak, Steve 46n20
The Wrecking Crew 64–65
Wright, Bradford 165

The X-Files 186n6
X-Men 1, 12, 39, 46n10, 49–51, 53, 59–60, 92, 169, 171, 185, 203; *Dark Phoenix Saga* 1
Xavier, Charles (Professor X) 12, 39–41, 44, 46n9, 46n16, 51, 81–82, 88n17, 104
Xavin 51

Yallow, Marcus 51–54
Yeats, William Butler 3, 7n1
Young Avengers 48–49, 51, 53
Youngstown Sheet and Tube Co. v. Sawyer 24n9

Zenari, Vivian 60
Zinsmeister, Karl 211n2
Zogby, John 154

www.ingramcontent.com/pod-product-compliance
Ingram Content Group UK Ltd.
Pitfield, Milton Keynes, MK11 3LW, UK
UKHW050532150426
5217IPUK00026B/1899